# CCNA Practical Studies

Gary Heap, CCIE #6411
and
Lynn Maynes, CCIE #6569

**Cisco Press**
201 W 103rd Street
Indianapolis, IN 46290 USA

# CCNA Practical Studies

Gary Heap and Lynn Maynes

Copyright© 2002 Cisco Press

Cisco Press logo is a trademark of Cisco Systems, Inc.

Published by:
Cisco Press
201 West 103rd Street
Indianapolis, IN 46290 USA

Printed in the United States of America

1 2 3 4 5 6 7 8 9 0

First printing April 2002

Library of Congress Cataloging-in-Publication Number: 2001090433

ISBN: 1-58720-046-5

## Warning and Disclaimer

This book is designed to provide information for CCNA candidates looking for hands-on study. Every effort has been made to make this book as complete and as accurate as possible, but no warranty or fitness is implied.

The information is provided on an "as is" basis. The authors, Cisco Press, and Cisco Systems, Inc., shall have neither liability nor responsibility to any person or entity with respect to any loss or damages arising from the information contained in this book or from the use of the discs or programs that may accompany it.

The opinions expressed in this book belong to the author and are not necessarily those of Cisco Systems, Inc.

## Trademark Acknowledgments

All terms mentioned in this book that are known to be trademarks or service marks have been appropriately capitalized. Cisco Press or Cisco Systems, Inc., cannot attest to the accuracy of this information. Use of a term in this book should not be regarded as affecting the validity of any trademark or service mark.

## Feedback Information

At Cisco Press, our goal is to create in-depth technical books of the highest quality and value. Each book is crafted with care and precision, undergoing rigorous development that involves the unique expertise of members from the professional technical community.

Readers' feedback is a natural continuation of this process. If you have any comments regarding how we could improve the quality of this book, or otherwise alter it to better suit your needs, you can contact us through e-mail at feedback@ciscopress.com. Please make sure to include the book title and ISBN in your message.

We greatly appreciate your assistance.

| | |
|---|---|
| Publisher | John Wait |
| Editor-in-Chief | John Kane |
| Cisco Systems Program Manager | Michael Hackert |
| Executive Editor | Brett Bartow |
| Managing Editor | Patrick Kanouse |
| Development Editor | Christopher Cleveland |
| Project Editor | Marc Fowler |
| Copy Editor | Krista Hansing |
| Technical Editors | Michael Ashton |
| | Brad Bonin |
| | Steve Kalman |
| Team Coordinator | Tammi Ross |
| Book Designer | Gina Rexrode |
| Cover Designer | Louisa Klucznik |
| Production Team | Argosy |
| Indexer | Tim Wright |

CISCO SYSTEMS

**Corporate Headquarters**
Cisco Systems, Inc.
170 West Tasman Drive
San Jose, CA 95134-1706
USA
http://www.cisco.com
Tel: 408 526-4000
 800 553-NETS (6387)
Fax: 408 526-4100

**European Headquarters**
Cisco Systems Europe
11 Rue Camille Desmoulins
92782 Issy-les-Moulineaux
Cedex 9
France
http://www-europe.cisco.com
Tel: 33 1 58 04 60 00
Fax: 33 1 58 04 61 00

**Americas Headquarters**
Cisco Systems, Inc.
170 West Tasman Drive
San Jose, CA 95134-1706
USA
http://www.cisco.com
Tel: 408 526-7660
Fax: 408 527-0883

**Asia Pacific Headquarters**
Cisco Systems Australia,
Pty., Ltd
Level 17, 99 Walker Street
North Sydney
NSW 2059 Australia
http://www.cisco.com
Tel: +61 2 8448 7100
Fax: +61 2 9957 4350

Cisco Systems has more than 200 offices in the following countries. Addresses, phone numbers, and fax numbers are listed on the Cisco Web site at www.cisco.com/go/offices

Argentina • Australia • Austria • Belgium • Brazil • Bulgaria • Canada • Chile • China • Colombia • Costa Rica • Croatia • Czech Republic • Denmark • Dubai, UAE • Finland • France • Germany • Greece • Hong Kong • Hungary • India • Indonesia • Ireland • Israel • Italy • Japan • Korea • Luxembourg • Malaysia • Mexico • The Netherlands • New Zealand • Norway • Peru • Philippines • Poland • Portugal • Puerto Rico • Romania • Russia • Saudi Arabia • Scotland • Singapore • Slovakia • Slovenia • South Africa • Spain Sweden • Switzerland • Taiwan • Thailand • Turkey • Ukraine • United Kingdom • United States • Venezuela • Vietnam • Zimbabwe

# About the Authors

**Gary Heap, CCIE #6411,** graduated with a Bachelor of Arts degree in Business Information Systems from Utah State University in 1998. He has worked for Novell, Lucent World-Wide Services (formerly International Network Services, INS), Sprint EISolutions, and Sprint Managed Network Services. Currently he is employed by Cornerstone Internetworking Solutions as a principal consultant. His responsibilities include the design, documentation, implementation, troubleshooting, and operational support of large-scale networks. Gary holds the following additional technical certifications: CCNP, CCNA, Master CNE, and MCSE.

**Lynn Maynes, CCIE #6569**, is a senior network engineer with Sprint Managed Network Services and is responsible for the design, implementation, and operation of large-scale networks worldwide. His network certifications include CCNP, CCNA, CCDA, Certified Internet Architect, Master CNE, and MCP. He has held technical positions with UPS, Novell, and most recently as a consultant for Sprint EISolutions, where he was involved in the design and optimization of a variety of large networks. He completed his Bachelor of Arts degree in international business from Westminster College in 1996.

## About the Technical Reviewers

**Michael Ashton** is a corporate systems engineer for Altiris. He has worked in technology for 13 years in a wide variety of positions in consulting, network administration, technical support, magazine publishing, and telecommunications.

Michael is certified in Cisco CCNP, MCSE, CNE, and Altiris ACE. He has written technical articles for *Microsoft Certified Professional Magazine*, *Smart Computing*, Earthweb's *Datamation*, *Y2K News*, *Computer Credible*, and several other publications. He can be reached at hmashton@earthlink.net or michael_ashton@yahoo.com.

**Brad Bonin, CCIE #4454**, is a systems engineer III for Cisco Systems in its service provider line of business, where he provides engineering support for various Cisco service provider customers. He has more than six years of experience in designing, deploying, and troubleshooting large-scale service provider and enterprise networks. Before joining Cisco Systems, Brad worked as a senior network engineer for EDS. His experience at EDS included assistance in the design and implementation of EDS's global IP network as well as the creation of new EDS IP service offerings. Brad has a Bachelor of Science degree in electrical engineering with a specialization in telecommunications from the University of Louisiana at Lafayette.

**Steven Kalman** is the principal officer at Esquire Micro Consultants, which operates in lecturing, writing, and consulting. He has more than 30 years of experience in data processing, with strengths in network design and implementation. Steven is an instructor and author for Learning Tree International and has written and reviewed many networking-related titles. He holds CCNA, CCDA, ECNE, CEN, and CNI certifications.

# Dedications

**Gary Heap:** To my wife, Alisha, thank you for all your love and support. To my children, Chance and Sawyer, and my dog, Maddy. Without a family, life would be meaningless. To my mother, Christine, for her kindness and encouragement throughout my life; and to my late father, Dan R. Heap, whose example and dedication I will always admire.

**Lynn Maynes:** To my wife, Alison: Thank you for your understanding and support through the entire process of writing this book. You truly are my love and inspiration.

To my parents, Ruth and Russ: Your love and devotion has been a key influence in my life, for which I'll always be grateful.

# Acknowledgments

This book would not have been possible without the efforts of many dedicated people. As authors, we would like to thank the following people for their contributions:

First, thanks to Chris Cleveland, senior development editor at Cisco Press, whose expertise, comments, and encouragement were essential during the writing of this book. To Brett Bartow, Cisco Press executive editor, for his vision, guidance, and patience.

Thanks to the technical editors, Michael Ashton, Brad Bonin, and Steve Kalman, whose attention to detail and subsequent advice was greatly appreciated and has enhanced this book.

Thanks to Matt Taylor for his suggestions on wording that didn't fit just right, to Keith Phillips for the use of some of his equipment, and to Phil Taylor, Chief Network Engineer at Sprint Managed Network Services, for his support during the writing of this book.

# Contents at a Glance

# Contents

# Foreword

*CCNA Practical Studies* is designed to provide you with another vehicle to obtain hands-on experience, which is a critical component of any preparation program for the Cisco Certified Network Associate exam. The detailed lab scenarios contained in this book illustrate the application of key internetworking concepts covered on the CCNA exam, helping you master the practical skills you need to install, configure, and operate LAN, WAN, and dial access services for small networks. With the introduction of performance-based testing elements to the CCNA exam, these hands-on skills are of critical importance to succeeding on the exam and in your daily job as a CCNA professional. This book was developed in cooperation with the Cisco Internet Learning Solutions Group. Cisco Press books are the only self-study books authorized by Cisco for CCNA exam preparation.

Cisco and Cisco Press present this material in text-based format to provide another learning vehicle for our customers and the broader user community in general. Although a publication does not duplicate the instructor-led or e-learning environment, we acknowledge that not everyone responds in the same way to the same delivery mechanism. It is our intent that presenting this material via a Cisco Press publication will enhance the transfer of knowledge to a broad audience of networking professionals.

Cisco Press will present lab manuals on existing and future exams through these Practical Studies titles to help achieve Cisco Internet Learning Solutions Group's principal objectives: to educate the Cisco community of networking professionals and to enable that community to build and maintain reliable, scalable networks. The Cisco Career Certifications and classes that support these certifications are directed at meeting these objectives through a disciplined approach to progressive learning. To succeed on the Cisco Career Certifications exams, as well as in your daily job as a Cisco-certified professional, we recommend a blended learning solution that combines instructor-led, e-learning, and self-study training with hands-on experience. Cisco Systems has created an authorized Cisco Learning Partner program to provide you with the most highly qualified instruction and invaluable hands-on experience in lab and simulation environments. To learn more about Cisco Learning Partner programs available in your area, please go to: www.cisco.com/go/training.

The books that Cisco Press creates in partnership with Cisco Systems meet the same standards for content quality demanded of our courses and certifications. It is our intent that you will find this and subsequent Cisco Press certification and training publications of value as you build your networking knowledge base.

Thomas M. Kelly
Vice-President, Internet Learning Solutions Group
Cisco Systems, Inc.
March 2002

# Introduction

Routing and switching concepts are the foundation upon which a solid network infrastructure is built. As networks increase in size and complexity, it becomes increasingly important to be able to apply conceptual knowledge effectively in a production environment as well as to understand how router configuration steps impact a network. It has been our experience that networking concepts often are learned independent of each other. Generally, this is intended to provide a focused learning approach. However, this often leaves gaps in how networking theory is applied in real-world scenarios. Real-world networks are seldom composed of a single WAN technology, routing protocol, or network topology. For this reason, a network engineer must have practical knowledge in applying networking concepts. *CCNA Practical Studies* is intended to help you move concepts and theories into practical experience on Cisco routers.

## Audience

*CCNA Practical Studies* is targeted toward networking professionals familiar with networking concepts as well as the principles of routing and switching theory, but who desire a hands-on approach to applying their knowledge. This book is designed to allow you, in a structured manner, to configure an entire network consisting of various topologies, technologies, and routing protocols from start to finish. In the process, you will gain not only more confidence in navigating within Cisco IOS Software but also an understanding of how networking concepts interrelate. The end result is that you become a more complete network engineer. *CCNA Practical Studies* is for individuals studying for the CCNA exam or those who have passed the CCNA exam and would like to apply their knowledge, preparing themselves for the next step. Some experience and knowledge level will be assumed of Cisco routers and routing protocols. Our objective is to help you prepare for the performance-based portion of the CCNA exam and make existing CCNAs confident in applying their knowledge in production environments.

## CCNA Exam 640-607 and  Performance-Based Testing

Cisco has introduced performance-based testing as part of the CCNA exam. Performance-based testing is the integration of interactive exercises that test a CCNA candidate's ability to configure a particular Cisco device through a simulation. Through performance-based testing, the candidate's ability to perform hands-on configuration tasks can be measured instead of just memorizing answers to questions. *CCNA Practical Studies* has been written to help you become comfortable with this area of the exam through learning to translate networking concepts into practical configuration steps on Cisco equipment.

## Chapter Organization

The seventeen chapters and four appendixes are divided into four parts.

Part I, "Basic Router Configuration," reviews Cisco router components and navigating within the Cisco IOS. The lab environment then is introduced with specific lab objectives that will be accomplished for each chapter within the book. Next, we review how to gain access to routers and switches and how a terminal server is configured to access each lab router. We then review bridging and switching and how these are configured in the lab. In addition, some general router configuration steps, such as configuring a host name or setting passwords, are covered. Finally, router interfaces such as Ethernet, Token Ring, loopback, and serial are configured per the objectives given to connect your network. Finally, the configuration of Frame Relay is explored.

Part II, "Configuring Routing Protocols, ISDN, and IPX," explores the configuration of multiple routing protocols such as RIP, IGRP, and EIGRP, as well as how basic route redistribution can be configured to share routing information between routing domains. Following this, ISDN dial-on-demand is configured to connect a remote office to the main network. Finally, IPX is introduced into the network and the configuration of IPX routing is covered.

Part III, "Access Lists, IOS Operations, and Troubleshooting," introduces the configuration of standard and extended access lists to accomplish a defined set of access rules within the network. Next, fundamental concepts of backing up the IOS and router configuration files are introduced. Finally, faults are introduced into the network, with the aim of resolving each of these issues through a logical troubleshooting process.

Part IV, "Appendixes," includes four appendixes with resources that allow you to check your work:

- Appendix A, "Master Lab Configurations and Lab Diagrams," includes router configurations on a per-chapter basis to allow you to check your router configurations for accuracy. It also includes as a master lab diagram showing all IP addressing and routing protocols.
- Appendix B contains the Frame Relay switch diagram and configuration.
- Appendix C is a self-study lab scenario that you can accomplish on an independent basis.
- Appendix D contains information on how the ISDN simulator is configured for use in the lab.

## How Best to Use This Book

This book is meant as a practical approach to learning networking concepts. Having your own equipment or access to the equipment described in Chapter 1 would be ideal. This allows you the opportunity to gain the hands-on experience of configuring each router according to the lab objectives.

## Getting Equipment

You can obtain reasonably priced equipment from various places. If your place of employment has spare equipment that you can use, this might be your first option. If you want to purchase equipment, numerous places exist on the Internet, a few of which are as follows:

www.optsys.net

www.iqsale.com

www.ebay.com

## How to Use The Book If You Cannot Get Equipment

If you are unable to get equipment, do not despair—you can still profit from this book. The book is structured to walk you through each configuration task step by step. If you pay close attention to the figures and examples within the chapter and observe the changes that are made to the network, you will begin to understand how configuration tasks are applied and impact the network. Because some experience and knowledge level has been assumed in the writing of this book, you might run into concepts for which you desire additional information. In such cases, we recommend using the following resources as reference material while reading the book:

- Interconnecting Cisco *Network Devices* by Steve McQuerry
- *Cisco CCNA Exam #640-607 Certification Guide* by Wendell Odom
- www.cisco.com

# Icons Used in This Book

 Router

 Bridge

 Hub

 DSU/CSU

 Catalyst Switch

 Multilayer Switch

 ATM Switch

 ISDN/Frame Relay Switch

 Communication Server

Gateway

Access Server

PC

PC with
Software

Sun
Workstation

Macintosh

Terminal

File
Server

Web
Server

Cisco Works
Workstation

Printer

Laptop

IBM
Mainframe

Front End
Processor

Cluster
Controller

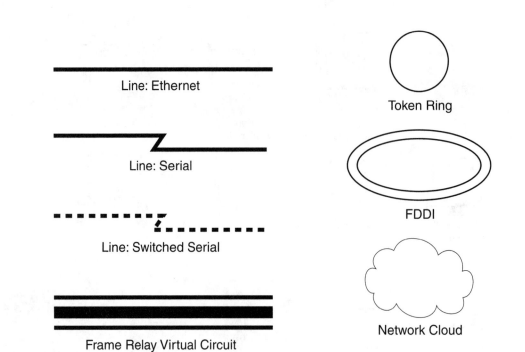

Line: Ethernet

Line: Serial

Line: Switched Serial

Frame Relay Virtual Circuit

Token Ring

FDDI

Network Cloud

## Command Syntax Conventions

The conventions used to present command syntax in this book are the same conventions used in the IOS Command Reference. The Command Reference describes these conventions as follows:

- Vertical bars (|) separate alternative, mutually exclusive elements.
- Square brackets [ ] indicate optional elements.
- Braces { } indicate a required choice.
- Braces within brackets [{ }] indicate a required choice within an optional element.
- **Boldface** indicates commands and keywords that are entered literally as shown. In actual configuration examples and output (not general command syntax), boldface indicates commands that are manually input by the user (such as a **show** command).
- *Italics* indicate arguments for which you supply actual values.

# Basic Router Configuration

## CHAPTER 1

# Practical Lab Methodology and Equipment

*CCNA Practical Studies* is a book dealing with the application of knowledge, not just the accumulation of knowledge. Our intention and hope is that, by the end of the book, your confidence and skill level in configuring and troubleshooting Cisco devices will have greatly increased. We ourselves came through the ranks of CCNA, CCNP, and CCIE, and through those experiences we learned that knowing networking theory is much different than configuring a networking device to operate according to that theory. During the certification process, we often experienced the frustration of understanding networking concepts but lacked the knowledge of how to configure networking devices according to those concepts in a real-world environment. These experiences made us feel that more hands-on experience was needed to help grasp the  configuration tasks necessary to configure Cisco devices from start to finish. For this purpose, we have developed this book. Our approach to this book is simple:

> To give you an opportunity to configure, step by step, a completely functional network with multiple routing protocols and ISDN dial backup

By doing so, you will be able to see and understand the impact that each command has and understand the method of configuring a network from scratch.

## OSI Reference Model

Our method to configuring this network will follow the OSI reference model. The OSI model was developed to help break internetworking concepts into areas that can be identified and separated from other concepts. This helps you to understand the different tasks that must be completed to obtain internetwork connectivity. The advantages of having a layered approach are listed here:

- Enables specialization in each of the layers
- Reduces the complexity of the entire process by breaking up complex operations into simple elements
- Provides an opportunity to define standards at each layer that are independent of the other layers
- Provides a method to troubleshooting internetworking issues

Table 1-1 illustrates the OSI reference model.

**Table 1-1**   *OSI Reference Model*

| Layer 7 | Application |
|---------|-------------|
| Layer 6 | Presentation |
| Layer 5 | Session |
| Layer 4 | Transport |
| Layer 3 | Network |
| Layer 2 | Data link |
| Layer 1 | Physical |

Before getting into the methodology behind the OSI model and this book, review Table 1-2, which delves into the seven layers of the OSI model individually.

**Table 1-2**   *OSI Reference Model Layers*

| Layer Name | Functional Description | Examples |
|------------|-----------------------|----------|
| Application (Layer 7) | An application that communicates with other computers is implementing OSI application layer concepts. The application layer refers to communications services to applications. For example, a word processor that lacks communications capabilities would not implement code for communications, and word processor programmers would not be concerned about OSI Layer 7. However, if an option for transferring a file were added, the word processor would need to implement OSI Layer 7 (or the equivalent layer in another protocol specification). | Telnet, HTTP, FTP, WWW browsers, NFS, SMTP gateways (Eudora, CC:mail), SNMP, X.400 mail, FTAM |
| Presentation (Layer 6) | This layer's main purpose is defining data formats, such as ASCII text, EBCDIC text, binary, BCD, and JPEG. Encryption also is defined by OSI as a presentation layer service. For example, FTP enables you to choose binary or ASCII transfer. If binary is selected, the sender and receiver do not modify the contents of the file. If ASCII is chosen, the sender translates the text from the sender's character set to a standard ASCII and sends the data. The receiver translates back from the standard ASCII to the character set used on the receiving computer. | JPEG, ASCII, EBCDIC, TIFF, GIF, PICT, encryption, MPEG, MIDI |

**Table 1-2**    *OSI Reference Model Layers (Continued)*

| Layer Name | Functional Description | Examples |
|---|---|---|
| Session (Layer 5) | The session layer defines how to start, control, and end conversations (called sessions). This includes the control and management of multiple bidirectional messages so that the application can be notified if only some of a series of messages are completed. This allows the presentation layer to have a seamless view of an incoming stream of data. The presentation layer can be presented with data if all flows occur, in some cases. For example, an automated teller machine transaction in which you withdraw cash from your checking account should not debit your account and then fail before handing you the cash, recording the transaction even though you did not receive money. The session layer creates ways to imply which flows are part of the same session and which flows must complete before any are considered complete. | RPC, SQL, NFS, NetBIOS names, AppleTalk ASP, DECnet SCP |
| Transport (Layer 4) | Layer 4 includes the choice of protocols that either do or do not provide error recovery. Multiplexing of incoming data for different flows to applications on the same host (for example, TCP sockets) also is performed. Reordering of the incoming data stream when packets arrive out of order is included. | TCP, UDP, SPX |
| Network (Layer 3) | This layer defines end-to-end delivery of packets. To accomplish this, the network layer defines logical addressing so that any endpoint can be identified. It also defines how routing works and how routes are learned so that the packets can be delivered. The network layer also defines how to fragment a packet into smaller packets to accommodate media with smaller maximum transmission unit sizes. (*Note:* Not all Layer 3 protocols use fragmentation.) The network layer of OSI defines most of the details that a Cisco router considers when routing. For example, IP running in a Cisco router is responsible for examining the destination IP address of a packet, comparing that address to the IP routing table, fragmenting the packet if the outgoing interface requires smaller packets, and queuing the packet to be sent out to the interface. | IP, IPX, AppleTalk DDP, ICMP |

*continues*

**Table 1-2**  *OSI Reference Model Layers (Continued)*

| Layer Name | Functional Description | Examples |
|---|---|---|
| Data link (Layer 2) | The data link (Layer 2) specifications are concerned with getting data across one particular link or medium. The data link protocols define delivery across an individual link. These protocols are necessarily concerned with the type of media in question; for example, 802.3 and 802.2 are specifications from the IEEE, which are referenced by OSI as valid data link (Layer 2) protocols. These specifications define how Ethernet works. Other protocols, such as High-Level Data Link Control (HDLC) for a point-to-point WAN link, deal with the different details of a WAN link. As with other protocol specifications, OSI often does not create any original specification for the data link layer but instead relies on other standards bodies such as IEEE to create new standards for the data link layer and the physical layer. | IEEE 802.3/802.2, HDLC, Frame Relay, PPP, FDDI, ATM, IEEE 802.5/802.2 |
| Physical (Layer 1) | These physical layer (Layer 1) specifications, which are also typically standards from other organizations that are referred to by OSI, deal with the physical characteristics of the transmission medium. Connectors, pins, use of pins, electrical currents, encoding, and light modulation are all part of different physical layer specifications. Multiple specifications are sometimes used to complete all details of the physical layer. For example, RJ-45 defines the shape of the connector and the number of wires or pins in the cable. Ethernet and 802.3 define the use of wires or pins 1, 2, 3, and 6. So, to use a Category 5 cable with an RJ-45 connector for an Ethernet connection, Ethernet and RJ-45 physical layer specifications are used. | EIA/TIA-232, V.35, EIA/TIA- 449, V.24, RJ45, Ethernet, 802.3, 802.5, FDDI, NRZI, NRZ, B8ZS |

As you configure the network, you will deal mostly in Layers 1 through 4. Our approach to the network configuration task is to start at the physical layer, complete the configuration task for the physical layer, move on to the data link layer configuration task, and so on until you have completed all the configuration tasks and the network is up and operational. Later chapters in the book get into more detail in terms of configuration tasks. This method enables you to identify all needed configuration tasks for each layer, remembering that if the physical layer configuration tasks are not completed, the data link configuration task will not produce the desired result because they are dependant on the physical layer. This is true with the network layer as well—if the data link configuration tasks are not completed or are completed incorrectly, the network layer (primarily routing) will not function correctly.

# Lab Equipment

Although lab equipment is not needed to benefit from this book, having your own equipment is highly recommended. By being able to follow the commands outlined in this book, you will experience for yourself the process of configuring a network from the ground up. If you choose to obtain your own equipment, Table 1-3 lists all the needed equipment for this lab network.

**Table 1-3**    *Lab Equipment*

| Hardware: | Quantity |
| --- | --- |
| Catalyst 1900 series switch | 1 |
| Cisco 2501 | 3 |
| Cisco 2504 | 2 |
| Cisco 2514 | 1 |
| Cisco 2523 | 1 |
| Cisco 2511 | 1 |
| Black Box ISDN Simulator | 1 |
| **Cables:** | |
| Cat 5 straight-through cables with RJ-45 connectors (for ISDN ports) | 2 |
| Cat 5 Ethernet cables with RJ-45 connectors | 6 |
| Token Ring DB9–to–Type 1 interface cable | 2 |
| Standard power cables | 9 |
| V.35 DTE-DCE back-to-back cables (DB60 to DB60) | 4 |
| Octal cable (For terminal server 2511) | 1 |
| **Miscellaneous:** | |
| Ethernet AUI–to–RJ-45 Transceiver | 6 |
| Token Ring MAU | 2 |
| Power strips[1] | *** |

1. ***Purchase as many power strips as needed to safely plug in all your devices.

To purchase the equipment, you can contact your local Cisco reseller. Also, many companies offer used or refurbished equipment at discounted rates. eBay, Iqsales.com, and others are great sources for used Cisco equipment available on the Internet.

With that being said, we are confident that through this book your internetworking skills and your ability to configure, maintain, and troubleshoot Cisco internetworking devices will increase tremendously. Begin by reviewing the hardware components of Cisco devices and Cisco IOS Software.

This chapter reviews the following key topics about router components:

- Memory
- Interfaces and ports
- The command-line interface (CLI)

## CHAPTER 2

# Cisco Router Review

The purpose of this chapter is to provide a brief review of Cisco's Internetwork Operating System (IOS) software and show how to use the command-line interface (CLI) to configure and manage a Cisco router. These skills are an essential part of successfully completing the lab scenarios. A thorough understanding of router hardware components and how Cisco IOS software controls these components is necessary to effectively configure, manage, and troubleshoot Cisco routers. If you already have training or experience with Cisco routers, much of the following information might be second nature. If not, a brief review follows to provide the general concepts necessary to understand the configuration process used during the lab scenarios.

This chapter begins by discussing the various memory types in a router, as well as the functions that each provides. Next, you will review interfaces and ports and their purpose within the router. Finally, you will review the CLI and how to navigate the CLI to configure and manage a Cisco router.

## Router Components

Cisco routers have various components that are controlled by the Cisco IOS. These components include such things as memory, interfaces, and ports. Each component has a purpose that provides added functionality to a router. A review of these components will be useful in understanding each of their roles within a router.

### Memory

A router contains different types of memory, where it can store images, configuration files, and microcode. The types of memory and their purposes are as follows:

- **RAM**—Often referred to as dynamic random-access memory (DRAM). RAM is the working area of memory storage used by the CPU to execute Cisco IOS software and to hold the running configuration file, routing tables, and ARP cache. The running configuration file (running-config) contains the current configuration of the software. Information in RAM is cleared when the router is power-cycled or reloaded.

- **ROM**—Sometimes referred to as erasable programmable read-only memory (EPROM). ROM is hard-wired read-only memory in the router. ROM contains power-on self-test (POST) diagnostics and the bootstrap or boot-loader software. This code allows the router to boot from ROM when it cannot find a valid Cisco IOS software image. This is known as *ROM Monitor mode*. This is a diagnostic mode that provides a user interface when the router cannot find a valid image.

- **Flash**—Available as EPROMs, single in-line memory modules (SIMMs), or PCMCIA cards. Flash is the default location where a router finds and boots its IOS image. On some platforms, additional configuration files or boot images can be stored in Flash. The contents of Flash are retained when the router is power-cycled or reloaded.

- **NVRAM**—Nonvolatile random-access memory. NVRAM stores the startup configuration file (startup-config), which is used during system startup to configure the software. In addition, NVRAM contains the software configuration register, a configurable setting in Cisco IOS software that determines which image to use when booting the router. The contents of NVRAM are retained when the router is power-cycled or reloaded.

Table 2-1 provides a summary of these memory types, their function, and useful Cisco IOS software commands when managing these different types of memory.

**Table 2-1**    *Memory Types*

| Memory Type | Contents | Useful Cisco IOS Software Commands |
|---|---|---|
| RAM | Running configuration file | **show running-config** |
|  | Routing tables | **show ip route** |
|  | ARP cache | **show arp** |
|  | Working memory | **show memory** |
| ROM | POST | — |
|  | Bootstrap |  |
|  | ROM Monitor mode |  |
|  | Locate and load IOS |  |
| Flash | IOS | **show flash** |
|  | Additional configuration files |  |
|  | Additional IOS images |  |
| NVRAM | Startup configuration file | **show startup-config** |
|  | Configuration register | **show version** |

An understanding of the different types of memory and their function within the router helps not only clarify where the IOS image and configuration files are stored, but also proves useful by allowing the user to manipulate these configuration files during the configuration process and understand what area of memory is being changed.

## Interfaces and Ports

Routers contain different types of interfaces and ports. Interfaces assist the router in routing packets and bridging frames between network segments, and they provide a connection point to different types of transmission media. Ports, on the other hand, provide management access to the router.

Some common interface types are as follows:

- Serial
- Ethernet
- Token Ring
- Asynchronous
- FDDI

The preceding types of interfaces are some of the most common; however, interface types are in no way static. Interface types are added as new technologies evolve and methods are needed to interconnect and integrate network devices. An example of this is the voice interface available in the Cisco 2600 series that connects to a private branch exchange (PBX) or standard analog phone.

Ports on the router enable a user to connect to the router for management and configuration purposes. You can connect either a terminal (DTE) or a modem (DCE) to these ports. Some of the common ports are:

- Console
- Auxiliary (AUX)

The console and auxiliary ports are physical ports on the router that provide management access to the router. In addition to these, there are also vty lines, which are software-defined lines that allow Telnet access to the router. The default vty configuration is vty lines 0 through 4, allowing five simultaneous Telnet sessions to the router. Passwords can be configured on each vty line to secure access to the router.

## Command-Line Interface

CLI is the acronym used by Cisco to denote the command-line interface of the IOS. CLI is the primary interface used to configure, manage, and troubleshoot Cisco devices. This user interface enables you to directly execute IOS commands, and it can be accessed through a console, modem, or Telnet connection. Access by any of these methods is generally referred to as an EXEC session.

## EXEC Levels or Modes

Two different EXEC sessions exist, user EXEC level and privileged EXEC level. Each level provides a different amount of access to the commands within the IOS. User EXEC provides access to a limited number of commands that allow basic troubleshooting and monitoring of the router. Privileged EXEC level allows access to all router commands, such as configuration and management settings. Password protection to the privileged EXEC level is highly recommended to prevent unauthorized configuration changes from being made to the router. Upon initiating an EXEC session on the router, a user is placed in user EXEC mode. This is denoted in the router with the > prompt—for example:

```
Router>
```

To change to the privileged EXEC level, type in the command **enable**, as shown:

```
Router> enable
Password: [enable password]
```

If an enable password has been set, the router prompts you for it. When you enter the correct enable password, the prompt changes from **Router>** to **Router#**. This indicates that you have successfully entered into privileged EXEC mode, as shown:

```
Router>
Password: [enable password]
Router#
```

---

**TIP**     Enable passwords show up as clear text in the running configuration file. If this is undesirable for your environment, Cisco IOS software offers another option—encrypt the enable password using the **enable secret** command. Using the **enable secret** command ensures that the password is not displayed as clear text in the running configuration file.

---

## IOS CLI Hierarchy

Cisco IOS software is structured in a hierarchical manner. It is important to understand this structure to successfully navigate within Cisco IOS software. As mentioned previously, there are two EXEC modes: user EXEC and privileged EXEC. Privileged EXEC mode is composed of various configuration modes:

- Global configuration mode
- Interface configuration mode
- Router configuration mode
- Line configuration mode

Figure 2-1 provides a visual breakdown of the configuration modes.

**Figure 2-1**    *Cisco IOS Software CLI Hierarchy*

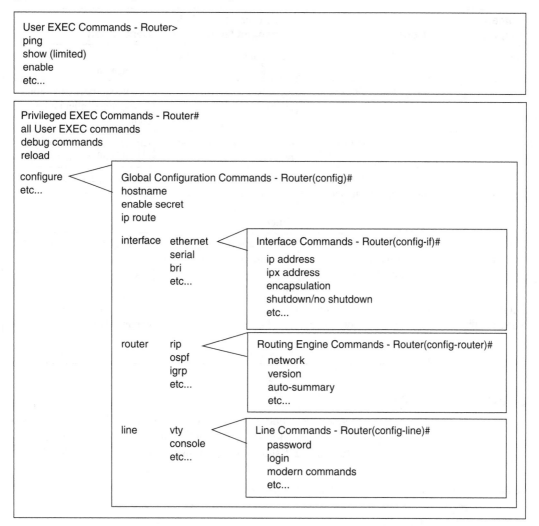

Within each mode, certain commands are available for execution. Using the context-sensitive help, you can see a list of which commands are available. While navigating the CLI, the router prompt changes to reflect your current position within the CLI hierarchy. Table 2-2 summarizes the main command prompts within the CLI hierarchy.

**Table 2-2**    *CLI Command Prompts by Mode*

| Command Prompt | Mode | IOS Command to Enter Command Mode | Description |
|---|---|---|---|
| **Router>** | User EXEC mode | Default mode upon login | Limited inspection of router information |
| **Router #** | Privileged EXEC mode | From **Router>**, type **enable** | Detailed inspection, testing, debug, and configuration commands |
| **Router(config)#** | Configuration mode | From **Router#**, type **config terminal** | High-level configuration or global configuration changes |
| **Router (config-if)#** | Interface level (submenu of configuration mode) | From **Router(config)#**, type **interface** [*interface name*]—for example, **Ethernet0** | Interface-specific commands |
| **Router (config-router)#** | Routing engine level (submenu of configuration mode) | From **Router(config)#**, type **router** [*routing protocol*]—for example, **rip**, **igrp**, and so forth | Routing engine commands |
| **Router (config-line)#** | Line level (submenu of configuration mode) | From **Router(config)#**, type **line** [*port*]—for example, **aux0**, **console0**, **vty 0 4** | Line-configuration commands |

## Context-Sensitive Help

In both user and privileged EXEC modes, you can see a listing of available commands by typing a question mark (**?**) at the **Router>** or **Router#** prompts. This is referred to as *context-sensitive help*. Example 2-1 shows context-sensitive help from user EXEC mode.

**Example 2-1**    *Context-Sensitive Help from User EXEC Mode*

```
Router>?
Exec commands:
  <1-99>          Session number to resume
  access-enable   Create a temporary Access-List entry
  clear           Reset functions
  connect         Open a terminal connection
  disable         Turn off privileged commands
  disconnect      Disconnect an existing network connection
  enable          Turn on privileged commands
  exit            Exit from the EXEC
  help            Description of the interactive help system
  lat             Open a lat connection
  lock            Lock the terminal
```

**Example 2-1**  *Context-Sensitive Help from User EXEC Mode (Continued)*

```
login             Log in as a particular user
logout            Exit from the EXEC
mrinfo            Request neighbor and version information from a multicast
                  router
mstat             Show statistics after multiple multicast traceroutes
mtrace            Trace reverse multicast path from destination to source
name-connection   Name an existing network connection
pad               Open a X.29 PAD connection
ping              Send echo messages
ppp               Start IETF Point-to-Point Protocol (PPP)
--More--
```

Example 2-1 displays the commands available for execution from user EXEC mode. When the number of commands available exceed that which can be displayed on the screen, the IOS displays the **--More--** prompt. Pressing the Spacebar presents the next page of commands, often followed by another **--More--** until all remaining commands are displayed and you're returned to the **Router>** prompt, as demonstrated in Example 2-2.

**Example 2-2**  *Hitting the Spacebar Continues the Context-Sensitive Help Listing and Returns You to the User EXEC Mode Prompt*

```
Logout            Exit from the EXEC
  mrinfo          Request neighbor and version information from a multicast
                  router
  mstat           Show statistics after multiple multicast traceroutes
  mtrace          Trace reverse multicast path from destination to source
  name-connection Name an existing network connection
  pad             Open a X.29 PAD connection
  ping            Send echo messages
  ppp             Start IETF Point-to-Point Protocol (PPP)
  resume          Resume an active network connection
  rlogin          Open an rlogin connection
  show            Show running system information
  slip            Start Serial-line IP (SLIP)
  systat          Display information about terminal lines
  telnet          Open a telnet connection
  terminal        Set terminal line parameters
  tn3270          Open a tn3270 connection
  traceroute      Trace route to destination
  tunnel          Open a tunnel connection
  where           List active connections
  x3              Set X.3 parameters on PAD
  xremote         Enter XRemote mode

Router>
```

You can repeat the same process to get a list of available commands from privileged EXEC mode. The only difference is that more commands are available within privileged EXEC mode.

To find out what commands are available that begin with the letter *c*, you would type the letter **c** immediately followed by a **?**. This is referred to as *word help*, and it is useful when you know what the command begins with, but not the exact syntax. Example 2-3 demonstrates this concept.

**Example 2-3**  *Using Word Help to Find the Exact Syntax of a Command*

```
Router#c?
clear  clock  configure  connect  copy
```

As more letters are added to the command you need help for, the context-sensitive help feature narrows down the available commands to choose from. Example 2-4 demonstrates what you would see if you narrowed your search by adding additional letters such as **co?** or **con?**.

**Example 2-4**  *Adding Characters in a Command Immediately Followed by a* **?** *Helps You Narrow Your Command Search*

```
Router#c?
clear  clock  configure  connect  copy

Router#co?
configure  connect  copy

Router#con?
configure  connect
```

Suppose that you need more information on the syntax of the **configure** command. Command help is available to list arguments that are available with a given command by typing the command, followed by a space and a **?**. For example, if you want to find out what commands were available to use with the **configure** command, you would type **configure ?**, as demonstrated in Example 2-5.

**Example 2-5**  *Entering Characters in a Command Followed by* **?** *Helps You Find the Exact Syntax of a Command*

```
Router#configure ?
  memory             Configure from NV memory
  network            Configure from a TFTP network host
  overwrite-network  Overwrite NV memory from TFTP network host
  terminal           Configure from the terminal
  <cr>
```

Finally, the command parser has the capability to distinguish erroneous commands that are entered incorrectly, as well as prompt you when more specific command arguments are needed. When an erroneous command is entered, the help feature returns the output shown in Example 2-6.

**Example 2-6** *Entering an Erroneous Command Generates a Message to Indicate the Syntax Error*

```
Router#show rnning-config
            ^
% Invalid input detected at '^' marker.
```

The ^ marker indicates where the error in the syntax occurred. When a more specific command argument is needed to distinguish among multiple possibilities, the help feature returns **%Ambiguous command:**, as shown in Example 2-7.

**Example 2-7** *Entering a Command Requiring More Specific Parameters Generates an Ambiguous Command Message*

```
Router#show access
% Ambiguous command:   "show access"
```

This is easily corrected by typing more of the command so that multiple possibilities no longer exist, as shown in Example 2-8.

**Example 2-8** *Entering a Command with the Required Arguments to Eliminate the Ambiguous Command Error*

```
Router#show access-lists
Standard IP access list 1
    permit any
```

Each of these context-sensitive help features is useful in helping you determine whether the command syntax is incorrect.

## Hot Keys

The CLI also provides hot keys for easier navigation within the IOS and provide shortcuts for editing functions. Table 2-3 provides a list of shortcuts that are available.

**Table 2-3** *CLI Hot Keys for Cisco IOS Software Command Editing Functions*

| Key Sequence | Description |
|---|---|
| Ctrl-A | Moves the cursor to the beginning of the current line |
| Ctrl-R | Redisplays a line |
| Ctrl-U | Erases a line |
| Ctrl-W | Erases a word |
| Ctrl-Z | Ends configuration mode and returns to privileged EXEC mode |
| Tab | Finishes a partial command |
| Backspace | Removes one character to the left of the cursor |
| Ctrl-P or Up Arrow | Allows you to scroll forward through former commands |
| Ctrl-N or Down Arrow | Allows you to scroll backward through former commands |
| Ctrl-E | Moves the cursor to the end of the current line |
| Ctrl-F or right arrow | Moves forward one character |
| Ctrl-B or left arrow | Moves back one character |
| Esc+B | Moves back one word |
| Esc+F | Moves forward one word |

# Summary

This chapter was intended as a brief review of the following router components:

- **Memory**—It is important to understand each type of memory and the function each provides.

- **Interfaces and ports**—Interfaces route packets or bridge frames between network segments, while ports provide management access to the router. You should understand the difference between interfaces and port and where each is configured within the CLI.

- **Command-line interface (CLI)**—Learning to navigate the CLI is essential to successfully being able to configure, manage, and troubleshoot Cisco devices. Hands-on practice will help you master the CLI.

This base knowledge is essential before moving into the lab scenario. For a more in-depth look at these topics, refer to Chapter 3, "Operating and Configuring a Cisco IOS Device," in the book *Interconnecting Cisco Network Devices*, by Steve McQuerry (published by Cisco Press). In addition, hands-on experience is the key to feeling comfortable navigating the CLI and understanding the different components of Cisco routers.

Now with the review complete, let's examine the lab environment in the next chapter.

This chapter outlines the lab objectives and physical topology. The following sections contain the lab objectives that will be completed in subsequent chapters:

- Terminal server configuration
- Cisco Catalyst switch configuration
- Cisco router configuration
- IP addressing
- Routing Information Protocol (RIP)
- Interior Group Routing Protocol (IGRP)
- Enhanced IGRP (EIGRP)
- Route redistribution
- ISDN dial-on-demand routing (DDR)
- Internetwork Packet Exchange (IPX)
- IPX EIGRP
- IPX RIP
- IPX routing redistribution
- Standard access lists
- Extended access lists
- Cisco router operations
- Physical layer configuration
- Basic router and data link layer configurations
- Network layer configurations (routing)

## CHAPTER 3

# Lab Environment

The lab has two components—the physical topology and the lab objectives that you must complete. This chapter reviews the physical topology and provides lab objectives to complete. Each following chapter focuses on one section of the lab objectives and takes you step by step through the configuration process for that section. Don't be too worried if some of the objectives don't make sense. We will explain in detail what is to be done to complete the objective in the chapter that covers that task.

The first step is to review the lab diagram. To make certain that you understand the lab objectives, take a look at the physical topology of the lab in Figure 3-1.

**Figure 3-1** *Lab Topology*

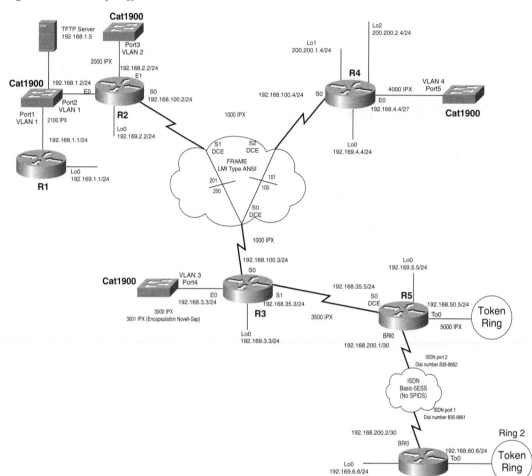

# Lab Inventory and Physical Connections

Let's take a look at R1. (Each router will be given a host name during the lab. We will use the host name as it appears on the lab diagram to refer to the different routers.) R1 is a Cisco 2500 series router with two serial ports and one Ethernet port. It is on the same segment as R2's Ethernet 0, and a TFTP server is running on the same segment (you will be using the TFTP server later in the lab). R1's Ethernet 0 and R2's Ethernet 0 are connected to a Cisco Catalyst 1900 (Cat 1900) on ports 1 and 2, respectively.

R2 is a 2514 series router. It has two serial ports and two Ethernet ports. R2's Ethernet 0 is connected to port 2 on Cat 1900, and Ethernet 1 is connected to port 3 on Cat 1900 as well. R2's Serial 0 is connected to Serial 1 on the Frame Switch router.

R3 is a Cisco 2500 series router with two serial ports and one Ethernet port. R3's Ethernet port is connected to Cat 1900 on port 4, and Serial 0 is connected to Serial 0 on the Frame Switch router. R3's Serial 1 port is connected to R5's Serial 0 port. R4 is a Cisco 2500 series router as well. It has two serial ports and one Ethernet port. R4's Ethernet port is connected to Cat 1900 on port 5. R4's Serial 0 is connected to Serial 2 on the Frame Switch router.

R5 is a Cisco 2500 series router. It has two serial ports, one Token Ring port and one ISDN BRI port. R5's Serial 0 port is connected to R3's Serial 1 port. Serial 0 on R5 is the DCE. R5's Token Ring port is connected to a standard media access unit (MAU). The BRI0 port is connected to port 2 on the Black Box ISDN simulator.

R6 is a Cisco 2500 series router. It has two serial ports, one Token Ring port and 1 ISDN BRI port. R6's Token Ring port is connected to a standard MAU. The BRI0 port is connected to port 1 on the Black Box ISDN simulator.

The terminal server is a Cisco 2511 router with 16 asynchronous ports. Each asynchronous port is connected to the console port on the back of each router in sequential order (that is, R1's console port is connected to asynchronous port 1 on the terminal server, R2's console port is connected to asynchronous port 2 on the terminal server, and so on). You will be accessing all the routers and the Catalyst 1900 switch through the terminal server. Chapter 4, "Gaining Access to the Routers and Switches," discusses the terminal server configuration.

The Frame Relay switch router is a Cisco 2523 router. It has ten serial ports, one ISDN BRI port, and one Token Ring port. The configuration of the Frame Relay switch will not be part of this lab. If you are unfamiliar with how a Frame Relay Switch operates or how to configure a Cisco router to be a Frame Relay switch, see Appendix B, "Frame Relay Switch Configuration," for more information.

---

**NOTE**      The Frame Relay switch is a very important piece of the lab. Without the Frame Switch operating correctly, you will not be able to complete the lab. We *highly* recommend reviewing Appendix B before continuing with the lab objectives.

---

# Lab Objectives

The lab objectives are divided into several sections. Each of the following chapters focuses on one of the sections and completes each section step by step. Before you actually start configuring the lab, it is highly recommended that you read completely all the lab objectives. It is important that you gain a high level understanding of what you will be doing before you start. One suggestion is to redraw the entire lab diagram on a separate piece of paper. Include router names, interfaces (including loopback interfaces), IP addresses, and all routing domain borders. If you are unsure of what your diagram should look like, refer to Appendix A, "Lab Configurations and Diagrams," for an example.

Reread the lab objectives until your diagram contains all devices, IP address, routing domains, and media types. The sections that follow lay out all the lab objectives.

## Terminal Server Configuration

Configure the Cisco 2511 router to be the terminal server for this lab. The terminal server is connected to each device's console port. Port assignments are as follows:

- **R1**—2001
- **R2**—2002
- **R3**—2003
- **R4**—2004
- **R5**—2005
- **R6**—2006
- **Catalyst Switch**—2007

---

**NOTE**     A terminal server is a router (or other device) that will provide one point of contact for gaining access to all the routers in the lab. Chapter 4 covers the concept of a terminal server and shows how to configure one.

---

Figure 3-2 depicts the physical connections from the terminal server to the lab routers.

**Figure 3-2**    *Terminal Server Connections*

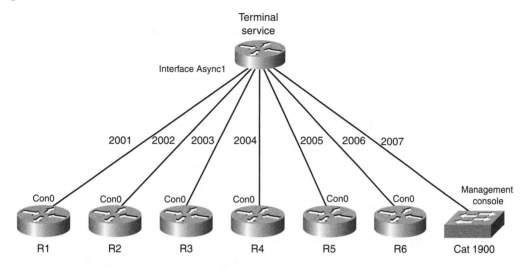

# Cisco Catalyst Switch Configuration

- Configure the switch with a host name of Cat1900.

- Set the enable password to falcons.

- Assign the management console an IP address of 192.168.1.3/24 and a default gateway of 192.168.1.10 (the terminal server).

- Configure ports 1 and 2 (refer to Figure 3-2, if needed) to be in VLAN 1, and name the VLAN vlan-r1r2.

- Configure port 3 for VLAN 2, and name the VLAN vlan-r2e1.

- Configure port 4 for VLAN 3, and name the VLAN vlan-r3e0.

- Configure port 5 for VLAN 4, and name the VLAN vlan-r4e0.

# Cisco Router Configuration

Configure all routers to have the following:

- Host name (that is, host names are to be according to the number R1, R2, R3, and so on).

- Enable password of falcons.

- Enable console login with password falcons.

- Telnet access (vty 0 4), password falcons.

- No DNS resolution (no domain name lookups).

- Configure all routers so that the console port will not time out your connection.

- Configure all routers so that messages from the router to the console screen will not be appended to the command line.

- Configure all routers to have a description on all active interfaces (except loopback interfaces) stating to which router they are connected and which interface they are using.

- Configure all routers to show a banner when you log into the console port. In the banner, state which router you are logging into. For example, on Router 1, the banner should read "This is Router 1."

- Create a host table on all routers using the loopback addresses you just created for each router.

# IP Addressing

- Create loopback interfaces on all routers. Use IP address 192.169.*X.X*/24 (where *X* is the router number). So, R1 would have a loopback address of 192.169.1.1/24, R2 would be 192.169.2.2/24, and so on.

Look at the network diagram for IP addressing assignments. Don't forget to look at the netmasks! The BRI ports on R5 and R6 should use the IP addresses 192.168.200.1/30 and 192.168.200.2/30, respectively.

# Routing Information Protocol

Routing Information Protocol (RIP) is a very common routing protocol used in small to medium-size networks. RIP is very important to the CCNA exam, and, in addition, you should have a working knowledge of configuring and troubleshooting routing issues in RIP.

- Place R2's loopback 0, E0, and E1 networks into RIP.

- R1's E0 and loopback 0 networks should be configured for RIP as well.

Figure 3-3 shows the routers that you will be working with in this section.

**Figure 3-3**  *IP RIP Routers*

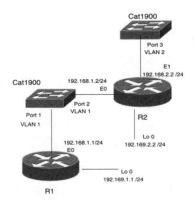

# Interior Gateway Routing Protocol

Interior Gateway Routing Protocol (IGRP) is a similar routing protocol to RIP. We have included a section in the lab so that you can see the configuration commands and routing issues with IGRP.

- Place R3's S1, loopback 0, and R5's To0, loopback 0, and S0 networks into IGRP autonomous system 200.

Figure 3-4 depicts the routers that you will configure in this section.

**Figure 3-4**   *IP IGRP Routers*

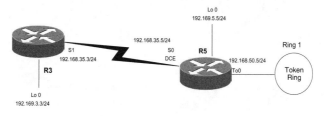

# Enhanced IGRP

Enhanced IGRP (EIGRP) is a very common routing protocol, and you will see it used many networks. It is very important that you understand the configuration process of EIGRP and know some troubleshooting processes for EIGRP. Having a strong working knowledge of EIGRP will be very beneficial in the real world. We have included EIGRP even though the CCNA exam does not cover it in depth.

- Place R3's S0, R2's S0, R4's S0, and R4's Loopback 0 networks into EIGRP autonomous System 100.
- Place R3's E0 network and R4's E0 into EIGRP AS 100.
- Create two loopback interfaces on R4 with the following addresses: loopback 1 = 200.200.1.4/24, loopback 2 = 200.200.2.4/24.
- Add these two networks into the EIGRP routing domain, and configure R4 so that all other routers see only one route to these two addresses.

Figure 3-5 shows the router setup involved in this section.

**Figure 3-5**   *IP EIGRP Routers*

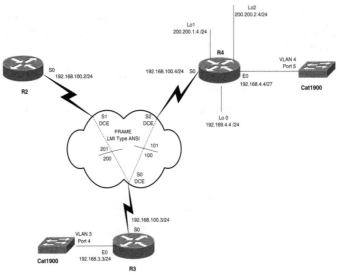

## Route Redistribution

Route redistribution is not covered on the CCNA exam, but it is imperative in a working environment that you understand how different routing processes interact. You will see very few networks that do not have some sort of route redistribution occurring at some level.

- On R2, redistribute RIP into EIGRP and redistribute EIGRP into RIP.

- On R3, redistribute EIGRP into IGRP and redistribute IGRP into EIGRP.

- Fix any routing problems that you encounter as you see fit.

All routers should be capable of pinging all interfaces at the end of this section.

## ISDN Dial-on-Demand Routing

Dial backup is an important element in most networks. We have included a basic dial-on-demand routing (DDR) situation so that you can see the configuration commands and see how it affects the network logically.

- Configure the BRI interfaces on R5 and R6. See Figure 12-2 for ISDN information such as switch type and dial numbers.

- Use PPP encapsulation.

- The ISDN link should be active only when IP traffic is present. R6 should call R5. No routing protocols are to be used across the link. Use static routes on R5 and R6, but ensure that workstations on R6's Token Ring network (192.168.60.0) can reach the rest of your network.

- The link should be brought down after 5 minutes of inactivity.

- Test R6 connectivity to the rest of your network through Telnet. You must use the host name of each router, which was configured previously (that is, R1, R2, R3, and so on), to initiate the Telnet session.

Figure 3-6 shows the routers involved in configuring DDR.

**Figure 3-6**   *ISDN DDR Routers*

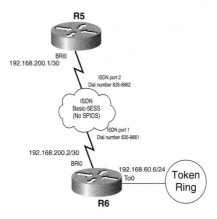

## Internetwork Packet Exchange

Internetwork Packet Exchange (IPX) is a very common protocol. Although its popularity has diminished, it can be found in many networks. You will find it very helpful to have a good understanding of how IPX is configured on Cisco routers and how the Cisco routers route between IPX networks.

- Configure R2's S0, R3's S0, and R4's S1 with IPX network number 1000.

- Configure R3's S1 and R5's S0 for IPX network number 3500.

- Configure R5's To0 for IPX network number 5000.

- Configure R4's E0 for IPX network 4000.

- Configure R1's E0 and R2's E0 for IPX network 2100.

- Configure R2's Ethernet 1 for IPX network 2000.

- Configure R3's E0 with IPX network 3000. Use the default encapsulation type.

- Configure a secondary IPX network number 3001 on R3's E0. Make the encapsulation Novell SAP.

Figure 3-7 shows the IPX network topology. Note that we will not be configuring ISDN DDR for IPX in this book.

**Figure 3-7** *IPX Network Topology*

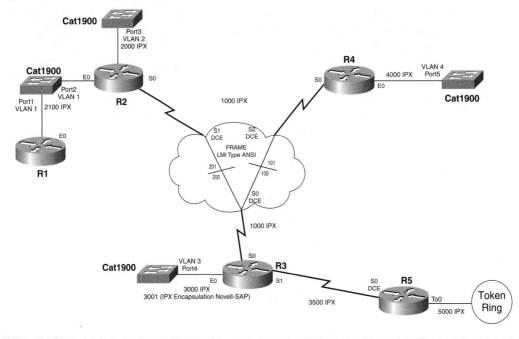

## IPX EIGRP

- Use IPX EIGRP as the routing protocol for the interfaces in the Frame Relay cloud and R4's E0. Figure 3-8 identifies the router interfaces that will be configured for IPX EIGRP.

**Figure 3-8** *IPX EIGRP Routers*

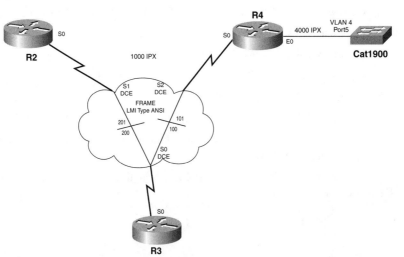

## IPX RIP

- Use IPX RIP for all other router interfaces that are *not* configured for IPX EIGRP. Figure 3-9 identifies the IPX networks that will be configured for IPX RIP.

**Figure 3-9**   *IPX RIP Routers*

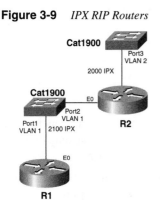

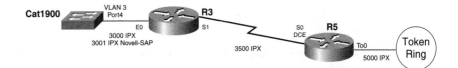

## IPX Routing Redistribution

- To make all IPX networks reachable by all IPX routers, redistribute IPX EIGRP and IPX RIP. Make sure that all IPX networks are reachable by using the IPX **ping** command.

## Standard Access Lists

Create a standard outgoing access list and apply it on R2's S0 that fulfills the following requirements:

- Deny access to users on network 192.168.12.0 to the Frame Relay network. (Assume that this network exists off R1.)

## Extended Access Lists

- Create an extended incoming access list and apply it on R3's S0 that fulfills the following requirements:

  — Deny HTTP (www) traffic from reaching the Token Ring 1s network.

  — Deny SMTP traffic from reaching R3's E0 network.

  — Permit anything else.

## Cisco Router Operations

The CCNA exam covers some basic router commands and operations. We have included a section that will help you master these commands and give you an understanding of how these commands are applied on routers in a working network environment.

- **Cisco Router Boot Configuration**—Configure R1 to boot from the TFTP server and then Flash. (Use the Cisco IOS Software image filename igs-j-l.111-18.bin.).

- **Cisco Router IOS Software Backup**—Backup the Cisco IOS Software image on R1 to the TFTP server 192.168.1.5.

- **Cisco Router IOS Software Upgrade**—Upgrade the Cisco IOS Software on R1 to image c2500-js-l_112-17.bin from the TFTP server.

- **Cisco Router Configuration Backup**—Backup the current configurations of R1 to the TFTP server.

- **Cisco Router Configuration Restore**—Restore the startup config on R1 from the saved image on the TFTP server.

Figure 3-10 gives a depiction of how the TFTP server is incorporated into the network.

**Figure 3-10**  *TFTP Server Topology*

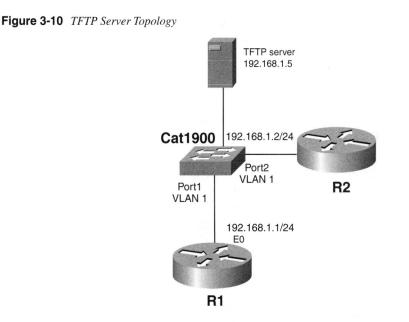

# Recommendations and Methodology

As mentioned earlier, redrawing the entire lab environment will be very helpful in understanding the lab objectives. In the next chapter, you will start configuring the devices. The methodology to configuring devices is quite simple. Start with the physical layer first, then configure the data link layer, and then move on to the network layer. This gives you a structured and repeatable process to ensure that no configuration steps are left out. This is also the same process in which you will troubleshoot any issues that arise.

## Physical Layer Configuration

Regarding the physical layer, you will have to trust us on this one! We will make sure that the physical cabling is correct.

## Basic Router and Data Link Layer Configurations

You then configure the switch, which is a data link layer device. After you have configured the switch, you will start configuring the routers. All routers will have the same basic configurations, including passwords, host names, host tables, and other items. When all the basic configurations are done, you will start configuring the interfaces. Each interface will have a data link layer configuration, such as Frame Relay, Ethernet, or Token Ring, as well as a network layer configuration (assigning IP addresses). Depending on each data link layer technology, some interfaces might not have any data link layer configuration commands needed (such as Ethernet) to bring up the interface, other than removing the interface from shutdown mode. When the interface has been configured for the data link layer, you will assign an IP address to the interface and verify connectivity (you will use the **ping** command to verify IP connectivity) to its directly connected neighbor(s).

## Network Layer Configurations (Routing)

In the previous section, you assigned IP addresses to all the interfaces. This is actually a network layer configuration task, but it makes more sense to assign the IP addresses as you bring up the interface. When all the interfaces have been configured and connectivity verified, you will configure the routing protocols. Each routing technology will be configured according to the objectives outlined in their respective sections. After all the routing technologies have been configured, you will redistribute the routing domains so that you have interconnectivity among all routing domains.

# Summary

This chapter reviewed the physical topology of the lab and identified all the configuration tasks that you will complete throughout this book. The rest of this book focuses on these objectives and walks you through the configuration tasks step by step to complete these objectives. By the end of the book, you should have a complete, functional network with multiple routing domains and ISDN DDR.

Upon completion all the lab objectives, we introduce problems into the lab environment to provide you with an opportunity to troubleshoot the different data link and network layer technologies.

This chapter describes how to access a router through the following methods:

- Through a direct console connection
- Over the LAN via Telnet
- Through a terminal server

## CHAPTER 4

# Gaining Access to
# the Routers and Switches

In this chapter, you learn how to access a router and switch through a direct console connection, over the LAN via Telnet, and finally through a terminal server. To begin, this chapter reviews how to access a router or switch through a direct console connection. Next, you will configure the terminal server router for Telnet access. Then you will access the terminal server over the LAN via Telnet using a terminal application program running on your PC. Finally, you will configure the 2511 router as the lab terminal server for reverse Telnet to access the lab routers.

Routers and switches can be accessed and configured through various means. To initially configure a Cisco device, you will need to connect directly through the console port. The console port exists on both routers and switches and is available to configure and monitor the device.

## Direct Access to Routers and
## Switches Through a Console Port

Most Cisco devices use a rollover cable connected to the console port on the router or switch. For exceptions, consult the product documentation to verify whether you should use a straight-through or rollover cable. The cable is then connected to an RJ-45–to–DB-9 or RJ-45–to–DB-25 terminal adapter that is attached to a serial communications port (COM1, COM2, or other COM port) on the PC. Figure 4-1 shows how this is done.

**Figure 4-1**    *Connecting a Device with a Console Cable*

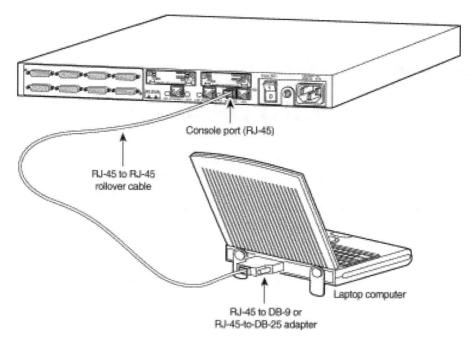

When the physical connection is in place, configure the terminal application program on the PC with the following COM settings:

- 9600 bps
- 8 data bits
- No parity
- 1 stop bit
- No flow control

In the lab, you will be using the terminal application program HyperTerminal to connect to the terminal server's console port. Any terminal application could be used based on your personal preference. If another terminal application is used, consult the product documentation for configuration and setup procedures.

---

**NOTE**    The version of HyperTerminal has changed over the years to address functionality problems within the application. For example, older versions that came with Windows 95 and NT could not send the Ctrl-Break sequence (needed to break into the router). An early version that came with NT Service Pack 2 or 3 fixed this issue but had a problem when pasting several commands into the configuration script—it took about 5 seconds per line while it sent CPU utilization to 100 percent. The version that comes with NT-SP5, 98, and 2000 is fine. The authors of the program (Hilgraeve) provide a free update. To obtain the free update, open HyperTerminal, click Help, About, Upgrade Information, and then follow the upgrade instructions, or visit http://www.hilgraeve.com.

Let's demonstrate how this is done.

## Accessing the Lab Terminal Server Through the Console Port

The physical cabling between your PC and the router acting as the terminal server has been configured as shown in Figure 4-1. With the physical cabling in place, start the program HyperTerminal on the PC. To do so, click Start, Programs, Accessories, Communications, HyperTerminal. Then double-click the HyperTerminal executable (hypertrm.exe) from within Windows, as shown in Figure 4-2.

**Figure 4-2**   *Starting the HyperTerminal Application*

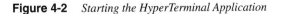

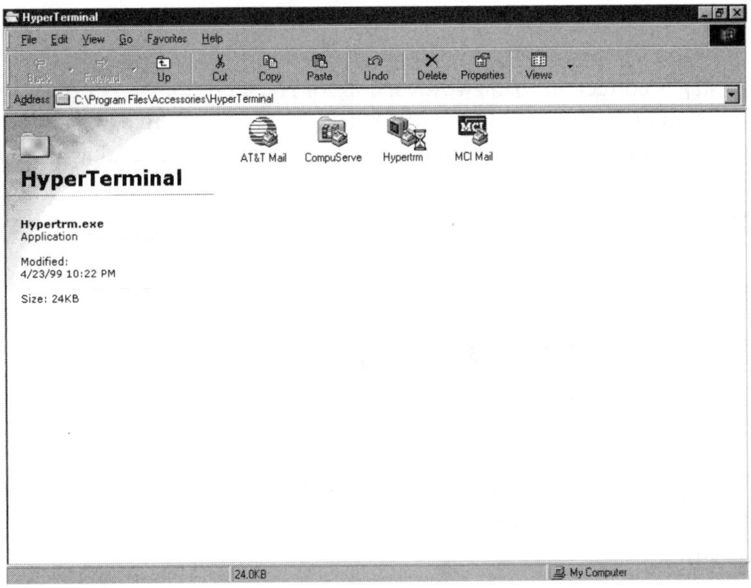

Give the new connection a name of LAB, and then click OK, as shown in Figure 4-3.

**Figure 4-3**   *Giving the Connection a Name*

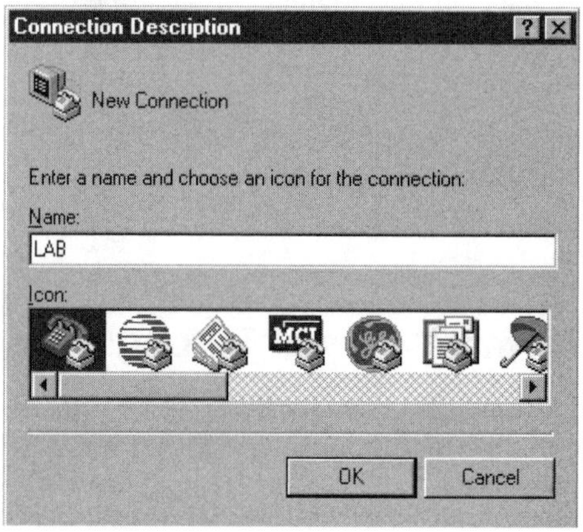

In the Connect Using field, select Direct to Com1 from the drop-down menu, as shown in Figure 4-4.

---

**NOTE**      This step is correct for the newest versions of HypterTerminal. For older versions of HyperTerminal, it is done differently. Hilgraeve provides a free update to HyperTerminal when used for personal use. Visit http://www.hilgraeve.com and download HyperTerminal Private Edition.

---

**Figure 4-4**   *Selecting the COM Port on PC*

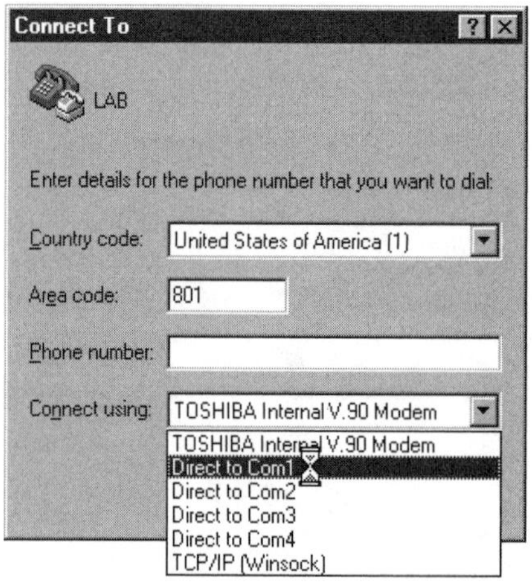

Now configure the port settings as follows and as shown in Figure 4-5. When finished, click OK:

- Bits per second: 9600
- Data bits: 8
- Parity: none
- Stop bits: 1
- Flow control: none

**Figure 4-5**    *Configuring HyperTerminal Port Settings*

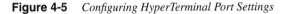

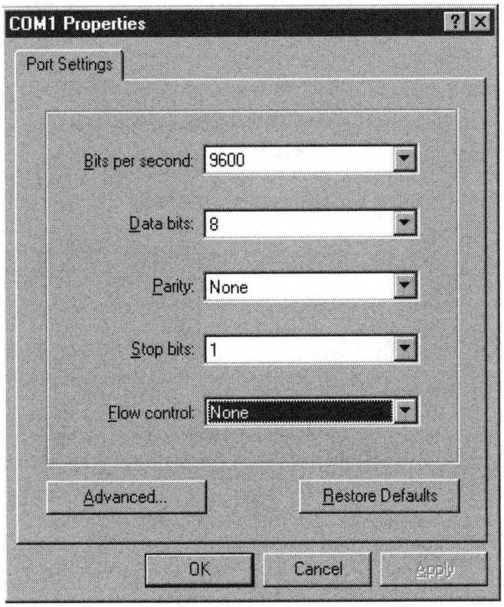

You are initially placed in user EXEC mode of the terminal server. If you do not see a prompt, hit the Enter key a few times, and then type enable and hit Enter. You are put into privileged EXEC mode without being prompted for a password because an enable password has not yet been set, as shown in Figure 4-6.

**Figure 4-6**    *Successful Establishment of EXEC Session Through a Direct Console Connection*

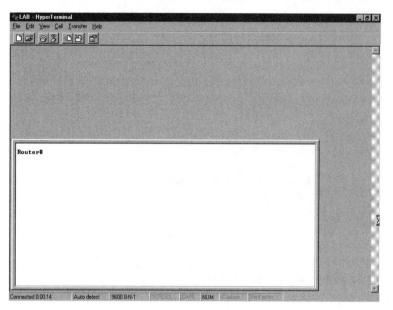

If you still do not get a console prompt, verify that it shows Connected in the bottom-left corner of the HyperTerminal application, as shown in Figure 4-6. If not, check the physical cabling as well as the port settings, and verify that the router has been powered on.

Now that you have successfully connected to the console port of the terminal server, you will configure the terminal server for Telnet access.

# Configuring the Terminal Server for Telnet Access

In this section, you will configure the terminal server so that you can Telnet to it across the network. When you are connected to the terminal server, the terminal server will be the single point from which you may access all other lab routers through reverse Telnet. A terminal server provides out-of-band access to several devices. Out-of-band access is through a router's console or aux port versus in-band access that occurs over a network through Telnet or SNMP. Telnet, reverse Telnet, and a terminal server overview are covered in greater detail later in the chapter.

The next step is to make the terminal server accessible over your Ethernet network so that you can access it from any workstation on the LAN, as shown in Figure 4-7.

**Figure 4-7**    *LAN Configuration for Telnet Access*

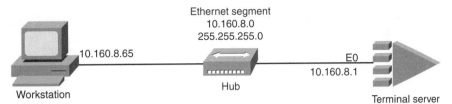

Telnet access is useful because it eliminates the requirement to be physically at the terminal server router to gain access. Instead, you can configure the terminal server so that you can Telnet to it over the LAN, as shown in Figure 4-7. Then, from the terminal server, you will be able to access each lab router through reverse Telnet, as shown in Figure 4-8. Reverse Telnet will be explained and demonstrated later in this chapter.

**Figure 4-8**    *Terminal Server Logical Diagram*

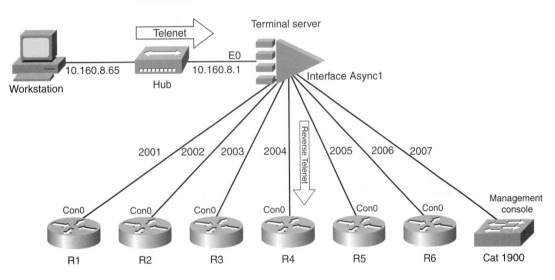

Begin by configuring the terminal servers' host name, Ethernet IP address, and vty lines. Because you're still attached via a direct connection to the terminal server's console port, ensure you're in privileged EXEC mode by typing **enable** from user EXEC mode, as in Example 4-1.

**Example 4-1** *Entering Enable Mode on Terminal Server*

```
Router>enable
Router#
```

Because the privileged EXEC password has not yet been set, you are allowed directly into privileged EXEC mode without entering a password, as denoted by the **Router#** prompt in Example 4-1. To change the host name on the router, type **configure terminal** to enter global configuration mode. Next, issue the **hostname** command followed by **Termserver**, as shown in Example 4-2.

**Example 4-2** *Changing the Host Name on the Terminal Server*

```
Router>enable

Router#configure terminal

Enter configuration commands, one per line.  End with CNTL/Z.

Router(config)#hostname Termserver
Termserver(config)#
```

Notice that the prompt has changed from **Router(config)#** to **Termserver(config)#**.

Next, from global configuration mode, enter interface configuration mode by typing **interface ethernet0**, and assign the IP address of 10.160.8.1 with a mask of 255.255.255.0 to the Ethernet0 interface. In addition, ensure that the interface is *not* shut down by typing **no shutdown** from interface configuration mode for Ethernet 0, as demonstrated in Example 4-3.

**Example 4-3**  *Assign the Terminal Server's Ethernet 0 Interface an IP Address and Bring the Interface Out of Shutdown Mode*

```
Router>enable
Router#configure terminal
Enter configuration commands, one per line.  End with CNTL/Z.

Router(config)#hostname Termserver
Termserver(config)#
Termserver(config)#interface ethernet0
Termserver(config-if)#ip address 10.160.8.1 255.255.255.0
Termserver(config-if)#no shutdown
Termserver(config-if)#
%LINEPROTO-5-UPDOWN: Line protocol on Interface Ethernet0, changed state to up
Termserver(config-if)#
%LINK-3-UPDOWN: Interface Ethernet0, changed state to up
Termserver(config-if)#
```

Notice that you receive a console message indicating that the line protocol on Ethernet 0 is up and the interface is up. You can verify that Ethernet 0 is up and configured with the proper IP address by typing **show interface ethernet0**, as shown in Example 4-4.

**Example 4-4**  *Verifying that Ethernet 0 Is Up and Configured with the Correct IP Address*

```
Termserver#show interface ethernet0
Ethernet0 is up, line protocol is up
  Hardware is Lance, address is 0000.0c47.351c (bia 0000.0c47.351c)
  Internet address is 10.160.8.1/24
  MTU 1500 bytes, BW 10000 Kbit, DLY 1000 usec, rely 255/255, load 1/255
  Encapsulation ARPA, loopback not set, keepalive set (10 sec)
  ARP type: ARPA, ARP Timeout 04:00:00
  Last input 00:00:00, output 00:00:00, output hang never
  Last clearing of "show interface" counters never
  Queueing strategy: fifo
  Output queue 0/40, 0 drops; input queue 1/75, 0 drops
  5 minute input rate 0 bits/sec, 1 packets/sec
  5 minute output rate 0 bits/sec, 1 packets/sec
     6674 packets input, 1267069 bytes, 0 no buffer
     Received 6252 broadcasts, 0 runts, 0 giants, 0 throttles
     0 input errors, 0 CRC, 0 frame, 0 overrun, 0 ignored, 0 abort
     0 input packets with dribble condition detected
     12718 packets output, 1199744 bytes, 0 underruns
     0 output errors, 0 collisions, 0 interface resets
     0 babbles, 0 late collision, 0 deferred
     0 lost carrier, 0 no carrier
     0 output buffer failures, 0 output buffers swapped out
```

You can see that Ethernet 0 is up as shown in the highlighted lines of Example 4-4 because the interface is up and the line protocol is up. In addition, you see that the IP address of 10.160.8.1 and mask of 255.255.255.0 (/24) are configured on the interface.

The workstation has been assigned an IP address of 10.160.8.65 with a subnet mask of 255.255.255.0. From the workstation, verify that you can **ping** the newly assigned IP address on your terminal server's Ethernet 0 interface, as shown in Figure 4-9.

**Figure 4-9** *Verify IP Connectivity Between Workstation and Terminal Server*

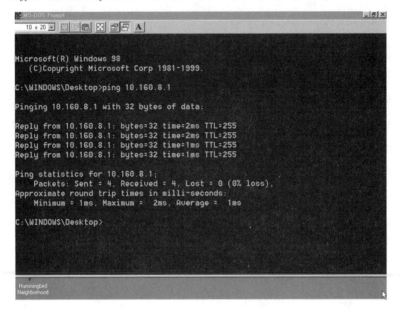

Success!

# vty Line Configuration for Telnet Access

Virtual terminal lines are used to allow remote access to a router. A virtual terminal line is not associated with either the auxiliary or console port; instead, it is a "virtual port" on the router. The router has five virtual terminal lines, by default. You will configure the five vty lines (vty 0 through 4) for Telnet access and set a password of falcons on these lines. In addition, you want to ensure that, after 15 minutes of inactivity on the vty lines, the connection times out. To configure the vty lines, you will do the following from global configuration mode:

**Step 1** Enter line configuration mode.

**Step 2** Enable login on the vty lines.

**Step 3** Set a password for Telnet access.

**Step 4** Set the **exec-timeout** interval.

To examine how this is done, first enter line configuration mode for vty lines 0 through 4, as shown in Example 4-5.

**Example 4-5**   *Line Configuration Mode for vty 0 Through 4*

```
Termserver#configure terminal
Enter configuration commands, one per line.  End with CNTL/Z.

Termserver(config)#line vty 0 4
Termserver(config-line)#
```

You can verify that you have successfully entered line configuration mode because the prompt has changed, as shown in the highlighted portion of Example 4-5. Next, enable login on the vty lines and set a Telnet password of falcons on the terminal server, as in Example 4-6.

**Example 4-6**   *Configure vty Lines with Login and Password Checking*

```
Termserver(config-line)#login
Termserver(config-line)#password falcons
```

**TIP**        Remember that if an enable password has not been set on the router, you cannot Telnet into the router. This is true even when a password has been set on the vty lines. Although not shown here, assume that the terminal server has been configured with the enable password **falcons**.

Finally, it is a good idea to set timeout values on your vty lines so that idle Telnet sessions will not remain up indefinitely. By default, the **exec-timeout** is set to 10 minutes on both the console and the vty ports.

The timeout value is specified in minutes and seconds. You will set the timeout value to 15 minutes and 0 seconds on vty lines 0 through 4 using the **exec-timeout** command. If you are unsure of the order in which to specify minutes and seconds, use context-sensitive help, as shown in Example 4-7.

**Example 4-7**   *Setting the* **exec-timeout** *Value to 15 Minutes and 0 Seconds on vty Lines 0 Through 4*

```
Termserver(config-line)#exec-timeout ?
  <0-35791>  Timeout in minutes

Termserver(config-line)#exec-timeout 15 ?
  <0-2147483>  Timeout in seconds
  <cr>

Termserver(config-line)#exec-timeout 15 0
Termserver(config-line)#
```

Verify the configuration changes in your running-config by exiting back to privileged EXEC with CTRL-Z and then using a **show running-config c**ommand. The highlighted section of Example 4-8 shows the last portion of the running-config with the configuration of the five vty lines.

**Example 4-8**  *Verify Changes with* **show running-config** *Command*

```
Termserver(config-line)#^Z
Termserver#show running-config

line con 0
 login
line 1 16
line aux 0
line vty 0 4
 exec-timeout 15 0
 password 7 15140A0007252537
 login
```

The end of the config shows all lines on the router, as well as the changes you have made to the vty lines.

## Saving the Running Configuration

Save the configuration by typing **copy running-config startup-config** from global configuration mode, as shown in Example 4-9.

**Example 4-9**  **Copy running-config** *to* **startup-config**

```
Termserver#copy running-config startup-config
Building configuration...
[OK]
Termserver#
```

**NOTE**      If you are running Cisco IOS software Release 12.0 or later, the **copy** command may ask for a confirmation in this form: **Destination file [startup-config]?**.

The configuration has been successfully copied from the running configuration to the startup configuration, as denoted by the **[OK]** highlighted in Example 4-9.

## Accessing the Terminal Server from a PC over a LAN/WAN via Telnet

Now you will test to see if you can Telnet to the terminal server at 10.160.8.1. To do so, configure the terminal application program (HyperTerminal) to Telnet to the router. This is done by starting HyperTerminal and, instead of selecting a COM port to connect through, selecting TCP/IP (Winsock), as shown in Figure 4-10.

**NOTE**    If the TCP/IP option is not available, you have an older version of the HypterTerminal Application. You can upgrade it at www.hilgraeve.com.

**Figure 4-10**  *HyperTerminal Configured to Use TCP/IP*

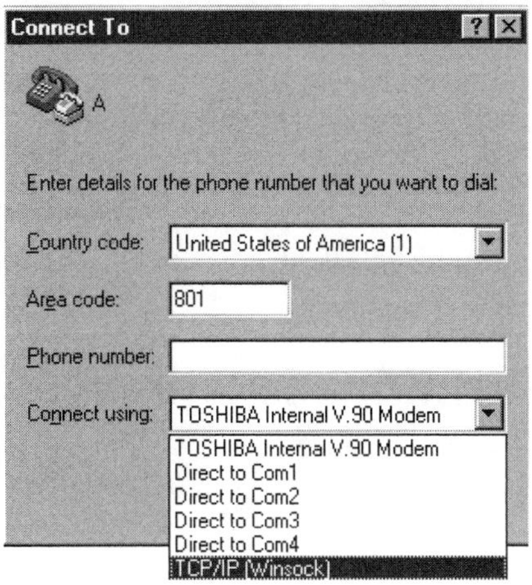

Next, enter the IP address of 10.160.8.1, as shown in Figure 4-11.

**Figure 4-11**   *Telnet to Ethernet 0 10.160.8.1*

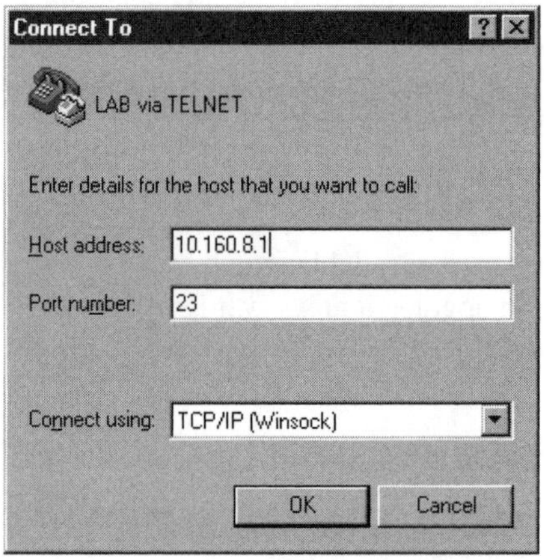

You are first prompted for the Telnet password of falcons that you configured previously in Example 4-6. When this password is successfully supplied, you are taken into user EXEC mode. From there, you can type **enable** to gain access to privileged EXEC mode.

You have now successfully Telnetted to the terminal server.

# Configuring the Terminal Server

This section demonstrates how to configure a terminal server to provide access to the rest of the routers in the lab. Once configured, you will be able access each lab router's console port through reverse Telnet.

## Lab Objective

In this chapter, you will accomplish the following lab objective:

- Configure the Cisco 2511 router to be the terminal server for this lab. The terminal server is connected to each device's console port. Port assignments are as follows:
  - **R1**—2001
  - **R2**—2002
  - **R3**—2003
  - **R4**—2004
  - **R5**—2005
  - **R6**—2006
  - **Catalyst Switch**—2007

After completing this objective, you will learn how to maneuver from the terminal server to each individual lab router and then back to the terminal server.

# Terminal Server Overview

A terminal server provides out-of-band access for several devices. Out-of-band access is through a router's console or aux port versus in-band access that occurs over the network using telnet. Generally, a terminal server is a router with multiple, asynchronous ports that are connected to other devices, such as the console port of other routers or switches, as shown previously in Figure 4-8. To get a better idea of what the ports look like on the back of a terminal server, see Figure 4-12, which shows the back of a Cisco 2511.

**Figure 4-12** *A Cisco 2511 to Be Configured as the Lab Terminal Server*

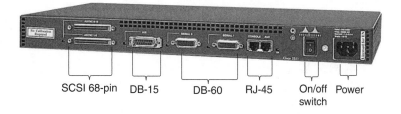

# Cabling

The Cisco 2511 series router uses a 68-pin connector and breakout cable (see Figure 4-13).

**Figure 4-13** *CAB-OCTAL-ASYNC Cable*

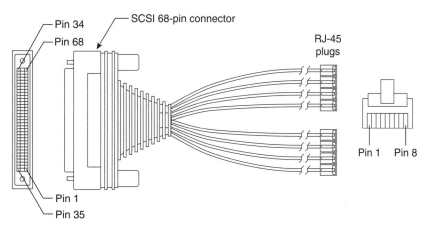

This cable is referred to as a *CAB-OCTAL-ASYNC cable* or just *OCTAL cable*. It provides eight RJ-45 rolled cable asynchronous (async) ports on each 68-pin connector. The 68-pin connector is attached to Interface Async 1 of the terminal server. Each RJ-45 rolled cable is connected to the console port of each router in the lab. For configuration purposes, each rolled cable is referred to as an *asynchronous line* in the configuration. Each line is numbered beginning with 2001 to 2008. So, R1 is attached to async 2001, R2 is connected to 2002, and so on up to 2007, which is connected to the Catalyst 1900 switch, leaving 2008 unused. See Figure 4-14 for an example.

**Figure 4-14** *Terminal Server Connectivity to Lab Routers*

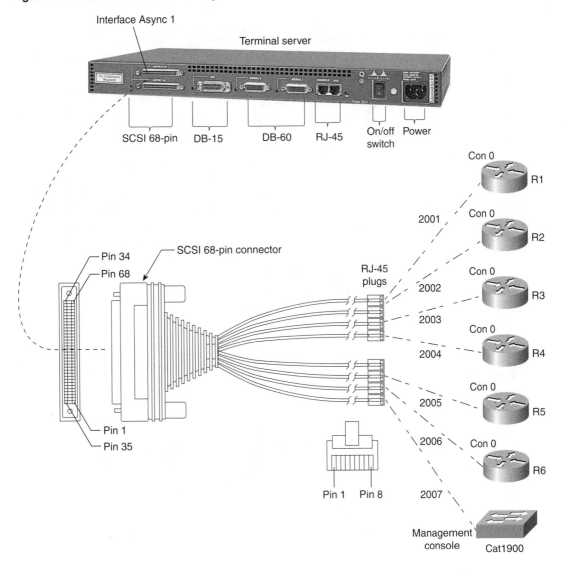

**NOTE**    The async ports from the 68-pin connector are data terminal equipment (DTE) devices.
DTE-to-DTE connections require a rolled (null modem) cable. DTE-to-DCE devices
require a straight-through cable. Because the Octal cable is rolled, you can connect each
cable directly to the RJ-45 console port of each lab router. However, some routers have
console ports that are 25-pin interfaces instead of RJ-45. If so, remember that the 25-pin
interface is a DCE, and you must use the RJ-45-to-25 pin adapter marked "modem" to
reverse the roll and complete the connection.

The major benefit of a terminal server is that it allows you a single point from which to
access the console ports of many devices. This is helpful initially in the lab because the lab
routers will not have any configuration settings such as IP addresses or Telnet parameters.
Without the terminal server, you would have the tedious process of manually switching
between each router's console port to gain access. A second benefit is that a terminal server
can provide fault tolerance in case the routers become inaccessible because of a network
failure. This is because you can configure a modem on the auxiliary or asynchronous port
of the terminal server, allowing dialup connectivity to the terminal server and thus to each
router that the terminal server is connected to.

In the lab, the terminal server will be the single point from which you may access all other
lab routers through reverse telnet.

## Reverse Telnet

Most Telnet connections are considered forward connections, or connections accepted into
a line or interface. Reverse Telnet means that the Telnet session is initiated out of the line
(like an asynchronous line) instead of accepting a connection into the line. Thus, reverse
Telnet allows you to Telnet out from a device that you are Telnetting to, but on a different
interface, such as an asynchronous port. For example, the terminal server has a LAN
(Ethernet) IP address of 10.160.8.1. If you want to connect to R1 on asynchronous line
2001, you would issue the following command from the terminal server:

```
Termserver#telnet 10.160.8.1 2001
```

Essentially, you are telling the router to connect to its own Ethernet 0 IP address of
10.160.8.1 via Telnet but to initiate the connection out line 2001. This will be a fundamental
part of the lab exercises, so let's demonstrate how this is done.

In the lab, you will do reverse Telnet using an IP address assigned to a loopback interface.
Loopback addresses are preferred because they are virtual and thus always available. For
reverse Telnet to work, the interface that is used must be up and the line protocol must be

up. Because of this, using a loopback interface is advantageous because it never goes down, as opposed to an Ethernet interface, which might go down and prevent reverse Telnet from working.

# Terminal Server Configuration

Now that you have an understanding of how the terminal server is physically connected and how reverse Telnet functions, it's time to examine how to configure the terminal server.

The steps to configure the terminal server are as follows:

**Step 1**  Create a loopback interface.

**Step 2**  Assign an IP address to the loopback interface.

**Step 3**  Allow Telnet as a transport across asynchronous lines 1 to 16.

**Step 4**  Create a host table that maps a router's host name (such as R1, R2, and so on) to the asynchronous line it is connected to on the terminal server (such as 2001, 2002, and so on).

## Steps 1 and 2: Creating a Loopback Interface and Assigning an IP Address

Begin by creating the loopback interface from global configuration mode. Going into interface configuration mode for the loopback 0 interface creates the loopback interface and brings up the interface, as highlighted in Example 4-11. You can assign the interface any number in the range of 0 to 2147483647. Use loopback 0 and assign it an IP address of 192.168.10.10 with a mask of 255.255.255.0, as shown in Example 4-10.

**Example 4-10**  *Creating loopback 0 and Assigning It an IP Address*

```
Termserver(config)#
Termserver(config)#interface loopback0
Termserver(config-if)#
%LINEPROTO-5-UPDOWN: Line protocol on Interface Loopback0, changed state to up
Termserver(config-if)#
%LINK-3-UPDOWN: Interface Loopback0, changed state to up

Termserver(config-if)#ip address 192.168.10.10 255.255.255.0
```

Exit interface configuration mode by doing a CTRL-Z and do a **show running-config** to show how this interface now appears in the output in Example 4-11.

**Example 4-11** *loopback0 Interface as It Appears in Running-Config After Creation*

```
Termserver(config-if)#^Z
Termserver#show running-config

Current configuration:
!
version 11.2
service password-encryption
no service udp-small-servers
no service tcp-small-servers
!
hostname Termserver
!
enable password 7 0200055708090132
!
interface Loopback0
 ip address 192.168.10.10 255.255.255.0
 !
```

You can also do a **show interface loopback0** to verify that the loopback interface is up and has the correct IP address, as in Example 4-12.

**Example 4-12 show interface loopback0** *Command Output Verifies Interface Status and IP Address*

```
Termserver#show interface loopback0
Loopback0 is up, line protocol is up
  Hardware is Loopback
  Internet address is 192.168.10.10/24
  MTU 1514 bytes, BW 8000000 Kbit, DLY 5000 usec, rely 255/255, load 1/255
  Encapsulation LOOPBACK, loopback not set, keepalive set (10 sec)
  Last input never, output never, output hang never
  Last clearing of "show interface" counters never
  Queueing strategy: fifo
  Output queue 0/0, 0 drops; input queue 0/75, 0 drops
  5 minute input rate 0 bits/sec, 0 packets/sec
  5 minute output rate 0 bits/sec, 0 packets/sec
     0 packets input, 0 bytes, 0 no buffer
     Received 0 broadcasts, 0 runts, 0 giants, 0 throttles
     0 input errors, 0 CRC, 0 frame, 0 overrun, 0 ignored, 0 abort
     0 packets output, 0 bytes, 0 underruns
     0 output errors, 0 collisions, 0 interface resets
     0 output buffer failures, 0 output buffers swapped out
Termserver#
```

## Step 3: Allowing Telnet as a Transport Across Asynchronous Lines 1 to 16

Now that the loopback 0 interface is created, you need to ensure that the asynchronous lines allow Telnet to traverse the lines.

This is done using the **transport input** *x* command, where *x* is the protocol that you want to allow, such as Telnet. The command allows the granularity of permitting only certain protocols to cross the asynchronous lines. The allowed protocols are shown using context-sensitive help, as demonstrated in Example 4-13.

**Example 4-13** *Available Protocols Configurable for Transport Across the Asynchronous Lines*

```
Termserver(config)#line 1 16
Termserver(config-line)#transport input ?
  all     All protocols
  lat     DEC LAT protocol
  mop     DEC MOP Remote Console Protocol
  nasi    NASI protocol
  none    No protocols
  pad     X.3 PAD
  rlogin  Unix rlogin protocol
  telnet  TCP/IP Telnet protocol
  v120    Async over ISDN

Termserver(config-line)#transport input
```

In the lab, you will do a **transport input telnet** to allow Telnet to cross the lines.

Enter line configuration mode for asynchronous lines 1 through 16. To do this, type **line 1 16** from privileged EXEC mode.

**NOTE**    In the lab, you are really concerned with only Lines 1 to 7 (2001 to 2007) because they are the only asynchronous lines that have routers connected to them. However, because a Cisco 2511 has two asynchronous interfaces, 16 lines total are available (8 per asynchronous interface) for configuration.

Upon entering line configuration mode, allow all protocols to be transported across the lines, as shown in Example 4-15.

**Example 4-14** *Allow All Protocols to Cross the Asynchronous Lines*

```
Termserver(config)#line 1 16
Termserver(config-line)#transport input telnet
Termserver(config-line)#^Z
```

## Step 4: Creating a Host Table That Maps a Router's Host Name to the Asynchronous Line to Which It Is Connected on the Terminal Server

At this point, the terminal server is configured and should be functional; however, as a timesaver, you will create a host table that maps the router name to the loopback 0 interface and then specify the asynchronous port out which to initiate the reverse Telnet session. This is done using the **ip host** command. The **ip host** command is a static DNS entry used by the router. The router will translate "R1" to 192.168.10.10 port 2001. When this host table is completed, you will access each router by typing the host name of the router. For example, typing **R1** initiates a reverse Telnet session out asynchronous line 1 (2001). Create the table from global configuration mode as shown in Example 4-15.

**Example 4-15** *Creating IP Host Table for Reverse Telnet*

```
Termserver#config t
Enter configuration commands, one per line.  End with CNTL/Z.

Termserver(config)#ip host r1 2001 192.168.10.10
Termserver(config)#ip host r2 2002 192.168.10.10
Termserver(config)#ip host r3 2003 192.168.10.10
Termserver(config)#ip host r4 2004 192.168.10.10
Termserver(config)#ip host r5 2005 192.168.10.10
Termserver(config)#ip host r6 2006 192.168.10.10
Termserver(config)#ip host cat19 2007 192.168.10.10
Termserver(config)#
```

## Saving and Testing the Terminal Server Configuration

Exit back to global configuration mode by doing a CTRL-Z and then save the configuration. Next, test reverse Telnet functionality by typing **r1** from user EXEC or privileged EXEC mode, as shown in Example 4-16.

**Example 4-16** *Successful Reverse Telnet to R1*

```
Termserver#^Z
Termserver#copy running startup
Building configuration...
[OK]
Termserver#r1
Trying r1 (192.168.10.10, 2001)... Open   Hit enter key

Router>
```

You can see from Example 4-16 that the terminal server initiates a connection to R1. It does this by connecting to its own loopback 0 address of 192.168.10.10 (via Telnet) and then redirecting the connection out asynchronous port 2001. Because the Telnet connection is "redirected," it is referred to a reverse Telnet connection. Next, hit the Enter key to get the

**Router>** prompt. R1's console port is connected to asynchronous line 1 (port 2001) of the terminal server. By hitting the Enter key, you are placed into R1's user EXEC mode. At this point, give the router a host name of R1 to avoid confusion about which router you are connected to. Change the host name to R1, and save the changes, as shown in Example 4-17.

**Example 4-17** *Hostname Changed from Router to R1*

```
Router>enable
Router#conf t
Enter configuration commands, one per line.  End with CNTL/Z.

Router(config)#hostname R1
R1(config)#^Z
R1#copy running startup
Building configuration...
[OK]
R1#
```

To get back to the terminal server, type **Ctrl-Shift-6, x** from R1, as in Example 4-18.

**Example 4-18** *Return to the Terminal Server via the Escape Sequence*

```
R1#Ctrl-Shift-6, x
Termserver#
```

Upon doing the escape sequence (**Ctrl-Shift-6, x**), notice that you have been returned to the terminal server, as shown by the change from the **R1#** prompt to the **Termserver#** prompt in Example 4-18.

## Connecting, Disconnecting, and Verifying Reverse Telnet Sessions

From the terminal server, you can view active reverse Telnet connections by doing **show sessions**, as in Example 4-19.

**Example 4-19** *Established Sessions on the Terminal Server*

```
Termserver#show sessions

Conn Host            Address           Byte  Idle Conn Name
*  1 r1               192.168.10.10        0     3 R1

Termserver#
```

When a reverse Telnet session is established, the session is given a connection number. The asterisk preceding the connection number indicates that the session is active, as highlighted in Example 4-19.

To return to an active session, you can simply enter the connection number. Upon seeing the message **[Resuming connection 1 to R1 ... ]**, press the Enter key and you are taken to R1, as demonstrated in Example 4-20.

**Example 4-20** *Resuming an Active Reverse Telnet Session Using the Connection Number*

```
Termserver#1
[Resuming connection 1 to r1 ... ]
      Hit Enter key
R1#
```

Occasionally, when initiating the reverse Telnet session, the connection might be refused and you will not be able to get into a router; you will see a message as shown in Example 4-21.

**Example 4-21** *Reverse Telnet Session Refused by Remote Host*

```
Termserver#r1
Trying r1 (192.168.10.10, 2001)...
% Connection refused by remote host

Termserver#
```

When the connection is refused, you need to clear the asynchronous line and attempt the reverse Telnet again. This is done by doing a **clear line 1**, confirming the request by pressing Enter, and then entering **r1** to reinitiate the reverse Telnet connection, as shown in Example 4-22.

**Example 4-22** *Clearing the Asynchronous Line 1 After a Connection Is Refused and Reinitiating the Reverse Telnet Connection*

```
Termserver#r1
Trying r1 (192.168.10.10, 2001)...
% Connection refused by remote host

Termserver#clear line 1
[confirm]
 [OK]
Termserver#r1
Trying r1 (192.168.10.10, 2001)... Open

R1>
```

**TIP**      You might need to clear the line a few times before it completely clears.

You have now successfully connected to R1 through reverse Telnet.

Return to the terminal server from R1 using **Ctrl-Shift-6, x**. Execute a **show sessions** command on the terminal server to display that connection 1 is an established reverse Telnet session to R1. To disconnect a previously established reverse Telnet session, you can enter **disconnect** and the connection number, and then hit Enter to confirm the disconnect, as shown in Example 4-23.

**Example 4-23** *Disconnecting an Established Reverse Telnet Session*

```
R1>
Termserver#show sessions
Conn Host              Address           Byte  Idle Conn Name
*  1 r1                192.168.10.10        0     0 R1

Termserver#disconnect 1
Closing connection to r1 [confirm]
Termserver#
```

Now if you do a **show sessions** on the terminal server, as demonstrated in Example 4-24, you can see that the reverse Telnet session to R1 was disconnected.

**Example 4-24** *No Active Reverse Telnet Session After Doing a Disconnect*

```
Termserver#show sessions
% No connections open
Termserver#
```

To finish, set up a reverse Telnet connection to each of the lab devices, R1 through R6. First, you'll connect to each router by typing the router's host name, hitting Enter, and then entering the escape sequence **Ctrl-Shift-6, x** to get back to the terminal server to repeat the process for the next router (see Example 4-25).

**Example 4-25** *Setting Up a Reverse Telnet Session to Each Lab Router*

```
Termserver#r1
Trying r1 (192.168.10.10, 2001)... Open

R1>
Termserver#r2
Trying r2 (192.168.10.10, 2002)... Open

Router>
Termserver#r3
Trying r3 (192.168.10.10, 2003)... Open

Router>
Termserver#r4
```

*continues*

**Example 4-25** *Setting Up a Reverse Telnet Session to Each Lab Router (Continued)*

```
Trying r4 (192.168.10.10, 2004)... Open

Router>
Termserver#r5
Trying r5 (192.168.10.10, 2005)... Open

Router>
Termserver#r6
Trying r6 (192.168.10.10, 2006)... Open

Router>
Termserver#
```

Notice in Example 4-25 that the reverse Telnet session is successful because the connection shows **Open** and you are taken to the router prompt of each respective device. R1 is the only router with a configured host name because it is the only router that you have configured with a host name so far. Thus, the remaining routers take you to the **Router>** prompt.

---

**NOTE**    Individual host names for the remaining routers will be configured in Chapter 6, "General Router Configurations."

---

## Reverse Telnetting to the Catalyst 1900 Switch

Next, establish a reverse Telnet session to the Catalyst 1900 switch by entering **cat1900** and pressing Enter, as shown in Example 4-26.

**Example 4-26** *Setting Up a Reverse Telnet Session to the Catalyst 1900 Switch*

```
Termserver#cat1900
Trying cat1900 (192.168.1.3, 2007)... Open




-----------------------------------------------
Catalyst 1900 Management Console
Copyright (c) Cisco Systems, Inc.  1993-1997
All rights reserved.

Ethernet address: 00-C0-1D-80-C7-5E
-----------------------------------------------



1 user(s) now active on Management Console.

Enter password:
Termserver#
```

Now from the terminal server, do a **show sessions** and notice that each reverse Telnet session has been assigned a connection number (see Example 4-27).

**Example 4-27** *Connections Numbers Assigned to Each Lab Device*

```
Termserver#show sessions
Conn Host              Address           Byte  Idle Conn Name
   1 r1                192.168.10.10        0     0 R1
   2 r2                192.168.10.10        0     0 r2
   3 r3                192.168.10.10        0     0 r3
   4 r4                192.168.10.10        0     0 r4
   5 r5                192.168.10.10        0     0 r5
   6 r6                192.168.10.10        0     0 r6
   7 cat1900           192.168.10.10        0     0 cat1900
```

From this point on, when configuring lab devices, you can access each device by simply entering the connection number associated with the device from the terminal server (that is, **1** to access R1, **2** to access R2, and so on).

# Summary

You have now successfully completed the configuration of the terminal server. Table 4-1 summarizes the commands to maneuver between the terminal server and the lab routers, as well as manage reverse Telnet connections on the terminal server.

**Table 4-1**    *Chapter Command Summary*

| Command | Purpose |
|---|---|
| **show sessions** | Displays all open sessions |
| **disconnect** *connection #* | Disconnects the desired connection |
| **clear line** *line #* | Clears the desired asynchronous line (1 to 16, where 1 = 2001, 2 = 2002 and so on) |
| **Ctrl-Shift-6, x** | Escapes the current session and returns to the terminal server |
| **line 1 16** | Enters line configuration mode for asynchronous lines 1 through 16 on the terminal server |
| **line vty 0 4** | Enters line configuration mode for vty lines 0 through 4 |
| **transport input** *protocol* | Defines what protocols are allowed across the asynchronous or vty lines |
| **ip host [hostname] [port] [ip-address]** | Adds an entry to the IP host name table |
| **Copy running-config startup-config** | Copies the running configuration to the startup configuration |

This chapter covers the following key topics:

- Transparent bridging
- Switching
- Using virtual LANS
- Configuring the Catalyst 1900 switch

## CHAPTER 5

# Bridging and Switching

Before configuring the Catalyst 1900 switch, you should briefly review bridging and switching technologies.

Bridges and switches are two data link layer technologies designed to increase bandwidth utilization and reduce collisions. This chapter briefly reviews each technology and then completes the configuration tasks set by the lab objectives for this chapter.

## Transparent Bridging

The most common bridging technology is transparent bridging. Other forms of bridging exist, such as source-route bridging, source-route transparent bridging, and source-route translation bridging, but are out of the scope of this book and will not be covered. A transparent bridge learns the MAC address of each host on a segment by looking at the source MAC address in the frame and forwarding the frame out only the port where the destination MAC address resides.

As the transparent bridge discovers the MAC addresses, it builds a table mapping the MAC address to the port on which it was learned. This way, the bridge does not have to rediscover the destination port every time a frame is received. As a frame is received, it can refer to the table and thus know the destination port and forward the frame appropriately. In essence, bridges build their table on source MAC addresses and filter on the destination MAC address. Bridges help segment traffic to local resources and save bandwidth. Each port on a bridge is a collision domain, and all ports on a bridge constitute a broadcast domain (meaning that all ports on a bridge belong to the same IP or IPX network). Figure 5-1 illustrates how ports on a bridge relate to collision domains and broadcast domains.

**Figure 5-1**    *A Standard Bridge*

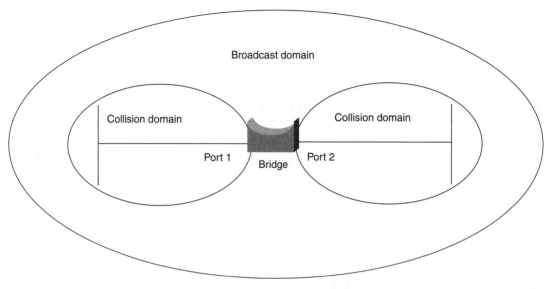

Although both bridges and switches operate with similar technique, switches have more functionality.

# Switching

As mentioned earlier, switches use the same technique as transparent bridges to learn of hosts on each of their ports. They, too, forward frames only out the port where the destination MAC address resides. Because of the large number of ports that switches have, several switching technologies have been developed to speed the process of switching frames from the source port to the destination port.

Three types of switching technologies exist:

- **Cut-through**—The switch performs the MAC address table query as soon as the destination address field in the frame header is received. The first part of the frame can be sent out the destination port before the remainder of the incoming frame is received. The major concern with this technique is that the switch can forward incomplete or damaged frames, consequently introducing more unneeded traffic and bandwidth utilization. This is the most commonly used type of switching in the industry.

- **Store-and-forward**—The switch completely receives the whole frame before forwarding the frame. This enables the switch to check the frame check sequence (FCS) before forwarding the frame. This form of switching enables the switch to drop frames that are incomplete or damaged, thus reducing unneeded traffic. Bridges use store-and-forward technology.

- **FragmentFree**—This technique is similar to cut-through switching, in that it forwards part of the frame before receiving the entire frame, but the switch waits for 64 bytes to be received before forwarding the first part of the frame. This is to check for collisions, which should be detected in the first 64 bytes of the frame. FragmentFree switching checks for collisions, but it does not check the FCS in the frame. On some switches, including the Catalyst 1900 series, FragmentFree is also known as FastForward.

# Virtual LANs

A *virtual LAN (VLAN)* is a broadcast domain created by one or more switches. On a switch, a VLAN is a collection of ports among which received broadcast frames are forwarded. Such frames are never forwarded outside the member port group. VLANs are what make a switch so versatile: They give the switches the capability to operate in different broadcast domains. Remember, all ports on a bridge constitute a broadcast domain. Well, with VLANs, you can configure certain ports on a switch to be in one broadcast domain and then configure other ports to be in a different broadcast domain. Each port on a switch is still a collision domain, but, depending on how you configure the switch, one or multiple broadcast domains (or IP network subnets) are possible. Figure 5-2 illustrates a four-port switch configured for two VLANs. Ports 1 and 2 are configured for VLAN 1. Ports 3 and 4 on the switch are configured for VLAN 2.

**Figure 5-2** *Switch Diagram with Two VLANs*

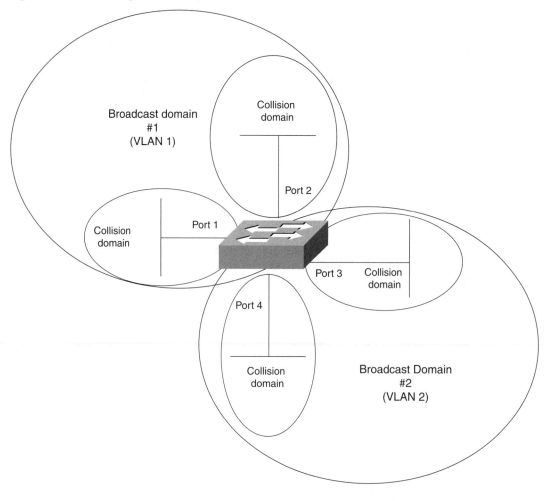

The Spanning-Tree Protocol will not have to be configured in the lab. The purpose of the Spanning-Tree Protocol is to dynamically discover one active path through a redundant bridged or switched network. Because the lab scenario does not have multiple switches, you do not have to concern yourself with redundant bridging paths, so the Spanning-Tree Protocol will not be covered in this book. If you need more information on the Spanning-Tree Protocol, refer to Chapter 5 of Steve McQuerry's book *Interconnecting Cisco Network Devices*, from Cisco Press.

# Configuring the Catalyst 1900 Switch

As covered in the *Interconnecting Cisco Network Devices* book, the Catalyst 1900 can be configured using three methods:

- Menu-driven interface from the management console
- Web-based Visual Switch Manager (VSM)
- Cisco IOS software command-line interface (CLI)

Because the ICND book focused on the CLI, this book uses the menu-driven interface so that you can get a feeling for configuration using both methods. It is also important to note that this chapter does not go through all the menu options—just those needed to complete the tasks in the lab objectives.

Before configuring the switch, you should review the physical configuration. Figure 5-3 reviews the lab diagram for the physical cabling of the Catalyst switch to the routers.

**Figure 5-3**   *Catalyst 1900 Switch Physical Configuration*

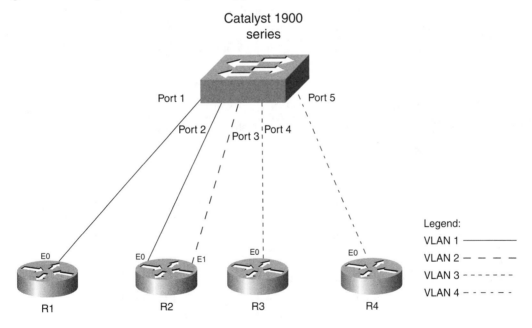

**NOTE**   Notice that VLAN 1 has two ports in the VLAN; the other VLANs have only one port assigned. Is that possible? Does it really matter? Well, in this situation, VLANs 2 through 4 are created just to provide you with the opportunity to configure multiple VLANs on a switch and to bring up the interfaces of those routers. If you did not connect the router's Ethernet ports to a switch or a hub, they would not become active. In the real world, you probably would not have one switch with one port belonging to one VLAN. That would mean that you would have only one host on one network.

Now that you understand how the routers are cabled to the switch, take a look at the specific lab objectives related to Cisco Catalyst switch configuration that you must complete for the switching section.

- Configure the switch with a host name of cat1900.
- Set the management console password to falcons.
- Assign the management console an IP address of 192.168.1.3/24 and the default gateway of 192.168.1.10 (the terminal server).
- Configure ports 1 and 2 (refer Figure 5-3, if needed) to be in VLAN 1. Name the VLAN vlan-r1r2.
- Configure port 3 for VLAN 2. Name the VLAN vlan-r2e1.
- Configure port 4 for VLAN 3. Name the VLAN vlan-r3e0.
- Configure port 5 for VLAN 4. Name the VLAN vlan-r4e0.

Let's go ahead and start configuring the switch.

**NOTE**   From here on out, you can assume that you will be starting from the terminal server. We won't cover gaining access to the terminal server to get to the switch or the routers.

## Accessing the Catalyst 1900 Switch

From the terminal server, access the switch as shown in Example 5-1. In the previous chapter, you established a session to all routers and the switch. To access the management console of the switch, all you need to do is press the number 7 and hit Return; that will take you to your previous connection on the switch.

**Example 5-1**   *Gaining Access to the Catalyst Switch*

```
Termserver#7
[Resuming connection 7 to cat1900...]




-------------------------------------------------
Catalyst 1900 Management Console
Copyright (c) Cisco Systems, Inc.  1993-1997
All rights reserved.

Ethernet address: 00-C0-1D-80-C7-5E
-------------------------------------------------



1 user(s) now active on Management Console.

Enter password:
```

There is no password on a Catalyst 1900 switch when it comes from the factory, so just press Enter. This takes you to the Catalyst 1900 main menu screen.

## Naming the Catalyst 1900 Switch

Here is the Catalyst 1900 main menu. Your first configuration task is to configure the switch with a host name of cat1900. So, you select **s** from the main menu, as demonstrated in Example 5-2.

---

**NOTE**         Feel free to go through all the options on the switch and get familiar with them. This chapter does not cover all the options in all the menus, but it is a good idea to get a general feeling of the menu system.

---

**Example 5-2**   *Catalyst 1900 Main Menu*

```
          Catalyst 1900 - Main Menu

      [C] Console Password
      [S] System
      [N] Network Management
      [P] Port Configuration
      [A] Port Addressing
      [D] Port Statistics Detail
```

*continues*

**Example 5-2** *Catalyst 1900 Main Menu (Continued)*

```
        [M] Monitoring
        [V] Virtual LAN
        [R] Multicast Registration
        [F] Firmware
        [I] RS-232 Interface
        [U] Usage Summaries
        [H] Help

        [X] Exit Management Console

Enter Selection: S
```

From the Catalyst 1900 System Configuration menu, you can then select **n** and type the name of the system, **cat1900**, as demonstrated in Example 5-3.

**Example 5-3** *Catalyst 1900 System Configuration Menu*

```
        Catalyst 1900 - System Configuration
        System Revision:  0   Address Capacity:  1024
        System Last Reset:  Sun Apr 15 22:29:45 2001

        ------------------Settings-----------------
        [N] Name of system
        [C] Contact name
        [L] Location
        [D] Date/time                             Tue Apr 17 14:24:41 2001
        [S] Switching mode                        FastForward
        [U] Use of store-and-forward for multicast  Disabled
        [A] Action upon address violation         Suspend
        [G] Generate alert on address violation   Enabled
        [M] Management Console inactivity timeout  None
        [I] Address aging time                    300 second(s)
        [P] Network Port                          A

        ------------------Actions------------------
        [R] Reset system                    [F] Reset to factory defaults

        ------------------Related Menus--------------
        [B] Broadcast storm control         [X] Exit to Main Menu
This command assigns an administrative name for this system. By convention, this is
the system's fully-qualified domain name.
Enter Selection:  N
```

Enter a name using a maximum of 255 characters, and then hit the Enter key:

```
Current setting ===>

    New setting ===> cat1900
```

After you type **cat1900** and hit Enter, the switch automatically sends you back to the Catalyst 1900 System Configuration menu.

# Setting a Password for the Catalyst 1900 Switch

The next task is to set the management console password to falcons. From the current menu, you need to exit back to the main menu by selecting **x** and then selecting **[C] Console Password** by typing **c**. This sends you to the Catalyst 1900 Console Password menu, as demonstrated in Example 5-4.

**Example 5-4**  *Navigating to the Catalyst 1900 Console Password Menu*

```
        Catalyst 1900 - Main Menu

    [C] Console Password
    [S] System
    [N] Network Management
    [P] Port Configuration
    [A] Port Addressing
    [D] Port Statistics Detail
    [M] Monitoring
    [V] Virtual LAN
    [R] Multicast Registration
    [F] Firmware
    [I] RS-232 Interface
    [U] Usage Summaries
    [H] Help

    [X] Exit Management Console

 Enter Selection:  C

        Catalyst 1900 - Console Password

        -----------------Settings-----------------
    [P] Password intrusion threshold          3 attempt(s)
    [S] Silent time upon intrusion detection  None

        -----------------Actions------------------
    [M] Modify password

    [X] Exit to Main Menu

 Enter Selection:
```

In Example 5-5, the only option is the **[M] Modify password** option. Selecting the **M** prompts you to enter the current console password (just press Enter) and then enter the new password (**falcons**). You must confirm the password selection by typing it again. After you re-enter the new password, you must hit any key to take you back to the Catalyst 1900

Console Password menu. Example 5-5 demonstrates the password creation/modification process.

**Example 5-5**    *Catalyst 1900 Console Password Menu*

```
         Catalyst 1900 - Console Password

         ------------------Settings-----------------
         [P] Password intrusion threshold                3 attempt(s)
         [S] Silent time upon intrusion detection        None

         ------------------Actions------------------
         [M] Modify password

         [X] Exit to Main Menu

  Enter Selection:  M



  The Management Console password can help prevent unauthorized accesses.
  When specifying a password, use a minimum of 4 characters and
  maximum of 8 characters.  The password is case insensitive and
  can contain any character with a legal keyboard representation.
  For the user's protection, the password must be entered the same
  way twice before it will be accepted.

         Enter current password:

           Enter new password:  *******
  Reenter to verify new password:  *******

  Password modified
  Press any key to continue.
```

Great, that's done—let's move on.

# Configuring an IP Address and Default Gateway for the Management Console

The next task is to configure the management console with an IP address of 192.168.1.3/24 and a default gateway of 192.168.1.10 (you will use the terminal server as your default gateway for the switch).

To do this, you need to exit out the Catalyst 1900 Console Password menu and get back to the main menu by selecting **[X] Exit to previous menu** and then the **[N] Network Management** option from the Catalyst 1900 main menu. Example 5-6 demonstrates the process of navigating to the Catalyst 1900 Network Management menu from the Catalyst 1900 main menu.

**Example 5-6**   *Navigating to the Catalyst 1900 Network Management Menu*

```
            Catalyst 1900 - Main Menu

    [C] Console Password
    [S] System
    [N] Network Management
    [P] Port Configuration
    [A] Port Addressing
    [D] Port Statistics Detail
    [M] Monitoring
    [V] Virtual LAN
    [R] Multicast Registration
    [F] Firmware
    [I] RS-232 Interface
    [U] Usage Summaries
    [H] Help

    [X] Exit Management Console

Enter Selection:  N


        Catalyst 1900 - Network Management

    [I] IP Configuration
    [S] SNMP Management
    [B] Bridge - Spanning Tree
    [C] Cisco Discovery Protocol
    [G] Cisco Group Management Protocol

    [X] Exit to Main Menu

Enter Selection:
```

Here you have several options, including an option to configure the Cisco Discovery Protocol (CDP). You won't be configuring CDP options on the switch; just know that it is enabled by default.

To assign an IP address and default gateway to the management console, you need to select the **[I] IP Configuration** option, as demonstrated in Example 5-7.

**Example 5-7**   *Navigating to the Catalyst 1900 IP Configuration Menu*

```
        Catalyst 1900 - Network Management

    [I] IP Configuration
    [S] SNMP Management
    [B] Bridge - Spanning Tree
    [C] Cisco Discovery Protocol
    [G] Cisco Group Management Protocol

    [X] Exit to Main Menu

Enter Selection:  I



        Catalyst 1900 - IP Configuration

        Ethernet Address:  00-C0-1D-80-C7-5E

    ------------------Settings------------------
    [I] IP address                      192.168.1.243
    [S] Subnet mask                     255.255.255.0
    [G] Default gateway                 192.168.1.100
    [V] Management VLAN                 1

    [X] Exit to previous menu

Enter Selection:
```

It is important to point out that the switch already has an IP address. By default, the Catalyst 1900 switch requests an IP address from a DHCP server, if available. The address in Example 5-7 was assigned by a DHCP server residing on the same segment as the switch. For the purposes of this exercise, you want to manually assign an IP address, so go ahead and select the **[I] IP address** option and assign the designated IP address of 192.168.1.3. Example 5-8 shows the Catalyst 1900 IP Configuration menu with the default settings and new IP address.

**Example 5-8**   *Catalyst 1900 IP Configuration Menu*

```
        Catalyst 1900 - IP Configuration

        Ethernet Address:  00-C0-1D-80-C7-5E

    ------------------Settings------------------
    [I] IP address                      192.168.1.243
    [S] Subnet mask                     255.255.255.0
    [G] Default gateway                 192.168.1.100
    [V] Management VLAN                 1

    [X] Exit to previous menu
This command assigns an administrative IP address to this switch. If an IP address
is assigned for the first time, the address will take immediate effect. Any
subsequent assignment will take effect on the next reset.
Enter the administrative IP address in dotted quad format (nnn.nnn.nnn.nnn):
```

**Example 5-8**  *Catalyst 1900 IP Configuration Menu (Continued)*

```
Enter Selection:  I
Current setting ===> 192.168.  1.243

     New setting ===> 192.168.1.3
```

You do not have to change the mask because the DHCP server assigned a 24-bit netmask by default. If it was different, you would need to change it by selecting the **[S] Subnet mask** option.

As you might have noticed, the default gateway is incorrect. You need to fix that by selecting the **[G] Default gateway** option, as demonstrated in Example 5-9. At this point, you can assign the correct default gateway (192.168.1.10, the terminal server).

**Example 5-9**  *Catalyst 1900 IP Configuration Menu*

```
        Catalyst 1900 - IP Configuration

        Ethernet Address:  00-C0-1D-80-C7-5E

        ------------------Settings-----------------
        [I] IP address                       192.168.1.3
        [S] Subnet mask                      255.255.255.0
        [G] Default gateway                  192.168.1.100
        [V] Management VLAN                  1

        [X] Exit to previous menu

Enter Selection:  G
The default gateway IP address is the address of the next-hop router the switch uses
to reach a non-local IP host when the switch does not know the return route. During
a normal management protocol exchange with an IP client host, the switch simply sends
its response onto the same route from which the request was received. The default
gateway route is only used when the switch itself initiates an exchange, e.g., a
TFTP upgrade, with the client.
The default gateway IP address is global to all VLANs. Type the address in dotted
quad format (nnn.nnn.nnn.nnn):
Current setting ===> 192.168.  1.100

     New setting ===> 192.168.1.10
```

The menu also prompts you to select a management VLAN. Because VLAN 1 will be configured for the IP segment of 192.168.1.X, you can leave the management VLAN as VLAN 1.

# VLAN Configuration

As you continue with the configuration tasks, you need to create the VLANs, name the VLANs, and assign the ports to the proper VLANs. To do this, exit back to the Catalyst 1900 main menu by hitting the X key twice and then selecting the **[V] Virtual LAN** option.

This takes you to the Catalyst 1900 Virtual LAN Configuration menu, as demonstrated in Example 5-10.

**Example 5-10** *Navigating to the Catalyst 1900 Virtual LAN Configuration Menu*

```
        Catalyst 1900 - Main Menu

    [C] Console Password
    [S] System
    [N] Network Management
    [P] Port Configuration
    [A] Port Addressing
    [D] Port Statistics Detail
    [M] Monitoring
    [V] Virtual LAN
    [R] Multicast Registration
    [F] Firmware
    [I] RS-232 Interface
    [U] Usage Summaries
    [H] Help

    [X] Exit Management Console

Enter Selection:  V



        Catalyst 1900 - Virtual LAN Configuration

    VLAN  Name                           Member ports
    ----  --------------------------     ------------
     1                                   1-24, AUI, A, B

    ------------------Actions------------------
    [C] Configure VLAN
    [X] Exit to Main Menu

Enter Selection:
```

From here, select the **[C] Configure VLAN** option and select the VLAN that you want to configure.

## Selecting VLAN 1 for Configuration

For the purposes of this lab exercise, you will configure VLAN 1 first. Example 5-11 demonstrates how to navigate through the Virtual LAN Configuration menu and select the **[C] Configure VLAN** option to select the VLAN that you want to configure.

**Example 5-11** *Selecting a Specific VLAN to Configure*

```
              Catalyst 1900 - Virtual LAN Configuration

     VLAN  Name                              Member ports
     ----  --------------------------  ------------
    1-24, AUI, A, B

            -----------------Actions-----------------
     [C] Configure VLAN
     [X] Exit to Main Menu

    Enter Selection:  C
    A VLAN is a collection of ports among which frames received are forwarded. Such
    frames are never forwarded outside of the member port group. Up to four VLANs may
    be configured on the switch.
    Identify VLAN 1 - VLAN 4:
    Select [1 - 4]:  1
```

## Naming VLAN 1

After selecting the VLAN to configure and hitting the Enter key, you come the Catalyst 1900 VLAN 1 Configuration menu. Now you can name the VLAN by selecting the **[V] VLAN name** option and typing the VLAN name for VLAN 1 (vlan-r1r2 will be the name for VLAN 1), as demonstrated in Example 5-12.

**Example 5-12** *Naming a VLAN*

```
              Catalyst 1900 - VLAN 1 Configuration

         Current member ports:  1-24, AUI, A, B

            -----------------Settings-----------------
     [V] VLAN name

            -----------------Actions-----------------
     [M] Move member ports from other VLANs

     [N] Next VLAN              [G] Goto VLAN
     [P] Previous VLAN          [X] Exit to previous Menu

    Enter Selection:  V

    A string of up to 60 characters may be specified to name or describe a VLAN.
      For example, VLAN 1 may be given a name such as 'Engineering LAN.'
```

*continues*

**Example 5-12** *Naming a VLAN (Continued)*

```
Enter VLAN name (60 characters max):

Current setting ===>

    New setting ===> vlan-r1r2
```

For VLAN 1, you do not need to add any ports to this VLAN. By default, all ports are members of VLAN 1. For the other VLANs, you will be reassigning ports from VLAN 1 to be members of the other VLANs.

## Selecting VLAN 2 for Configuration

When you have finished configuring VLAN 1, you can move on to VLAN 2. Notice in Example 5-13 that the name of the VLAN and the member ports are shown under the Catalyst 1900 Virtual LAN Configuration menu.

To configure VLAN 2, you need to exit VLAN 1 configuration by selecting the **[X] Exit to previous Menu** option, selecting **[C] Configure VLAN** from the Catalyst 1900 Virtual LAN Configuration menu, and typing **2** for VLAN 2, as demonstrated in Example 5-13.

**Example 5-13** *Configuring VLAN 2*

```
        Catalyst 1900 - Virtual LAN Configuration

   VLAN  Name                         Member ports
   ----  -------------------------    ------------
    1    vlan-r1r2                    1-24, AUI, A, B


   ------------------Actions------------------
   [C] Configure VLAN
   [X] Exit to Main Menu

Enter Selection:  C
A VLAN is a collection of ports among which frames received are forwarded.
Such frames are never forwarded outside of the member port group.
Up to 4 VLANs may be configured on the switch.
Identify VLAN 1 - VLAN 4:
Select [1 - 4]:  2


            Catalyst 1900 - VLAN 2 Configuration

        Current member ports:

        ------------------Settings------------------
        [V] VLAN name
```

**Example 5-13** *Configuring VLAN 2 (Continued)*

```
------------------Actions------------------
[M] Move member ports from other VLANs

[N] Next VLAN                 [G] Goto VLAN
[P] Previous VLAN             [X] Exit to previous Menu

Enter Selection:
```

## Naming VLAN 2

To name the VLAN, repeat the process used for VLAN 1 by selecting the **[V] VLAN name** option and typing **vlan-r2e1**, as done in Example 5-14.

**Example 5-14** *Naming VLAN 2*

```
          Catalyst 1900 - VLAN 2 Configuration

          Current member ports:

          ------------------Settings------------------
          [V] VLAN name

          ------------------Actions------------------
          [M] Move member ports from other VLANs

          [N] Next VLAN                 [G] Goto VLAN
          [P] Previous VLAN             [X] Exit to previous Menu

Enter Selection:  V


A string of up to 60 characters may be specified to name or describe a
VLAN.  For example, VLAN 1 may be given a name such as 'Engineering LAN.'
Enter VLAN name (60 characters max):

Current setting ===>

    New setting ===> vlan-r2e1
```

## Adding Member Ports to VLAN 2

Unlike VLAN 1, you need to add a member port to VLAN 2. If you refer back to Figure 5-3, you see that port 3 is assigned to VLAN 2. Make port 3 a member port in VLAN 2 by selecting the **[M] Move member ports from other VLANs** option and typing **3** for port 3, as demonstrated in Example 5-15.

If you look at the syntax for the command, you can specify several consecutive ports by using a hyphen (-),as in **3-8**, or you can specify individual ports by using a comma (for example, **3,5,7**). One port exists in this VLAN, so you need to type only **3**.

**Example 5-15** *Adding a Member Port to VLAN 2*

```
                Catalyst 1900 - VLAN 2 Configuration

            Current member ports:

            ------------------Settings------------------
            [V] VLAN name                              vlan-r2e1

            ------------------Actions-------------------
            [M] Move member ports from other VLANs

            [N] Next VLAN                 [G] Goto VLAN
            [P] Previous VLAN             [X] Exit to previous Menu

    Enter Selection:  M


    This command moves ports from other VLANs into this VLAN, removing
    them from containing VLANs.

    Port numbers should be separated by commas or spaces.  A port
    number range may also be specified. The word ALL indicates all ports.
    Example:  1, 7-11, AUI, 4, A
    Enter port numbers:  3
```

## Selecting VLAN 3 for Configuration

Now do the same for VLAN 3 and VLAN 4. Hit the X key to return to the Catalyst 1900 Virtual LAN Configuration menu; select the **[C] Configure VLAN** option and type **3**. See Example 5-16.

**NOTE**    It is important to note that VLAN 2 was added to the list of VLANs under the Catalyst 1900 Virtual LAN Configuration menu, along with a list of member ports belonging to each VLAN, as shown in Example 5-16. This helps you know which ports you have configured for each VLAN.

**Example 5-16** *Selecting VLAN 3 for Configuration*

```
                Catalyst 1900 - Virtual LAN Configuration

        VLAN  Name                         Member ports
        ----  --------------------------   -----------
          1   vlan-r1r2                     1-2, 4-24, AUI, A, B
          2   vlan-r2e0                     3


        ------------------Actions------------------
        [C] Configure VLAN
        [X] Exit to Main Menu

   Enter Selection:  C



   A VLAN is a collection of ports among which frames received are forwarded.
     Such frames are never forwarded outside of the member port group.
     Up to 4 VLANs may be configured on the switch.

   Identify VLAN 1 - VLAN 4:
   Select [1 - 4]:  3
```

## Naming VLAN 3

Select the **[V] VLAN name** option and type **vlan r3e0** to name the VLAN, as demonstrated in Example 5-17.

**Example 5-17** *Naming VLAN 3*

```
                Catalyst 1900 - VLAN 3 Configuration

        Current member ports:

        ------------------Settings------------------
        [V] VLAN name

        ------------------Actions------------------
        [M] Move member ports from other VLANs

        [N] Next VLAN                [G] Goto VLAN
        [P] Previous VLAN            [X] Exit to previous Menu

   Enter Selection:  V



   A string of up to 60 characters may be specified to name or describe a VLAN.
     For example, VLAN 1 may be given a name such as 'Engineering LAN.'

   Enter VLAN name (60 characters max):

   Current setting ===>

      New setting ===> vlan-r3e0
```

## Adding Member Ports to VLAN 3

Now add port 4 to be a member port of VLAN 3 by selecting the **[M] Move member ports from other VLANs** option and typing **4** for port 4 on the switch, as demonstrated in Example 5-18.

**Example 5-18** *Adding Port 4 as a Member Port of VLAN 3*

```
               Catalyst 1900 - VLAN 3 Configuration

          Current member ports:

          ------------------Settings------------------
          [V] VLAN name                           vlan-r3e0

          ------------------Actions-------------------
          [M] Move member ports from other VLANs

          [N] Next VLAN                 [G] Goto VLAN
          [P] Previous VLAN             [X] Exit to previous Menu

     Enter Selection:  M


     This command moves ports from other VLANs into this VLAN, removing
     them from containing VLANs.

     Port numbers should be separated by commas or spaces.  A port
     number range may also be specified. The word ALL indicates all ports.
     Example:  1, 7-11, AUI, 4, A

     Enter port numbers:   4
```

## Selecting VLAN 4 for Configuration

Now for your last VLAN, VLAN 4. To get back to the Catalyst 1900 Virtual LAN Configuration menu, select the **[X] Exit to previous Menu** option. To configure VLAN 4, select the **[C] Configure VLAN** option and type **4** for Catalyst 1900 VLAN 4 Configuration, as demonstrated in Example 5-19.

**Example 5-19** *Selecting VLAN 4 for Configuration*

```
               Catalyst 1900 - Virtual LAN Configuration

        VLAN  Name                          Member ports
        ----  --------------------------    -----------
           1  vlan-r1r2                      1-2, 5-24, AUI, A, B
           2  vlan-r2e0                      3
           3  vlan-r3e0                      4
```

**Example 5-19** *Selecting VLAN 4 for Configuration (Continued)*

```
            ------------------Actions------------------
          [C] Configure VLAN
          [X] Exit to Main Menu

    Enter Selection:  C


    A VLAN is a collection of ports among which frames received are forwarded. Such
    frames are never forwarded outside of the member port group. Up to 4 VLANs may be
    configured on the switch.

    Identify VLAN 1 - VLAN 4:
    Select [1 - 4]:  4
```

## Naming VLAN 4

From the Catalyst 1900 VLAN 4 Configuration menu, select the **[V] VLAN name** option
and type **vlan-r4e0**, as demonstrated in. Example 5-20.

**Example 5-20** *Naming VLAN 4*

```
                  Catalyst 1900 - VLAN 4 Configuration

              Current member ports:

              ------------------Settings------------------
             [V] VLAN name


              ------------------Actions------------------
             [M] Move member ports from other VLANs

             [N] Next VLAN            [G] Goto VLAN
             [P] Previous VLAN        [X] Exit to previous Menu

     Enter Selection:  V


     A string of up to 60 characters may be specified to name or describe a VLAN.  For
     example, VLAN 1 may be given a name such as 'Engineering LAN.'

     Enter VLAN name (60 characters max):

     Current setting ===>

        New setting ===> vlan-r4e0
```

## Adding Member Ports to VLAN 4

Don't forget to add port 5 to be a member port to VLAN 4. Select the **[M] Move member ports from other VLANs** option and type **5** for port 5, as demonstrated in Example 5-21.

**Example 5-21** *Adding Port 5 as a Member Port of VLAN 4*

```
              Catalyst 1900 - VLAN 4 Configuration

          Current member ports:

          ------------------Settings-----------------
          [V] VLAN name                            vlan-r4e0

          ------------------Actions------------------
          [M] Move member ports from other VLANs

          [N] Next VLAN                [G] Goto VLAN
          [P] Previous VLAN            [X] Exit to previous Menu

     Enter Selection:  M


     This command moves ports from other VLANs into this VLAN, removing
     them from containing VLANs.

     Port numbers should be separated by commas or spaces.  A port
     number range may also be specified. The word ALL indicates all ports.
     Example:  1, 7-11, AUI, 4, A

     Enter port numbers:  5
```

## Verifying VLAN Configuration

Now you are finished configuring the VLANs. Double-check your configuration by selecting the **[X] Exit to Main Menu** option to get back to the Catalyst 1900 Virtual LAN Configuration menu, which displays the VLAN names and associated member ports for each VLAN (see Example 5-22).

**Example 5-22** *Catalyst 1900 Virtual LAN Configuration Menu*

```
              Catalyst 1900 - Virtual LAN Configuration

     VLAN  Name                          Member ports
     ----  ---------------------------   ------------
      1    vlan-r1r2                      1-2, 6-24, AUI, A, B
      2    vlan-r2e1                      3
      3    vlan-r3e0                      4
      4    vlan-r4e0                      5

     -------------------Actions------------------
```

**Example 5-22** *Catalyst 1900 Virtual LAN Configuration Menu (Continued)*

```
        [C] Configure VLAN
        [X] Exit to Main Menu

Enter Selection:
```

As you can see, the VLANs are named correctly and have the correct member ports.

Leave the switch on this menu and go back to the terminal server (hitting Ctrl-Shift-6, x simultaneously) and get ready to configure the routers in Chapter 6, "General Router Configurations."

This chapter covers the following key topics:

- Configuring a host name
- Configuring enable, console, and vty passwords
- Configuring a message of the day (MOTD) banner
- Enabling and disabling DNS lookup
- Configuring a console port
- Creating a host table for Telnet access
- Writing a basic configuration script in Notepad

## CHAPTER 6

# General Router Configurations

This chapter covers the basic router configuration steps, with demonstrations on how to configure host names; set the enable, console, and vty passwords; configure a message of the day banner; and configure each router for Telnet access. You will learn how to enable and disable DNS resolution, ensure that your console connection does not time out, and configure the console port so that console messages do not append to the command line. Finally, you will create a host file on each router to facilitate Telnet access.

Each router in the lab will have some basic router configuration requirements that are the same. Although these steps are basic, they are an essential component to successfully administering Cisco routers.

## Lab Objectives

Configure all routers to have the following:

- Host name (that is, host names are to be according to the number R1, R2, R3, and so on).
- Enable password of falcons.
- Enable console login with password falcons.
- Telnet access (vty 0 4) with password falcons.
- No DNS resolution (no domain name lookups).
- Configure all routers so that the console port will not time out your connection.
- Configure all routers so that messages from the router to the console screen do not append to the command line.
- Configure all routers to show a banner when you log into the console port. In the banner, state which router you are logging into (for example, on Router 1, the banner should read "This is Router 1.")
- Create a host table on all routers using the loopback addresses that you created for each router.

Initially, you will configure a host name on each lab router. Next, you will learn how to manually configure each required lab objective task on R1. After this, you will learn how to write a basic configuration script in Notepad that will configure these same items. This script will then be applied to the remaining routers (R2 through R6) in the lab.

# Configuring a Host Name

To this point, you have configured only a host name on R1 and the Catalyst 1900 switch. The other lab routers have the router prompt of **Router>**. In the lab, you will give each router a host name as a means of identifying the router.

To begin, configure a host name on each router. Host names are useful in that they identify the router and help you know which router you are working on. Because R1 is already configured with a hostname of R1, you will reverse Telnet to the remaining lab routers, configure a host name, and then save the configuration. In addition, remember that the terminal server has an established reverse Telnet session to each lab router. Thus, you will reverse Telnet to each lab router by the connection number. To configure the host name, enter global configuration mode and use the following command:

```
Router(config)#hostname {name}
```

After you have saved the configuration, remember to issue the escape sequence **Ctrl-Shift-6, x** to get back to the terminal server and proceed to the next router. Example 6-1 demonstrates how to configure the host name for R2 through R6 and save the configuration.

**Example 6-1**   *Configuring a Host Name on Each Lab Router and Saving the Configuration*

```
Termserver#2
[Resuming connection 2 to r2 ... ]

Router>enable
Router#configure terminal
Enter configuration commands, one per line.  End with CNTL/Z.
Router(config)#hostname R2
R2(config)#exit
R2#
%SYS-5-CONFIG_I: Configured from console by console
R2#copy running-config startup-config
Building configuration...
[OK]
R2#    Ctrl-Shift-6, x

Termserver#3
[Resuming connection 3 to r3 ... ]

Router>enable
Router#configure terminal
Enter configuration commands, one per line.  End with CNTL/Z.
Router(config)#hostname R3
R3(config)#exit
```

**Example 6-1**  *Configuring a Host Name on Each Lab Router and Saving the Configuration (Continued)*

```
R3#
%SYS-5-CONFIG_I: Configured from console by console
R3#copy running-config startup-config
Building configuration...
[OK]
R3#
```

```
Termserver#4
[Resuming connection 4 to r4 ... ]

Router>enable
Router#configure terminal
Enter configuration commands, one per line.  End with CNTL/Z.
Router(config)#hostname R4
R4(config)#exit
R4#
%SYS-5-CONFIG_I: Configured from console by console
R4#copy running-config startup-config
Building configuration...
[OK]
R4#
```

```
Termserver#5
[Resuming connection 5 to r5 ... ]

Router>enable
Router#configure terminal
Enter configuration commands, one per line.  End with CNTL/Z
Router(config)#hostname R5
R5(config)#exit
R5#
%SYS-5-CONFIG_I: Configured from console by console
R5#copy running-config startup-config
Building configuration...
[OK]
R5#
```

```
Termserver#6
[Resuming connection 6 to r6 ... ]

Router>enable
Router#configure terminal
Enter configuration commands, one per line.  End with CNTL/Z
Router(config)#hostname R6
R6(config)#exit
R6#
%SYS-5-CONFIG_I: Configured from console by console
R6#copy running-config startup-config
Building configuration...
```

*continues*

**Example 6-1**   *Configuring a Host Name on Each Lab Router and Saving the Configuration (Continued)*

```
[OK]
R6#

Termserver#
```

Now each router has been assigned its respective host name.

# Setting the Enable, Console, and vty Passwords

Next, configure the enable, console, and vty passwords for R1. To set the enable password, enter global configuration mode and enter the following:

```
Router(config)#enable password password
```

To set the console and vty passwords, enter line configuration mode for line con0 and line vty 0 4, and use the following command:

```
Router(config-line)#password password
```

Then set the enable, console, and vty passwords to be falcons, as demonstrated in Example 6-2.

**Example 6-2**   *Setting the Enable, Console, and vty Passwords on R1*

```
R1>enable
R1#configure terminal
Enter configuration commands, one per line.  End with CNTL/Z.
R1(config)#enable password falcons
R1(config)#line con 0
R1(config-line)#password falcons
R1(config-line)#exit
R1(config)#line vty 0 4
R1(config-line)#password falcons
R1(config-line)#^Z
R1#
%SYS-5-CONFIG_I: Configured from console by console
R1#copy running-config startup-config
Building configuration...
[OK]
R1#
```

| NOTE | In a production environment, it is wise to set the enable, console, and vty passwords to be different so that access to the router is controlled in a secure manner. In addition, it is highly recommended that in production environments, you use the enable secret password, which is encrypted, instead of the enable password. For the purposes of the lab, the enable password is used and all three passwords are set to falcons, for simplicity's sake. You will have a chance to configure the enable secret password in Appendix C, "Self-Study Lab." |
|------|------|

After configuring each password, save the configuration to ensure that the passwords remain in effect after the router is power-cycled.

# Configuring a Message of the Day (MOTD) Banner

When configured, a message of the day (MOTD) banner displays a configured message to all connecting terminals. In this section, you will configure a MOTD banner on R1 that indicates which router you have connected to—that is, "This is Router 1." To do so, enter global configuration mode and issue the following command, followed by a delimiting character:

```
Router#banner motd #
```

Example 6-3 demonstrates configuring the message of the day and using # as the delimiting character.

**Example 6-3**    *Configuring a Message of the Day (MOTD) Banner on R1*

```
Termserver#1
[Resuming connection 1 to r1 ... ]

R1>enable
R1#configure terminal
Enter configuration commands, one per line.  End with CNTL/Z.
R1(config)#banner motd #
Enter TEXT message.  End with the character '#'.
This is Router 1
#
R1(config)#

Termserver#1
```

After issuing the **banner motd** command, you determine a delimiting character that Cisco IOS software will interpret to mean that you are finished with the banner. It is essential to choose a delimiting character that will not be in your message banner; otherwise, when you key the character as part of your message, Cisco IOS software will interpret the character to mean that you are finished with your message and will return you to global configuration mode. Example 6-2 uses # as the delimiting character, as highlighted.

Now exit global configuration mode and privileged EXEC mode. After exiting these modes, hit the Enter key. You should see the banner that you just configured. Example 6-4 demonstrates this process.

**Example 6-4**    *The Configured Message of the Day Banner Is Displayed When Entering User Exec Mode*

```
R1(config)#exit
R1#
%SYS-5-CONFIG_I: Configured from console by console
R1#exit


R1 con0 is now available




Press RETURN to get started.




This is Router 1

R1>
```

The message of the day banner has been successfully set.

# Enabling and Disabling DNS Lookup

IP domain name lookups or DNS resolution is enabled by default. To disable DNS resolution, use the following command:

```
Router(config)#no ip domain-lookup
```

When DNS has been disabled, you can enable DNS lookups with the following command:

```
Router(config)#ip domain-lookup
```

This command is executed from global configuration mode. DNS resolution is useful on a network because it enables you to Telnet between routers by name instead of by IP address. In large networks, DNS resolution is not only useful, but also necessary. Without it, it would be similar to surfing the Internet using only the IP address as the URL instead of typing the domain name of the web site.

**NOTE**    The **no ip domain-lookup** command disables only DNS packets generated by Cisco IOS software. IP packets carrying DNS requests/responses for end users are not affected and will be routed correctly.

The lab in this book does not have a configured DNS server in the network, so you need to disable DNS resolution. In addition, when DNS is not in use on the network, it is recommended that you disable IP domain lookup. This is because when a router cannot distinguish between a mistyped command and a possible host name, it tries to resolve the host through DNS. Often this might take several seconds as the router tries to translate the name to an IP address before the request times out and you are returned to a command prompt. Example 6-5 demonstrates what happens when you erroneously type **sxow** instead of **show** and hit the Enter key. The router responds by trying to do a name lookup on the network for the host sxow.

**Example 6-5**    *Router Doing a Name Lookup on a Mistyped Command*

```
R1#sxow
Translating "sxow"...domain server (255.255.255.255)
% Unknown command or computer name, or unable to find computer address
R1#
```

Disabling DNS resolution prevents the router from doing name lookups on mistyped commands. Example 6-6 demonstrates disabling DNS resolution on R1.

**Example 6-6**    *Disabling IP Domain Lookup on R1*

```
R1#configure terminal
Enter configuration commands, one per line.  End with CNTL/Z.
R1(config)#no ip domain-lookup
R1(config)#
```

In Example 6-7, enter the same erroneously typed command **sxow**, as done in Example 6-5.

**Example 6-7**    *Typing an Erroneous Command with IP Domain Lookup Disabled*

```
R1#sxow
Translating "sxow"
% Unknown command or computer name, or unable to find computer address
R1#
```

Notice that, this time, a DNS request is not sent out as before in Example 6-5. The result is that you are immediately returned to the command prompt. You have now successfully disabled IP domain lookup on R1.

# Console Port Configuration

In the lab, you need to ensure that your connection to the console port does not time out, consequently disconnecting the reverse Telnet session. This is done from the line configuration mode of the console port using the following command:

```
Router(config-line)#no exec-timeout
```

Example 6-8 demonstrates how to prevent your connection to the console port on R1 from timing out.

**Example 6-8**  *Disabling* **exec-timeout** *on the Console Port*

```
R1#configure terminal
Enter configuration commands, one per line.  End with CNTL/Z.
R1(config)#line con 0
R1(config-line)#no exec-timeout
R1(config-line)#
```

NOTE    In Example 6-8, the command **exec-timeout 0 0** is the same as **no exec-timeout**. The **exec-timeout** command also can be set to an arbitrary number of minutes and seconds. For example, you could set the timeout value to 10 minutes and 5 seconds using the command **exec-timeout 10 5**. In live environments, it is recommended that you avoid using the **no exec-timeout** command because this provides unlimited access on the console port and the potential for a security breach.

In addition, another useful command helps with readability. Often when you are configuring a router, you will receive a console message that is generated by the router. If this happens while you are typing a command, your command is interrupted and the console message is inserted from where you entered your last keystroke. Example 6-9 highlights an occurrence of this. As you begin to type the command **configure terminal**, the console message inserts itself and the **configure** command is split between two lines of screen output.

**Example 6-9**  *Console Message Interrupts When Typing the* **configure terminal** *Command*

```
R1(config-line)#^Z
R1#confi
%SYS-5-CONFIG_I: Configured from console by consolegure
Enter configuration commands, one per line.  End with CNTL/Z.
R1(config)#
```

This becomes problematic when typing long commands because you might lose track of where you left off in the command syntax, consequently typing an erroneous command. To prevent this, enable synchronous logging on the console port. This is done from line configuration mode of the console port using the following command:

```
Router(config-line)#logging synchronous
```

Example 6-10 demonstrates enabling synchronous logging on the console port of R1.

**Example 6-10** *Enabling Synchronous Logging on the Console Port*

```
R1(config)#line con 0
R1(config-line)#logging synchronous
R1(config-line)#
```

With synchronous logging enabled on the console port, when you begin to type the same configure terminal command, the console message is displayed; however, this time it does not interrupt the command flow. Instead, the keystrokes that you have entered to that point (that is, **confi**) are redrawn on the line following the console message. Then you can finish typing and the completed command appears uninterrupted on the screen. Example 6-11 demonstrates this.

**Example 6-11** *With Logging Synchronous Enabled, Command Flow Is Not Interrupted when a Console Message Is Displayed*

```
R1#confi
%SYS-5-CONFIG_I: Configured from console by console
R1#configure
```

Synchronous logging has now been successfully enabled on R1.

# Creating a Host Table for Telnet Access

The host table defines a static name-to-address mapping on the router. This host table enables you to Telnet to the router defined in the host table by its name that is defined in the table. To create an IP host table, enter global configuration mode and use the following command:

```
Router#ip host name address
```

For demonstration purposes, create a host table on R1 for each lab router that will map the router name to its loopback IP address. (You will assign them to the routers in Chapter 7, "Router Interface Configuration.") Example 6-12 shows the host table configuration.

**Example 6-12** *Configuring and IP Host Table Mapping the Router Name to Its Loopback IP Address*

```
R1#configure terminal
Enter configuration commands, one per line.  End with CNTL/Z.
R1(config)#ip host R1 192.169.1.1
R1(config)#ip host R2 192.169.2.2
R1(config)#ip host R3 192.169.3.3
R1(config)#ip host R4 192.169.4.4
R1(config)#ip host R5 192.169.5.5
R1(config)#ip host R6 192.169.6.6
R1(config)#exit
R1#
```

**NOTE**  In Example 6-12, 192.169.*x.x* is within the public addressing space used on the Internet. For our purposes, this is not an issue because the lab routers are not connected to the Internet. If your lab equipment is connected to the Internet, use RFC 1918 addressing instead.

Now examine the host table as it appears in the configuration by doing a **show running-config**. The highlighted portion of Example 6-13 displays the host table as it appears in the running-config.

**Example 6-13** *Host Table Configuration as it Appears in the Running-Config*

```
R1#show running-config
Building configuration...

Current configuration:
!
version 11.2
no service password-encryption
no service udp-small-servers
no service tcp-small-servers
!
hostname R1
!
enable password falcons
!
no ip domain-lookup
ip host R1 192.169.1.1
ip host R2 192.169.2.2
ip host R3 192.169.3.3
```

**Example 6-13** *Host Table Configuration as it Appears in the Running-Config (Continued)*

```
ip host R4 192.169.4.4
ip host R5 192.169.5.5
ip host R6 192.169.6.6
!
interface Ethernet0
 no ip address
 shutdown

R1#
```

Now test the connection to R2 via a regular Telnet session. From R1, Telnet to R2 by its name-to-address mapping that you configured in the host table, as shown in Example 6-14.

**Example 6-14** *Telnet Attempt to R2 Using Host Table Mapping Fails*

```
R1#R2
Trying R2 (192.169.2.2)...
% Destination unreachable; gateway or host down

R1#
```

Why did the attempt fail? For it to work, you must have IP connectivity to the loopback interface that was defined in the host table. In addition, the destination router must have Telnet access configured on its vty lines. When IP connectivity is established and each router has the appropriate loopback IP address assigned, you'll be able to Telnet to each router by host name. Chapter 7 covers these configuration steps in greater detail.

# Writing a Basic Script in Notepad

Your objective is to configure R2 through R6 with the same items just configured on R1. You can do this either manually or through an automated method. When generic configuration commands are configured on multiple routers, it is useful to create a script that will expedite the configuration process.

In this scenario, use Notepad to write the script and then paste what was scripted to the desired router as you are connected to the router through reverse Telnet.

To accomplish this, open the text editor Notepad by clicking Start, Run, and typing **notepad**, as shown in Figure 6-1.

**Figure 6-1**    *Starting the Notepad Application to Use when Writing the Router Script*

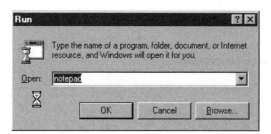

Notepad then opens, as shown in Figure 6-2.

**Figure 6-2**    *Notepad Application Opened to Use when Writing Script*

The next step is to enter the configuration commands in Notepad as if you are beginning from a particular configuration point in the CLI.

For the purposes of this chapter, the configuration point begins in enable mode. Because of this choice, you will need to ensure that the script begins with the **configure terminal** command, which gets you into the correct mode so that the scripted commands will execute in the proper mode. The following configuration items must be included in the script:

- Enable password
- Password of falcons on line con0 and vty 0 4

- No IP domain lookup
- No exec timeout on line con0
- Logging synchronous on line con0
- IP host table
- MOTD banner

For the script in Notepad, you should order these items in such a way that the router can interpret them. The commands should follow a natural sequence within a script. For example, you must assign IP addresses to interfaces before you can advertise a network in a routing protocol. By placing them in the same sequence that you would when configuring the router, Cisco IOS software will be capable of interpreting and then executing them accordingly. End the script with the **banner motd** command. This is because the banner will have input unique to the router you are configuring. When the script is pasted, it will end with the **banner motd** command and you will need to manually enter the input appropriate for the respective router that you're configuring. Now enter each command in Notepad as shown in Figure 6-3.

**Figure 6-3**    *The Configuration Script as it Appears in Notepad*

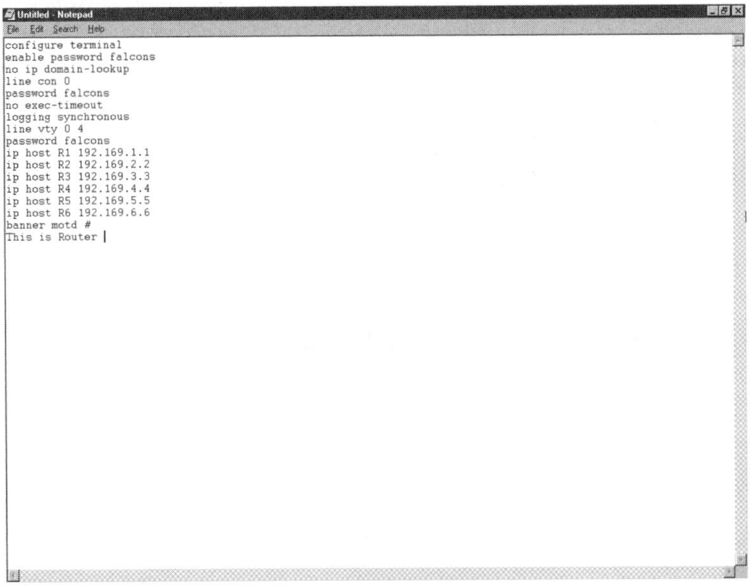

```
Untitled - Notepad
File  Edit  Search  Help
configure terminal
enable password falcons
no ip domain-lookup
line con 0
password falcons
no exec-timeout
logging synchronous
line vty 0 4
password falcons
ip host R1 192.169.1.1
ip host R2 192.169.2.2
ip host R3 192.169.3.3
ip host R4 192.169.4.4
ip host R5 192.169.5.5
ip host R6 192.169.6.6
banner motd #
This is Router |
```

As you will notice, the script in Figure 6-3 begins with the **configure terminal** command. This gets you into global configuration mode. In global configuration mode, you set the enable password, disable DNS lookup, and then enter line configuration mode for the console port. Then you set the password for console 0, ensure that the console connection won't time out with the **no exec-timeout** command, and enable synchronous logging. Then enter line configuration mode for vty lines 0 through 4. Then you set the password on the vty lines to falcons and exit line configuration mode again. Now you are back into global configuration mode and can issue the **ip host** commands for the host table. Finally, you issue the **banner motd** command and specify the delimiting character. You then type the banner and end with a space following **Router**. This enables you to manually type the number of the router that you are configuring, hit the Enter key, and then end the banner by typing the delimiting character **#**. Now the script is ready.

As R1 was manually configured with these items, begin with R2 using the script. Before pasting the script to the router, reverse Telnet to the router and enter enable mode, as shown in Example 6-15.

**Example 6-15** *Entering Enable Mode in Preparation to Paste Script*

```
Termserver#2
[Resuming connection 2 to r2 ... ]

R2>
2w1d: %SYS-5-CONFIG_I: Configured from console by console
R2>enable
R2#
```

Now switch back to Notepad and copy the script to the Clipboard by highlighting the scripted commands. Now copy the script to the Clipboard by selecting Edit and then Copy from within Notepad, as shown in Figure 6-4.

**Figure 6-4**   *Copying the Script from Notepad to the Clipboard in Preparation for the Paste to R2*

Now switch to HyperTerminal that is connected to R2 and, from enable mode, select Edit and Paste to Host, as shown in Figure 6-5.

**Figure 6-5**   *Pasting the Script to R2 using HyperTerminal*

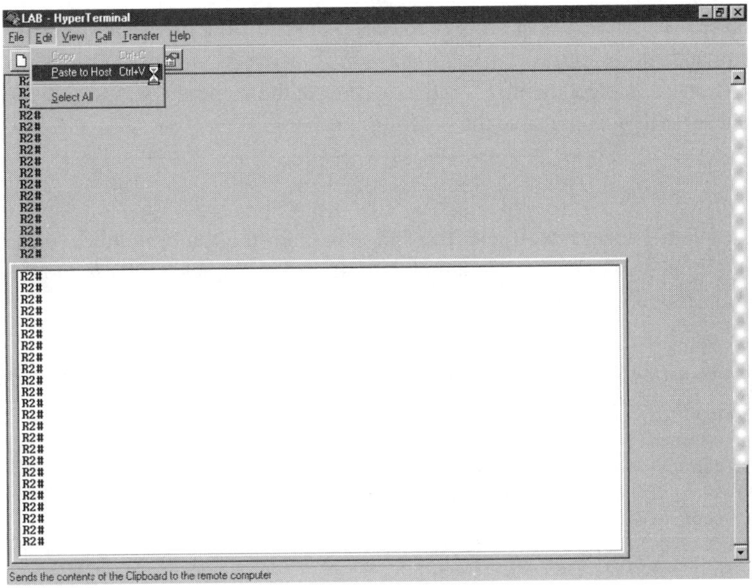

The configuration commands are pasted in the terminal application program, and the router executes each one as they were typed in the script, ending with the last configuration command, as shown in Example 6-16.

**Example 6-16** *Each Command Is Pasted as Type in the Script*

```
R2#configure terminal
Enter configuration commands, one per line.  End with CNTL/Z.
R2(config)#enable password falcons
R2(config)#no ip domain-lookup
R2(config)#line con 0
R2(config-line)#password falcons
R2(config-line)#no exec-timeout
R2(config-line)#logging synchronous
R2(config)#line vty 0 4
R2(config-line)#password falcons
R2(config)#ip host R1 192.169.1.1
R2(config)#ip host R2 192.169.2.2
R2(config)#ip host R3 192.169.3.3
R2(config)#ip host R4 192.169.4.4
R2(config)#ip host R5 192.169.5.5
R2(config)#ip host R6 192.169.6.6
R2(config)#banner motd #
Enter TEXT message.  End with the character '#'.
This is Router
```

**CAUTION** It is important to verify that each command was pasted properly and that no errors were reported for erroneous or ambiguous commands during the paste. If an ambiguous command was reported, you might have mistyped a command in your script. Simply return to the script, correct the error, and then repaste the corrected script to the router. When this is successful, you can save the configuration.

Example 6-16 leaves you with the option to enter the router number (that is, 2, 3, and so on), hit the Enter key, and then end with the delimiting character **#**. Do this now, as demonstrated in Example 6-17.

**Example 6-17** *Completing the Script Configuration by Finishing the Banner and Entering the Delimiting Character*

```
R2#configure terminal
Enter configuration commands, one per line.  End with CNTL/Z.
R2(config)#enable password falcons
R2(config)#no ip domain-lookup
R2(config)#line con 0
R2(config-line)#password falcons
R2(config-line)#no exec-timeout
R2(config-line)#logging synchronous
R2(config-line)#exit
R2(config)#line vty 0 4
R2(config-line)#password falcons
R2(config-line)#exit
R2(config)#ip host R1 192.169.1.1
R2(config)#ip host R2 192.169.2.2
R2(config)#ip host R3 192.169.3.3
R2(config)#ip host R4 192.169.4.4
R2(config)#ip host R5 192.169.5.5
R2(config)#ip host R6 192.169.6.6
R2(config)#banner motd #
Enter TEXT message.  End with the character '#'.
This is Router 2
#
R2(config)#exit
R2#
```

Now save the configuration, as shown in Example 6-18.

**Example 6-18** *Saving the Configuration After the Script Is Pasted Successfully*

```
R2#copy running-config startup-config
Building configuration...
[OK]
R2#
```

If you do a **show running-config**, you can see that all the information has been correctly configured per the script, as intended (see Example 6-19).

**Example 6-19** *The Configuration Changes Appear Correctly in the Running-Config*

```
R2#show running-config
Building configuration...

Current configuration:
!
version 12.0
service timestamps debug uptime
service timestamps log uptime
no service password-encryption
!
hostname R2
!
enable password falcons
!
ip subnet-zero
no ip domain-lookup
ip host R1 192.169.1.1
ip host R2 192.169.2.2
ip host R3 192.169.3.3
ip host R4 192.169.4.4
ip host R5 192.169.5.5
ip host R6 192.169.6.6
!
!
!
interface Ethernet0
 no ip address
 no ip directed-broadcast
 shutdown
!
interface Ethernet1
 no ip address
 no ip directed-broadcast
 shutdown
!
interface Serial0
 no ip address
```

*continues*

**Example 6-19** *The Configuration Changes Appear Correctly in the Running-Config (Continued)*

```
 no ip directed-broadcast
 no ip mroute-cache
 shutdown
!
ip classless
!
banner motd ^C
This is Router 2
^C
!
line con 0
 exec-timeout 0 0
 password falcons
 logging synchronous
 transport input none
line vty 0 4
 password falcons
 login
!
end

R2#
```

To finish, this process must be repeated for each remaining lab router, R3 through R6. Begin with R3 by reverse Telnetting to R3, entering enable mode, pasting the script, completing the appropriate message of the day banner, and then saving the configuration, as shown in Example 6-20.

**Example 6-20** *Pasting Script to R3, Completing the Banner, and Saving the Configuration*

```
Termserver#3
  [Resuming connection 3 to r3 ... ]

R3>
2w1d: %SYS-5-CONFIG_I: Configured from console by console
R3>enable

R3#configure terminal
Enter configuration commands, one per line.  End with CNTL/Z.
R3(config)#enable password falcons
R3(config)#no ip domain-lookup
R3(config)#line con 0
R3(config-line)#password falcons
R3(config-line)#no exec-timeout
R3(config-line)#logging synchronous
R3(config)#line vty 0 4
R3(config-line)#password falcons
R3(config)#ip host R1 192.169.1.1
```

**Example 6-20** *Pasting Script to R3, Completing the Banner, and Saving the Configuration (Continued)*

```
R3(config)#ip host R2 192.169.2.2
R3(config)#ip host R3 192.169.3.3
R3(config)#ip host R4 192.169.4.4
R3(config)#ip host R5 192.169.5.5
R3(config)#ip host R6 192.169.6.6
R3(config)#banner motd #
Enter TEXT message.  End with the character '#'.
This is Router 3
#
R3(config)#exit
R3#
%SYS-5-CONFIG_I: Configured from console by console
R3#copy running-config startup-config
Building configuration...
[OK]
R3#
```

Now escape back to the terminal server using **Ctrl-Shift-6, x** and repeat the process for R4, as shown in Example 6-21.

**Example 6-21** *Pasting Script to R4, Completing the Banner, and Saving the Configuration*

```
Termserver#4
[Resuming connection 4 to r4 ... ]

R4>
2w1d: %SYS-5-CONFIG_I: Configured from console by console
R4>enable

R4#configure terminal
Enter configuration commands, one per line.  End with CNTL/Z.
R4(config)#enable password falcons
R4(config)#no ip domain-lookup
R4(config)#line con 0
R4(config-line)#password falcons
R4(config-line)#no exec-timeout
R4(config-line)#logging synchronous
R4(config)#line vty 0 4
R4(config-line)#password falcons
R4(config)#ip host R1 192.169.1.1
R4(config)#ip host R2 192.169.2.2
R4(config)#ip host R3 192.169.3.3
R4(config)#ip host R4 192.169.4.4
R4(config)#ip host R5 192.169.5.5
R4(config)#ip host R6 192.169.6.6
R4(config)#banner motd #
Enter TEXT message.  End with the character '#'.
This is Router 4
```

*continues*

**Example 6-21** *Pasting Script to R4, Completing the Banner, and Saving the Configuration (Continued)*

```
#
R4(config)#exit
R4#
%SYS-5-CONFIG_I: Configured from console by console
R4#copy running-config startup-config
Building configuration...
[OK]
R4#
```

Next, escape back to the terminal server using **Ctrl-Shift-6, x** and repeat the process for R5, as shown in Example 6-22.

**Example 6-22** *Pasting Script to R5, Completing the Banner, and Saving the Configuration*

```
Termserver#5
[Resuming connection 5 to r5 ... ]

R5>
2w1d: %SYS-5-CONFIG_I: Configured from console by console
R5>enable

R5#configure terminal
Enter configuration commands, one per line.  End with CNTL/Z.
R5(config)#enable password falcons
R5(config)#no ip domain-lookup
R5(config)#line con 0
R5(config-line)#password falcons
R5(config-line)#no exec-timeout
R5(config-line)#logging synchronous
R5(config)#line vty 0 4
R5(config-line)#password falcons
R5(config)#ip host R1 192.169.1.1
R5(config)#ip host R2 192.169.2.2
R5(config)#ip host R3 192.169.3.3
R5(config)#ip host R4 192.169.4.4
R5(config)#ip host R5 192.169.5.5
R5(config)#ip host R6 192.169.6.6
R5(config)#banner motd #
Enter TEXT message.  End with the character '#'.
This is Router 5
#
R5(config)#exit
R5#
%SYS-5-CONFIG_I: Configured from console by console
R5#copy running-config startup-config
Building configuration...
[OK]
R5#
```

Finally, return back to the terminal server using **Ctrl-Shift-6, x** and repeat the process for R6, as shown in Example 6-23.

**Example 6-23** *Pasting Script to R6, Completing the Banner, and Saving the Configuration*

```
Termserver#6
[Resuming connection 6 to r6 ... ]

R6>
2w1d: %SYS-5-CONFIG_I: Configured from console by console
R6>enable

R6#configure terminal
Enter configuration commands, one per line.  End with CNTL/Z.
R6(config)#enable password falcons
R6(config)#no ip domain-lookup
R6(config)#line con 0
R6(config-line)#password falcons
R6(config-line)#no exec-timeout
R6(config-line)#logging synchronous
R6(config)#line vty 0 4
R6(config-line)#password falcons
R6(config)#ip host R1 192.169.1.1
R6(config)#ip host R2 192.169.2.2
R6(config)#ip host R3 192.169.3.3
R6(config)#ip host R4 192.169.4.4
R6(config)#ip host R5 192.169.5.5
R6(config)#ip host R6 192.169.6.6
R6(config)#banner motd #
Enter TEXT message.  End with the character '#'.
This is Router 6
#
R6(config)#exit
R6#
%SYS-5-CONFIG_I: Configured from console by console
R6#copy running-config startup-config
Building configuration...
[OK]
R6#
```

You have now completed the basic router configuration steps for the lab. You have configured each router with a host name; set the enable, console, and vty password; and created a message of the day banner. Each router is now configured for Telnet access, and you have created a host table that will be used to facilitate Telnet access after IP has been configured on the required interfaces. In addition, you have learned how to use a script to configure multiple routers with similar configuration information.

You are now ready to proceed to the router interface configuration section of the lab, covered in Chapter 7.

This chapter covers the following aspects of router interface configuration:

- Interface connectivity and IP addressing
- Frame Relay overview
- Configuring Frame Relay interfaces
- Configuring point-to-point serial interfaces
- Configuring Ethernet interfaces
- Configuring Token Ring interfaces
- Creating and configuring loopback interfaces
- Cisco Discovery Protocol (CDP)

## CHAPTER 7

# Router Interface Configuration Methodology

This chapter covers the methodology for configuring the router interfaces. The chapter begins with configuring the Frame Relay interfaces and then continues with configuring any other type of serial interfaces, Ethernet interfaces, and finally Token Ring interfaces. When you are familiar with how to configure the various interface types, you will learn how to create and configure loopback interfaces. The chapter concludes with a brief overview of the Cisco Discovery Protocol (CDP). CDP allows directly connected routers to learn of each other and their capabilities. It is also a very good tool in determining whether you have Layer 1 and Layer 2 connectivity.

## Interface Connectivity and IP Addressing

The approach used in this chapter to configuring each of the router interfaces is based on types of interfaces. For example, you will configure all the Frame Relay interfaces first. You will enter all the necessary commands to bring up the Frame Relay connection and assign an IP address to the interface, and then you will verify connectivity to all directly connected interfaces by using the **ping** command.

After the Frame Relay interfaces are configured, you will configure all of the point-to-point serial interfaces and assign them IP addresses; then you'll move on to Ethernet and then Token Ring. This will give you the opportunity to focus on each of the data link layer technologies and how to configure them. This is an important section of the lab because you cannot configure the different routing protocols until you have all interfaces configured with IP addresses and have complete IP connectivity to directly connected interfaces. (*Directly connected interfaces* refers to router interfaces connected to the same physical segment.)

The lab objectives to complete in this chapter are as follows:

- Configure all routers to have a description on all active interfaces (except loopback interfaces) stating the router and interface to which they are connected.

- Create loopback interfaces on all routers. Use IP address 192.169.*X.X*/24 (where *X* is the router number). So, R1 would have a loopback address of 192.169.1.1/24, R2 would be 192.169.2.2/24, and so on.

## IP Addressing

Refer to the lab diagram in Figure 7-1 for IP addressing assignments. Don't forget to look at the network mask. The BRI ports on R5 and R6 should use the IP addresses 192.168.200.1/30 and 192.168.200.2/30, respectively.

**Figure 7-1**   *Lab Diagram*

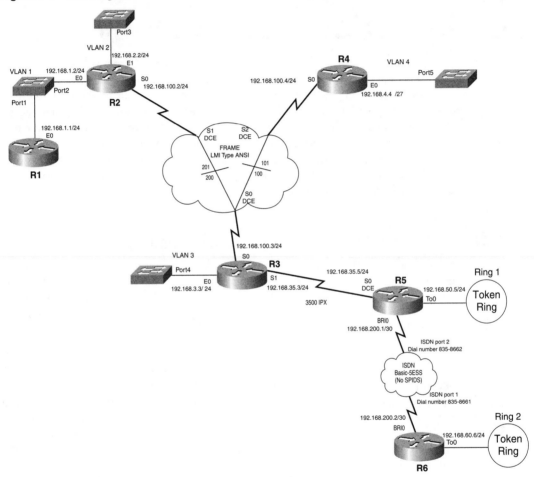

As mentioned earlier, you begin configuring the lab with the routers that have interfaces connected to the Frame Relay network. Before you start configuring the routers, however, you should briefly review Frame Relay and its components.

# Frame Relay Overview

Frame Relay is a very popular technology for connectivity across WAN links. Before configuring the interfaces, you probably should gain a basic familiarity with Frame Relay. We will not cover Frame Relay technology in depth; we will just review the essentials so that you understand how Frame Relay is operating in the lab for configuration and troubleshooting tasks. For a complete review of Frame Relay, see Chapter 13 of *Interconnecting Cisco Network Devices* from Cisco Press.

Frame Relay is a physical and data link layer encapsulation technology, as depicted in Figure 7-2.

**Figure 7-2**    *Frame Relay and OSI Reference Model Correlation*

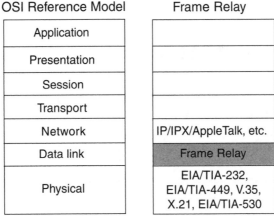

Frame Relay is an ITU-T (CCITT) and American National Standards Institute (ANSI) defined standard that outlines sending data over a public network.

## Frame Relay Components

You should be familiar with several Frame Relay components before going through the Frame Relay interface configuration process:

- **Data-link connection identifier (DLCI)**—This is a number that identifies the logical circuit between the router and the Frame Relay switch. The Frame Relay switch maps the DLCIs between each pair of routers to create a PVC. DLCIs have local significance in that the identifier references the point between the local router and the Frame Relay switch to which it is connected. Thus, the same (or different) DLCI numbers can be used on both ends and it still would work properly.

- **Permanent virtual circuit (PVC)**—This is a virtual circuit that is permanently established. A PVC is an end-to-end path (that is, router-to-router path through a Frame Relay cloud). One or more DLCIs form a PVC in a Frame Relay network. PVCs save bandwidth associated with the establishment and teardown of circuits.

- **Local Management Interface (LMI)**—This is a signaling standard between the router device and the Frame Relay switch that is responsible for managing the connection and maintaining status between the devices.

**NOTE**    Not all Frame Relay terminology is reviewed here. Frame Relay is a useful technology, and there are several different applications of Frame Relay. Again, we will review only what is needed to complete the lab.

## Frame Relay Address Mappings

An important part of Frame Relay is the mapping of IP addresses to DLCIs. Two methods exist for Cisco routers to form these mappings:

- **Frame Relay Inverse ARP (dynamic)**—This is a method of dynamically associating a network layer address with a DLCI. It allows a router to discover the network address of a device associated with a DLCI. Inverse ARP normally is used in fully meshed networks (networks in which all routers have PVCs to each other). The environment in this lab is a hub-spoke topology, so you will encounter some limitations with Frame Relay Inverse ARP.

- **Static (manual) mappings**—In this method, you manually map a network layer address, such as IP or IPX, to a DLCI. This is done under the interface configuration mode for the serial interface configured for Frame Relay. It is important to note that when you manually map an IP address to a DLCI, Frame Relay Inverse ARP is disabled for that interface. You will have an opportunity to manually map IP addresses to DLCIs in this lab.

# Configuring Frame Relay Interfaces

**NOTE**    If you have not configured the Frame Relay Switch router (the Cisco 2523 router), you need to do so before continuing. See Appendix B, "Frame Relay Switch Configuration," for the configuration steps.

Before you configure the Frame Relay interfaces, review the Frame Relay network for the lab environment. Figure 7-3 shows the Frame Relay cloud and the router interfaces that you will be configuring for Frame Relay.

**Figure 7-3**   *Frame Relay Cloud*

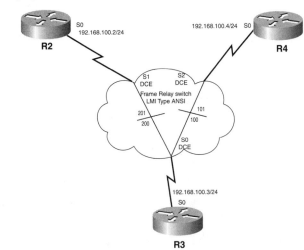

As you can see, R2's S0, R3's S0, and R4's S0 are the three interfaces that you need to configure for Frame Relay. Because R3 is the "hub" router (meaning that all other Frame Relay connections terminate on R3), you will start there.

From the terminal server, let's resume the connection to R3 by typing **3**, as in Example 7-1.

**Example 7-1**   *Gaining Access to R3*

```
Termserver#3
[Resuming connection 3 to r3 ... ]

R3#
```

If the **R3#** does not appear right away, hit the Enter key several times.

---

**NOTE**    If for some reason you are not in privileged exec mode, type **enable** and type the password **falcons** before executing any commands.

---

The first step is to get into global configuration mode by typing **config t**. To get into interface configuration mode, enter the **interface** command with the appropriate interface type and number. The options for the **interface** command are listed here:

```
Router#(config)interface [async | dialer | ethernet | group-async | lex | loopback |
    null | serial | tunnel | virtual-template] number
```

As you can see, Cisco IOS Software supports several different types of interfaces. After you specify the type of interface, you need to indicate the number of that particular interface. In the example, R3 has only two serial interfaces: Serial 0 and Serial 1. Remember, all interface numbering starts at 0.

Example 7-2 illustrates the commands executed on R3.

**Example 7-2**  *Serial 0 Interface Configuration Mode*

```
R3#config t
Enter configuration commands, one per line.  End with CNTL/Z.
R3(config)#interface serial 0
R3(config-if)#
```

Because Frame Relay is a type of encapsulation, you need to change the default encapsulation type of HDLC on S0 to Frame Relay. This is done in interface configuration mode using the following command:

```
Router(config-if)#encapsulation frame-relay [cisco ¦ ietf]
```

Two types of Frame Relay encapsulation exist: Cisco and IEFT. Cisco is the default encapsulation and should be used when connecting to another Cisco router. IETF should be used if you are connecting to a non-Cisco device.

The next step is to specify that the LMI type (provided in Figure 7-3) coming from the Frame Relay switch is ANSI. The command to use is this:

```
Router(config-if)#frame-relay lmi-type [cisco ¦ ansi ¦ q933a]
```

Cisco routers support three different LMI types:

- **cisco**—An LMI type defined together by Cisco, StrataCom, Northern Telecom, and Digital Equipment Corporation
- **ansi–AnnexD**—Defined by the ANSI standard T1.617
- **a33a**—ITU-T Q.933 Annex A

Because the Frame Relay switch was configured for LMI type ansi, that is what you must use on the Frame Relay routers. LMI type is from the local router to the switch. The Frame Relay encapsulation type must be consistent from router to router.

Example 7-3 shows the configuration task completed on R3.

**Example 7-3**  **frame-relay** *Interface Commands*

```
R3(config-if)#encapsulation frame-relay
R3(config-if)#frame-relay lmi-type ansi
R3(config-if)#
```

Now assign the interface the IP address 192.168.100.3 with a mask of /24 (which is 255.255.255.0 in decimal format) by using the following command:

```
Router(config-if)#ip address A.B.C.D A.B.C.D [secondary]
```

The first four letters represent the IP address in decimal form. The second four letters represent the subnet mask in decimal form. You can specify a secondary IP address on the interface as well by using the **secondary** option at the end of the command line.

By default, physical interfaces on a router are "shut down." To bring the port into service, you must enter the command **no shutdown** in the interface configuration mode.

Example 7-4 shows the completed commands for R3.

**Example 7-4**  *IP Address Assignment*

```
R3(config-if)#ip address 192.168.100.3 255.255.255.0
R3(config-if)#no shutdown
```

If you have done things correctly, you should receive several messages indicating that the interfaces are up and that the line protocol is up. In addition, you should see LMI messages stating what PVC or DLCIs you are seeing from your Frame Relay switch and stating whether they are active. The messages are shown in Example 7-5.

**Example 7-5**  *Router Console Messages*

```
R3(config-if)#no shutdown
%LINEPROTO-5-UPDOWN: Line protocol on Interface Serial0, changed state to up
R3(config-if)#
%LINK-3-UPDOWN: Interface Serial0, changed state to up
R3(config-if)#
%FR-5-DLCICHANGE: Interface Serial0 - DLCI 100 state changed to ACTIVE
%FR-5-DLCICHANGE: Interface Serial0 - DLCI 200 state changed to ACTIVE

%FR-5-DLCICHANGE: Interface Serial0 - DLCI 100 state changed to INACTIVE
%FR-5-DLCICHANGE: Interface Serial0 - DLCI 200 state changed to INACTIVE
```

From the messages in Example 7-5, you know that R3 is seeing two DLCIs, 100 and 200. It is interesting to note that the DLCIs go into an ACTIVE state first and then go back to an INACTIVE a few moments later. This is because no other routers are configured for Frame Relay at this point. When routers R2 and R4 are configured for Frame Relay, the DLCI should stay in an ACTIVE state.

The **show frame-relay pvc** command is useful for troubleshooting because it displays more information regarding the DLCIs, as demonstrated in Example 7-6.

**Example 7-6**  **show frame-relay pvc** *Command Output*

```
R3#show frame-relay pvc

PVC Statistics for interface Serial0 (Frame Relay DTE)

DLCI = 100, DLCI USAGE = LOCAL, PVC STATUS = INACTIVE, INTERFACE = Serial0

    input pkts 0            output pkts 0           in bytes 0
    out bytes 0            dropped pkts 0          in FECN pkts 0
    in BECN pkts 0         out FECN pkts 0         out BECN pkts 0
    in DE pkts 0           out DE pkts 0
    out bcast pkts 0        out bcast bytes 0
    pvc create time 00:00:44, last time pvc status changed 00:00:23

DLCI = 200, DLCI USAGE = LOCAL, PVC STATUS = INACTIVE, INTERFACE = Serial0

    input pkts 0            output pkts 0           in bytes 0
    out bytes 0            dropped pkts 0          in FECN pkts 0
    in BECN pkts 0         out FECN pkts 0         out BECN pkts 0
    in DE pkts 0           out DE pkts 0
    out bcast pkts 0        out bcast bytes 0
    pvc create time 00:00:47, last time pvc status changed 00:00:16
R3#
```

With R3 having multiple DLCIs, one going to R2 and the other to R4, this command separates DLCI numbers and gives you individual statistics for each DLCI. If you could not communicate with the Frame Relay switch, you would not have any entries in the output. Remember, LMI is communicating with the Frame Relay switch to provide information on what, if any, DLCIs are advertised on each interface.

The highlighted text in Example 7-6 shows some important information gleaned from this **show** command. The output shows the DLCI number(s), the PVC state, and the interfaces on which these DLCI were received. Another important piece of information is **pvc create time** and **last time pvc status changed**. From these fields, you can determine when the router or the PVC to the switch went down, which is very useful information for troubleshooting purposes.

Another useful troubleshooting command is **show frame-relay lmi**, as demonstrated in Example 7-7.

**Example 7-7** **show frame-relay pvc** *Command Output*

```
R3(config-if)#end
R3#show frame-relay lmi

LMI Statistics for interface Serial0 (Frame Relay DTE) LMI TYPE = ANSI
  Invalid Unnumbered info 0          Invalid Prot Disc 0
  Invalid dummy Call Ref 0           Invalid Msg Type 0
  Invalid Status Message 0           Invalid Lock Shift 0
  Invalid Information ID 0           Invalid Report IE Len 0
  Invalid Report Request 0           Invalid Keep IE Len 0
  Num Status Enq. Sent 13        Num Status msgs Rcvd 10
  Num Update Status Rcvd 0           Num Status Timeouts 5
R3#
```

The highlighted text in Example 7-7 depicts some important information. You can see the interface that is receiving LMI (Serial0) and the LMI type (ANSI). You also see the number of LMI keepalives being sent and received. Usually these values will not be equal. It takes a few moments for the DLCI to become active, so a few LMI timeouts will occur.

**show frame-relay map** is an additional helpful command for troubleshooting. There are no options for this command. The output from this command reveals the mapping of network address (IP or IPX) to DLCI. If you issued this command at this point, you would not see any mappings because no other routers are configured for Frame Relay. Demonstration of this command appears later after the configuration of R2 for Frame Relay.

Next, place a description on the interface that indicates to whom this interface connects.

The **description** command is issued under interface configuration mode:

```
Router#(config-if)description {text}
```

This command is very helpful in managing your routers. By placing a description on each active interface with information such as which router the interface connects to, the private line number or circuit number, DLCI numbers, and other helpful information, you can reduce the time to resolve issues because you have the information located on the router and not on some spreadsheet tucked away somewhere.

Example 7-8 demonstrates this task.

**Example 7-8** *Interface Description Task*

```
R3#config t
Enter configuration commands, one per line.  End with CNTL/Z.
R3(config)#interface serial 0
R3(config-if)#description This interface connects to R2's S0 (DLCI 200) and R4's S0
  (DLCI 100)
```

You will be placing descriptions on the interfaces at the same time that you assign IP addresses. Before leaving R3 and configuring R2 and R4, take a look at the running-config to see what the configuration looks like for interface Serial 0. Example 7-9 reveals only the interface section of the running-config.

**Example 7-9** **show running-config** *Command Output*

```
R3#show running-config
Building configuration...

Current configuration:
.
.
.
!
interface Ethernet0
 no ip address
 shutdown
!
interface Serial0
 description This interface connects to R2's S0 (DLCI 200) and R4's S0 (DLCI 100)
 ip address 192.168.100.3 255.255.255.0
 encapsulation frame-relay
 frame-relay lmi-type ansi
 !
interface Serial1
 no ip address
 shutdown
```

The highlighted text in Example 7-9 illustrates what the configuration should look like. You do not see any Frame Relay DLCI information in the configuration. This is because Frame Relay Inverse ARP will take care of the DLCI mappings on R3. This will not be the case for R2 and R4, as explained later in the chapter.

Next, save the configuration to NVRAM and move on to R2.

---

**TIP**      It is always good to save your configuration before leaving the router. Remember, **Ctrl-Shift-6, x** will take you back to the terminal server.

---

Example 7-10 walks you through the process.

**Example 7-10** *Save Configuration and Return to Term Server*

```
R3#copy running-config startup-config
Building configuration...
[OK]
R3#<ctrl-shft-6><x>
    Termserver#2
[Resuming connection 2 to r2 ... ]

R2#
```

From the lab diagram that hopefully you have printed and are updating, you know that you need to configure R2's Serial 0 interface for Frame Relay. Configuring R2's S0 interface for Frame Relay works the same way as what you did for R3's S0 interface. After you change the encapsulation to Frame Relay and specify the Frame Relay LMI type, you can assign the IP address to the main interface and remove it from shutdown state. Example 7-11 demonstrates this process.

**Example 7-11** *R2's Serial 0 Frame Relay Configuration*

```
R2#config t
Enter configuration commands, one per line.  End with CNTL/Z.
R2(config)#interface serial 0
R2(config-if)#encapsulation frame-relay
R2(config-if)#frame-relay lmi-type ansi
R2(config-if)#ip address 192.168.100.2 255.255.255.0
R2(config-if)#description This interface connects to R3's S0 (DLCI 201)
R2(config-if)#no shutdown
```

Again, if the configuration is correct, you should see console messages like those shown in Example 7-12.

**Example 7-12** *R2 Console Messages*

```
2w3d: %LINK-3-UPDOWN: Interface Serial0, changed state to up
R2(config-if)#
2w3d: %FR-5-DLCICHANGE: Interface Serial0 - DLCI 201 state changed to ACTIVE
2w3d: %LINEPROTO-5-UPDOWN: Line protocol on Interface Serial0, changed state to
  up
R2(config-if)#
```

As the output in Example 7-12 reveals, both the interface and the line protocol came up. As you can see, the LMI reveals that DLCI 201 is being advertised from the Frame Relay switch. This matches the diagram of the Frame Cloud in Figure 7-3. R2 should be receiving DLCI 201. IP connectivity to R3 should be established. To **ping** R3, you need to have an IP address-to-DLCI mapping. Issuing the **show frame-relay map** command reveals whether

Frame Relay Inverse ARP is working. Example 7-13 contains the output from the **show frame-relay map** command.

**Example 7-13 show frame-relay map** *Command Output*

```
R2#show frame-relay map
Serial0 (up): ip 192.168.100.3 dlci 201(0xC9,0x3090), dynamic,
              broadcast,, status defined, active
R2#
```

The highlighted sections of Example 7-13 illustrate the important information of this command. The output shows that the interface that the mapping was learned on (Serial 0) and its status (up), the IP address of R3 (192.168.100.3), and the DLCI number (201). In addition, "dynamic" tells you that Frame Relay Inverse ARP was used to discover this mapping. If you used a **frame-relay map** statement to manually map the IP address to the DLCI, the output would show "static" where "dynamic" is now. One more piece of information tells you whether the mapping is active or inactive. If the PVC is to be disconnected, you would see "deleted" in that field. In short, the IP address-to-DLCI mapping tells the router that any packets destined to the IP address, or where the IP address is the next hop to the destination address in the IP packet, is to be sent out DLCI 201 (or to R3).

With a valid IP address-to-DLCI mapping, try to **ping** R3's Serial 0 IP address (192.168.100.3). The command syntax is shown here:

```
Router#ping [word | apollo | appletalk | clns | decnet | ip | ipx |vines | xns ] {address}
```

**ping** is actually an acronym for Packet INternet Groper. It is a mechanism for devices to test Layer 3b (network) connectivity to other devices. The Cisco implementation of the **ping** command supports several different protocols. For this example, you want to test IP connectivity. The router is smart enough to understand the different protocol address format, so you need to type only the command and the destination IP address that you want to test. When testing IP connectivity, the router sends an ICMP echo-request packet; if the destination router receives the packet, it will send an ICMP echo-reply packet. The command will display a "!" when it receives an echo-reply packet. If it never receives the packet, it displays a "." (period) indicating that it waited 2 seconds and did not receive a response to its ICMP echo-request. This will be a very useful command throughout the lab.

Example 7-14 shows the result of issuing the **ping** command on R3's Serial 0 IP address (192.168.100.3).

**Example 7-14** *R2-to-R3* **ping** *Result*

```
R2#ping 192.168.100.3

Type escape sequence to abort.
Sending 5, 100-byte ICMP Echos to 192.168.100.3, timeout is 2 seconds:
!!!!!
Success rate is 100 percent (5/5), round-trip min/avg/max = 32/34/36 ms
R2#
```

You got 100 percent success! Looks like you are on the right track. Before leaving R2 to configure R4, take a look at the running-config for R2 and save the configuration to NVRAM. Example 7-15 illustrates the running-config output.

**Example 7-15** *R2's Running-Config*

```
R2#show run
Building configuration...

Current configuration:
!
version 12.0
service timestamps debug uptime
service timestamps log uptime
no service password-encryption
!
hostname R2
.

.
!
interface Ethernet0
 no ip address
 no ip directed-broadcast
 shutdown
!
interface Ethernet1
 no ip address
 no ip directed-broadcast
 shutdown
!
interface Serial0
description This interface connects to R3's S0 (DLCI 201)
 ip address 192.168.100.2 255.255.255.0
 no ip directed-broadcast
 encapsulation frame-relay
 no ip mroute-cache
 frame-relay lmi-type ansi
!
.

.
```

*continues*

**Example 7-15** *R2's Running-Config (Continued)*

```
R2#copy running-config startup-config
Building configuration...
[OK]
R2#
```

The **encapsulation frame-relay** and **frame-relay lmi-type** commands are present along with the IP address. You have saved the running-config to the startup-config, so move on to R4.

To get to R4, go back to the terminal server, resume the reverse Telnet session to R4, and go into global configuration mode and then interface configuration mode for interface Serial 0. Example 7-16 takes you through the commands to do this.

**Example 7-16** *R4 Interface Configuration Mode*

```
R2#
R2#<ctrl-shft-6><x>
    Termserver#4
[Resuming connection 4 to r4 ... ]

R4#config t
Enter configuration commands, one per line.  End with CNTL/Z.
R4(config)#interface serial 0
R4(config-if)#
```

Now that you are in interface configuration mode for R4's S0, go ahead and configure Frame Relay on S0; assign it an IP address and remove it from shutdown mode. The commands are exactly like R2's, except that the IP address changes to 192.168.100.4 with a network mask of 255.255.255.0. See Example 7-17.

**Example 7-17** *R4 Frame Relay Configuration*

```
R4(config-if)#encapsulation frame-relay
R4(config-if)#frame-relay lmi-type ansi
R4(config-if)#ip address 192.168.100.4 255.255.255.0
R4(config-if)#description This interface connects to R3's S0 (DLCI 101)
R4(config-if)#no shutdown
R4(config-if)#
```

The highlighted text in Example 7-17 shows the commands for Frame Relay and IP address assignment. You should see console messages, as you did on R2, to inform you that the interface and line protocols came up and that LMI is discovering DLCIs. Example 7-18 illustrates what you should see when the interface becomes active.

**Example 7-18** *R4 Console Messages*

```
%LINK-3-UPDOWN: Interface Serial0, changed state to up
R4(config-if)#
%LINEPROTO-5-UPDOWN: Line protocol on Interface Serial0, changed state to up
R4(config-if)#
%FR-5-DLCICHANGE: Interface Serial0 - DLCI 101 state changed to ACTIVE
R4(config-if)#
```

The interface is up and the DLCI is active. You now should be capable of **ping**ing R3. Example 7-19 shows the result.

**Example 7-19** *R4-to-R3* **ping** *Result*

```
R4(config-if)#end
R4#
%SYS-5-CONFIG_I: Configured from console by console
R4#ping 192.168.100.3
Type escape sequence to abort.
Sending 5, 100-byte ICMP Echos to 192.168.100.3, timeout is 2 seconds:
!!!!!
Success rate is 100 percent (5/5), round-trip min/avg/max = 60/60/60 ms
R4#
```

Okay, 100 percent success! Now try to **ping** R2. After all, it is configured for Frame Relay, right? Example 7-20 illustrates what happens when you try to **ping** R2's S0 interface IP address.

**Example 7-20** *R4-to-R2* **ping** *Result*

```
R4#ping 192.168.100.2
Type escape sequence to abort.
Sending 5, 100-byte ICMP Echos to 192.168.100.2, timeout is 2 seconds:
.....
Success rate is 0 percent (0/5)
R4#
```

What happened? You can **ping** R3, right? R2 is on the same IP segment (IP subnet 192.168.100.0), right? Why is the **ping** to R2 from R4 not successful? Frame Relay Inverse ARP is the reason. Remember, for Inverse ARP to operate correctly, you need to have a fully meshed network. The Frame Relay network in this lab is a hub-spoke topology. This means that R2 and R3 have a PVC connecting each other; R4 and R3 do, too, but R2 and R4 do not. If two routers do not have a direct PVC linking them, Frame Relay Inverse ARP will not resolve the IP address. As demonstrated in Example 7-21, you can issue a **show frame-relay map** command to take a look at the Frame Relay DLCI mappings to see if a mapping to R2's IP address exists.

**Example 7-21** show frame-relay map *Output*

```
R4#show frame-relay map
Serial0 (up): ip 192.168.100.3 dlci 101(0x65,0x1850), dynamic,
              broadcast,, status defined, active
R4#
```

As you can see from Example 7-21, there is a mapping for R3's S0, but not for R2's. You can resolve this problem by also mapping R2's IP address to DLCI 101. It is important to understand, however, that R4 does not send packets directly to R2. R4 sends any packet destined to R2 out DLCI 101, which terminates on R3, and then R3 redirects the packet to R2. Remember, just because you make a manual DLCI-to-IP-address mapping, you have not created a PVC to R2; you are just forwarding everything to R3. Another important item to remember is that when you issue a manual **map** statement on an interface, you disable Frame Relay Inverse ARP for that interface. This means that any mappings that were discovered using Frame Relay Inverse ARP are removed when the router is rebooted or a **clear frame-relay inverse arp** command is issued. So, you need to map not only R2's IP address, but R3's as well, or you will lose connectivity to R3.

The command to manually map IP addresses to DLCIs is as follows:

```
Router(config-if)#frame-relay map [ip | apollo | appletalk | bridge | clns |
    decnet | dlsw | ip | ipx | llc2 | qllc | rsrb | stun | vines | xns]
    {a.b.c.d} {dlci-number} [active | broadcast | cisco | ietf | nocompress |
    payload-compression | tcp]
```

The first option in the command is the protocol type. The **frame-relay map** command supports several protocols, but the only one to be concerned with in this chapter is IP. The second option in the command syntax (*a.b.c.d*) is the destination address. If you specify IP as the protocol that you want to map, the command expects an IP address. If you choose IPX (as covered in Chapter 13, "IPX"), the command expects an IPX address. The third option in the command is the DLCI number. This is the local DLCI number that you want any packets destined for the address to be forwarded out this DLCI. The last option provides several options, but you need to be concerned with only the **broadcast** option. Frame Relay, by default, will not forward Layer 3 broadcasts. You can override that default value by specifying the **broadcast** option here. This is important because, later in the lab, you will be configuring routing protocols over the Frame Relay network that will need to use broadcast packets to exchange routing tables (RIP or IGRP) or to establish neighbor adjacencies (EIGRP).

Example 7-22 demonstrates how to manually map an IP address to a DLCI. Because the DLCI is being advertised to the interface, you create the IP address-to-DLCI mapping on that interface (in this case, interface S0).

**Example 7-22** *Frame Relay Manual Map*

```
R4#config t
Enter configuration commands, one per line.  End with CNTL/Z.
R4(config)#interface serial 0
R4(config-if)#frame-relay map ip 192.168.100.2 101 broadcast
R4(config-if)#frame-relay map ip 192.168.100.3 101 broadcast
R4(config-if)#
```

Before trying to **ping** R2 again, go back and place the **frame-relay map** statements of R2's Serial 0 interface. Example 7-23 walks you through the process.

**Example 7-23** *Adding* **frame-relay map** *Statements on R2*

```
R4#copy running-config startup-config
Building configuration...
[OK]
R4#<ctrl-shft-6><x>
    Termserver#2
[Resuming connection 2 to r2 ... ]
```

```
R2#config t
Enter configuration commands, one per line.  End with CNTL/Z.
R2(config)#interface serial 0
R2(config-if)#frame-relay map ip 192.168.100.4 201 broadcast
R2(config-if)#frame-relay map ip 192.168.100.3 201 broadcast
R2(config-if)#
```

Now that you have manually mapped the IP addresses to the DLCI, take a look at how the mapping table changed from the output in Example 7-24.

**Example 7-24** **show frame-relay map** *Command Output*

```
R2#show frame-relay map
Serial0 (up): ip 192.168.100.3 dlci 201(0xC9,0x3090), static,
              broadcast,
              CISCO, status defined, active
Serial0 (up): ip 192.168.100.4 dlci 201(0xC9,0x3090), static,
              broadcast,
              CISCO, status defined, active
R2#
```

The output of Example 7-24 shows a couple of changes. First, now two mappings exist—one to 192.168.100.3 (R3) and one to 192.168.100.4 (R4). Both go out DLCI 201. The other major change is that the mapping changed from dynamic (meaning that they were learned by Inverse ARP) to static (meaning that the IP address to the DLCI under the interface was manually mapped). With the correct mappings, you should be capable of **ping**ing R3 as well as R4. Example 7-25 shows the result of the **ping** command to R3 and R4.

**Example 7-25** *R2-to-R3 and R2-to-R4* **ping** *Result*

```
R2#ping 192.168.100.3

Type escape sequence to abort.
Sending 5, 100-byte ICMP Echos to 192.168.100.3, timeout is 2 seconds:
!!!!!
Success rate is 100 percent (5/5), round-trip min/avg/max = 32/36/44 ms

R2#ping 192.168.100.4

Type escape sequence to abort.
Sending 5, 100-byte ICMP Echos to 192.168.100.4, timeout is 2 seconds:
!!!!!
Success rate is 100 percent (5/5), round-trip min/avg/max = 88/94/112 ms
R2#
```

With R2 capable of **ping**ing both routers, full IP connectivity through the Frame Relay network now exists.

---

**NOTE**    R3 will not need manual **frame-relay map** statements because R3 has a direct PVC to both R2 and R4. Frame Relay Inverse ARP will operate correctly for R3.

---

Now you can move on and configure the point-to-point serial link between R3 and R5.

# Configuring Point-to-Point Serial Interfaces

The point-to-point serial link is a little different than the Frame Relay serial link. As you recall, Frame Relay is used in many cases in a point-to-multipoint environment. To create a point-to-point connection between two routers, you can use other types of WAN encapsulations, such as HDLC, PPP, and SLIP. For a complete review of these encapsulations, refer to Chapter 11 of the ICDN book. We will use the default serial encapsulation, which is HDLC.

For two serial interfaces to communicate, you must provide the clock rate. The clock rate provides bit synchronization and has other uses that are beyond the scope of this chapter's purposes. The device that provides this clock rate is the data circuit-terminating equipment (DCE). The other device is denoted as the data terminal equipment (DTE). In the real world, the router is the DTE. The telecom equipment, such as the Frame Relay switch, is the DCE. Because the lab scenario bypasses the telecom equipment, you need to specify which router is the DTE and which one is the DCE; you also need to provide the clock rate. To bypass the telecom equipment, you need to directly connect the routers with a DTE–DCE crossover cable. Each end of this cable is labeled as DTE or DCE. Whichever router is plugged into the DCE end of the cable will need to provide the clock rate. In the Frame Relay network, the Frame Relay switch is the DCE, so none of the Frame Relay routers needs to provide clock rate. For more information on WAN serial cabling and signaling, refer to Chapter 2 of *Interconnecting Cisco Network Devices* from Cisco Press.

First, review the routers that you are going to use to configure a point-to-point serial connection. Figure 7-4 shows routers R3 and R5. This is the only point-to-point connection in the lab.

**Figure 7-4**    *Point-to-Point Serial Connection*

In the figure, you can see the R5 has been cabled as the DCE, so it will need to supply the clock rate.

Begin by configuring the serial link and assign IP addresses to the interfaces. Start with R5.

You last configured R2, so you need to go back to the terminal server and resume the connection to R5. When there, you need to go into global configuration mode and then into the appropriate interface configuration. For R5, that would be Serial 0. Example 7-26 walks you through these initial configuration steps.

**Example 7-26** *R5 Serial Configuration*

```
R2#
R2#<crtl-shft-6-x>

    Termserver#5
[Resuming connection 5 to r5 ... ]

R5#config t
Enter configuration commands, one per line.  End with CNTL/Z.
R5(config)#interface serial 0
R5(config-if)#
```

Now that you are in interface configuration mode for R5's Serial 0, you can execute the necessary configuration commands. The first thing to do is make the encapsulation type HDLC for the interface. Because HDLC is the default encapsulation method, you really don't need to execute the command. However, just for the sake of practice, and so that you understand that there is a data link layer configuration command for the serial link, specify HDLC as the encapsulation by entering it as a command option. This is the same command issued previously when specifying the encapsulation type for routers R2, R3, and R4; the only difference is that you specify the **hdlc** option instead of **frame-relay**.

This is the command for R2's S0, R3's S0, and R4's S0:

```
Router(config-if)#encapsulation frame-relay [cisco | ietf]
```

This is the command for R3's S1 and R5's S0:

```
Router(config-if)#encapsulation hdlc
```

Unlike Frame Relay, there aren't any different types of HDLC encapsulation. After you specify the encapsulation type as HDLC, you can assign the appropriate IP address to the interface.

---

**NOTE**   We will not review previous commands that already have been demonstrated. Refer back to the previous examples if you are unsure of the command syntax, or use the help menu in Cisco IOS Software.

---

Example 7-27 shows the commands executed on R5.

**Example 7-27** *R5 Configuration Commands*

```
R5(config-if)#encapsulation hdlc
R5(config-if)#ip address 192.168.35.5 255.255.255.0
R5(config-if)#
```

Before removing the interface from shutdown mode, you need to provide the clock rate to R3 using the following command:

```
Router(config-if)#clock rate {300-8000000 bps}
```

The only option in this command is to give the speed of the link in bits per second. Because this is a T1 or E1 interface, you can specify an easy-to-remember value of 2,000,000. This is the equivalent of an E1 link, which will work for this lab environment. As mentioned earlier, in the real world, you will not have to configure this parameter. The telecom service provider will set this value on its equipment. After you set this value, give the interface a description and remove the interface from shutdown mode, as demonstrated in Example 7-28.

**Example 7-28** clock rate *Command*

```
R5(config-if)#clock rate 2000000
R5(config-if)#description This interface connects to R3's S1 (DTE)
R5(config-if)#no shutdown
R5(config-if)#
%LINK-3-UPDOWN: Interface Serial0, changed state to down
R5(config-if)#
```

At first glance, you might get a little nervous that the interface did not come up, but that is normal. R3's serial interface has not been configured yet, so the R5 interface is not receiving any signaling from R3; thus, the interface will remain in the down state until R3 is configured and removed from shutdown mode. Before you get too far into this configuration, you should know about a very helpful **show** command:

```
Router#show interfaces [bri | null | serial | tokenring | accounting | crb | irb]
  {number}
```

This command is very useful in troubleshooting and verifying interface configuration. The first option is to choose which type of interface you would like to see; the second option is to select the number of the interface. If you do not select any type of interface, the command shows you all the interfaces that the router has. Example 7-29 demonstrates sample output of the command on R5.

**Example 7-29** show interfaces serial 0 *Command Output*

```
R5#show interfaces serial 0
Serial0 is down, line protocol is down
  Hardware is HD64570
  Description: This interface connects to R3's S1 (DTE)
  Internet address is 192.168.35.5/24
  MTU 1500 bytes, BW 1544 Kbit, DLY 20000 usec, rely 255/255, load 1/255
  Encapsulation HDLC, loopback not set, keepalive set (10 sec)
  Last input never, output 2w5d, output hang never
  Last clearing of "show interface" counters never
  Queueing strategy: fifo
  Output queue 0/40, 0 drops; input queue 0/75, 0 drops
  5 minute input rate 0 bits/sec, 0 packets/sec
  5 minute output rate 0 bits/sec, 0 packets/sec
     0 packets input, 0 bytes, 0 no buffer
     Received 0 broadcasts, 0 runts, 0 giants, 0 throttles
     0 input errors, 0 CRC, 0 frame, 0 overrun, 0 ignored, 0 abort
     212 packets output, 18206 bytes, 0 underruns
     0 output errors, 0 collisions, 37557 interface resets
     0 output buffer failures, 0 output buffers swapped out
     111 carrier transitions
     DCD=up  DSR=up  DTR=down  RTS=down  CTS=up
```

The highlighted text reveals some important information regarding the interface Serial 0. The first thing that you see is the state in which the interface resides: "Serial0 is down, line protocol is down." The first "down" (this is referred to as *interface* or the physical layer state) tells you that there is a physical problem. A physical problem might result from a cable not being plugged in, or the connected device might not be receiving any electrical signaling, which is the case here. The "line protocol down" means that Layer 2 is not functional, meaning that HDLC is not operating correctly for some reason. It is important to note that the line protocol will never be up if the interface is in the down state. Next, the output shows the description placed on the Serial 0 interface. You see the IP address that you assigned earlier. This is a good place to review your configuration and make sure that what you typed in the interface configuration mode was correct. You also see the encapsulation type here. For a complete review of the output, refer to Chapter 3 of *Interconnecting Cisco Network Devices*. You will see this command again after configuring R3's serial interface to see what changes.

To configure R3, you need to go back to the terminal server and resume the session with R3, but don't forget to save the configuration before leaving. When at R3, you need to enter global configuration mode and then go into interface configuration mode for Serial 1. Remember, you will configure Serial 0 for Frame Relay. Serial 1 connects to R5's S0 interface. (Refer to your lab diagram.) See Example 7-30.

**Example 7-30** *R3 Interface Configuration Mode*

```
R5#copy running-config startup-config
Building configuration...
[OK]
R5#<ctrl-shft-6><x>
    Termserver#3
[Resuming connection 3 to r3 ... ]
R3#
R3#config t
Enter configuration commands, one per line.  End with CNTL/Z.
R3(config)#interface serial 1
R3(config-if)#
```

Now you are in interface configuration mode for Serial 1 on R3, and you can assign the appropriate IP address and mask. After that, don't forget to remove the interface from shutdown mode. Example 7-31 illustrates the commands.

**Example 7-31** *R3 Serial 1 Configuration Commands*

```
R3(config-if)#encapsulation hdlc
R3(config-if)#ip address 192.168.35.3 255.255.255.0
R3(config-if)#description This interface connects to R5's S0 (DCE)
R3(config-if)#no shutdown
R3(config-if)#
%LINK-3-UPDOWN: Interface Serial1, changed state to up
```

**Example 7-31** *R3 Serial 1 Configuration Commands (Continued)*

```
R3(config-if)#
%LINEPROTO-5-UPDOWN: Line protocol on Interface Serial1, changed state to up
R3(config-if)#
```

As you can see, the interface came up, and so did the line protocol. Return to R5 and see how the **show interface** command output has changed. Example 7-32 shows the changes in the output.

**Example 7-32** *R5* **show interface serial 0** *Command Output*

```
R3(config-if)#end
%SYS-5-CONFIG_I: Configured from console by console
R3#copy running-config startup-config
Building configuration...
[OK]
R3#<ctrl-shft-6-x>
    Termserver#5
[Resuming connection 5 to r5 ... ]

R5#
R5#show interface serial 0
Serial0 is up, line protocol is up
  Hardware is HD64570
  Description: This interface connects to R3's S1 (DTE)
  Internet address is 192.168.35.5/24
  MTU 1500 bytes, BW 1544 Kbit, DLY 20000 usec, rely 255/255, load 1/255
  Encapsulation HDLC, loopback not set, keepalive set (10 sec)
  Last input 00:00:01, output 00:00:01, output hang never
  Last clearing of "show interface" counters never
  Queueing strategy: fifo
  Output queue 0/40, 0 drops; input queue 0/75, 0 drops
  5 minute input rate 0 bits/sec, 0 packets/sec
  5 minute output rate 0 bits/sec, 0 packets/sec
    25 packets input, 1865 bytes, 0 no buffer
    Received 25 broadcasts, 0 runts, 0 giants, 0 throttles
    0 input errors, 0 CRC, 0 frame, 0 overrun, 0 ignored, 0 abort
    236 packets output, 20009 bytes, 0 underruns
    0 output errors, 0 collisions, 37629 interface resets
    0 output buffer failures, 0 output buffers swapped out
    112 carrier transitions
    DCD=up  DSR=up  DTR=up  RTS=up  CTS=up
R5#
```

Great! You now should be capable of **ping**ing R3 from R5, as demonstrated in Example 7-33.

**Example 7-33** *R5* **ping** *Result*

```
R5#ping 192.168.35.3

Type escape sequence to abort.
Sending 5, 100-byte ICMP Echos to 192.168.35.3, timeout is 2 seconds:
!!!!!
Success rate is 100 percent (5/5), round-trip min/avg/max = 4/4/8 ms
R5#
```

You got 100 percent success! R3 and R5 have full IP connectivity. Question: Should R5 be capable of **ping**ing R3's Serial 0 IP address? Why not? Even though R5 can reach R3 through interface Serial 1, R5 cannot **ping** R3's Serial 0 interface. This is because you do not have any routing protocols configured to let R5 know about the 192.168.100.0 network, to which R3's Serial 0 interface belongs. When you have configured all the interfaces on all the routers, you will start configuring the routing protocols. Then you should be capable of **ping**ing any interface on any router.

# Configuring Ethernet Interfaces

The configuration tasks for Ethernet interfaces are quite simple. In fact, you only need to assign the IP address and remove the interface from shutdown mode. Because the configuration tasks are so straightforward, an overview of Ethernet technology is not really necessary here. Begin with a review of the routers that have Ethernet interfaces that you will need to configure. Figure 7-5 illustrates the Ethernet interfaces on the routers.

**Figure 7-5**   *Ethernet Routers*

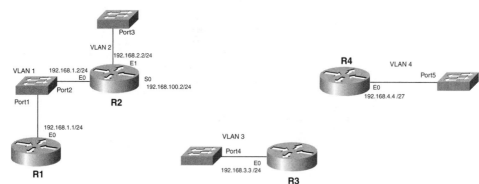

Start with configuring R1, then configure R2, and go up to R4. To assign the IP address and remove the interface from shutdown mode, you need to be in interface configuration mode for the Ethernet interface. Example 7-34 takes you through the process of configuring the

Ethernet interface on R1. Refer to Figure 7-5 for the interface number, IP address, and subnet mask.

**Example 7-34** *R1 Ethernet Configuration*

```
R5#<ctrl-shft-6-x>
     Termserver#1
[Resuming connection 1 to r1 ... ]

R1#config t
Enter configuration commands, one per line.  End with CNTL/Z.
R1(config)#interface ethernet0
R1(config-if)#ip address 192.168.1.1 255.255.255.0
R1(config-if)#description This interface connects to R2's E0
R1(config-if)#no shut
R1(config-if)#
%LINEPROTO-5-UPDOWN: Line protocol on Interface Ethernet0, changed state to up
R1(config-if)#
R1#
%SYS-5-CONFIG_I: Configured from console by console
R1(config-if)#
%LINK-3-UPDOWN: Interface Ethernet0, changed state to up
```

R1's Ethernet 0 came up fine, so go to R2. Example 7-35 demonstrates the steps in configuring R2's Ethernet interfaces.

**Example 7-35** *R2 Ethernet Interface Configuration*

```
R1#copy running-config startup-config
Building configuration...
[OK]
R1#<ctrl-shft-6><x>
     Termserver#2
[Resuming connection 2 to r2 ... ]

R2#
R2#config t
Enter configuration commands, one per line.  End with CNTL/Z.
R2(config)#interface ethernet 0
R2(config-if)#ip address 192.168.1.2 255.255.255.0
R2(config-if)#description This interface connects to R1's E0
R2(config-if)#no shutdown
R2(config-if)#
1d17h: %LINK-3-UPDOWN: Interface Ethernet0, changed state to up
1d17h: %LINEPROTO-5-UPDOWN: Line protocol on Interface Ethernet0, changed state
to up
R2(config-if)#
R2(config-if)#exit
R2(config)#interface ethernet 1
R2(config-if)#ip address 192.168.2.2 255.255.255.0
R1(config-if)#description This interface does not connect with another IP device
```

*continues*

**Example 7-35** *R2 Ethernet Interface Configuration (Continued)*

```
R2(config-if)#no shutdown
R2(config-if)#
1d17h: %LINK-3-UPDOWN: Interface Ethernet1, changed state to up
1d17h: %LINEPROTO-5-UPDOWN: Line protocol on Interface Ethernet1, changed state
to up
R2(config-if)#
```

Both Ethernet interfaces came up. You should be capable of **ping**ing R1's Ethernet 0 interface for R2, as demonstrated in Example 7-36.

**Example 7-36** *R2 to R1* **ping** *Results*

```
R2(config-if)#end
R2#ping 192.168.1.1

Type escape sequence to abort.
Sending 5, 100-byte ICMP Echos to 192.168.1.1, timeout is 2 seconds:
.!!!!
Success rate is 80 percent (4/5), round-trip min/avg/max = 1/1/1 ms
R2#
```

Okay, R1 and R2 have IP connectivity. You can verify that Ethernet 1 is functional by looking at the interface. Example 7-37 shows the output of the **show interfaces** command, which displays all of R2's interfaces; however, only the Ethernet interfaces are of interest for this part of the lab.

**Example 7-37 show interfaces** *Command Output on R2*

```
R2#show interfaces
Ethernet0 is up, line protocol is up
  Description: This interface connects to R1's E0
  Hardware is QUICC Ethernet, address is 0010.7bf9.4912 (bia 0010.7bf9.4912)
  Internet address is 192.168.1.2/24
  MTU 1500 bytes, BW 10000 Kbit, DLY 1000 usec, rely 255/255, load 1/255
  Encapsulation ARPA, loopback not set, keepalive set (10 sec)
  ARP type: ARPA, ARP Timeout 04:00:00
  Last input 00:00:20, output 00:00:06, output hang never
  Last clearing of "show interface" counters never
  Queueing strategy: fifo
  Output queue 0/40, 0 drops; input queue 0/75, 0 drops
  5 minute input rate 0 bits/sec, 0 packets/sec
  5 minute output rate 0 bits/sec, 0 packets/sec
     41 packets input, 4110 bytes, 0 no buffer
     Received 36 broadcasts, 0 runts, 0 giants, 0 throttles
     0 input errors, 0 CRC, 0 frame, 0 overrun, 0 ignored, 0 abort
     0 input packets with dribble condition detected
     159 packets output, 16101 bytes, 0 underruns
     0 output errors, 0 collisions, 1 interface resets
```

**Example 7-37** show interfaces *Command Output on R2 (Continued)*

```
        0 babbles, 0 late collision, 0 deferred
        0 lost carrier, 0 no carrier
        0 output buffer failures, 0 output buffers swapped out
Ethernet1 is up, line protocol is up
  Hardware is QUICC Ethernet, address is 0010.7bf9.4913 (bia 0010.7bf9.4913)
  Description: This interface does not connect with another IP device
  Internet address is 192.168.2.2/24
  MTU 1500 bytes, BW 10000 Kbit, DLY 1000 usec, rely 255/255, load 1/255
  Encapsulation ARPA, loopback not set, keepalive set (10 sec)
  ARP type: ARPA, ARP Timeout 04:00:00
  Last input 00:00:23, output 00:00:09, output hang never
  Last clearing of "show interface" counters never
  Queueing strategy: fifo
  Output queue 0/40, 0 drops; input queue 0/75, 0 drops
  5 minute input rate 0 bits/sec, 0 packets/sec
  5 minute output rate 0 bits/sec, 0 packets/sec
      19 packets input, 1729 bytes, 0 no buffer
      Received 19 broadcasts, 0 runts, 0 giants, 0 throttles
      0 input errors, 0 CRC, 0 frame, 0 overrun, 0 ignored, 0 abort
      0 input packets with dribble condition detected
      136 packets output, 13770 bytes, 0 underruns
      0 output errors, 0 collisions, 1 interface resets
      0 babbles, 0 late collision, 0 deferred
      0 lost carrier, 0 no carrier
      0 output buffer failures, 0 output buffers swapped out
--More--
```

The most important information right now is to see that both interfaces are up. This signifies that link keepalives are being exchanged between the interfaces and the switch. No other devices exist off Ethernet 1, so you cannot verify connectivity. However, because both interfaces are up, you can assume that they are configured and working properly.

Example 7-38 consolidates the configuration of both R3 and R4 to save time. Make sure that you see the console messages stating that the interfaces are up, but there is no need to **ping** anything at this point. Be sure to look at the subnet mask on R4's Ethernet 0. It has a mask of /27. That is a 255.255.255.224 mask in decimal notation.

**Example 7-38** *R3 and R4 Ethernet Configuration*

```
R2#copy running-config startup-config
Destination filename [startup-config]?
Building configuration...
[OK]
R2#<ctrl-shft-6><x>
    Termserver#3
[Resuming connection 3 to r3 ... ]

R3#config t
Enter configuration commands, one per line.  End with CNTL/Z.
```

*continues*

**Example 7-38** *R3 and R4 Ethernet Configuration (Continued)*

```
R3(config)#interface ethernet 0
R3(config-if)#ip address 192.168.3.3 255.255.255.0
R3(config-if)#description This interface does not connect with another IP device
R3(config-if)#no shutdown
R3(config-if)#
%LINEPROTO-5-UPDOWN: Line protocol on Interface Ethernet0, changed state to up
R3(config-if)#
%LINK-3-UPDOWN: Interface Ethernet0, changed state to up
R3(config-if)#end
R3#
%SYS-5-CONFIG_I: Configured from console by console
R3#copy running-config  startup-config
Building configuration...
[OK]
R3#<ctrl-shft-6><x>
    Termserver#4
[Resuming connection 4 to r4 ... ]

R4#config t
Enter configuration commands, one per line.  End with CNTL/Z.
R4(config)#interface  ethernet 0
R4(config-if)#ip address 192.168.4.4 255.255.255.224
Bad mask /27 for address 192.168.4.4
R4(config-if)#
```

Notice the error message "Bad mask /27 for address 192.168.4.4." Why is /27 (or 255.255.255.2250) a bad mask? In IP subnetting, you cannot use the first group of IP addresses or the last group of a subnetted address space. Does 192.168.4.4 fall into the first group of addresses? To find out, break up the /27 bit mask (255.255.255.224). The result is eight different groups of IP addresses:

> 0 to 31
> 32 to 63
> 64 to 95
> 96 to 127
> 128 to 159
> 160 to 191
> 192 to 123
> 224 to 255

The address of 192.168.4.4 does fall into the first group. Cisco has a command that will overcome this limitation:

```
Router(config)#ip subnet-zero
```

There are no options on this command, and it is executed under global configuration mode. This command enables you to use the first and last groups of a subnetted address space. Example 7-39 uses this command to configure R4.

**NOTE**    In Cisco IOS Software Release 12.*x*, the command **ip subnet-zero** is on by default. If you are using this version, you will not see the error, nor will you need to execute the command.

**Example 7-39** *R4 Configuration for* **ip subnet-zero**

```
R4(config-if)#exit
R4(config)#ip subnet-zero
R4(config)#interface ethernet 0
R4(config-if)#ip address 192.168.4.4 255.255.255.224
R4(config)-if)#$cription This interface does not connect with another IP device
R4(config-if)#no shutdown
R4(config-if)#
%LINEPROTO-5-UPDOWN: Line protocol on Interface Ethernet0, changed state to up
R4(config-if)#
%LINK-3-UPDOWN: Interface Ethernet0, changed state to up
R4(config-if)#end
%SYS-5-CONFIG_I: Configured from console by console
R4#copy running-config startup-config
Building configuration...
[OK]
R4#
```

You get no error messages this time. The IP address successfully is assigned to the interface and is removed from the shutdown state. Console messages indicate that the interface and line protocol for Ethernet 0 are up. The configuration is saved, and you are ready to configure the Token Ring interfaces on R5 and R6.

# Configuring Token Ring Interfaces

Token Ring interfaces have similar configuration tasks to Ethernet, but the technologies are very different. For lab purposes, those differences are out of the scope of this book.

The only configuration difference in Token Ring versus Ethernet interfaces is that, on Token Ring, you need to specify a ring speed, either 4 or 16 Mbps. Begin by reviewing the routers that you will be configuring as Token Ring, as shown in Figure 7-6.

**Figure 7-6** *Router Interfaces to Configure as Token Ring*

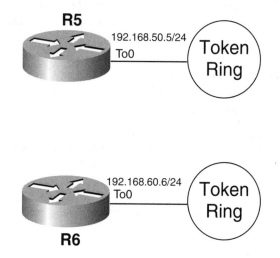

To set the ring speed, you must be in interface configuration mode for the Token Ring interface and must use this command:

```
Router(config-if)#ring-speed {4 |16}
```

As mentioned earlier, Token Ring supports two speeds: 4 and 16 Mbps. For this lab, use 16 Mbps. For Token Ring to operate correctly, every device belonging to a certain Ring must be configured for the same ring speed. After you set the speed, you can assign an IP address to the interface. Example 7-40 completes the commands on R5.

**Example 7-40** *R5 Token Ring Interface Configuration*

```
R4#<ctrl-shft-6><x>
    Termserver#5
[Resuming connection 5 to r5 ... ]

R5#config t
Enter configuration commands, one per line.  End with CNTL/Z.
R5(config)#interface tokenRing 0
R5(config-if)#ring-speed 16
R5(config-if)#ip address 192.168.50.5 255.255.255.0
R5(config-if)#$iption This interface does not connect with another IP device
R5(config-if)#no shutdown
R5(config-if)#
%LINK-5-CHANGED: Interface TokenRing0, changed state to initializing
R5(config-if)#
%LINEPROTO-5-UPDOWN: Line protocol on Interface TokenRing0, changed state to up
R5(config-if)#
%LINK-3-UPDOWN: Interface TokenRing0, changed state to up
R5(config-if)#
```

Example 7-40 shows a console message a little differently than on other interfaces. "%LINK-5-CHANGED: Interface TokenRing0, changed state to initializing" means that the router is trying to insert the Token Ring into the main network ring. If that is successful, you will get the interface up and line protocol up messages. This looks good, so save the configuration and complete R6. See Example 7-41.

**Example 7-41** *Token Ring Interface Configuration on R6*

```
R5#copy running-config startup-config
Building configuration...
[OK]
R5#<ctrl-shft-6><x>
    Termserver#6
[Resuming connection 6 to r6 ... ]

R6#config t
Enter configuration commands, one per line.  End with CNTL/Z.
R6(config)#interface tokenRing 0
R6(config-if)#ring-speed 16
R6(config-if)#ip address 192.168.60.6 255.255.255.0
R6(config-if)#$iption This interface does not connect with another IP device
R6(config-if)#no shutdown
R6(config-if)#
%LINK-5-CHANGED: Interface TokenRing0, changed state to initializing
R6(config-if)#
%LINEPROTO-5-UPDOWN: Line protocol on Interface TokenRing0, changed state to up
R6(config-if)#
%LINK-3-UPDOWN: Interface TokenRing0, changed state to up
R6(config-if)#
```

Everything looks good. Next you will learn how to create and configure loopback interfaces.

# Creating and Configuring Loopback Interfaces

A loopback interface is a virtual interface that resides on a router. It is not connected to any other device. Loopback interfaces are very useful because they will never go down, unless the entire router goes down. This helps in managing routers because there will always be at least one active interface on the routers, the loopback interface.

To create a loopback interface, all you need to do is enter configuration mode for the interface:

```
Router(config)#interface loopback {number}
```

The only option on this command is to specify a number between 0 and 2,147,483,647. Cisco IOS Software gives you plenty of loopback interfaces, if you want to use all of them. When entering this command, Cisco IOS Software automatically creates the loopback interface, places you into interface configuration mode, and removes the interface from shutdown mode. When that is complete, you only need to assign an IP address to the interface. The criteria for the IP addresses of the loopback interfaces is as follows:

> Create loopback interfaces on all routers using IP address 192.169.X.X/24 (where X is the router number). So, R1 would have a loopback address of 192.169.1.1/24, R2 would be 192.169.2.2/24, and so on.

Because you are already on R6, create and configure the loopback interface on R6; then go to R1, R2, and so on, and create and configure all the loopback interfaces and assign appropriate IP addresses. Example 7-42 takes you through the process on R6.

**Example 7-42** *R6 Loopback Interfaces Configuration*

```
R6(config)#interface loopback 0
R6(config-if)#
%LINEPROTO-5-UPDOWN: Line protocol on Interface Loopback0, changed state to up
R6(config-if)#ip address 192.169.6.6 255.255.255.0
```

Because the router automatically removes the loopback from shutdown state, you receive the console message indicating that the interface is up.

Now configure the rest of the routers, starting with R1. Don't forget to save the running-config to NVRAM (startup-config) before leaving the routers. See Example 7-43.

**Example 7-43** *Loopback Interface Configuration*

```
R6#<ctrl-shft-6><x>
    Termserver#1
[Resuming connection 1 to r1 ... ]
[OK]


R1#config t
Enter configuration commands, one per line.  End with CNTL/Z.
R1(config)#interface loopback 0
%LINEPROTO-5-UPDOWN: Line protocol on Interface Loopback0, changed state to up
R1(config-if)#ip address 192.169.1.1 255.255.255.0
R1(config-if)#end
%SYS-5-CONFIG_I: Configured from console by console
R1#copy running-config startup-config
Building configuration...
[OK]
R1#<ctrl-shft-6><x>
Termserver#2
 [Resuming connection 2 to r2 ... ]


R2#
R2#config t
```

**Example 7-43** *Loopback Interface Configuration (Continued)*

```
Enter configuration commands, one per line.  End with CNTL/Z.
R2(config)#interface loopback 0
R2(config-if)#ip address 192.169.2.2 255.255.255.0
R2(config-if)#end
R2#copy running-config startup-config
Destination filename [startup-config]?
Building configuration...
[OK]
R2#<ctrl-shft-6><x>
    Termserver#3
[Resuming connection 3 to r3 ... ]
[OK]
```

```
R3#config t
Enter configuration commands, one per line.  End with CNTL/Z.
R3(config)#interface loopback 0
%LINEPROTO-5-UPDOWN: Line protocol on Interface Loopback0, changed state to up
R3(config-if)#ip address 192.169.3.3 255.255.255.0
R3(config-if)#end
R3#copy running-config startup-config
Building configuration...
[OK]
R3#<ctrl-shft-6><x>
    Termserver#4
[Resuming connection 4 to r4 ... ]
```

```
R4#config t
R4(config)#interface loopback 0
%LINEPROTO-5-UPDOWN: Line protocol on Interface Loopback0, changed state to up
R4(config-if)#ip address 192.169.4.4 255.255.255.0
R4(config-if)#end
R4#copy running-config startup-config
Building configuration...
[OK]
R4#<ctrl-shft-6><x>
Termserver#5
[Resuming connection 5 to r5 ... ]
```

```
R5#config t
Enter configuration commands, one per line.  End with CNTL/Z.
R5(config)#interface loopback 0
%LINEPROTO-5-UPDOWN: Line protocol on Interface Loopback0, changed state to up
R5(config-if)#ip address 192.169.5.5 255.255.255.0
R5(config-if)#end
R5#copy running-config startup-config
Building configuration...
[OK]
R5#
```

Everything looks okay. A router interface description is not necessary here because no other type of device can connect to a loopback interface. Now that you have configured all the interfaces and have IP connectivity, you should familiarize yourself with the Cisco Discovery Protocol (CDP). CDP is an information-gathering tool that enables you to discover directly connected Cisco devices and their network layer addresses.

# Cisco Discovery Protocol (CDP)

CDP is a Cisco proprietary data link layer protocol that operates over any medium that supports the Subnetwork Access Protocol (SNAP) encapsulation (LANs, most WANs, and ATM). It is important to understand that because CDP operates at Layer 2 (data link layer of the OSI model), it functions independently of the Layer 3 (network) protocol (IP or IPX). CDP is on by default, but it can be disabled. In many cases, CDP is disabled on dial backup links, such as ISDN, so as to not keep the link up constantly. Chapter 4 of *Interconnecting Cisco Network Devices* provides more detailed information about CDP.

To display what CDP has discovered, issue this command:

```
Router#show cdp [entry | interface | neighbors | traffic]
```

This command offers several options. For purposes here, look at the **interface** and **neighbors** options only, but feel free to become familiar with the other options.

The first option to look at is the **interface** option:

```
Router#show cdp interface [ethernet | loopback | null | serial] [number]
```

The first option on this command is to specify the type of interface that you want to see CDP information on. The last option is to specify the interface number. Example 7-44 uses the **show cdp interface** command to examine R5's Serial 0 interface.

**Example 7-44** **show cdp interface serial 0** *Command Output*

```
R5#show cdp interface serial 0
Serial0 is up, line protocol is up
  Encapsulation HDLC
  Sending CDP packets every 60 seconds
  Holdtime is 180 seconds
R5#
```

It does not give a whole lot of information, but it is a "quick and dirty" way of seeing some CDP information. The second option of the **show cdp** command that we are going to look at is this:

```
Router#show cdp neighbors [bri | loopback | null | serial | tokenring | detail]
```

As you can see, this command provides the option to see CDP information by interface, but the last option, **detail**, gives a complete summary of all Cisco devices that CDP was capable of discovering and displays information about those devices. Example 7-45 displays the output of the **show cdp neighbors detail** command.

**Example 7-45** **show cdp neighbors detail** *Command Output*

```
R5#show cdp neighbors detail
-------------------------
Device ID: R3
Entry address(es):
  IP address: 192.168.35.3
Platform: cisco 2500,  Capabilities: Router
Interface: Serial0,  Port ID (outgoing port): Serial1
Holdtime : 164 sec

Version :
Cisco Internetwork Operating System Software
IOS (tm) 2500 Software (C2500-JS-L), Version 11.2(17), RELEASE SOFTWARE (fc1)
Copyright (c) 1986-1999 by cisco Systems, Inc.
Compiled Mon 04-Jan-99 17:27 by ashah

R5#
```

The first piece of information that the output shows is the device ID, usually the hostname of the device. As you can see, R5 has discovered R3.

The second field is the IP address of R3. This is very useful if you have several routers and you are not sure of the IP address of the desired router. You can use this command to find that instead of trying to track down a network map.

The third field is the platform and capability. R3 is a 2500 and is a router. If you issue this same command on R1, you will see the Catalyst 1900 switch in the summary as well.

The fourth item is the interface on R5 that the device was discovered and the port on R3 to which R5 is connected. The command also displays the Cisco IOS Software version of your neighbor.

You will see this command revisited throughout the rest of the book, to demonstrate the different ways to utilize this command to help configure and troubleshoot the network.

Now that you have all the interfaces configured and have established IP connectivity, you can move on to the next chapter and start configuring the different routing protocols.

# Configuring Routing Protocols, ISDN, and IPX

This chapter covers the following key topics:

- RIP routing updates
- RIP routing metric
- RIP scalability and limitations
- RIP stability features
- Configuring RIP

# ation

___

eristics and limitations of the distance vector routing
des with an exercise on configuring RIP between two
p with useful commands to verify and troubleshoot your

ol (RIP) is a comparatively old interior gateway protocol
Ps are used for routing within networks that are under a
, whereas exterior gateway protocols are used to exchange
works. As an IGP, RIP performs routing only within a
is a classical distance vector routing protocol that uses hop
ing the best route to a given destination.

ges at regular 30-second intervals and when the network
adcast User Datagram Protocol (UDP) data packets to
The routing update process is termed *advertising*. When a
that includes changes to an entry, it updates its routing table
tric value for the path is increased by 1, and the sender is
uters maintain only the best route (the route with the lowest
after updating its routing table, the router immediately
ates to inform other network routers of the change. These
e regularly scheduled 30-second interval updates that RIP

c (hop count) to measure the distance between the source
hop in a path from source to destination is assigned a hop-
a router receives a routing update that contains a new or

changed destination-network entry, the router adds 1 to the metric value indicated in the update and enters the network in the routing table. The IP address of the sender is used as the next hop.

RIP prevents routing loops from continuing indefinitely by implementing a limit on the number of hops allowed in a path from the source to a destination. The maximum number of hops in a path is 15. If a router receives a routing update that contains a new or changed entry, and if increasing the metric value by 1 causes the metric to be infinity (defined as 16), the network destination is considered unreachable.

## RIP Scalability and Limitations

The low hop count of RIP is considered a scalability limitation for large networks. Another limitation is that RIP Version 1 (RIP-1) is a classful routing protocol and does not carry subnet mask information in its routing updates.

**NOTE**       RIP Version 2 (RIP-2) was introduced to address this limitation. The RIP-2 specification (described in RFC 1723) allows more information, such as the subnet mask, to be included in RIP packets and provides a simple authentication mechanism.

Because of this, RIP-1 does not support the use of variable-length subnet masking (VLSM). VLSM provides the capability to specify a different subnet mask for the same network number, but on different subnets. Before RIP-1 sends out an update, it performs a check against the subnet mask of the network that is about to be advertised. If a VLSM has been assigned, the subnet gets dropped from the advertisement. This limitation also poses scalability issues for large networks in which address space is limited.

## RIP Stability Features

RIP implements mechanisms such as split horizon, hold-down timers, hop-count limits, and poison reverse to prevent routing loops and maintain network stability, as explained in the list that follows:

- **Split horizon**—If a route is learned on an interface, the information about that route is not sent back out the interface where it was learned. In this way, split horizon prevents routing loops within the network.

- **Hold-down timers**—These timers ignore routing update information for a specified period of time. Hold-down timers can be reset when the timer expires, a routing update is received that has a better metric, or a routing update is received indicating that the original route to the network is valid. Hold-down timers are useful in preventing routing information from flooding the network when network links are unstable.

- **Hop-count limit**—This limits the number of hops allowed in a path from source to destination. The maximum is 15, and 16 is deemed unreachable. The hop-count limit prevents routing loops from continuing indefinitely.

- **Poison reverse**—A route is "poisoned" when a router marks a route as unreachable by setting the hop count to 16 and then passes this route out to a neighboring router, causing the neighboring router to remove the route from its routing table. This speeds network convergence by preventing invalid routes from being propagated throughout the network.

These features allow RIP to adjust to network-topology changes and prevent routing loops from being propagated and continuing indefinitely.

Now that you are familiar with the fundamentals of RIP, you should be able to begin the lab for this chapter.

# RIP Lab Objective

Configure RIP using the following criteria:

- Place R2's E0 and E1 networks into RIP.
- R1's E0 network should be configured for RIP as well.
- Place R1 and R2's loopback interfaces into RIP.

Figure 8-1 depicts that portion of the lab where RIP will be configured.

**Figure 8-1**  *IP RIP Routers*

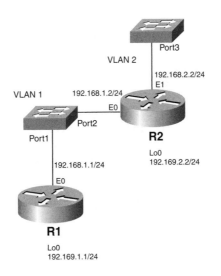

# Configuring RIP Between R1 and R2

Before configuring RIP, look at the existing IP routing table of both R1 and R2 to get an idea of the routes that each device currently has in its routing table. Display the IP routing table of a router using the following command:

Router#**show ip route**

To do this on R1, first resume your reverse Telnet session to R1 and, from privileged EXEC mode, enter the **show ip route** command as demonstrated in Example 8-1.

**Example 8-1** *IP Routing Table on R1 Before the Configuration of IP RIP*

```
Termserver#1
[Resuming connection 1 to r1 ... ]

R1#show ip route
Codes: C - connected, S - static, I - IGRP, R - RIP, M - mobile, B - BGP
       D - EIGRP, EX - EIGRP external, O - OSPF, IA - OSPF inter area
       N1 - OSPF NSSA external type 1, N2 - OSPF NSSA external type 2
       E1 - OSPF external type 1, E2 - OSPF external type 2, E - EGP
       i - IS-IS, L1 - IS-IS level-1, L2 - IS-IS level-2, * - candidate default
       U - per-user static route, o - ODR

Gateway of last resort is not set

C    192.169.1.0/24 is directly connected, Loopback0
C    192.168.1.0/24 is directly connected, Ethernet0
R1#
```

At the top of the routing table, a legend displays the various routes that may exist in a routing table. Each route type corresponds to a letter. These letters appear next to the route in the routing table. Paying attention to these letters enables you to better understand how the router learned each route in the routing table.

Currently, the only routes that exist on R1 are routes to directly connected interfaces. The letter *C* preceding the actual route denotes a directly connected route to 192.168.1.0/24 through Ethernet0. In addition, you should see a route to 192.169.1.0/24 directly connected to Loopback0. These routes were created in the IP routing table when you assigned an IP address to each interface and brought the interface up and out of shutdown mode. Loopback interfaces come up out of shutdown mode upon creation and then are placed in the routing table. This was done in Chapter 7, "Router Interface Configuration." Essentially, this means that R1 knows how to route to its directly connected networks, but nothing else.

Next, observe the routing table on R2 by returning to the terminal server, resuming the connection to R2, and then displaying the IP routing table with the **show ip route** command, as shown in Example 8-2.

**Example 8-2**  *IP Routing Table on R2 Before the Configuration of IP RIP*

```
Termserver#2
[Resuming connection 2 to r2 ... ]

R2#show ip route
Codes: C - connected, S - static, I - IGRP, R - RIP, M - mobile, B - BGP
       D - EIGRP, EX - EIGRP external, O - OSPF, IA - OSPF inter area
       N1 - OSPF NSSA external type 1, N2 - OSPF NSSA external type 2
       E1 - OSPF external type 1, E2 - OSPF external type 2, E - EGP
       i - IS-IS, L1 - IS-IS level-1, L2 - IS-IS level-2, * - candidate default
       U - per-user static route, o - ODR

Gateway of last resort is not set

C    192.168.1.0/24 is directly connected, Ethernet0
C    192.168.2.0/24 is directly connected, Ethernet1
C    192.169.2.0/24 is directly connected, Loopback0
C    192.168.100.0/24 is directly connected, Serial0
R2#
```

As the output in Example 8-2 shows, R2 has directly connected routes off each of its configured interfaces—Ethernet0, Ethernet1, Loopback0, and Serial0. These also were created in the IP routing table when each interface on R2 was assigned an IP address and was brought out of shutdown using the **no shutdown** command on the interface.

Suppose that, from R1, you need to get to R2's network of 192.168.2.0. You can check to see if this works by initiating a **ping** from R1 to R2's Ethernet1 interface of 192.168.2.2. If the **ping** succeeds, you know that R1 can reach the destination network. To do this, return to R1 and, from privileged EXEC mode, use the following command:

```
Router#ping 192.168.2.2
```

Example 8-3 demonstrates this series of transactions.

**Example 8-3**  *R1 Incapable of pinging 192.168.2.2*

```
Termserver#1
[Resuming connection 1 to r1 ... ]

R1#ping 192.168.2.2

Type escape sequence to abort.
Sending 5, 100-byte ICMP Echos to 192.168.2.2, timeout is 2 seconds:
.....
Success rate is 0 percent (0/5)
```

A standard **ping** request sends five ICMP echo packets. Receiving an ICMP echo reply in response to the ICMP echo request indicates a successful **ping**. A successful reply is denoted by an exclamation mark (!). In Example 8-3, no reply was received, as indicated by the five periods (.); this indicates zero replies received to the five ICMP echo packets that were sent. As a result, the success rate was 0 percent, indicating the request failed and that R1 cannot get to the network 192.168.2.0.

It is possible that the **ping** failed because of physical connectivity problems. In addition, R1 is incapable of **ping**ing R2's Loopback0 interface of 192.169.2.2, as shown in Example 8-4.

**Example 8-4**   *R1 Incapable of **ping**ing R2's Loopback0 Interface*

```
R1#ping 192.169.2.2

Type escape sequence to abort.
Sending 5, 100-byte ICMP Echos to 192.169.2.2, timeout is 2 seconds:
.....
Success rate is 0 percent (0/5)
R1#
```

Example 8-5 demonstrates R1's attempt to **ping** R2's Ethernet0 interface of 192.168.1.2.

**Example 8-5**   *R1 Successfully **ping**s R2's Ethernet0 Interface*

```
R1#ping 192.168.1.2

Type escape sequence to abort.
Sending 5, 100-byte ICMP Echos to 192.168.1.2, timeout is 2 seconds:
!!!!!
Success rate is 100 percent (5/5), round-trip min/avg/max = 1/2/4 ms
R1#
```

R1 successfully can **ping** R2's Ethernet0 interface, but it cannot **ping** any of the other directly connected interfaces of R2. This result indicates that physical connectivity between R1 and R2 exists.

The reason that R1 cannot **ping** R2's Ethernet1 or Loopback0 interface is that it does not have a route to networks 192.168.2.0 and 192.169.2.0.

This also is verified by R1's routing table, as indicated earlier in Example 8-1. R1 had a route to its directly connected network of 192.168.1.0, but no route to 192.168.2.0 or 192.169.2.0. For this reason, you can **ping** R2's Ethernet0 interface from R1, but you cannot **ping** R2's Ethernet1 or Loopback0 interfaces.

**NOTE**        When you type the command **ping 192.169.2.2**, the router creates an IP packet with a
               destination IP address of 192.169.2.2. The router then looks in its routing table to determine
               what interface it should send the packet out to get to 192.169.2.2. Because the router does
               not have an entry in its routing table for the IP network 192.169.2.0 where 192.169.2.2
               resides, the router discards the packet.

You can resolve this issue by configuring R1 with a static route to the destination networks
of 192.168.2.0 and 192.169.2.0; or, you could configure a routing protocol between R1 and
R2 that would advertise these routes. For purposes here, configure RIP between R1 and R2.
Through RIP, R2 will advertise the routes of its directly connected networks of 192.168.2.0
and 192.169.2.0 to R1. After R1 has received these routes, R1 will be capable of **ping**ing
192.168.2.2 and 192.169.2.2. In addition, you should be capable of Telnetting from R1 to
R2 using the host table configured in Chapter 6, "General Router Configurations," which
mapped R2's host name to its Loopback0 interface.

Configuring RIP requires the following steps:

**Step 1**    Enable the RIP routing process, which places you in router configuration
              mode via the Router#**router rip** command.

**Step 2**    Specify those networks that should be advertised using RIP via the
              Router(config-router)#**network** [*network-number*] command.

Begin the RIP configuration by resuming the reverse Telnet session to R1. On R1, you enter
global configuration mode and start the RIP routing process. This places you in router
configuration mode. Then use the **network** command to specify networks 192.168.1.0 and
192.169.1.0 to be advertised using RIP. Example 8-6 demonstrates this series of transactions.

**Example 8-6**  *Starting the RIP Routing Process on R1 and Advertising Networks 192.168.1.0 and 192.169.1.0*
               *Through RIP*

```
Termserver#1
[Resuming connection 1 to r1 ... ]

R1#configure terminal
Enter configuration commands, one per line.  End with CNTL/Z.
R1(config)#router rip
R1(config-router)#network 192.168.1.0
R1(config-router)#network 192.169.1.0
R1(config-router)#end
R1#
%SYS-5-CONFIG_I: Configured from console by console
R1#
```

To get an idea of how this should appear, look at the highlighted portion of the RIP configuration of R1 in Example 8-7.

**Example 8-7** *Running Configuration of R1 After Configuration of RIP*

```
R1#show running-config
Building configuration...

Current configuration:
!
version 11.2
no service password-encryption
no service udp-small-servers
no service tcp-small-servers
!
hostname R1
!
enable password falcons
!
no ip domain-lookup
ip host R1 192.169.1.1
ip host R2 192.169.2.2
ip host R3 192.169.3.3
ip host R4 192.169.4.4
ip host R5 192.169.5.5
ip host R6 192.169.6.6
!
interface Loopback0
 ip address 192.169.1.1 255.255.255.0
!
interface Ethernet0
 description This interface connects to R2's E0
 ip address 192.168.1.1 255.255.255.0
!
interface Serial0
 no ip address
 shutdown
!
interface Serial1
 no ip address
 shutdown
!
router rip
 network 192.168.1.0
 network 192.169.1.0
!
no ip classless
!
banner motd ^C
This is Router 1
^C
!
line con 0
```

**Example 8-7**    *Running Configuration of R1 After Configuration of RIP (Continued)*

```
 exec-timeout 0 0
 password falcons
 logging synchronous
line aux 0
line vty 0 4
 password falcons
 login
 !
end
```

Next, you need to configure R2 with RIP and add networks 192.168.1.0, 192.168.2.0, and
192.169.2.0 to be advertised using RIP. Return to the terminal server, resume the
connection with R2, and configure RIP with each of these **network** statements, as
demonstrated in Example 8-8.

**Example 8-8**    *Starting the RIP Routing Process on R2 and Advertising Networks 192.168.1.0, 192.168.2.0, and
192.169.2.0 Through RIP*

```
Termserver#2
[Resuming connection 2 to r2 ... ]

R2#configure terminal
Enter configuration commands, one per line.  End with CNTL/Z.
R2(config)#router rip
R2(config-router)#network 192.168.1.0
R2(config-router)#network 192.168.2.0
R2(config-router)#network 192.169.2.0
R2(config-router)#end
R2#
%SYS-5-CONFIG_I: Configured from console by console
R2#
```

When a network is added to RIP, RIP not only advertises this network route, but it also
sends updates on the interface corresponding to this network. R2 now broadcasts RIP
advertisements to R1 through its Ethernet0 interface. This ensures that R1 receives the
routes that it needs to get to R2's directly connected networks.

As done with R1, examine the RIP configuration on R2 as it appears in the running
configuration in Example 8-9. As highlighted in the running configuration of R2, three
networks on R2 are configured to be a part of the RIP routing process.

**Example 8-9**    *Running Configuration of R2 After Configuration of RIP*

```
R2#show running-config
Building configuration...

Current configuration:
```

*continues*

**Example 8-9** *Running Configuration of R2 After Configuration of RIP (Continued)*

```
!
version 12.0
service timestamps debug uptime
service timestamps log uptime
no service password-encryption
!
hostname R2
!
enable password falcons
!
ip subnet-zero
no ip domain-lookup
ip host R1 192.169.1.1
ip host R2 192.169.2.2
ip host R3 192.169.3.3
ip host R4 192.169.4.4
ip host R5 192.169.5.5
ip host R6 192.169.6.6
!
!
!
interface Loopback0
 ip address 192.169.2.2 255.255.255.0
 no ip directed-broadcast
!
interface Ethernet0
 ip address 192.168.1.2 255.255.255.0
 no ip directed-broadcast
!
interface Ethernet1
 description This interface does not connect with another IP device
 ip address 192.168.2.2 255.255.255.0
 no ip directed-broadcast
!
interface Serial0
 description This interface connects to R3's S0 (201)
 ip address 192.168.100.2 255.255.255.0
 no ip directed-broadcast
 encapsulation frame-relay
 no ip mroute-cache
 frame-relay map ip 192.168.100.3 201 broadcast
 frame-relay map ip 192.168.100.4 201 broadcast
 frame-relay lmi-type ansi
!
router rip
 network 192.168.1.0
 network 192.168.2.0
 network 192.169.2.0
!
ip classless
!
banner motd ^CCC
```

**Example 8-9**  *Running Configuration of R2 After Configuration of RIP (Continued)*

```
This is Router 2
^C
!
line con 0
 exec-timeout 0 0
 password falcons
 logging synchronous
 transport input none
line vty 0 4
 password falcons
 login
!
end

R2#
```

# Verifying RIP Configuration and Operation

Besides viewing the running configuration to ensure that RIP appears with the desired networks as expected, you can use a few commands to help you verify the RIP configuration, fine tune it where necessary, and ensure that it is operating properly.

These commands include the following:

> **show ip protocols**
> **show ip route**
> **ping**
> **debug ip rip**
> **passive-interface**

## Verifying RIP Configuration with the **show ip protocols** Command

Begin verifying the RIP configuration using the **show ip protocols** command, as demonstrated in Example 8-10.

**Example 8-10 show ip protocols** *Command Output on R1 Displays Detailed Information About RIP Configuration*

```
R1#show ip protocols
Routing Protocol is "rip"
  Sending updates every 30 seconds, next due in 20 seconds
  Invalid after 180 seconds, hold down 180, flushed after 240
  Outgoing update filter list for all interfaces is not set
  Incoming update filter list for all interfaces is not set
  Redistributing: rip
  Default version control: send version 1, receive any version
    Interface        Send  Recv   Key-chain
    Ethernet0          1    1 2
```

*continues*

**Example 8-10** **show ip protocols** *Command Output on R1 Displays Detailed Information About RIP Configuration (Continued)*

```
  Loopback0          1      1 2
 Routing for Networks:
   192.168.1.0
   192.169.1.0
 Routing Information Sources:
   Gateway          Distance       Last Update
   192.168.1.2           120       00:00:06
 Distance: (default is 120)

R1#
```

Review the highlighted fields in the **show ip protocols** output from Example 8-10. First, you see the following:

```
 Sending updates every 30 seconds, next due in 20 seconds
```

This indicates that RIP is advertising routes every 30 seconds and that the next advertisement is expected in 20 seconds; this means that R1 just received an update 10 seconds ago. Next, you get the following:

```
 Invalid after 180 seconds, hold down 180, flushed after 240
```

This means that if R1 does not receive an update from R2 for 180 seconds or more, it marks the routes advertised by R2 as being unusable. If R1 still doesn't receive an update from R2 after 240 seconds, R1 removes the routing table entries that it received from R2. This line also shows that the hold-down timer is set to 180.

The next highlighted line indicates that the default configuration for RIP is to send RIP-1 updates and to receive both RIP-1 and RIP-2 updates.

The last highlighted lines verify that RIP is configured for networks 192.168.1.0 and 192.169.1.0. Each of these networks will be advertised in RIP routing updates.

Compare the **show ip protocols** output for R1 in Example 8-10 to the **show ip protocols** output on R2, as shown in Example 8-11.

**Example 8-11** **show ip protocols** *on R2*

```
R2#show ip protocols
Routing Protocol is "rip"
  Sending updates every 30 seconds, next due in 28 seconds
  Invalid after 180 seconds, hold down 180, flushed after 240
  Outgoing update filter list for all interfaces is
  Incoming update filter list for all interfaces is
  Redistributing: rip
  Default version control: send version 1, receive any version
    Interface       Send  Recv   Key-chain
    Ethernet0        1     1 2
    Ethernet1        1     1 2
    Loopback0        1     1 2
```

**Example 8-11 show ip protocols** *on R2 (Continued)*

```
    Routing for Networks:
      192.168.1.0
      192.168.2.0
      192.169.2.0
    Routing Information Sources:
      Gateway         Distance      Last Update
      192.168.1.1          120      00:00:08
    Distance: (default is 120)

R2#
```

The highlighted areas show that the only difference is that R2 also is configured to send and receive RIP updates for the 192.168.2.0 network on its Ethernet1 interface. Ideally, you do not want RIP updates to be broadcast out the Ethernet1 interface. The section "Preventing RIP Updates with the **passive-interface** Command" goes into more detail about this.

## Confirming RIP Advertisement Receipt with the **show ip route** Command

The **show ip protocols** command indicates that the proper networks are configured for RIP advertisements. You can confirm that these RIP advertisements are being received by looking at the routing table of R1 and R2 using the **show ip route** command. Example 8-12 provides the output from this command on R1.

**Example 8-12** *Routing Table of R1 After Successful RIP Configuration*

```
R1#show ip route
Codes: C - connected, S - static, I - IGRP, R - RIP, M - mobile, B - BGP
       D - EIGRP, EX - EIGRP external, O - OSPF, IA - OSPF inter area
       N1 - OSPF NSSA external type 1, N2 - OSPF NSSA external type 2
       E1 - OSPF external type 1, E2 - OSPF external type 2, E - EGP
       i - IS-IS, L1 - IS-IS level-1, L2 - IS-IS level-2, * - candidate default
       U - per-user static route, o - ODR

Gateway of last resort is not set

C    192.169.1.0/24 is directly connected, Loopback0
C    192.168.1.0/24 is directly connected, Ethernet0
R    192.168.2.0/24 [120/1] via 192.168.1.2, 00:00:09, Ethernet0
R    192.169.2.0/24 [120/1] via 192.168.1.2, 00:00:09, Ethernet0
R1#
```

R1 has received two RIP routes from R2: one to network 192.168.2.0 and one to 192.169.2.0. These correspond to Ethernet1 and Loopback0 on R2. Each route is preceded by an *R*, indicating that the route was learned through RIP.

Example 8-13 shows the routing table of R2.

**Example 8-13** *R2 Routing Table*

```
R2#show ip route
Codes: C - connected, S - static, I - IGRP, R - RIP, M - mobile, B - BGP
       D - EIGRP, EX - EIGRP external, O - OSPF, IA - OSPF inter area
       N1 - OSPF NSSA external type 1, N2 - OSPF NSSA external type 2
       E1 - OSPF external type 1, E2 - OSPF external type 2, E - EGP
       i - IS-IS, L1 - IS-IS level-1, L2 - IS-IS level-2, * - candidate default
       U - per-user static route, o - ODR

Gateway of last resort is not set

C    192.168.1.0/24 is directly connected, Ethernet0
R    192.169.1.0/24 [120/1] via 192.168.1.1, 00:00:19, Ethernet0
C    192.168.2.0/24 is directly connected, Ethernet1
C    192.169.2.0/24 is directly connected, Loopback0
C    192.168.100.0/24 is directly connected, Serial0
R2#
```

R2 has received one RIP route of 192.169.1.0 from R1. This corresponds to R1's Loopback0 interface and was learned via a RIP advertisement from R1.

## Verifying Router Interconnectivity with the **ping** Command

With the correct routes in R1's and R2's routing tables, R1 and R2 should be capable of **ping**ing each other's Loopback0 interface. In addition, R1 now should be capable of **ping**ing R2's Ethernet1 address of 192.168.2.2. To verify this, first initiate a **ping** from R2 to R1's Loopback0 address of 192.169.1.1, as shown in Example 8-14.

**Example 8-14** *Successful **ping** from R2 to R1's Loopback0 Address*

```
R2#ping 192.169.1.1

Type escape sequence to abort.
Sending 5, 100-byte ICMP Echos to 192.169.1.1, timeout is 2 seconds:
!!!!!
Success rate is 100 percent (5/5), round-trip min/avg/max = 1/6/24 ms
R2#
```

Success! Now initiate a **ping** from R1 to R2's Loopback0 address of 192.169.2.2 and to R2's Ethernet1 address of 192.168.2.2, as shown in Example 8-15.

**Example 8-15** *Successful* **ping** *from R1 to R2's Loopback0 and Ethernet1 Addresses*

```
Termserver#1
[Resuming connection 1 to r1 ... ]

R1#ping 192.169.2.2

Type escape sequence to abort.
Sending 5, 100-byte ICMP Echos to 192.169.2.2, timeout is 2 seconds:
!!!!!
Success rate is 100 percent (5/5), round-trip min/avg/max = 1/3/4 ms
R1#ping 192.168.2.2

Type escape sequence to abort.
Sending 5, 100-byte ICMP Echos to 192.168.2.2, timeout is 2 seconds:
!!!!!
Success rate is 100 percent (5/5), round-trip min/avg/max = 4/4/4 ms
R1#
```

Success! R1 now has successfully learned the routes necessary to **ping** R2's Loopback0 and Ethernet1 addresses.

## Analyzing Router Processes with the **debug ip rip** Command

In the lab examples, R1 and R2 learned the desired routes without any problems; however, in the real world, problems might arise where the configuration appears correct but RIP routes are not appearing in the routing table as expected. For more complex scenarios, you can use a **debug** command to see what is going on in the background RIP process of the router. The command used is **debug ip rip** and is executed from privileged EXEC mode as follows:

```
Router#debug ip rip
```

To turn off IP RIP debugging, use the **no** form of the preceding command, as follows:

```
Router#no debug ip rip
```

To turn off all debugging on the router, you can use either of the following commands:

```
Router#undebug all
Router#no debug all
```

Observe the RIP routing process on R1 by turning on IP RIP debugging and then turning off all debugging, as shown in Example 8-16.

**Example 8-16 debug ip rip** *Command Output on R1*

```
R1#debug ip rip
RIP protocol debugging is on
R1#
RIP: received v1 update from 192.168.1.2 on Ethernet0
     192.168.2.0 in 1 hops
     192.169.2.0 in 1 hops
R1#
RIP: sending v1 update to 255.255.255.255 via Ethernet0 (192.168.1.1)
     network 192.169.1.0, metric 1

RIP: sending v1 update to 255.255.255.255 via Loopback0 (192.169.1.1)
     network 192.168.1.0, metric 1
     network 192.168.2.0, metric 2
     network 192.169.2.0, metric 2

R1#undebug all
All possible debugging has been turned off
R1#
```

The **debug ip rip** output reveals the following information:

- R1 received a Version 1 update from 192.168.1.2 (R2) on its Ethernet0 interface. This update contained the two routes configured on R2 to be advertised (that is, 192.168.2.0 and 192.169.2.0).

- R1 sent a RIP broadcast on its Ethernet0 interface advertising the network 192.169.1.0.

- R1 sent a RIP broadcast on its Loopback0 interface advertising networks 192.168.1.0, 192.168.2.0, and 192.169.2.0.

## Preventing RIP Updates with the **passive-interface** Command

R1 is sending RIP updates via its Loopback0 interface because when a network is added to RIP, RIP not only advertises this network route but also sends updates on the interface corresponding to this network. This is the case with Loopback0 on R1. When R1's Loopback0 network 192.169.1.0 was added to RIP to ensure that it was advertised to R2, RIP also began sending updates on the interface corresponding to network 192.169.1.0 or Loopback0. Because loopback interfaces are virtual interfaces, there is no purpose in sending updates out this interface. Remember that the reason to include the Loopback0 network in RIP was to ensure that it was advertised to R2. You can prevent RIP from sending updates via Loopback0 by configuring Loopback0 to be a passive interface in the

RIP routing process. You can do this from router configuration mode using the following command:

```
R1(config-router)#passive-interface [interface#]
```

Example 8-17 demonstrates how to configure Loopback0 as a passive interface.

**Example 8-17** *R1 Loopback0 Configured as a Passive Interface*

```
R1#conf t
Enter configuration commands, one per line.  End with CNTL/Z.
R1(config)#router rip
R1(config-router)#passive-interface loopback0
R1(config-router)#end
R1#
%SYS-5-CONFIG_I: Configured from console by console
R1#
```

Now turn on IP RIP debugging again and observe the difference in the **debug** output after Loopback0 has been configured as a passive interface, as shown in Example 8-18.

**Example 8-18 debug ip rip** *Output on R1 After Loopback0 Configured as a Passive Interface*

```
R1#debug ip rip
RIP protocol debugging is on
R1#
RIP: received v1 update from 192.168.1.2 on Ethernet0
     192.168.2.0 in 1 hops
     192.169.2.0 in 1 hops
R1#
RIP: sending v1 update to 255.255.255.255 via Ethernet0 (192.168.1.1)
     network 192.169.1.0, metric 1
R1#
RIP: received v1 update from 192.168.1.2 on Ethernet0
     192.168.2.0 in 1 hops
     192.169.2.0 in 1 hops
R1#
RIP: sending v1 update to 255.255.255.255 via Ethernet0 (192.168.1.1)
     network 192.169.1.0, metric 1
R1#
```

The **debug** output represents two 30-second RIP interval updates. Notice that after you have configured Loopback0 to be a passive interface, RIP no longer sends updates via Loopback0.

R2 has a similar situation. You do not want RIP updates to be sent out Loopback0 or
Ethernet1. Switch over to R2 and observe the current **debug ip rip** information, as shown
in Example 8-19.

**Example 8-19** *RIP Debug Information on R2 Before Passive Interface Configuration*

```
Termserver#2
[Resuming connection 2 to r2 ... ]

R2#debug ip rip
RIP protocol debugging is on
R2#
RIP: received v1 update from 192.168.1.1 on Ethernet0
     192.169.1.0 in 1 hops
R2#
RIP: sending v1 update to 255.255.255.255 via Ethernet0 (192.168.1.2)
     network 192.168.2.0, metric 1
     network 192.169.2.0, metric 1
RIP: sending v1 update to 255.255.255.255 via Ethernet1 (192.168.2.2)
     network 192.168.1.0, metric 1
     network 192.169.1.0, metric 2
     network 192.169.2.0, metric 1
RIP: sending v1 update to 255.255.255.255 via Loopback0 (192.169.2.2)
     network 192.168.1.0, metric 1
     network 192.169.1.0, metric 2
     network 192.168.2.0, metric 1
R2#undebug all
All possible debugging has been turned off
R2#
```

The output indicates that R2 still is receiving network 192.169.1.0 from R1. This corresponds
to R1's Loopback0 and verifies that even though Loopback0 was configured as a passive
interface on R1, R1 still is advertising this network to R2 as desired. In addition, notice that
R2 is sending updates out Ethernet0, Ethernet1, and Loopback0. To remedy this, configure
Ethernet1 and Loopback0 to be passive interfaces on R2, as shown in Example 8-20.

**Example 8-20** *Ethernet1 and Loopback0 Configured as Passive Interface on R2*

```
R2#conf t
Enter configuration commands, one per line.  End with CNTL/Z.
R2(config)#
%SYS-5-CONFIG_I: Configured from console by console
R2(config)#router rip
R2(config-router)#passive-interface ethernet1
R2(config-router)#passive-interface loopback0
R2(config-router)#end
R2#
%SYS-5-CONFIG_I: Configured from console by console
R2#
```

Example 8-21 shows the change to the **debug ip rip** information after the new passive interface configuration.

**Example 8-21** **debug ip rip** *Output After Loopback0 and Ethernet1 Configured as Passive Interfaces on R2*

```
R2#debug ip rip
RIP protocol debugging is on
R2#
RIP: sending v1 update to 255.255.255.255 via Ethernet0 (192.168.1.2)
      network 192.168.2.0, metric 1
      network 192.169.2.0, metric 1
R2#
RIP: received v1 update from 192.168.1.1 on Ethernet0
      192.169.1.0 in 1 hops
R2#
```

RIP updates no longer are being sent via Loopback0 and Ethernet1, as intended.

## Saving the New Configuration

At this point, turn off all debugging and save the configuration on R1 and R2, as shown in Example 8-22.

**Example 8-22** *Turning Off All Debugging and Saving Configuration on R1 and R2*

```
R2#undebug all
All possible debugging has been turned off
R2#copy running startup
Building configuration...
[OK]
R2#
Termserver#1
[Resuming connection 1 to r1 ... ]

R1#undebug all
All possible debugging has been turned off
R1#copy running startup
Building configuration...
[OK]
R1#
```

Next, you can verify that the host table mapping that was set up in Chapter 6 pointing to the loopback interface works between R1 and R2. This is because RIP is advertising the routes to these loopback interfaces via RIP between R1 and R2. Test this on R1 by typing **r2** from the privileged EXEC mode, and see if a Telnet session is opened up to R2, as shown in Example 8-23.

**Example 8-23** *Successful Telnet from R1 to R2 Using Host Table Entry*

```
R1#r2
Trying R2 (192.169.2.2)... Open

This is Router 2


User Access Verification

Password:
R2>enable
Password:
R2#
```

Example 8-23 verifies that the host table worked as designed. R1 initiated a Telnet session to 192.169.2.2 (R2's Loopback0 interface), the banner is displayed, and you are prompted for the vty password and finally the enable password. Quit the Telnet session to R2 using the **quit** command, as demonstrated in Example 8-24.

**Example 8-24** *Ending Telnet Session Between R1 and R2*

```
R2#quit

[Connection to r2 closed by foreign host]
R1#
```

The Telnet session has been terminated, and you are returned to R1.

## Lab Follow-up Tasks

You now have successfully configured RIP and verified its proper operation. Now that RIP has been configured between R1 and R2, draw the RIP routing domains on the master lab diagram to help you to see and understand routing boundaries. For example, because you have configured RIP between R1 and R2, you should draw a line encompassing all interfaces that have been included in the RIP routing process. In this way, you can have a visual representation of what routes you'd expect to be advertised to neighboring RIP routers. See Figure 8-2 for an example.

**Figure 8-2**    *RIP Routing Domain*

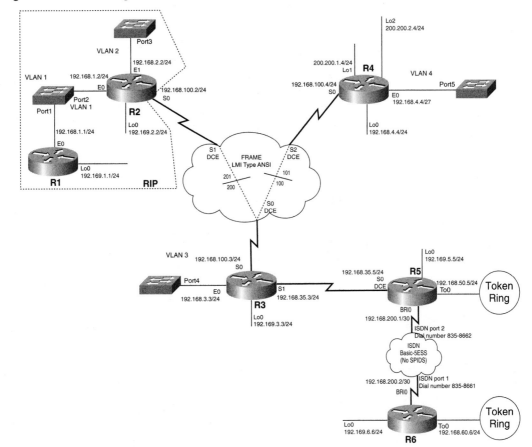

You now are prepared to move on to IGRP configuration and operation.

This chapter covers the following key topics:

- IGRP fundamentals
- Configuring IGRP

CHAPTER **9**

# Interior Gateway Routing Protocol (IGRP)

This chapter briefly reviews the IGRP routing protocol and then completes the lab objectives associated with this protocol. You also will learn about several commands to help troubleshoot and debug IGRP. Note that, for a full review of the IGRP protocol, you should review Chapter 8 of *Interconnecting Cisco Network Devices* from Cisco Press.

## IGRP Fundamentals

The Interior Gateway Routing Protocol (IGRP) is an advanced distance vector routing protocol. Because it is a Cisco-developed routing protocol, only Cisco devices can utilize this protocol for routing purposes. Like RIP, it, too, is a classful protocol, meaning that it does not send the subnet mask with routing updates. For this reason, it cannot support VLSMs.

## IGRP Routing Updates

A router running IGRP sends an update broadcast every 90 seconds, by default. When an update from the originating router is not received within three update periods (270 seconds), it declares a route invalid. After seven update periods (630 seconds), which include the three update periods, the router removes the route from the routing table. IGRP advertises three types of routes:

- **Interior**—Routes between subnets in the network attached to a router interface.

- **System**—Routes to networks within an autonomous system. The router derives system routes from directly connected network interfaces and system route information provided by other IGRP-speaking routers.

- **Exterior**—Routes to networks outside the autonomous system that are considered when identifying a *gateway of last resort*. The router chooses a gateway of last resort from the list of exterior routes that IGRP provides. The router uses the gateway (router) of last resort if it does not have a better route for a packet and the destination is not a connected network. If the autonomous system has more than one connection to an external network, different routers can choose different exterior routers as the gateway of last resort.

## IGRP Routing Metric

IGRP uses a composite metric of internetwork delay, bandwidth, reliability, MTU, and load to determine the best path for each packet. The values are important, but because of the simple network topology of this lab environment, they will not be too critical for the lab objectives. However, they will be important when you implement route redistribution in Chapter 11, "Basic Route Redistribution and Static Routing." When redistributing routes from one routing protocol into another (RIP to IGRP, for example) you lose all metrics, so you will have to manually specify those values; for now, though, you will not change any metric values for IGRP.

## IGRP Scalability Features

IGRP is an advanced distance vector protocol. Several features distinguish it from other distance vector routing protocols, such as RIP:

- **Increased scalability**—Improved for routing in larger networks compared to networks that use RIP, IGRP can be used to overcome RIP's 15-hop limit. IGRP has a default maximum hop count of 100 hops, which can be configured to a maximum of 255 hops.

- **Sophisticated metric**—IGRP uses a composite metric that provides significant flexibility in route selection. By default, internetwork delay and bandwidth are used to arrive at a composite metric. Reliability, load, and MTU may be included in the metric computation as well.

- **Multiple path support**—IGRP can maintain up to six unequal-cost paths between a network source and destination, but only the route with the lowest metric is placed in the routing table. RIP, on the other hand, keeps only the route with the best metric and disregards the rest. Multiple paths can be used to increase available bandwidth or for router redundancy.

IGRP is a worthy candidate for IP networks that require a simple but more robust and scalable routing protocol than RIP Version 1 (RIP-1). Another advantage that IGRP has over RIP-1 is that it may be configured to perform triggered updates. It is important to point out that IGRP, even with advanced features, still uses techniques such as split horizon, hold-down timer (which is 280 seconds), and poison reverse updates to avoid routing loops.

# Configuring IGRP

Figure 9-1 illustrates the routers on which you will be configuring IGRP.

**Figure 9-1**    *IGRP Routers*

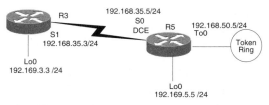

The objectives for this lab are as follows:

- Place R3's S1, loopback 0 and R5's To0, loopback 0, and S1 networks into IGRP autonomous system 200.

Without any routing protocols configured, R3's IP routing table would be similar to what you saw in the beginning of Chapter 8, "Routing Information Protocol (RIP)"—only directly connected networks would be seen. R3 can **ping** R5's S0 interface; however, you cannot **ping** R5's Token Ring 0 interface from R3 because R3 doesn't know that it exists at this point. After completing the lab objectives, you should be capable of **ping**ing R5's To0 interface from R3, as verified in the next section. First, you need to configure IGRP.

## Enabling and Configuring IGRP on Router R3

The first step in configuring IGRP is to enable the routing process on the router. From global configuration mode, issue the following command:

```
Router(config)# router igrp autonomous-system
```

The autonomous system is a collection of networks (routers) under common administration that share a common routing strategy. The autonomous system (AS) number identifies the collection of networks. The AS number for IGRP will be 200. The AS number must be the same for all routers that are going to exchange IGRP routes. Begin by configuring R3. Example 9-1 illustrates the command to enable IGRP on R3.

**Example 9-1**   *IGRP Configuration on R3*

```
Termserver#3
[Resuming connection 3 to r3 ... ]

R3#config t
Enter configuration commands, one per line.  End with CNTL/Z.
R3(config)#router igrp 200
R3(config-router)#
```

Upon issuing the **router igrp** command, you are placed into the IGRP routing process configuration mode. From here, you need to place any networks that you want IGRP to propagate into the routing process with the following command:

```
Router(config-router)# network network-number
```

The *network number* is the network address of the IP subnet that you want to associate with IGRP. In the case of this lab, you need to place R3's S0 network and Loopback 0 network into IGRP. The IP address for R3's S0 network is 192.168.35.3 with a /24 bit mask. The network address for this interface is 192.168.35.0. For Loopback 0, the network address is 192.169.3.0. Without understanding IP subnetting, you would not know what the network address was for that particular interface. For this reason, IP subnetting is important to routing. It is with the network addresses that routers populate their routing tables. Knowing which interfaces of a router belong to which routing table entries is a basic concept that CCNAs should understand. Proceed and place the network into the IGRP process as demonstrated in Example 9-2.

**Example 9-2**   *IGRP Network Configuration on R3*

```
R3(config-router)#network 192.168.35.0
R3(config-router)#network 192.169.3.0
```

With only two networks to associate with IGRP on R3, the configuration tasks are quite simple.

# Enabling and Configuring IGRP on Router R5

The tasks for configuring R5 are the same as for R3, except that R5 has three networks, 192.168.35.0 (Serial 0), 192.168.50.0 (Token Ring 0), and 192.169.5.0 (Loopback 0). Example 9-3 takes you through the IGRP configurations task on R5.

**Example 9-3**   *IGRP Configuration on R5*

```
Termserver#5
[Resuming connection 5 to r5 ... ]

R5#config t
```

**Example 9-3**  *IGRP Configuration on R5 (Continued)*

```
Enter configuration commands, one per line.  End with CNTL/Z.
R5(config)#
R5(config)#router igrp 200
R5(config-router)#network 192.168.35.0
R5(config-router)#network 192.168.50.0
R5(config-router)#network 192.169.5.0
R5(config-router)#
```

The configuration tasks for both R3 and R5 are complete. Make sure that you save your configurations before verifying that IGRP is configured correctly and is operating as expected.

# Verifying IGRP Configuration and Operation

Chapter 8 introduced several commands that help you verify that RIP is configured and working properly. You can use some of those same commands for IGRP. To verify that the configuration commands are valid, look at the running-config of R5, as demonstrated in Example 9-4.

**Example 9-4**  *R5's Running-Config*

```
R5#show running-config
Building configuration...

Current configuration:
!
version 11.2
no service password-encryption
no service udp-small-servers
no service tcp-small-servers
!
hostname R5
!
enable password falcons
!
no ip domain-lookup
ip host R1 192.169.1.1
ip host R2 192.169.2.2
ip host R3 192.169.3.3
ip host R4 192.169.4.4
ip host R5 192.169.5.5
ip host R6 192.169.6.6
!
interface Loopback0
 ip address 192.169.5.5 255.255.255.0
!
interface Serial0
 description This interface connects to R3's S1 (DTE)
```

*continues*

**Example 9-4**    *R5's Running-Config (Continued)*

```
ip address 192.168.35.5 255.255.255.0
no fair-queue
clockrate 2000000
!
interface Serial1
 no ip address
 shutdown
!
interface TokenRing0
 description This interface does not connect with another IP device
 ip address 192.168.50.5 255.255.255.0
 ring-speed 16
!
interface BRI0
 no ip address
 shutdown
!
router igrp 200
 network 192.168.35.0
 network 192.168.50.0
 network 192.169.5.0
!
no ip classless
!
banner motd ^C
This is Router 5
^C
!
line con 0
 exec-timeout 0 0
 password falcons
 logging synchronous
line aux 0
line vty 0 4
 password falcons
 login
!
end

R5#
```

The highlighted portion of Example 9-4 illustrates the IGRP configuration commands as they appear in the running-config. The entire configuration file was preserved here so that you can see where the IGRP configuration commands fall in the sequence of the running-config file—specifically that they fall after the interfaces are configured and initialized.

With the configuration file appearing correct, look at R5's IP routing table to see if R3's Loopback 0's network is present. R3's S1 network is present already because it is directly connected via R5's S0 interface. Example 9-5 shows the output from the **show ip route** command on R5.

**Example 9-5**  show ip route *Command Output*

```
R5#show ip route
Codes: C - connected, S - static, I - IGRP, R - RIP, M - mobile, B - BGP
       D - EIGRP, EX - EIGRP external, O - OSPF, IA - OSPF inter area
       N1 - OSPF NSSA external type 1, N2 - OSPF NSSA external type 2
       E1 - OSPF external type 1, E2 - OSPF external type 2, E - EGP
       i - IS-IS, L1 - IS-IS level-1, L2 - IS-IS level-2, * - candidate default
       U - per-user static route, o - ODR

Gateway of last resort is not set

C    192.168.35.0/24 is directly connected, Serial0
C    192.168.50.0/24 is directly connected, TokenRing0
I    192.169.3.0/24 [100/8976] via 192.168.35.3, 00:00:03, Serial0
C    192.169.5.0/24 is directly connected, Loopback0
R5#
```

Just as expected. R3's Loopback 0's network has been advertised to R5 via IGRP. The **I** in the output next to the route identifies the route as being learned by IGRP. Example 9-6 demonstrates a **ping** of R3's Loopback 0 interface to verify connectivity.

**Example 9-6**  *R5-to-R3* **ping** *Result*

```
R5#ping 192.169.3.3

Type escape sequence to abort.
Sending 5, 100-byte ICMP Echos to 192.169.3.3, timeout is 2 seconds:
!!!!!
Success rate is 100 percent (5/5), round-trip min/avg/max = 4/5/8 ms
R5#
```

That gives 100 percent success! Example 9-7 displays the **show ip protocols** command output after configuring IGRP.

**Example 9-7**  show ip protocols *Command Output*

```
R5#show ip protocols
Routing Protocol is "igrp 200"
  Sending updates every 90 seconds, next due in 24 seconds
  Invalid after 270 seconds, hold down 280, flushed after 630
  Outgoing update filter list for all interfaces is not set
  Incoming update filter list for all interfaces is not set
  Default networks flagged in outgoing updates
  Default networks accepted from incoming updates
  IGRP metric weight K1=1, K2=0, K3=1, K4=0, K5=0
  IGRP maximum hopcount 100
  IGRP maximum metric variance 1
  Redistributing: igrp 200
  Routing for Networks:
```

*continues*

**Example 9-7** **show ip protocols** *Command Output (Continued)*

```
    192.168.35.0
    192.168.50.0
    192.169.5.0
  Routing Information Sources:
    Gateway         Distance      Last Update
    192.168.35.3         100      00:00:32
  Distance: (default is 100)

R5#
```

The routing protocol says "igrp 200." This output shows several important configuration values for IGRP. The one of most interest is the "Routing for Networks:" field. This field shows that 192.168.35.0, 192.169.50.0, and 192.168.5.0 are configured for IGRP. Another way to verify that IGRP is sending and receiving the correct routes is to issue the following command:

```
Router#debug ip igrp {events | transactions}
```

You want the **transactions** option because the output of this option informs you of routing updates being sent and received from adjacent routers. Example 9-8 shows output from the **debug ip igrp** command using the **transactions** option.

**Example 9-8** **debug ip igrp transactions** *Command Output*

```
R5#debug ip igrp transactions
IGRP protocol debugging is on

IGRP: received update from 192.168.35.3 on Serial0
      network 192.169.3.0, metric 8976 (neighbor 501)
IGRP: edition is now 2


IGRP: sending update to 255.255.255.255 via Serial0 (192.168.35.5)
      network 192.168.50.0, metric=688
      network 192.169.5.0, metric=501

IGRP: sending update to 255.255.255.255 via Loopback0 (192.169.5.5)
      network 192.168.35.0, metric=8476
      network 192.168.50.0, metric=688
      network 192.169.3.0, metric=8976

IGRP: sending update to 255.255.255.255 via TokenRing0 (192.168.50.5)
      network 192.168.35.0, metric=8476
      network 192.169.3.0, metric=8976
      network 192.169.5.0, metric=501
R5#
```

Chapter 8 covered the details of the output, so we will not cover it again. You just need to verify that the network received from R3 is 192.169.3.0 (highlighted in the first section of output) and that you are sending the correct routes (192.168.50.0 and 192.169.5.0), as depicted in the second highlighted section of output.

The third highlighted section of output verifies that an update was sent via Loopback 0. This is pointless because you cannot have any other devices off that interface, but the router does it anyway. To prevent IGRP updates from being sent out the loopback interface on R5, use the **passive-interface** command (in this case, specifying loopback0). Example 9-9 demonstrates the **passive-interface** command on R5.

**Example 9-9    passive-interface** *Command*

```
R5#config t
Enter configuration commands, one per line.  End with CNTL/Z.
R5(config)#router igrp 200
R5(config-router)#passive-interface loopback 0
R5(config-router)#end
```

The output reveals that updates no longer are being sent out Loopback 0. Example 9-10 illustrates how the output has changed for the command **debug ip igrp transactions**.

**Example 9-10** *Modified* **debug ip igrp transactions** *Command Output*

```
IGRP: received update from 192.168.35.3 on Serial0
      network 192.169.3.0, metric 8976 (neighbor 501)
IGRP: edition is now 4
IGRP: sending update to 255.255.255.255 via Serial0 (192.168.35.5)
      network 192.168.50.0, metric=688
      network 192.169.5.0, metric=501
IGRP: sending update to 255.255.255.255 via TokenRing0 (192.168.50.5)
      network 192.168.35.0, metric=8476
      network 192.169.3.0, metric=8976
      network 192.169.5.0, metric=501
R5#
```

As you can see, IGRP did not send any routing updates out interface Loopback 0, as it did before the **passive-interface** command. This is very useful if you want to hide a segment of your network from others. Notice that the "IGRP: edition is now 4" output has incremented since the last output. Each time IGRP sends out an update, it increments the edition by 1. So, this would be the fourth update that this router has sent. Another item to notice is the metrics: They are different from RIP metrics. RIP uses hop counts, and IGRP uses a composite metric of bandwidth, delay, load, reliability, and MTU size. The metrics that you see in the output are the IGRP composite metrics for each of those routers, not the hop count, as in RIP.

Now verify the configuration of R3 using the output from the **show ip route** command in Example 9-11.

**Example 9-11** *R3's IP Routing Table*

```
Termserver#3
[Resuming connection 3 to r3 ... ]

R3#show ip route
Codes: C - connected, S - static, I - IGRP, R - RIP, M - mobile, B - BGP
       D - EIGRP, EX - EIGRP external, O - OSPF, IA - OSPF inter area
       N1 - OSPF NSSA external type 1, N2 - OSPF NSSA external type 2
       E1 - OSPF external type 1, E2 - OSPF external type 2, E - EGP
       i - IS-IS, L1 - IS-IS level-1, L2 - IS-IS level-2, * - candidate default
       U - per-user static route, o - ODR

Gateway of last resort is not set

C    192.168.100.0/24 is directly connected, Serial0
C    192.168.35.0/24 is directly connected, Serial1
I    192.168.50.0/24 [100/8539] via 192.168.35.5, 00:00:54, Serial1
C    192.169.3.0/24 is directly connected, Loopback0
C    192.168.3.0/24 is directly connected, Ethernet0
I    192.169.5.0/24 [100/8976] via 192.168.35.5, 00:00:54, Serial1
R3#
```

From the highlighted portions of the output, you can see the route to R5's Loopback 0 network (192.169.5.0) and to R5's Token Ring network (192.168.50.0).

Confirm IP connectivity to those networks using the **ping** command. Example 9-12 shows the results of **ping**ing R5's Loopback 0 and Token Ring interfaces (192.169.5.5 and 192.168.50.5).

**Example 9-12 ping** *Result from R3 to R5*

```
R3#ping 192.169.5.5

Type escape sequence to abort.
Sending 5, 100-byte ICMP Echos to 192.169.5.5, timeout is 2 seconds:
!!!!!
Success rate is 100 percent (5/5), round-trip min/avg/max = 4/5/8 ms
R3#ping 192.168.50.5

Type escape sequence to abort.
Sending 5, 100-byte ICMP Echos to 192.168.50.5, timeout is 2 seconds:
!!!!!
Success rate is 100 percent (5/5), round-trip min/avg/max = 4/4/4 ms
R3#
```

Success! This confirms that IGRP is operating correctly. If you want to, you could execute the same **show** and **debug** commands that you did on R5 for R3; to eliminate redundancy, though, this isn't necessary. The output from **show** and **debug** from R5 to R3 would have the same results.

Before you leave the routers, turn off debugging (Router#**undebug all**), save the configurations, and update the master diagram to reflect the addition of the IGRP AS 200 routing domain. Figure 9-2 illustrates the updated diagram.

**Figure 9-2**    *IGRP Routing Domain*

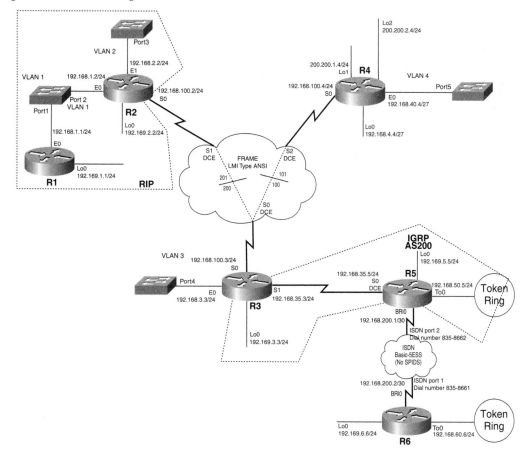

Now you have configured IGRP and are routing between R3 and R5. As you noted, the commands were similar to the commands executed to configure and verify RIP. It will be the same for EIGRP, as covered in the next chapter.

This chapter covers the following key topics:

- EIGRP fundamentals
- Lab objective: configuring EIGRP

## CHAPTER 10

# Enhanced Interior Gateway Protocol (EIGRP)

This chapter introduces the features, concepts, and configurations associated with Enhanced Interior Gateway Protocol (EIGRP). You will learn how to configure EIGRP between R2, R3, and R4. The chapter also provides some useful commands to verify and troubleshoot your EIGRP configuration.

## EIGRP Fundamentals

Enhanced Interior Gateway Protocol (EIGRP) is a proprietary hybrid routing protocol developed by Cisco Systems. EIGRP uses the same distance vector algorithm and distance information as IGRP. However, as its name implies, EIGRP has been enhanced in convergence properties and operating efficiency over IGRP. Principally, EIGRP has been enhanced to use more advanced features to avoid routing loops and to speed convergence time. In addition, EIGRP transmits the subnet mask for each routing entry, enabling EIGRP to support features such as VLSM and route summarization.

## EIGRP Features

EIGRP provides advanced features over its predecessors IGRP and RIP:

- **Increased network width**—With IP RIP, the largest possible width of your network is 15 hops. When IP EIGRP is enabled, the largest possible width is 224 hops.

- **Fast convergence**—EIGRP uses an algorithm called the Diffusing Update Algorithm (DUAL). This algorithm guarantees loop-free operation at every instant throughout a route computation and allows all routers involved in a topology change to synchronize at the same time. Routers that are not affected by topology changes are not involved in recomputations. DUAL provides a system for routers to not only calculate the best current route to each subnet, but also to calculate alternative routes that could be used if the current route fails. The alternate route, called the *feasible successor route*, is guaranteed to be loop-free, so convergence can happen quickly. Because of DUAL, the convergence time of EIGRP rivals that of other existing routing protocols.

- **Partial updates**—EIGRP sends incremental updates when the state of a destination changes, instead of sending the entire contents of the routing table. This feature reduces the bandwidth required for EIGRP packets and also reduces CPU processing.

- **Neighbor-discovery mechanism**—This is a simple hello mechanism used to learn about neighboring routers. It is protocol-independent.

- **VLSM and route summarization**—EIGRP supports variable-length subnet masks and route summarization.

- **Automatic redistribution**—Because IGRP and EIGRP share the same metrics, IP IGRP routes can be automatically redistributed into EIGRP, and IP EIGRP routes can be automatically redistributed into IGRP. If desired, you can turn off redistribution. Redistribution is covered in more detail in Chapter 11, "Route Redistribution."

## EIGRP Components

EIGRP has four basic components:

- **Neighbor discovery/recovery**—Routers use this process to dynamically learn of other routers on their directly attached networks. Routers also must discover when their neighbors become unreachable or inoperative. Neighbor discovery/recovery is achieved with low overhead by periodically sending small hello packets. As long as hello packets are received, a router can determine that a neighbor is alive and functioning. When this status is determined, the neighboring routers can exchange routing information.

- **Reliable transport protocol**—This protocol is responsible for guaranteed, ordered delivery of EIGRP packets to all neighbors. It supports intermixed transmission of multicast and unicast packets. Some EIGRP packets must be transmitted reliably and others need not be. For efficiency, reliability is provided only when necessary. For example, on a multi-access network that has multicast capabilities, such as Ethernet, it is not necessary to send hellos reliably to all neighbors individually. Therefore, EIGRP sends a single multicast hello with an indication in the packet informing the receivers that the packet need not be acknowledged. Other types of packets, such as updates, require acknowledgment, and this is indicated in the packet. The reliable transport has a provision to send multicast packets quickly when there are unacknowledged packets pending. Doing so helps ensure that convergence time remains low in the presence of varying speed links.

- **DUAL finite state machine**—This embodies the decision process for all route computations. It tracks all routes advertised by all neighbors. DUAL uses the distance information, known as a metric, to select efficient, loop-free paths. DUAL selects routes to be inserted into a routing table based on feasible successors. A successor is a neighboring router used for packet forwarding that has a least-cost path to a destination that is guaranteed not to be part of a routing loop. When there are no feasible successors but there are neighbors advertising the destination, a recomputation must occur. This is called "going active." A router asks all of its neighbors if they have a feasible successor to the destination. If none replies, the neighbors go active and the process repeats. This is the process whereby a new successor is determined. The amount of time that it takes to recompute a route affects the convergence time. Even though the recomputation is not processor-intensive, it is advantageous to avoid recomputation if it is not necessary. When a topology change occurs, DUAL tests for changes to feasible successors. If feasible successors exist, it uses any that it finds, to avoid unnecessary recomputation.

# EIGRP Concepts

The sections that follow describe these EIGRP concepts in greater detail:

- Neighbor tables
- Topology tables
- Feasible successors
- Route states
- Packet formats
- Internal vs. external routes
- DUAL

## Neighbor Tables

Each router keeps state information about adjacent neighbors. When newly discovered neighbors are learned, the address and interface of the neighbor are recorded. This information is stored in the neighbor table. When a neighbor sends a hello packet, it advertises a hold time, which is the amount of time that a router treats a neighbor as reachable and operational. In other words, if a hello packet isn't heard within the hold time, the hold time expires and DUAL is informed of the topology change.

## Topology Tables

The topology table contains all destinations advertised by neighboring routers. Associated with each entry are the destination address and a list of neighbors that have advertised the destination. For each neighbor, the advertised metric is recorded. This is the metric that the neighbor stores in its routing table. If the neighbor is advertising this destination, it must be using the route to forward packets.

Also associated with the destination is the metric that the router uses to reach the destination. This is the sum of the best-advertised metric from all neighbors, plus the link cost to the best neighbor. This is the metric that the router uses in the routing table and when advertising to other routers.

## Feasible Successors

A destination entry is moved from the topology table to the routing table when there is a feasible successor. All minimum-cost paths to the destination form a set. From this set, the neighbors that have an advertised metric less than the current routing table metric are considered feasible successors. A router views feasible successors as neighbors that are downstream with respect to the destination. These neighbors and the associated metrics are placed in the forwarding table. When a neighbor changes the metric that it has been advertising or a topology change occurs in the network, the set of feasible successors might have to be re-evaluated. However, this is not categorized as a route recomputation.

## Route States

A topology table entry for a destination can have one of two states:

* **Passive**—A route is considered in passive state when a router is not performing a route recomputation.

* **Active**—A route is in active state when a router is undergoing a route recomputation.

If there are always feasible successors, a route never has to go into active state and it avoids a route recomputation. When there are no feasible successors, a route goes into active state and a route recomputation occurs. A route recomputation commences with a router sending a query packet to all neighbors. Neighboring routers either can reply if they have feasible successors for the destination or optionally can return a query indicating that they are performing a route recomputation. While in active state, a router cannot change the next-hop neighbor that it is using to forward packets. When all replies are received for a given query, the destination can transition to passive state and a new successor can be selected. When a link to a neighbor that is the only feasible successor goes down, all routes through that neighbor commence a route recomputation and enter the active state.

## Packet Formats

EIGRP uses the following five packet types:

* **Hello/Acks**—Hello packets are sent for neighbor discovery/recovery and do not require acknowledgment.

* **Updates**—Update packets are used to convey reachability of destinations. When a new neighbor is discovered, update packets are sent so that the neighbor can build up its topology table.

* **Queries**—Query packets are sent when a destination has no feasible successors.

- **Replies**—Reply packets are sent when a destination has no feasible successors and are sent in response to query packets to instruct the originator not to recompute the route because feasible successors exist.

- **Requests**—Request packets are used to get specific information from one or more neighbors.

## Internal Versus External Routes

EIGRP has the notion of internal and external routes. Internal routes have been originated within an EIGRP autonomous system (AS). Therefore, a directly attached network that is configured to run EIGRP is considered an internal route and is propagated with this information throughout the EIGRP AS. External routes have been learned by another routing protocol or reside in the routing table as static routes. These routes are tagged individually with the identity of their origination. Internal EIGRP routes are denoted in the routing table with the letter *D* preceding the route. External EIGRP routes are denoted in the routing table with a "D EX" preceding the route.

## DUAL Example

The topology in Figure 10-1 illustrates how the DUAL algorithm converges. The example focuses on destination to Router X only. Each node shows its cost to X in hops. The arrows show the node's successor. For example, Router C uses Router A to reach X, and the cost is 2.

**Figure 10-1**  *Example of DUAL Convergence*

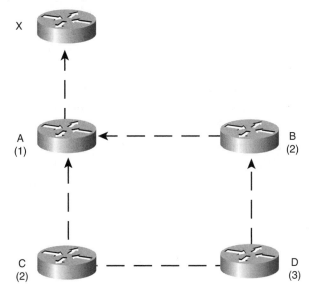

If the link between routers A and B fails, Router B sends a query informing its neighbors that it has lost its feasible successor. Router D receives the query and determines whether it has any other feasible successors. If it does not, it must start a route computation and enter the active state. However, in this case, Router C is a feasible successor because its cost (2) is less than Router D's current cost (3) to destination Router X. Router D can switch to Router C as its successor. In this scenario, routers A and C did not participate because they were unaffected by the change.

Now let's cause a route computation to occur. In this scenario, the link between routers A and C fails. Router C determines that it has lost its successor and that it has no other feasible successors. Router D is not considered a feasible successor because its advertised metric (3) is greater then C's current cost (2) to reach destination Router X. Router C must perform a route computation for destination Router X. Router C sends a query to its only neighbor, Router D. Router D replies because its successor has not changed. Router D does not need to perform a route computation. When Router C receives the reply, it knows that all neighbors have processed the news about the failure to destination Router X. At this point, Router C can choose its new feasible successor of Router D, with a cost of 4 to reach destination Router X. Note that routers A and B were unaffected by the topology change, and Router D needed only to reply to Router C.

This completes the introductory text about EIGRP. Next, review the lab objective that you will accomplish in this chapter.

# Lab Objective: Configuring EIGRP

In this chapter, you will learn how to configure EIGRP by accomplishing the following lab objectives, based on the network topology in Figure 10-2:

- Place R3's S0, R2's S0, R4's S0, and R4's Loopback0 networks into EIGRP autonomous system (AS) 100.
- Place R3's E0 and R4's E0 networks into EIGRP 100.
- Create two loopback interfaces on R4 with the following addresses: loopback1=200.200.1.4/24 and loopback2=200.200.2.4/24.
- Add these two networks into the EIGRP routing domain, and configure R4 so that all other routers see only one route to these two addresses.

Review the routers that will be configured for EIGRP. Figure 10-2 depicts that portion of the lab in which EIGRP will be configured.

**Figure 10-2** *IP EIGRP Routers*

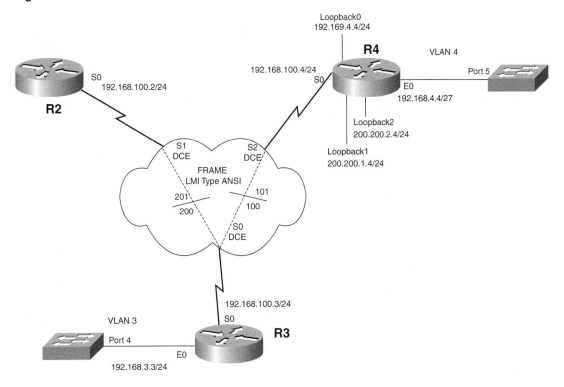

## Configuring EIGRP Between R2, R3, and R4

Table 10-1 outlines the two required steps and corresponding commands for configuring EIGRP.

**Table 10-1** *Steps for Configuring EIGRP*

| Step | Command |
|---|---|
| 1. Enable the EIGRP routing process in global configuration mode. | Router(config)#**router eigrp** [*autonomous-system*] |
| 2. Associate networks with an EIGRP routing process in router configuration mode. | Router(config-router)#**network** [*network-number*] |

EIGRP will send updates only to the interfaces in the networks specified. If you do not specify an interface's network, it will not be advertised in any IP EIGRP update.

## Lab Task 1: Place R3's S0, R2's S0, R4's S0, and R4's Loopback0 Networks into EIGRP AS 100

Begin by configuring EIGRP as the routing protocol between R2, R3, and R4. Use the autonomous system 100. Resume the connection to R2 and place S0 into EIGRP 100, as shown in Example 10-1.

**Example 10-1** *Configuring EIGRP on R2 and Placing S0 into EIGRP Autonomous System 100*

```
Termserver#2
[Resuming connection 2 to r2 ... ]

R2#conf t
Enter configuration commands, one per line.  End with CNTL/Z.
R2(config)#router eigrp 100
R2(config-router)#network 192.168.100.0
R2(config-router)#
```

Now return to the terminal server, and resume the connection to R3 and subsequently to R4. Enable the EIGRP routing process on each router. Then add R3 and R4's S0 interface into EIGRP AS 100, and add R4's loopback0 into EIGRP AS 100, as shown in Example 10-2.

**Example 10-2** *Enabling EIGRP on R3 and R4 and Placing R3 and R4's S0 Interface and R4's Loopback0 Interface Into EIGRP Autonomous System 100*

```
Termserver#3
[Resuming connection 3 to r3 ... ]

R3#conf t
Enter configuration commands, one per line.  End with CNTL/Z.
R3(config)#router eigrp 100
R3(config-router)#network 192.168.100.0
R3(config-router)#^Z
R3#
%SYS-5-CONFIG_I: Configured from console by console
R3#
```

```
Termserver#4
[Resuming connection 4 to r4 ... ]

R4#conf t
Enter configuration commands, one per line.  End with CNTL/Z.
R4(config)#router eigrp 100
R4(config-router)#network 192.168.100.0
R4(config-router)#network 192.169.4.0

R4(config-router)#^Z
R4#
%SYS-5-CONFIG_I: Configured from console by console
R4#
```

After EIGRP has been configured, R2 and R4 each should form a neighbor relationship to R3. In addition, R3 should form two neighbor relationships, one to R2 and one to R4. You can verify that this has occurred using the following command:

```
Router#show ip eigrp neighbors
```

Now go to each individual router in EIGRP AS 100 and verify that you have the proper EIGRP neighbor relationships. First, examine the neighbor relationship on R2, as shown in Example 10-3.

**Example 10-3** *R2 EIGRP Neighbor Relationship to R3*

```
Termserver#2
[Resuming connection 2 to r2 ... ]

R2#show ip eigrp neighbors
IP-EIGRP neighbors for process 100
H   Address              Interface   Hold Uptime   SRTT   RTO   Q   Seq
                                     (sec)         (ms)         Cnt Num
0   192.168.100.3        Se0          162 00:07:39    0   5000   0   1
R2#
```

The output in Example 10-3 shows that R2 has successfully formed a neighbor relationship to R3's S0 address of 192.168.100.3.

Next, examine the neighbor relationship on R4, as shown in Example 10-4.

**Example 10-4** *R4 EIGRP Neighbor Relationship to R3*

```
Termserver#4
[Resuming connection 4 to r4 ... ]

R4#show ip eigrp neighbors
IP-EIGRP neighbors for process 100
H    Address             Interface   Hold Uptime   SRTT   RTO   Q   Seq
                                     (sec)         (ms)         Cnt Num
0    192.168.100.3       Se0          170 00:07:45    0   5000   0   1
R4#
```

Again, the output from **show ip eigrp neighbors** shows that R4 has successfully formed a neighbor relationship to R3's S0 address of 192.168.100.3.

Finally, examine R3 to see its neighbor relationships, as shown in Example 10-5.

**Example 10-5** *R3 Neighbor Relationships to R4 and R2*

```
Termserver#3
[Resuming connection 3 to r3 ... ]

R3#show ip eigrp neighbors
IP-EIGRP neighbors for process 100
H   Address              Interface   Hold Uptime   SRTT   RTO  Q  Seq
                                     (sec)         (ms)        Cnt Num
1   192.168.100.4        Se0         163 00:08:26   0    5000  0  1
0   192.168.100.2        Se0         147 00:08:40   0    3000  0  1
R3#
```

The output in Example 10-5 shows that R3 has two neighbor relationships, one to R2 and one to R4, as expected.

Although EIGRP has been configured properly, if you examine the routing table on R3, you can see that only one EIGRP route exists in the routing table to R4's loopback0 network of 192.169.4.0. The letter *D* precedes the EIGRP route to depict internal routes learned through EIGRP. Example 10-6 displays the routing table on R3.

**Example 10-6** *Only One EIGRP Route on R3*

```
R3#show ip route
Codes: C - connected, S - static, I - IGRP, R - RIP, M - mobile, B - BGP
       D - EIGRP, EX - EIGRP external, O - OSPF, IA - OSPF inter area
       N1 - OSPF NSSA external type 1, N2 - OSPF NSSA external type 2
       E1 - OSPF external type 1, E2 - OSPF external type 2, E - EGP
       i - IS-IS, L1 - IS-IS level-1, L2 - IS-IS level-2, * - candidate default
       U - per-user static route, o - ODR

Gateway of last resort is not set

C    192.168.100.0/24 is directly connected, Serial0
C    192.168.35.0/24 is directly connected, Serial1
I    192.168.50.0/24 [100/8539] via 192.168.35.5, 00:01:02, Serial1
C    192.169.3.0/24 is directly connected, Loopback0
C    192.168.3.0/24 is directly connected, Ethernet0
I    192.169.5.0/24 [100/8976] via 192.168.35.5, 00:01:02, Serial1
D    192.169.4.0/24 [90/2297856] via 192.168.100.4, 00:06:28, Serial0
R3#
```

The output shows only one EIGRP route on R3, even though you placed two networks into EIGRP on R4. This is expected because the network of 192.168.100.0 is already in the routing table as a directly connected route. So, even though it was added to EIGRP, you should expect to see it as a directly connected route, not an EIGRP route. This appears in the routing table where 192.168.100.0 appears as a directly connected route represented by a *C* preceding the route instead of an EIGRP route represented by and *EX*.

## Lab Task 2: Add R3 and R4's EO Network into EIGRP AS 100

Next, add R3 and R4's E0 network into EIGRP AS 100. After doing so, you should expect to see additional EIGRP routes being advertised to these networks through EIGRP. Example 10-7 shows how these networks are added on R3 and R4.

**Example 10-7** *Configuring R3 and R4's E0 Network as Part of AS 100*

```
R3#conf t
Enter configuration commands, one per line.  End with CNTL/Z.
R3(config)#router eigrp 100
R3(config-router)#network 192.168.3.0
R3(config-router)#end
R3#
%SYS-5-CONFIG_I: Configured from console by console
R3#

Termserver#4
[Resuming connection 4 to r4 ... ]


R4#conf t
Enter configuration commands, one per line.  End with CNTL/Z.
R4(config)#router eigrp 100
R4(config-router)#network 192.168.4.0
R4(config-router)#end
R4#
%SYS-5-CONFIG_I: Configured from console by console
R4#
```

Now, if you display the routing table on R3, you should see that R3 has learned R4's E0 network in addition to R4's Loopback0 network, which were advertised through EIGRP, as shown in Example 10-8.

**Example 10-8** *R3 Displays EIGRP Route to R4's E0 Network of 192.168.4.0 and to R4's Loopback0 Network of 192.169.4.0*

```
Termserver#3
[Resuming connection 3 to r3 ... ]

R3#show ip route
Codes: C - connected, S - static, I - IGRP, R - RIP, M - mobile, B - BGP
       D - EIGRP, EX - EIGRP external, O - OSPF, IA - OSPF inter area
       N1 - OSPF NSSA external type 1, N2 - OSPF NSSA external type 2
       E1 - OSPF external type 1, E2 - OSPF external type 2, E - EGP
       i - IS-IS, L1 - IS-IS level-1, L2 - IS-IS level-2, * - candidate default
```

*continues*

**Example 10-8** *R3 Displays EIGRP Route to R4's E0 Network of 192.168.4.0 and to R4's Loopback0 Network of 192.169.4.0 (Continued)*

```
          U - per-user static route, o - ODR

Gateway of last resort is not set

C    192.168.100.0/24 is directly connected, Serial0
C    192.168.35.0/24 is directly connected, Serial1
I    192.168.50.0/24 [100/8539] via 192.168.35.5, 00:00:35, Serial1
C    192.169.3.0/24 is directly connected, Loopback0
C    192.168.3.0/24 is directly connected, Ethernet0
D    192.168.4.0/24 [90/2195456] via 192.168.100.4, 00:00:49, Serial0
D    192.169.4.0/24 [90/2297856] via 192.168.100.4, 00:06:28, Serial0
I    192.169.5.0/24 [100/8976] via 192.168.35.5, 00:00:35, Serial1
R3#
```

Conversely, R4's routing table shows that R3's E0 network of 192.168.3.0 was learned through EIGRP, as shown in the highlighted section of Example 10-9.

**Example 10-9** *R4 Displays EIGRP Route to R3's E0 Network of 192.168.3.0*

```
R4#show ip route
Codes: C - connected, S - static, I - IGRP, R - RIP, M - mobile, B - BGP
       D - EIGRP, EX - EIGRP external, O - OSPF, IA - OSPF inter area
       N1 - OSPF NSSA external type 1, N2 - OSPF NSSA external type 2
       E1 - OSPF external type 1, E2 - OSPF external type 2, E - EGP
       i - IS-IS, L1 - IS-IS level-1, L2 - IS-IS level-2, * - candidate default
       U - per-user static route, o - ODR

Gateway of last resort is not set

C    192.168.100.0/24 is directly connected, Serial0
D    192.168.3.0/24 [90/2195456] via 192.168.100.3, 00:04:15, Serial0
     192.168.4.0/24 is variably subnetted, 2 subnets, 2 masks
D    192.168.4.0/24 is a summary, 00:04:33, Null0
C    192.168.4.0/27 is directly connected, Ethernet0
C    192.169.4.0/24 is directly connected, Loopback0
R4#
```

Finally, examine the routing table of R2, as shown in Example 10-10. Based on what you've seen regarding how EIGRP works on R3 and R4, at first glance you might expect R2 to learn, through EIGRP, routes to R4 and R3's E0 networks and R4's Loopback0 network—more specifically, routes to 192.168.3.0, 192.168.4.0, and 192.169.4.0.

**Example 10-10** *R2's Routing Table Shows Route to 192.168.3.0 but Not to 192.168.4.0*

```
Termserver#2
[Resuming connection 2 to r2 ... ]

R2#show ip route
Codes: C - connected, S - static, I - IGRP, R - RIP, M - mobile, B - BGP
       D - EIGRP, EX - EIGRP external, O - OSPF, IA - OSPF inter area
       N1 - OSPF NSSA external type 1, N2 - OSPF NSSA external type 2
       E1 - OSPF external type 1, E2 - OSPF external type 2, E - EGP
       i - IS-IS, L1 - IS-IS level-1, L2 - IS-IS level-2, * - candidate default
       U - per-user static route, o - ODR

Gateway of last resort is not set

C    192.168.1.0/24 is directly connected, Ethernet0
R    192.169.1.0/24 [120/1] via 192.168.1.1, 00:00:08, Ethernet0
C    192.168.2.0/24 is directly connected, Ethernet1
C    192.169.2.0/24 is directly connected, Loopback0
C    192.168.100.0/24 is directly connected, Serial0
D    192.168.3.0/24 [90/2195456] via 192.168.100.3, 00:00:56, Serial0
R2#
```

Notice that R2 has learned the route to 192.168.3.0 through EIGRP but not to 192.168.4.0 or 192.169.4.0. Because you know that R4 advertised the 192.168.4.0 and 192.169.4.0 routes to R3 and each route shows up correctly in R3's routing table (see Example 10-8), you might wonder why these routes were not passed on to R2. The rule of split horizon explains this:

> Information about routes is prevented from exiting the router interface through which that information was received.

Although these routes were learned by R3, split horizon prevents them from being passed out R3's S0 interface to R2 because it is the same interface that the routes were learned on initially. To disable split horizon for EIGRP, enter interface configuration mode and use the following command:

```
Router(config-if)#no ip split-horizon eigrp [autonomous-system]
```

Split horizon is a key consideration in hub-and-spoke Frame Relay networks when not using point-to-point subinterfaces. Disable EIGRP split horizon on R3 by entering the interface configuration mode of S0 and executing the command shown in Example 10-11.

**Example 10-11** *Disabling EIGRP Split Horizon on R3's S0 Interface*

```
R3#conf t
Enter configuration commands, one per line.  End with CNTL/Z.
R3(config)#int s0
R3(config-if)#no ip split-horizon eigrp 100
R3(config-if)#end
R3#
```

Now that split horizon has been disabled for EIGRP on R3's S0 interface, when you return
to R2 and display the routing table, you should see that R2 has learned the routes to network
192.168.4.0 and 192.169.4.0, as shown in Example 10-12. These routes were passed on to
R2 through R3 after split horizon was disabled on the R3's S0 interface.

**Example 10-12** *After Split Horizon Is Disabled on R3's S0 Interface, R2 Successfully Learns Routes to 192.168.4.0*
*and 192.169.4.0*

```
R2#show ip route
Codes: C - connected, S - static, I - IGRP, R - RIP, M - mobile, B - BGP
       D - EIGRP, EX - EIGRP external, O - OSPF, IA - OSPF inter area
       N1 - OSPF NSSA external type 1, N2 - OSPF NSSA external type 2
       E1 - OSPF external type 1, E2 - OSPF external type 2, E - EGP
       i - IS-IS, L1 - IS-IS level-1, L2 - IS-IS level-2, * - candidate default
       U - per-user static route, o - ODR

Gateway of last resort is not set

D     192.168.4.0/24 [90/2707456] via 192.168.100.3, 00:02:08, Serial0
D     192.169.4.0/24 [90/2809856] via 192.168.100.3, 00:02:08, Serial0
C     192.168.1.0/24 is directly connected, Ethernet0
R     192.169.1.0/24 [120/1] via 192.168.1.1, 00:00:11, Ethernet0
C     192.168.2.0/24 is directly connected, Ethernet1
C     192.169.2.0/24 is directly connected, Loopback0
C     192.168.100.0/24 is directly connected, Serial0
D     192.168.3.0/24 [90/2195456] via 192.168.100.3, 00:02:09, Serial0
R2#
```

Now that R2 has a route to R4's E0 network of 192.168.4.0 and to R4's Loopback0 network
of 192.169.4.0, R2 should be capable of **ping**ing 192.168.4.4 and 192.169.4.4, as shown in
Example 10-13.

**Example 10-13** *R2 Can Ping R4's E0 and Loopback0 Interfaces After the Route Is Learned Through EIGRP*

```
R2#ping 192.168.4.4

Type escape sequence to abort.
Sending 5, 100-byte ICMP Echos to 192.168.4.4, timeout is 2 seconds:
!!!!!
Success rate is 100 percent (5/5), round-trip min/avg/max = 88/92/104 ms
R2#


R2#ping 192.169.4.4

Type escape sequence to abort.
Sending 5, 100-byte ICMP Echos to 192.168.4.4, timeout is 2 seconds:
!!!!!
Success rate is 100 percent (5/5), round-trip min/avg/max = 88/92/104 ms
R2#
```

With the proper routes in the routing table, R2 successfully **ping**s R4's E0 and loopback0 interfaces.

## Lab Task 3 & 4: Create Two Loopback Interfaces on R4 with Specified Network Addresses, and Place R4's Loopback0 into EIGRP 100

Next, resume the connection to R4 and configure two new additional loopback interfaces. Create loopback1 with an address of 200.200.1.4 and loopback2 with an address of 200.200.2.4, as shown in Example 10-14.

**Example 10-14** *Configuring R4 with Loopback Interfaces 200.200.1.4 and 200.200.2.4*

```
Termserver#4
[Resuming connection 4 to r4 ... ]

R4#conf t
Enter configuration commands, one per line.  End with CNTL/Z.
R4(config)#int loopback1
R4(config-if)#ip addre
%LINEPROTO-5-UPDOWN: Line protocol on Interface Loopback1, changed state to up
R4(config-if)#ip address 200.200.1.4 255.255.255.0
R4(config-if)#exit
R4(config)#int loopback2
R4(config-if)#
%LINEPROTO-5-UPDOWN: Line protocol on Interface Loopback2, changed state to up
R4(config-if)#ip address 200.200.2.4 255.255.255.0
R4(config-if)#^Z
R4#
```

## Lab Task 5: Add the Two Networks into the EIGRP Routing Domain, and Configure R4 So That All Other Routers See Only One Route to These Two Addresses

Each loopback interface represents a network. These two networks are advertised in the EIGRP routing process on R4 to R3 and R2 and are used to demonstrate route summarization. Route summarization is the process of condensing routing information. This process also is referred to as route aggregation, classless interdomain routing (CIDR), or supernetting. Without summarization, each router in a network must retain a route to every subnet in the network. With summarization, routers can reduce a group of routes to a single advertisement called a *summary route*. Route summarization reduces the load on the router by decreasing the number of CPU processing cycles required for route propagation and routing information overhead.

In large networks, summarization is a useful technique to consolidate hundreds or possibly thousands of routes propagated within an autonomous system. Instead, a summary route is advertised that represents the path to multiple routes. As the network increases in size, the more important route summarization becomes. The simplest form of route summarization is collapsing all the subnet routes into a single network route at the classful bit boundary. By default, EIGRP automatically summarizes in this fashion; however, EIGRP also supports route summarization at any bit boundary rather than just at the major network number boundary. This is possible because EIGRP supports VLSM.

Next, add the two loopback networks created on R4 to EIGRP AS 100, as shown in Example 10-15.

**Example 10-15** *Adding Loopback1 and Loopback2 to EIGRP AS 100 on R4*

```
R4#conf t
Enter configuration commands, one per line.  End with CNTL/Z.
R4(config)#router eigrp 100
R4(config-router)#network 200.200.1.0
R4(config-router)#network 200.200.2.0
R4(config-router)#^Z
R4#
```

Go to R3 and examine the routing table of R3 to verify that the loopback networks added on R4 are being advertised through EIGRP. Example 10-16 shows that networks 200.200.1.0 and 200.200.2.0 have been advertised and that R3 learned these through EIGRP.

**Example 10-16** *Networks 200.200.1.0 and 200.200.2.0 Advertised to R3 Through EIGRP*

```
Termserver#3
[Resuming connection 3 to r3 ... ]

R3#show ip route
Codes: C - connected, S - static, I - IGRP, R - RIP, M - mobile, B - BGP
       D - EIGRP, EX - EIGRP external, O - OSPF, IA - OSPF inter area
       N1 - OSPF NSSA external type 1, N2 - OSPF NSSA external type 2
       E1 - OSPF external type 1, E2 - OSPF external type 2, E - EGP
       i - IS-IS, L1 - IS-IS level-1, L2 - IS-IS level-2, * - candidate default
       U - per-user static route, o - ODR

Gateway of last resort is not set

D    200.200.1.0/24 [90/2297856] via 192.168.100.4, 00:00:03, Serial0
D    200.200.2.0/24 [90/2297856] via 192.168.100.4, 00:00:03, Serial0
C    192.168.100.0/24 is directly connected, Serial0
C    192.168.35.0/24 is directly connected, Serial1
I    192.168.50.0/24 [100/8539] via 192.168.35.5, 00:00:03, Serial1
C    192.169.3.0/24 is directly connected, Loopback0
C    192.168.3.0/24 is directly connected, Ethernet0
I    192.169.5.0/24 [100/8976] via 192.168.35.5, 00:00:03, Serial1
D    192.168.4.0/24 [90/2195456] via 192.168.100.4, 00:00:03, Serial0
D    192.169.4.0/24 [90/2297856] via 192.168.100.4, 00:00:03, Serial0
R3#
```

To ensure that split horizon is not an issue, verify that R2 is receiving these EIGRP loopback networks through EIGRP from R3, as shown in Example 10-17.

**Example 10-17** *R2 Receives R4 Loopback Networks as Expected*

```
Termserver#2
[Resuming connection 2 to r2 ... ]

R2#show ip route
Codes: C - connected, S - static, I - IGRP, R - RIP, M - mobile, B - BGP
       D - EIGRP, EX - EIGRP external, O - OSPF, IA - OSPF inter area
       N1 - OSPF NSSA external type 1, N2 - OSPF NSSA external type 2
       E1 - OSPF external type 1, E2 - OSPF external type 2, E - EGP
       i - IS-IS, L1 - IS-IS level-1, L2 - IS-IS level-2, * - candidate default
       U - per-user static route, o - ODR

Gateway of last resort is not set

D    200.200.1.0/24 [90/2809856] via 192.168.100.3, 00:01:13, Serial0
D    200.200.2.0/24 [90/2809856] via 192.168.100.3, 00:01:14, Serial0
D    192.168.4.0/24 [90/2707456] via 192.168.100.3, 00:01:14, Serial0
C    192.168.1.0/24 is directly connected, Ethernet0
R    192.169.1.0/24 [120/1] via 192.168.1.1, 00:00:16, Ethernet0
C    192.168.2.0/24 is directly connected, Ethernet1
C    192.169.2.0/24 is directly connected, Loopback0
C    192.168.100.0/24 is directly connected, Serial0
D    192.168.3.0/24 [90/2195456] via 192.168.100.3, 00:36:35, Serial0
D    192.169.3.0/24 [90/2809856] via 192.168.100.3, 00:36:35, Serial0
R2#
```

You can see that R2 has received network 200.200.1.0 and 200.200.2.0 as desired and that split horizon is not an issue. Verify that R2 can **ping** these newly created loopbacks on R4, as shown in Example 10-18.

**Example 10-18** *R2 Can* **ping** *R4's Newly Created Loopback Addresses*

```
R2#ping 200.200.1.4

Type escape sequence to abort.
Sending 5, 100-byte ICMP Echos to 200.200.1.4, timeout is 2 seconds:
!!!!!
Success rate is 100 percent (5/5), round-trip min/avg/max = 88/92/104 ms

R2#ping 200.200.2.4

Type escape sequence to abort.
Sending 5, 100-byte ICMP Echos to 200.200.2.4, timeout is 2 seconds:
!!!!!
Success rate is 100 percent (5/5), round-trip min/avg/max = 88/91/100 ms
R2#
```

So far, so good. However, the lab objective explicitly states that these two loopbacks should be added to the EIGRP routing domain and that you need to configure R4 so that all other routers see only one route to these two addresses. This objective is accomplished through configuring route summarization. By doing so, you will summarize the two Class C loopback addresses into one Class B summary address that will be advertised from R4 to R3 and R2 through EIGRP. As mentioned previously, because EIGRP supports VLSM, you can summarize these two addresses at any bit boundary rather than just at the major Class B network number boundary if you desire. For the purposes here, however, you need to summarize at the Class B boundary.

A summary address is configured in interface configuration mode of the interface from which you want the summarized address to be advertised. In the lab, a summary address of 200.200.0.0 is configured on R4's S0 interface and is advertised out to the rest of the network. In addition, you will need to turn off autosummary within the EIGRP routing process of R4. Autosummary is on by default when the EIGRP routing process is started. Turn off autosummary so that *only* the summarized Class B route is advertised from R4. If autosummary was not turned off, R4 would advertise the Class B summary address that you will configure on R4's S0 interface in addition to the two Class C addresses of each loopback (that is, 200.200.1.0 and 200.200.2.0). By turning off autosummary, you ensure that *only* the Class B summary address is advertised to the rest of the network.

To configure a summary address and ensure that only one summary route is advertised from R4, two steps are required, as shown in Table 10-2.

**Table 10-2**    *Configuring a Summary Address and Ensuring That Only One Summary Route Is Advertised*

| Step | Command |
|------|---------|
| 1. Disable automatic route summarization in router configuration mode. | Router(config-router)#**no auto-summary** |
| 2. Configure a summary address in interface configuration mode of the desired interface from which the summary address will be advertised. | Router(config-if)# **ip summary-address eigrp** [*autonomous-system #*] [*network address*] [*mask*] |

After a summary address is configured, if there are any more specific routes in the routing table, EIGRP will advertise the summary address out the interface with a metric equal to the minimum of all more specific routes.

First, disable autosummary within the EIGRP routing process on R4, as shown in Example 10-19.

**Example 10-19** *Disabling Autosummary on R4 to Prevent Route Advertisements of 200.200.1.0 and 200.200.2.0*

```
R4#conf t
Enter configuration commands, one per line.  End with CNTL/Z.
R4(config)#router eigrp 100
R4(config-router)#no auto-summary
R4(config-router)#^Z
```

**Example 10-19** *Disabling Autosummary on R4 to Prevent Route Advertisements of 200.200.1.0 and 200.200.2.0*

```
R4#
%SYS-5-CONFIG_I: Configured from console by console
R4#
```

As mentioned previously, this prevents routes 200.200.1.0 and 200.200.2.0 from being automatically summarized at their default major network boundary and being subsequently advertised through EIGRP to R3 and R2.

Next, configure a summary address of 200.200.0.0 on R4's S0. This is the interface that you want the summary address to be advertised from. Example 10-20 shows the summary address configuration.

**Example 10-20** *Configuring a Summary Address on R4 of 200.200.200.0 to Be Advertised Out S0*

```
R4#conf t
Enter configuration commands, one per line.  End with CNTL/Z.
R4(config)#int s0
R4(config-if)#ip summary-address eigrp 100 200.200.0.0 255.255.0.0
R4(config-if)#^Z
R4#
%SYS-5-CONFIG_I: Configured from console by console
R4#
```

R4 now has been configured to advertise the summary address of 200.200.0.0 out its S0 interface to the rest of the network. Now examine the routing table on R4 to see how the summary address appears in the routing table as shown in Example 10-21.

**Example 10-21** *R4 Routing Table Show How the Summary Address Appears After Configuration*

```
R4#show ip route
Codes: C - connected, S - static, I - IGRP, R - RIP, M - mobile, B - BGP
       D - EIGRP, EX - EIGRP external, O - OSPF, IA - OSPF inter area
       N1 - OSPF NSSA external type 1, N2 - OSPF NSSA external type 2
       E1 - OSPF external type 1, E2 - OSPF external type 2, E - EGP
       i - IS-IS, L1 - IS-IS level-1, L2 - IS-IS level-2, * - candidate default
       U - per-user static route, o - ODR

Gateway of last resort is not set

C    200.200.1.0/24 is directly connected, Loopback1
C    200.200.2.0/24 is directly connected, Loopback2
C    192.168.100.0/24 is directly connected, Serial0
D    192.168.3.0/24 [90/2195456] via 192.168.100.3, 00:00:00, Serial0
     192.168.4.0/27 is subnetted, 1 subnets
C    192.168.4.0 is directly connected, Ethernet0
```

*continues*

**Example 10-21** *R4 Routing Table Show How the Summary Address Appears After Configuration (Continued)*

```
C     192.169.4.0/24 is directly connected, Loopback0
D     200.200.0.0/16 is a summary, 00:00:36, Null0
R4#
```

R4's routing table has added a summary route of 200.200.0.0/16 pointing to Null0. Null0 is also known as the *bit bucket*, meaning that the router drops all packets routed to Null0. Essentially, the summary address route is displayed on R4's routing table for informational purposes. It does not affect the routing of packets because R4 has more specific routes pointing to the specific networks of 200.200.1.0 and 200.200.2.0. Thus, the summary route of 200.200.0.0 is advertised to the rest of the network, but when packets are forwarded to R4 destined for either network, R4 forwards the packets to the more specific routes of 200.200.1.0 or 200.200.2.0. In this way, you can consolidate these two routes using summarization and then advertise the summary route to the remainder of the network, while still maintaining specific routes to these destinations on R4.

---

**NOTE**     This concept is known as longest match routing. The router selects a route from its routing table that has the longest matching value to the destination IP address in the IP packet. For example, assume that router R4 receives an IP packet with a destination IP address of 200.200.1.1. The router will parse through its routing table to determine which route has the longest match to 200.200.1.1. R4 will choose 200.200.1.0 instead of 200.200.0.0 because 200.200.1.0 matches the first three octets instead of only the first two octets. When the longest match is found, the router forwards the packet to the loopback interface.

---

Now that you've configured a summary address of 200.200.0.0 on R4, check R3 and R2's routing table to see if the summary route has been advertised as designed. Resume the connection to R3 to check the routing table, as demonstrated in Example 10-22.

**Example 10-22** *Summary Address of 200.200.0.0 Advertised Successfully from R4 to R3*

```
Termserver#3
[Resuming connection 3 to r3 ... ]

R3#show ip route
Codes: C - connected, S - static, I - IGRP, R - RIP, M - mobile, B - BGP
       D - EIGRP, EX - EIGRP external, O - OSPF, IA - OSPF inter area
       N1 - OSPF NSSA external type 1, N2 - OSPF NSSA external type 2
       E1 - OSPF external type 1, E2 - OSPF external type 2, E - EGP
       i - IS-IS, L1 - IS-IS level-1, L2 - IS-IS level-2, * - candidate default
       U - per-user static route, o - ODR

Gateway of last resort is not set
```

**Example 10-22**  *Summary Address of 200.200.0.0 Advertised Successfully from R4 to R3 (Continued)*

```
C    192.168.100.0/24 is directly connected, Serial0
C    192.168.35.0/24 is directly connected, Serial1
I    192.168.50.0/24 [100/8539] via 192.168.35.5, 00:01:06, Serial1
C    192.169.3.0/24 is directly connected, Loopback0
C    192.168.3.0/24 is directly connected, Ethernet0
     192.168.4.0/27 is subnetted, 1 subnets
D    192.168.4.0 [90/2195456] via 192.168.100.4, 00:01:24, Serial0
D    192.169.4.0 [90/2297856] via 192.168.100.4, 00:01:24, Serial0
I    192.169.5.0/24 [100/8976] via 192.168.35.5, 00:01:07, Serial1
D    200.200.0.0/16 [90/2297856] via 192.168.100.4, 00:01:24, Serial0
R3#
```

The output in Example 10-22 shows that R3 has received the summary address configured on R4's S0 interface. Next, check R2's routing table. Remember that before configuring a summary address on R4, R3 and R2 were receiving two loopback routes—one to 200.200.1.0 and one to 200.200.2.0 (see Example 10-17). Now, if you display R2's routing table, you should see the results in Example 10-23.

**Example 10-23**  *Summary Address of 200.200.0.0 Advertised Successfully Propagated to R2*

```
Termserver#2
[Resuming connection 2 to r2 ... ]

R2#show ip route
Codes: C - connected, S - static, I - IGRP, R - RIP, M - mobile, B - BGP
       D - EIGRP, EX - EIGRP external, O - OSPF, IA - OSPF inter area
       N1 - OSPF NSSA external type 1, N2 - OSPF NSSA external type 2
       E1 - OSPF external type 1, E2 - OSPF external type 2, E - EGP
       i - IS-IS, L1 - IS-IS level-1, L2 - IS-IS level-2, * - candidate default
       U - per-user static route, o - ODR

Gateway of last resort is not set

     192.168.4.0/27 is subnetted, 1 subnets
D    192.168.4.0 [90/2707456] via 192.168.100.3, 00:01:35, Serial0
C    192.168.1.0/24 is directly connected, Ethernet0
R    192.169.1.0/24 [120/1] via 192.168.1.1, 00:00:10, Ethernet0
C    192.168.2.0/24 is directly connected, Ethernet1
C    192.169.2.0/24 is directly connected, Loopback0
C    192.168.100.0/24 is directly connected, Serial0
D    192.168.3.0/24 [90/2195456] via 192.168.100.3, 00:42:24, Serial0
D    192.169.3.0/24 [90/2809856] via 192.168.100.3, 00:42:24, Serial0
D    200.200.0.0/16 [90/2809856] via 192.168.100.3, 00:01:35, Serial0
R2#
```

R2 now is getting only the summarized route of 200.200.0.0, as designed. Thus, you know that these two Class C routes have been properly summarized on R4 and advertised successfully through EIGRP to R3 and R2, per the lab objective.

With only a summary address in the routing table of R2, you need to determine whether R2 can still **ping** the loopback addresses of R4 by initiating a **ping** to each of R4's loopback addresses, as shown in Example 10-24.

**Example 10-24**  *After Receiving the Summary Address of 200.200.0.0, R2 Still Can Successfully* **ping** *Each of R4's Loopback Addresses*

```
R2#ping 200.200.1.4

Type escape sequence to abort.
Sending 5, 100-byte ICMP Echos to 200.200.1.4, timeout is 2 seconds:
!!!!!
Success rate is 100 percent (5/5), round-trip min/avg/max = 88/92/100 ms

R2#ping 200.200.2.4

Type escape sequence to abort.
Sending 5, 100-byte ICMP Echos to 200.200.2.4, timeout is 2 seconds:
!!!!!
Success rate is 100 percent (5/5), round-trip min/avg/max = 88/93/104 ms
R2#
```

You now have successfully configured EIGRP between R2, R3, and R4, adding the required networks into EIGRP AS 100. In addition, you have summarized the two loopback networks of 200.200.1.0 and 200.200.2.0 on R4 into one route of 200.200.0.0, and you have advertised this summary address to the rest of your network. The next section examines some commands useful to verifying the configuration and operation of EIGRP.

## Verifying EIGRP Configuration and Operation

To verify the EIGRP configuration and ensure that the proper networks are configured for EIGRP, a few commands are helpful. These two important **show** commands are used quite extensively while configuring EIGRP between R2, R3, and R4:

```
show ip eigrp neighbors
show ip route
```

The **show ip eigrp neighbors** command is useful for verifying that two neighboring routers configured for EIGRP have established a neighbor relationship and thus will be capable of exchanging EIGRP routing information. The **show ip route** command is useful for verifying that expected EIGRP routes have been learned and have made it into the routing table. If additional review of either command is needed, refer back within this chapter to see how each command was used to verify and troubleshoot the EIGRP configuration in the lab environment.

The remaining commands that provide helpful information concerning EIGRP configuration as well as foster an understanding of how the EIGRP configuration should appear in the running configuration are as follows:

```
show ip protocols
show running-config
show ip eigrp topology
```

## show ip protocols Command

Begin by returning to R3 and executing the **show ip protocols** command. Currently, R3 is configured for two routing protocols—IGRP and EIGRP. Execute the command on R3, and examine the EIGRP information as shown in Example 10-25.

**Example 10-25**  *Output of* **show ip protocols** *on R3*

```
R3#show ip protocols
Routing Protocol is "igrp 200"
  Sending updates every 90 seconds, next due in 41 seconds
  Invalid after 270 seconds, hold down 280, flushed after 630
  Outgoing update filter list for all interfaces is not set
  Incoming update filter list for all interfaces is not set
  Default networks flagged in outgoing updates
  Default networks accepted from incoming updates
  IGRP metric weight K1=1, K2=0, K3=1, K4=0, K5=0
  IGRP maximum hopcount 100
  IGRP maximum metric variance 1
  Redistributing: igrp 200
  Routing for Networks:
    192.168.35.0
    192.169.3.0
  Routing Information Sources:
    Gateway         Distance      Last Update
    192.168.35.5          100      00:00:02
  Distance: (default is 100)

Routing Protocol is "eigrp 100"
  Outgoing update filter list for all interfaces is not set
  Incoming update filter list for all interfaces is not set
  Default networks flagged in outgoing updates
  Default networks accepted from incoming updates
  EIGRP metric weight K1=1, K2=0, K3=1, K4=0, K5=0
  EIGRP maximum hopcount 100
  EIGRP maximum metric variance 1
  Redistributing: eigrp 100
  Automatic network summarization is in effect
  Automatic address summarization:
    192.168.100.0/24 for Ethernet0
```

*continues*

**Example 10-25** *Output of* **show ip protocols** *on R3 (Continued)*

```
      192.168.3.0/24 for Serial0
  Routing for Networks:
    192.168.100.0
    192.168.3.0
  Routing Information Sources:
    Gateway          Distance      Last Update
    192.168.100.4          90      00:55:52
    192.168.100.2          90      00:55:52
  Distance: internal 90 external 170

R3#
```

The output shows that that R3 is running IGRP and EIGRP. The EIGRP section shows that you are running EIGRP with AS 100, as displayed by the following information:

```
Routing Protocol is "eigrp 100"
```

Next, you can see that automatic network summarization is in effect for networks 192.168.100.0/24 (E0) and 192.168.3.0/24 (S0). When the EIGRP routing process is started on a router, automatic network summarization is on by default, and EIGRP automatically summarizes at the major network boundary, as you can see for E0 and S0. To turn it off, as you did on R4, you need to use the **no auto-summary** command under the EIGRP routing process.

Next, the output shows that EIGRP is advertising networks 192.168.100.0 and 192.168.3.0, as indicated by the following information:

```
Routing for Networks:
    192.168.100.0
    192.168.3.0
```

Finally, you can see that R3 has two EIGRP neighbors—one to R2 and one to R4. From these two sources, R3 is receiving EIGRP routing information, as shown from the following portion of the output:

```
Routing Information Sources:
    Gateway          Distance      Last Update
    192.168.100.4          90      00:55:52
    192.168.100.2          90      00:55:52
```

Now that you have a basic idea of some of the information available using the **show ip protocols** command for EIGRP, go to R4 and see how R4 differs from R3. Execute the **show ip protocols** command on R4 results in the output displayed in Example 10-26.

**Example 10-26** **show ip protocols** *Output on R4*

```
R4#show ip protocols
Routing Protocol is "eigrp 100"
  Outgoing update filter list for all interfaces is not set
  Incoming update filter list for all interfaces is not set
  Default networks flagged in outgoing updates
```

**Example 10-26** **show ip protocols** *Output on R4 (Continued)*

```
    Default networks accepted from incoming updates
    EIGRP metric weight K1=1, K2=0, K3=1, K4=0, K5=0
    EIGRP maximum hopcount 100
    EIGRP maximum metric variance 1
    Redistributing: eigrp 100
    Automatic network summarization is not in effect
    Address Summarization:
      200.200.0.0/16 for Serial0
        Summarizing with metric 128256
    Routing for Networks:
      192.168.100.0
      192.168.4.0
      200.200.1.0
      200.200.2.0
      192.169.4.0
    Routing Information Sources:
      Gateway          Distance      Last Update
      (this router)           5      3d05h
      192.168.100.3          90      00:36:05
    Distance: internal 90 external 170

R4#
```

R4 shows that automatic network summarization is not in effect. This is expected because you disabled autosummary on R4. In addition, R4 shows that you are summarizing 200.200.1.0 and 200.200.2.0 to 200.200.0.0/16 and that you are advertising this summarized route out the Serial0 interface. Lastly, you can see that R4 has five networks being advertised in EIGRP AS 100, two of which have been summarized.

## show running-config Command

If you look at the running configuration on R4, you should be able to derive much of the same information as the output from **show ip protocols**. The highlighted area of Example 10-27 shows the EIGRP configuration on R4.

**Example 10-27** *Running Configuration on R4 Shows EIGRP Configuration*

```
R4#show running-config
Building configuration...

Current configuration:
!
version 11.2
no service password-encryption
no service udp-small-servers
no service tcp-small-servers
!
hostname R4
```

*continues*

**Example 10-27** *Running Configuration on R4 Shows EIGRP Configuration (Continued)*

```
!
enable password falcons
!
ip subnet-zero
no ip domain-lookup
ip host R1 192.169.1.1
ip host R2 192.169.2.2
ip host R3 192.169.3.3
ip host R4 192.169.4.4
ip host R5 192.169.5.5
ip host R6 192.169.6.6
!
interface Loopback0
 ip address 192.169.4.4 255.255.255.0
!
interface Loopback1
 ip address 200.200.1.4 255.255.255.0
!
interface Loopback2
 ip address 200.200.2.4 255.255.255.0
!
interface Ethernet0
 description This interface does not connect to another IP device
 ip address 192.168.4.4 255.255.255.224
!
interface Serial0
 description This interface connects to R3's S0 (DLCI 101)
 ip address 192.168.100.4 255.255.255.0
 ip summary-address eigrp 100 200.200.0.0 255.255.0.0
 encapsulation frame-relay
 frame-relay map ip 192.168.100.2 101 broadcast
 frame-relay map ip 192.168.100.3 101 broadcast
 frame-relay lmi-type ansi
!
interface Serial1
 no ip address
 shutdown
!
router eigrp 100
 network 192.168.100.0
 network 192.168.4.0
 network 200.200.1.0
 network 200.200.2.0
 network 192.169.4.0
 no auto-summary
!
no ip classless
!
banner motd ^CC
This is Router 4
^C
!
```

**Example 10-27**  *Running Configuration on R4 Shows EIGRP Configuration (Continued)*

```
line con 0
 exec-timeout 0 0
 password falcons
 logging synchronous
line aux 0
line vty 0 4
 password falcons
 login

R4#
```

You can verify that what you see in the running configuration parallels what you saw in the **show ip protocols** output—namely, that five networks have been placed in EIGRP AS 100, two of which have been summarized to 200.200.0.0/16 and advertised out S0. In addition, autosummary has been disabled on R4 using the **no auto-summary** command. The EIGRP configuration looks exactly as expected.

## show ip eigrp topology Command

Another useful EIGRP troubleshooting command is **show ip eigrp topology**, which gives you the capability to view the EIGRP topology table, as demonstrated for R3 in Example 10-28.

**Example 10-28**  *EIGRP Topology Table on R3 Indicates That All Routes Are in the Passive State*

```
R3#show ip eigrp topology
IP-EIGRP Topology Table for process 100

Codes: P - Passive, A - Active, U - Update, Q - Query, R - Reply,
       r - Reply status

P 200.200.0.0/16, 1 successors, FD is 2297856
        via 192.168.100.4 (2297856/128256), Serial0
P 192.168.100.0/24, 1 successors, FD is 2169856
        via Connected, Serial0
P 192.168.3.0/24, 1 successors, FD is 281600
        via Connected, Ethernet0
P 192.168.4.0/27, 1 successors, FD is 2195456
        via 192.168.100.4 (2195456/281600), Serial0
P 192.169.4.0/24, 1 successors, FD is 2297856
        via 192.168.100.4 (2297856/128256), Serial0
R3#
```

As discussed earlier, EIGRP maintains a topology table that contains all destinations advertised by neighboring routers. A destination is moved from the topology table to the routing table when there is a feasible successor. An entry in the topology table can have one of two states—passive or active. A route in the topology table is in the passive state when the router is not performing a route recomputation. It is in an active state when undergoing a route recomputation. If there are always feasible successors, a route never has to go into the active state and avoids a route recomputation. Viewing the topology table can help you determine whether a route recomputation is occurring, causing you not to see expected EIGRP routes in the routing table. Currently, you can see that all of R3's routes in the topology table are in the passive state, so expected routes should be advertised properly into the routing table.

# Summary

You have now successfully configured EIGRP and verified its proper operation. Now that EIGRP has been configured between R2, R3, and R4, you should draw the EIGRP routing domains on the master lab diagram. This will help you to distinguish the RIP, IGRP, and EIGRP routing boundaries. In addition, this will be necessary to understanding route redistribution covered in the next chapter. Figure 10-3 shows a visual representation of the EIGRP routing domains you have just configured.

**Figure 10-3**  *EIGRP Routing Domain*

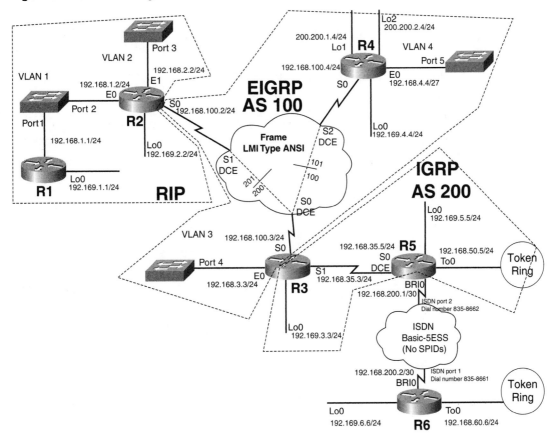

You are now ready to configure basic route redistribution and verify its operation.

This chapter covers the following key topics:

- Fundamentals of route redistribution
- Route redistribution between RIP and EIGRP
- Route redistribution between IGRP and EIGRP

## CHAPTER 11

# Route Redistribution

This chapter covers how to redistribute, or transfer, routes between routing domains and how to troubleshoot routing issues due to route redistribution. This is above and beyond the scope of the CCNA exam, but for practical knowledge it is very important. Route redistribution is a very popular way of exchanging routing information between two disparate routing protocols. Many organizations use route redistribution, so an introduction to this concept seemed prudent. This chapter might not give you direct help in passing the CCNA exam, but it will make you a better internetworking professional and a more capable network engineer.

## Fundamentals of Route Redistribution

Route redistribution involves placing the routes learned from one routing domain, such as RIP, into another routing domain, such as EIGRP. When this occurs, you have several issues to address, one of which is metrics.

Each routing protocol has its own way of determining the best path to a network. RIP uses hops, and EIGRP and IGRP both use a composite metric of bandwidth, delay, reliability, load, and MTU size. Because of the differences in metric calculations, when redistributing routes, you lose all metrics and must manually specify the cost metric for each routing domain. This is because RIP has no way of translating bandwidth, delay, reliability, load, and MTU size into hops, and vice versa. Another issue to address with route redistribution is that some routing protocols are classful, meaning that the routing protocol does not send subnet mask information in the routing updates (for example, in RIP and IGRP). In addition, some protocols are classless, meaning that the routing protocol does send subnet mask information in the routing updates (for example, in EIGRP). This poses a problem when variable-length subnet masking (VLSM, in which you use a netmask other than the default netmask for the IP address) and classless interdomain routing (CIDR, sometimes referred to as "supernetting" or route summarization) routes need to be redistributed from a classless routing protocol into a classful routing protocol.

Route redistribution can get very complex and can introduce many problems. Sometimes the solutions to the problems are even more complex than the problems themselves. This chapter keeps the situation as basic as possible, to help you understand the issues involved in route redistribution without being overwhelming. Just keep the issues outlined previously in mind as you configure route redistribution in the lab that follows. The lab discusses solutions to the problems as they arise.

# Lab Objectives

Before beginning, review the lab objectives and the routing domains in the network. This will help you understand where route redistribution needs to occur.

- On R2, redistribute RIP into EIGRP and redistribute EIGRP into RIP.

- On R3, redistribute EIGRP into IGRP and redistribute IGRP into EIGRP.

- Fix any routing problems that you encounter as you see fit.

All routers should be capable of **ping**ing all interfaces at the end of this section.

Figure 11-1 outlines the routing domains.

**Figure 11-1** *Routing Domains*

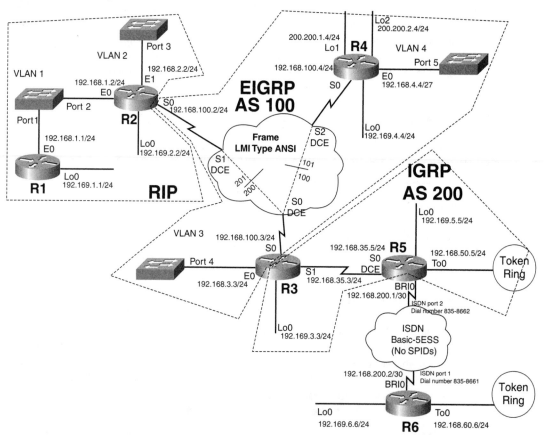

Before beginning with the route redistribution configuration, take a look at each of the router's routing table to see how it appears now and how it will change after redistributing the routes. Example 11-1 depicts the routing tables for the routers thus far.

**Example 11-1** *Router Routing Table*

```
R1#show ip route
Gateway of last resort is not set

C    192.169.1.0/24 is directly connected, Loopback0
C    192.168.1.0/24 is directly connected, Ethernet0
R    192.168.2.0/24 [120/1] via 192.168.1.2, 00:00:10, Ethernet0
R    192.169.2.0/24 [120/1] via 192.168.1.2, 00:00:10, Ethernet0


R2#show ip route
Gateway of last resort is not set

     192.168.4.0/27 is subnetted, 1 subnets
D       192.168.4.0 [90/2707456] via 192.168.100.3, 1d03h, Serial0
C    192.168.1.0/24 is directly connected, Ethernet0
R    192.169.1.0/24 [120/1] via 192.168.1.1, 00:00:02, Ethernet0
C    192.168.2.0/24 is directly connected, Ethernet1
C    192.169.2.0/24 is directly connected, Loopback0
C    192.168.100.0/24 is directly connected, Serial0
D    192.168.3.0/24 [90/2195456] via 192.168.100.3, 2d03h, Serial0
D    200.200.0.0/16 [90/2809856] via 192.168.100.3, 1d03h, Serial0


R3#show ip route
Gateway of last resort is not set

C    192.168.100.0/24 is directly connected, Serial0
C    192.168.35.0/24 is directly connected, Serial1
I    192.168.50.0/24 [100/8539] via 192.168.35.5, 00:01:02, Serial1
C    192.169.3.0/24 is directly connected, Loopback0
C    192.168.3.0/24 is directly connected, Ethernet0
     192.168.4.0/27 is subnetted, 1 subnets
D       192.168.4.0 [90/2195456] via 192.168.100.4, 1d03h, Serial0
D    192.169.4.0/24 [90/2297856] via 192.168.100.4, 00:06:19, Serial0
I    192.169.5.0/24 [100/8976] via 192.168.35.5, 00:01:02, Serial1
D    200.200.0.0/16 [90/2297856] via 192.168.100.4, 1d03h, Serial0


R4#show ip route
Gateway of last resort is not set

C    200.200.1.0/24 is directly connected, Loopback1
C    200.200.2.0/24 is directly connected, Loopback2
C    192.168.100.0/24 is directly connected, Serial0
D    192.168.3.0/24 [90/2195456] via 192.168.100.3, 1d03h, Serial0
     192.168.4.0/27 is subnetted, 1 subnets
C       192.168.4.0 is directly connected, Ethernet0
C    192.169.4.0/24 is directly connected, Loopback0
D    200.200.0.0/16 is a summary, 1d03h, Null0


R5#show ip route
Gateway of last resort is not set
```

*continues*

**Example 11-1** *Router Routing Table (Continued)*

```
C    192.168.35.0/24 is directly connected, Serial0
C    192.168.50.0/24 is directly connected, TokenRing0
I    192.169.3.0/24 [100/8976] via 192.168.35.3, 00:00:45, Serial0
C    192.169.5.0/24 is directly connected, Loopback0
```

Example 11-1 shows that each of the router's routing tables are fairly small and include only the routes pertaining to the routing protocol that each is using. When you have completed this chapter, you should see several more routes and should be able to **ping** every interface on every router, except R6. R6 is unreachable at this time because it will be connected to the network using dial-on-demand routing (DDR) in Chapter 12, "Integrated Services Digital Network (ISDN)."

## Redistributing Between RIP and EIGRP

As you can see, R2 is the boundary for RIP, and EIGRP and R3 is the boundary for EIGRP and IGRP. It is at these two "crossroads" that you will redistribute routes between the routing protocols.

The first lab objective is to redistribute between RIP and EIGRP. To redistribute routes from one protocol to another, you need to issue the **redistribute** command under the routing protocol in which you want to introduce the routes from the other routing protocol. The command syntax to accomplish this is as follows:

```
Router(config-router)# redistribute protocol autonomous-system-number metric
   [route-map map-tag]
```

You need to concern yourself only with the first three parameters of the command. For the *protocol* parameter of the command, you need to supply the routing protocol from which you want to redistribute routes. The *autonomous-system* parameter pertains only to those routing protocols that use autonomous system number identifiers. With the *metric* parameter you manually specify the metrics for the routes being introduced into the routing protocol.

Begin by configuring route redistribution on R2. Redistribute EIGRP routes into RIP and then RIP routes into EIGRP. Example 11-2 demonstrates the command for redistributing EIGRP routes into RIP.

**Example 11-2** *Route Redistribution for RIP on R2*

```
Termserver#2
[Resuming connection 2 to r2 ... ]

R2#
R2#config t
Enter configuration commands, one per line.  End with CNTL/Z.
```

**Example 11-2** *Route Redistribution for RIP on R2 (Continued)*

```
R2(config)#router rip
R2(config-router)#redistribute eigrp 100 metric 1
R2(config-router)#
```

Because RIP uses hop counts, you can set all routes coming from EIGRP as one hop away. As you know, most of these routes are not one hop away, but for RIP to be capable of placing them into the routing table, one hop count is the minimum that you can specify. It is important to review your routing environment before arbitrarily assigning metrics. Because of the simplicity of the lab topology, the metric assignment is not critical, but in a production environment, it is very critical to review metrics because they control the paths selected for your network traffic. Example 11-3 provides the configuration to now redistribute RIP routes into EIGRP AS 100.

**Example 11-3** *Redistributing RIP into EIGRP on R2*

```
R2(config-router)#exit
R2(config)#router eigrp 100


R2(config-router)#redistribute rip metric ?
  <1-4294967295>  Bandwidth metric in Kbits per second

R2(config-router)#redistribute rip metric 2000 ?
  <0-4294967295>  IGRP delay metric, in 10 microsecond units

R2(config-router)#redistribute rip metric 2000 200 ?
  <0-255>  IGRP reliability metric where 255 is 100% reliable

R2(config-router)#redistribute rip metric 2000 200 255 ?
  <1-255>  IGRP Effective bandwidth metric (Loading) where 255 is 100% loaded

R2(config-router)#redistribute rip metric 2000 200 255 1 ?
  <1-4294967295>  IGRP MTU of the path

R2(config-router)#redistribute rip metric 2000 200 255 1 1500
R2(config-router)#
```

Because EIGRP uses a more complex metric calculation for path selection, Example 11-3 employed the CLI inline help functionality to help you understand the metric sequence and available values.

The first metric option is bandwidth. Example 11-3 uses a standard 2000-bandwidth metric, but this will change according to the media to which you are attached.

The second metric is delay. Usually this is in direct correlation to the bandwidth. Example 11-3 uses a 200-microsecond delay value for this lab.

The third metric is reliability. Consider the links to be 100 percent reliable, thus equating to a 255 value (255 being 100 percent reliable).

The fourth metric is load. Consider all links to have minimum traffic. 255 is a fully loaded circuit, and 1 is not.

The fifth metric is MTU size. The standard MTU size for Ethernet is 1500, so this will be the default here.

Remember, these values can drastically change the way a real production network will route, so be very thoughtful and thorough before issuing the **redistribute** command.

After redistributing between RIP and EIGRP, you should see some changes. R2 will not show any changes because it is running both protocols, but R1, R3, and R4 should be very different. Go to R1 and take a look at the routing table as demonstrated in Example 11-4.

**Example 11-4** *R1's Routing Table*

```
Termserver#1
[Resuming connection 1 to r1 ... ]


R1#show ip route
Codes: C - connected, S - static, I - IGRP, R - RIP, M - mobile, B - BGP
       D - EIGRP, EX - EIGRP external, O - OSPF, IA - OSPF inter area
       N1 - OSPF NSSA external type 1, N2 - OSPF NSSA external type 2
       E1 - OSPF external type 1, E2 - OSPF external type 2, E - EGP
       i - IS-IS, L1 - IS-IS level-1, L2 - IS-IS level-2, * - candidate default
       U - per-user static route, o - ODR

Gateway of last resort is not set

R    192.168.100.0/24 [120/1] via 192.168.1.2, 00:00:11, Ethernet0
C    192.169.1.0/24 is directly connected, Loopback0
C    192.168.1.0/24 is directly connected, Ethernet0
R    192.168.2.0/24 [120/1] via 192.168.1.2, 00:00:12, Ethernet0
R    192.168.3.0/24 [120/1] via 192.168.1.2, 00:00:12, Ethernet0
R    192.169.2.0/24 [120/1] via 192.168.1.2, 00:00:12, Ethernet0
R    192.168.4.0/24 [120/1] via 192.168.1.2, 00:00:12, Ethernet0
R    192.169.4.0/24 [120/1] via 192.168.1.2, 00:00:12, Ethernet0
```

The highlighted portion in Example 11-4 illustrates the changes in the routing table, among which are several additions:

```
R    192.168.100.0/24 [120/1] via 192.168.1.2, 00:00:11, Ethernet0
```

This route is the Frame Relay network.

```
R    192.168.3.0/24 [120/1] via 192.168.1.2, 00:00:12, Ethernet0
```

This route is to R3's Ethernet 0 network.

```
R    192.169.4.0/24 [120/1] via 192.168.1.2, 00:00:12, Ethernet0
```

This route is R4's loopback 0 network.

```
R    192.168.4.0/24 [120/1] via 192.168.1.2, 00:00:12, Ethernet0
```

This route is to R4's Ethernet 0 network.

It is interesting to note that the subnet mask on R4's Ethernet 0 is a /27 bit mask, but the route on R1 is a /24 bit mask. This is because EIGRP will autosummarize the route to its classful boundary, 192.168.4.0 /24. It is important to understand this because RIP, being a classful routing protocol, would not understand a route with a /27 bit mask and would drop the route. Remember that RIP and IGRP do not send subnet mask information with their routing updates.

If a router running RIP or IGRP receives a route, such as a Class B or Class A address space, it checks to see if it has an interface configured in the same address space. If it does, it assumes that the same subnet mask on its interface is being used through the network and, by default, applies the subnet mask of its interface to the route that it received. If it does not have an interface configured in the same address space, it applies the classful subnet mask according to the route that it received. For example, if a router has an interface configured with an IP address of 172.16.2.1 /24, and it receives a route in the 172.16.5.0 address space, it applies the /24 mask to the route and the route looks like 172.16.5.0/24. If it does not have an interface configured in the 17.16.0.0 address space, it applies the default /16 bit mask (172.X.X.X being a Class B address) to the route; the route would be 172.16.0.0/16, pointing to the next hop that it learned through the routing update.

Notice that the two loopback interfaces configured on R4 and summarized to 200.200.0.0/ 16 are omitted from the routing table. Again, RIP and IGRP are classful routing protocols, meaning that they do not support VLSM or CIDR routing updates. The summary route to 200.200.0.0 is a Class C (200.X.X.X) address space being summarized to a Class B subnet mask (/16). This is known as classless interdomain routing (CIDR), although many network engineers refer to this as *supernetting* or *route summarizing*. CIDR is the act of summarizing several routes under one route. Earlier, the two loopback networks (200.200.1.0/ 24 and 200.200.2.0/24) were summarized into one route, 200.200.0.0/16, on R4. EIGRP understands this concept, but RIP and IGRP do not, so they disregard the route when EIGRP tries to redistribute it into RIP.

To **ping** the two loopback networks, you need to manually specify the route. You have three options:

- Set a default route.
- Set a default network.
- Set static routes to the individual networks.

You will encounter this same issue for IGRP, so use one solution here and another for IGRP. Resolve this issue on R1 by setting a default route.

In global configuration mode, the command for setting a default route is as follows:

```
Router(config)#ip route 0.0.0.0 0.0.0.0 next-hop-address [metric]
```

The *next-hop-address* parameter of this command is the IP address of the default gateway. This IP address must be a directly connected neighbor.

The *metric* parameter is the administrative distance of the route. For purposes here, do not change the default administrative distance for a static route (which is 1).

---

**NOTE**    Administrative distance is the first criterion that a router uses to determine which routing protocol to use if two protocols provide route information for the same destination. Table 11-1 shows the administrative distances for all routing protocols.

---

**Table 11-1**    *Administrative Distances by Routing Protocol*

| Route Source | Default Distance Values |
|---|---|
| Connected interface | 0 |
| Static route | 1 |
| Enhanced Interior Gateway Routing Protocol (EIGRP) summary route | 5 |
| External Border Gateway Protocol (BGP) | 20 |
| Internal EIGRP | 90 |
| IGRP | 100 |
| OSPF | 110 |
| Intermediate System-to-Intermediate System (IS-IS) | 115 |
| Routing Information Protocol (RIP) | 120 |
| Exterior Gateway Protocol (EGP) | 140 |
| External EIGRP | 170 |
| Internal BGP | 200 |
| Unknown | 255 |

With R1 having only one other router connected to it, you need to use the Ethernet IP address of R2 as the default gateway. Example 11-5 illustrates the command on R1.

**Example 11-5** *Configuring Default Route on R1*

```
R1#config t
Enter configuration commands, one per line.  End with CNTL/Z.
 R1(config)#ip route 0.0.0.0 0.0.0.0 192.168.1.2
R1(config)#
```

Next, look at R1's routing table in Example 11-6 to see how the default route appears in the table.

**Example 11-6** *R1's IP Routing Table*

```
R1#show ip route
Codes: C - connected, S - static, I - IGRP, R - RIP, M - mobile, B - BGP
       D - EIGRP, EX - EIGRP external, O - OSPF, IA - OSPF inter area
       N1 - OSPF NSSA external type 1, N2 - OSPF NSSA external type 2
       E1 - OSPF external type 1, E2 - OSPF external type 2, E - EGP
       i - IS-IS, L1 - IS-IS level-1, L2 - IS-IS level-2, * - candidate default
       U - per-user static route, o - ODR

Gateway of last resort is 192.168.1.2 to network 0.0.0.0

R     192.168.100.0/24 [120/1] via 192.168.1.2, 00:00:09, Ethernet0
C     192.169.1.0/24 is directly connected, Loopback0
C     192.168.1.0/24 is directly connected, Ethernet0
R     192.168.2.0/24 [120/1] via 192.168.1.2, 00:00:09, Ethernet0
R     192.168.3.0/24 [120/1] via 192.168.1.2, 00:00:09, Ethernet0
R     192.169.2.0/24 [120/1] via 192.168.1.2, 00:00:09, Ethernet0
R     192.168.4.0/24 [120/1] via 192.168.1.2, 00:00:10, Ethernet0
R     192.169.4.0/24 [120/1] via 192.168.1.2, 00:00:10, Ethernet0
S*    0.0.0.0/0 [1/0] via 192.168.1.2
R1#
```

The routing table now informs you in two ways of the default route. The first is highlighted in Example 11-6:

```
Gateway of last resort is 192.168.1.2 to network 0.0.0.0.
```

The second way is to display the default route as a static route:

```
S*    0.0.0.0/0 [1/0] via 192.168.1.2
```

It is important to note that default routes are considered static routes, denoted by the *S*. However, to distinguish a default route from a regular static route a * is placed after the *S*.

Now that R1 has a default route, you should be able to **ping** all interfaces from R1 that were learned through EIGRP. For brevity in the lab, you need only **ping** a few interfaces, but in a live environment, you should take the time to **ping** all the EIGRP interfaces from R1 and then **ping** all the RIP interfaces from R3 or R4.

Example 11-7 displays several **ping** results from R1 to R4's loopback 0 and loopback 1, and R3's Serial 0 and Ethernet 0.

**Example 11-7 ping** *Results from R1 to R4 and R3*

```
R1#ping 192.169.4.4

Type escape sequence to abort.
Sending 5, 100-byte ICMP Echos to 192.169.4.4, timeout is 2 seconds:
```

*continues*

**Example 11-7** **ping** *Results from R1 to R4 and R3 (Continued)*

```
!!!!!
Success rate is 100 percent (5/5), round-trip min/avg/max = 88/90/92 ms
R1#ping 200.200.1.4

Type escape sequence to abort.
Sending 5, 100-byte ICMP Echos to 200.200.1.8, timeout is 2 seconds:
!!!!!
Success rate is 100 percent (5/5), round-trip min/avg/max = 88/89/92 ms
R1#ping 200.200.2.4

Type escape sequence to abort.
Sending 5, 100-byte ICMP Echos to 200.200.2.8, timeout is 2 seconds:
!!!!!
Success rate is 100 percent (5/5), round-trip min/avg/max = 88/90/96 ms
R1#ping 192.168.100.3

Type escape sequence to abort.
Sending 5, 100-byte ICMP Echos to 192.168.100.3, timeout is 2 seconds:
!!!!!
Success rate is 100 percent (5/5), round-trip min/avg/max = 32/33/36 ms
R1#ping 192.168.3.3

Type escape sequence to abort.
Sending 5, 100-byte ICMP Echos to 192.168.3.3, timeout is 2 seconds:
!!!!!
Success rate is 100 percent (5/5), round-trip min/avg/max = 32/34/36 ms
R1#
```

The **ping** output indicates 100 percent success on all **ping**ed networks.

To verify that RIP is properly redistributed into EIGRP, go to R4 and take a look at its routing table in Example 11-8.

**Example 11-8** *R4's IP Routing Table*

```
Termserver#4
[Resuming connection 4 to r4 ... ]

R4#show ip route
Codes: C - connected, S - static, I - IGRP, R - RIP, M - mobile, B - BGP
       D - EIGRP, EX - EIGRP external, O - OSPF, IA - OSPF inter area
       N1 - OSPF NSSA external type 1, N2 - OSPF NSSA external type 2
       E1 - OSPF external type 1, E2 - OSPF external type 2, E - EGP
       i - IS-IS, L1 - IS-IS level-1, L2 - IS-IS level-2, * - candidate default
       U - per-user static route, o - ODR

Gateway of last resort is not set

C    200.200.1.0/24 is directly connected, Loopback1
C    200.200.2.0/24 is directly connected, Loopback2
```

**Example 11-8** *R4's IP Routing Table (Continued)*

```
C    192.168.100.0/24 is directly connected, Serial0
D EX 192.169.1.0/24 [170/2733056] via 192.168.100.3, 01:23:47, Serial0
D EX 192.168.1.0/24 [170/2733056] via 192.168.100.3, 02:13:53, Serial0
D EX 192.168.2.0/24 [170/2733056] via 192.168.100.3, 02:13:53, Serial0
D EX 192.169.2.0/24 [170/2733056] via 192.168.100.3, 02:13:53, Serial0
D    192.168.3.0/24 [90/2195456] via 192.168.100.3, 1d06h, Serial0
     192.168.4.0/27 is subnetted, 1 subnets
C        192.168.4.0 is directly connected, Ethernet0
C    192.169.4.0/24 is directly connected, Loopback0
D    200.200.0.0/16 is a summary, 1d06h, Null0
```

EIGRP makes it a little easier to determine which routes were redistributed. It denotes routes learned external to EIGRP with an "EX" symbol after the *D*. Take a look at the new routes individually:

```
D EX 192.169.1.0/24 [170/2733056] via 192.168.100.3, 01:23:47, Serial0
```

This route is to R1's loopback 0 network.

```
D EX 192.168.1.0/24 [170/2733056] via 192.168.100.3, 02:13:53, Serial0
```

This route is to R1 and R2's Ethernet 0 network.

```
D EX 192.168.2.0/24 [170/2733056] via 192.168.100.3, 02:13:53, Serial0
```

This route is to R2's Ethernet 1 network.

```
D EX 192.169.2.0/24 [170/2733056] via 192.168.100.3, 02:13:53, Serial0
```

This route is R2's loopback 0 network.

Before moving on to redistribute EIGRP and IGRP, **ping** R1's loopback 0 and R1's Ethernet 0 interfaces, just to verify IP connectivity, as done in Example 11-9.

**Example 11-9** *R4* **ping** *Results to R1*

```
R4#ping 192.169.1.1

Type escape sequence to abort.
Sending 5, 100-byte ICMP Echos to 192.169.1.1, timeout is 2 seconds:
!!!!!
Success rate is 100 percent (5/5), round-trip min/avg/max = 88/92/104 ms
R4#ping 192.168.1.1

Type escape sequence to abort.
Sending 5, 100-byte ICMP Echos to 192.168.1.1, timeout is 2 seconds:
!!!!!
Success rate is 100 percent (5/5), round-trip min/avg/max = 88/89/92 ms
```

RIP and EIGRP are redistributing correctly, and the default route statement is working properly on R1. Next, look at R1 and R2's configuration to understand how the commands that you entered appear in the configuration file. Example 11-10 depicts the output from the running config file on R1.

**Example 11-10** *Portion of R1's Running Config*

```
R1#show running-config
.
.
.
!
router rip
 network 192.168.1.0
 network 192.169.1.0
 !
no ip classless
ip route 0.0.0.0 0.0.0.0 192.168.1.2
 !
banner motd ^C
This is Router 1
^C
.
```

All static and default routes appear in the configuration file after the routing protocols. Actual redistribution commands appear under the routing protocol. Example 11-11 illustrates a portion of R2's configuration file.

**Example 11-11** *Portion of R2's Running Config File*

```
R2#show running-config
.
.
.
!
router eigrp 100
 redistribute rip metric 2000 200 255 1 1500
 network 192.168.100.0
 !
router rip
 redistribute eigrp 100 metric 1
 network 192.168.1.0
 network 192.168.2.0
 network 192.169.2.0
 !
.
.
.
```

When redistributing, the source protocol is redistributed into the destination protocol. You accomplish this by entering router configuration mode for the destination protocol and then using the **redistribute** command to bring in the source protocol's routes. All of the configuration files look good. In the next section, you will redistribute IGRP and EIGRP on R3.

# Redistributing Between IGRP and EIGRP

With the boundaries for EIGRP and IGRP meeting at R3, R3 is the place where you need to configure route redistribution. In this section, you will redistribute EIGRP into IGRP and then IGRP into EIGRP. The command syntax is the same here as it was on R2. Use the same values that you used for EIGRP on R2 for both routing protocols. Example 11-12 illustrates the configuration for redistributing EIGRP into IGRP on R3.

**Example 11-12** *Redistributing EIGRP into IGRP on R3*

```
Termserver#3
[Resuming connection 3 to r3 ... ]

R3#config t
Enter configuration commands, one per line.  End with CNTL/Z.
R3(config)#router igrp 200
R3(config-router)#redistribute eigrp 100 metric 2000 200 255 1 1500
R3(config-router)#
```

Now redistribute IGRP routes into EIGRP using the configuration for R3 in Example 11-13.

**Example 11-13** *Redistributing IGRP into EIGRP on R3*

```
R3(config-router)#exit
R3(config)#router eigrp 100
R3(config-router)#redistribute igrp 200 metric 2000 200 255 1 1500
R3(config-router)#
```

Next, look at R3's running configuration, the routing protocol portion of which is displayed in Example 11-14.

**Example 11-14** *R3's Running Configuration File*

```
R3#show running-config
 .
 .
interface Serial1
 description This interface connects to R5's S0 (DCE)
 ip address 192.168.35.3 255.255.255.0
!
router eigrp 100
 redistribute igrp 200 metric 2000 200 255 1 1500
 network 192.168.100.0
 network 192.168.3.0
!
router igrp 200
 redistribute eigrp 100 metric 2000 200 255 1 1500
 network 192.168.35.0
```

*continues*

**Example 11-14** *R3's Running Configuration File (Continued)*

```
 network 192.169.3.0
!
no ip classless
!
banner motd ^CCC
This is Router 3
^C
.
.
.
```

The highlighted portions illustrate where and how the commands appear in the configuration file. Next, go to R5 and take a look at the routing table to make sure that it is functioning correctly. Example 11-15 displays the IP routing table from R5.

**Example 11-15** *R5's IP Routing Table*

```
Termserver#5
[Resuming connection 5 to r5 ... ]


R5#show ip route
Codes: C - connected, S - static, I - IGRP, R - RIP, M - mobile, B - BGP
       D - EIGRP, EX - EIGRP external, O - OSPF, IA - OSPF inter area
       N1 - OSPF NSSA external type 1, N2 - OSPF NSSA external type 2
       E1 - OSPF external type 1, E2 - OSPF external type 2, E - EGP
       i - IS-IS, L1 - IS-IS level-1, L2 - IS-IS level-2, * - candidate default
       U - per-user static route, o - ODR

Gateway of last resort is not set

I    192.168.100.0/24 [100/10476] via 192.168.35.3, 00:00:51, Serial0
C    192.168.35.0/24 is directly connected, Serial0
C    192.168.50.0/24 is directly connected, TokenRing0
I    192.169.1.0/24 [100/10676] via 192.168.35.3, 00:00:52, Serial0
I    192.168.1.0/24 [100/10676] via 192.168.35.3, 00:00:52, Serial0
I    192.168.2.0/24 [100/10676] via 192.168.35.3, 00:00:52, Serial0
I    192.169.3.0/24 [100/8976] via 192.168.35.3, 00:00:52, Serial0
I    192.168.3.0/24 [100/8576] via 192.168.35.3, 00:00:52, Serial0
I    192.169.2.0/24 [100/10676] via 192.168.35.3, 00:00:52, Serial0
I    192.168.4.0/24 [100/10576] via 192.168.35.3, 00:00:52, Serial0
C    192.169.5.0/24 is directly connected, Loopback0
I    192.169.4.0/24 [100/10976] via 192.168.35.3, 00:00:52, Serial0
```

IGRP makes it a little more difficult to determine which routes were introduced into IGRP through redistribution, but you know from the network diagram in Figure 11-1 that the highlighted routes were not originally in the IGRP domain. Another interesting note is that all of the RIP routes show up in the routing table as well. This is because you already redistributed between RIP and EIGRP, so when EIGRP was redistributed into IGRP, all of the RIP routes in addition to EIGRP routes were redistributed. Take a look at the highlighted individual routes:

```
I    192.168.100.0/24 [100/10476] via 192.168.35.3, 00:00:51, Serial0
```
This route is to the Frame Relay network. It was learned through EIGRP.

```
I    192.169.1.0/24 [100/10676] via 192.168.35.3, 00:00:52, Serial0
```
This route is to R1's loopback 0 network. It was learned through EIGRP by RIP redistribution.

```
I    192.168.1.0/24 [100/10676] via 192.168.35.3, 00:00:52, Serial0
```
This route is to R1 and R2's Ethernet 0 network. It was learned through EIGRP by RIP redistribution.

```
I    192.168.2.0/24 [100/10676] via 192.168.35.3, 00:00:52, Serial0
```
This route is to R2's Ethernet 1 network. It was learned through EIGRP by RIP redistribution.

```
I    192.168.3.0/24 [100/8576] via 192.168.35.3, 00:00:52, Serial0
```
This route is to R3's Ethernet 0 network. It was learned through EIGRP redistribution.

```
I    192.169.2.0/24 [100/10676] via 192.168.35.3, 00:00:52, Serial0
```
This route is to R2's loopback 0 network. It was learned through EIGRP by RIP redistribution.

```
I    192.168.4.0/24 [100/10576] via 192.168.35.3, 00:00:52, Serial0
```
This route is to R4's Ethernet 0 network. Note that it was summarized to a /24 network. The actual subnet mask on R4's Ethernet 0 is /27. This is the same situation that was encountered on R2. EIGRP will autosummarize to the classful boundary before redistributing the route. IGRP is a classful routing protocol, so it does not understand any VLSMs.

```
I    192.169.4.0/24 [100/10976] via 192.168.35.3, 00:00:52, Serial0
```
This route is to R4's loopback 0 network. It was learned through EIGRP.

Notice that the 200.200.0.0/16 summary route is not present. This is the same situation as on R2. IGRP, being a classful routing protocol, does not understand CIDR. You can fix this problem using a default network. The key concept to remember when configuring a default network is that it does not have to be a directly connected network. This provides some flexibility in choosing how to route your network. The command to configure a default network is issued under the global configuration mode, and the syntax is as follows:

```
Router(config)#ip default-network network-address
```

The only thing to specify in this command is the network address. It is a good rule of thumb to choose a network that will nearly never go down. This is when a loopback interface is very useful. You could use R3's Ethernet 0 or Serial 0 interface, but once in a while the interface might go down. A loopback network will never go down unless the router goes down; then you might have more serious issues than a router that can't reach its default network! For purposes here, use R3's loopback 0 network (192.169.3.0) for the default network on R5. Example 11-16 displays the configuration command on R5.

**Example 11-16**  **ip default-network** *Command on R5*

```
R5#config t
Enter configuration commands, one per line.  End with CNTL/Z.
R5(config)#ip default-network 192.169.3.0
R5(config)#
```

Next, take a look at the routing table on R5 in Example 11-17 to see how the default
network appears in the routing table.

**Example 11-17** *R5's IP Routing Table*

```
R5(config)#end
R5#show ip route
%SYS-5-CONFIG_I: Configured from console by console
R5#sho ip route
Codes: C - connected, S - static, I - IGRP, R - RIP, M - mobile, B - BGP
       D - EIGRP, EX - EIGRP external, O - OSPF, IA - OSPF inter area
       N1 - OSPF NSSA external type 1, N2 - OSPF NSSA external type 2
       E1 - OSPF external type 1, E2 - OSPF external type 2, E - EGP
       i - IS-IS, L1 - IS-IS level-1, L2 - IS-IS level-2, * - candidate default
       U - per-user static route, o - ODR

Gateway of last resort is 192.168.35.3 to network 192.169.3.0

I    192.168.100.0/24 [100/10476] via 192.168.35.3, 00:00:57, Serial0
C    192.168.35.0/24 is directly connected, Serial0
C    192.168.50.0/24 is directly connected, TokenRing0
I    192.169.1.0/24 [100/10676] via 192.168.35.3, 00:00:58, Serial0
I    192.168.1.0/24 [100/10676] via 192.168.35.3, 00:00:58, Serial0
I    192.168.2.0/24 [100/10676] via 192.168.35.3, 00:00:58, Serial0
I*   192.169.3.0/24 [100/8976] via 192.168.35.3, 00:00:58, Serial0
I    192.168.3.0/24 [100/8576] via 192.168.35.3, 00:00:58, Serial0
I    192.169.2.0/24 [100/10576] via 192.168.35.3, 00:00:58, Serial0
I    192.168.4.0/24 [100/10576] via 192.168.35.3, 00:00:58, Serial0
C    192.169.5.0/24 is directly connected, Loopback0
I    192.169.4.0/24 [100/10976] via 192.168.35.3, 00:00:58, Serial0
R5#
```

From the highlighted portion in Example 11-17, the routing table shows two areas where the
default network is identified. The first is the gateway of last resort statement—R3's Serial 1
interface IP address at the top of the routing table. The second indicator of the location of the
default network is where the router to R3's loopback 0 network has a * next to it. Even though
the route was learned through IGRP (I), it can be a default network candidate. A default
network is similar to the default route, but, as you remember, the default route was added to
the routing table as a static route (S) with the * following it. A default network is *not*
considered a static route or a default route, and it will not add an additional route entry in the
routing table, as the default route statement will. It will designate an existing route in the
routing table as a default path to reach only networks not present in the routing table. A

default **network** statement can use any network in the routing table, not just a directly connected network. Example 11-18 displays the running configuration file of R5. Notice where the default network statement appears in the configuration file.

**Example 11-18** *R5's Running Configuration*

```
R5#show running-config
Building configuration...

Current configuration:
!
.
.
router igrp 200
 passive-interface Loopback0
 network 192.168.35.0
 network 192.168.50.0
 network 192.169.5.0
 !
no ip classless
ip default-network 192.169.3.0
!
banner motd ^CC
This is Router 5
^C
.
.
.
end

R5#
```

The **ip default-network** statement comes after the routing protocol configuration section.

Next, **ping** a few interfaces to verify connectivity into the EIGRP and RIP domains. For brevity in the lab we will not ping all of the interfaces, but in live environments you should **ping** all of the interfaces, just to verify for yourself. **ping** R1's Loopback 0 (192.169.1.1), R2's Ethernet 1 (192.168.2.2), R4's Loopback 1 (200.200.1.4), and R3's Serial 0 (192.168.100.3). Example 11-19 displays the results.

**Example 11-19** *R5* **ping** *Results*

```
R5#ping 192.169.1.1

Type escape sequence to abort.
Sending 5, 100-byte ICMP Echos to 192.169.1.1, timeout is 2 seconds:
!!!!!
Success rate is 100 percent (5/5), round-trip min/avg/max = 32/35/44 ms
R5#ping 192.168.2.2
```

*continues*

**Example 11-19** *R5* **ping** *Results (Continued)*

```
Type escape sequence to abort.
Sending 5, 100-byte ICMP Echos to 192.168.2.2, timeout is 2 seconds:
!!!!!
Success rate is 100 percent (5/5), round-trip min/avg/max = 32/36/44 ms
R5#ping 200.200.1.4

Type escape sequence to abort.
Sending 5, 100-byte ICMP Echos to 200.200.1.4, timeout is 2 seconds:
!!!!!
Success rate is 100 percent (5/5), round-trip min/avg/max = 60/62/64 ms
R5#ping 192.168.100.3

Type escape sequence to abort.
Sending 5, 100-byte ICMP Echos to 192.168.100.3, timeout is 2 seconds:
!!!!!
Success rate is 100 percent (5/5), round-trip min/avg/max = 4/5/8 ms
R5#
```

The 100-percent success rate confirms complete interrouting domain connectivity.

## Lab Summary

To quickly review this chapter, you learned how to redistribute routes from one routing
protocol to another. An issue that you need to remember when redistributing is that all
metrics are lost and need to be manually set in the **redistribute** command. Redistributing
routes between classful and classless routing protocols can cause some routes to be lost. Be
aware of VLSM and CIDR routes when redistributing from a classless routing protocol
(EIGRP) to a classful routing protocol (RIP or IGRP).

To compare the routing tables, Example 11-20 contains the routing tables for routers R1
through R5 after all of the route redistribution, default routes, and default networks have
been configured.

**Example 11-20** *Routing Tables*

```
R1#show ip route
Gateway of last resort is 192.168.1.2 to network 0.0.0.0

R    192.168.100.0/24 [120/1] via 192.168.1.2, 00:00:09, Ethernet0
R    192.168.35.0/24 [120/1] via 192.168.1.2, 00:00:10, Ethernet0
R    192.168.50.0/24 [120/1] via 192.168.1.2, 00:00:10, Ethernet0
C    192.169.1.0/24 is directly connected, Loopback0
C    192.168.1.0/24 is directly connected, Ethernet0
R    192.169.3.0/24 [120/1] via 192.168.1.2, 00:00:10, Ethernet0
R    192.168.2.0/24 [120/1] via 192.168.1.2, 00:00:10, Ethernet0
R    192.168.3.0/24 [120/1] via 192.168.1.2, 00:00:10, Ethernet0
R    192.169.2.0/24 [120/1] via 192.168.1.2, 00:00:10, Ethernet0
```

**Example 11-20** *Routing Tables (Continued)*

```
R    192.169.5.0/24 [120/1] via 192.168.1.2, 00:00:10, Ethernet0
R    192.168.4.0/24 [120/1] via 192.168.1.2, 00:00:10, Ethernet0
R    192.169.4.0/24 [120/1] via 192.168.1.2, 00:00:10, Ethernet0
S*   0.0.0.0/0 [1/0] via 192.168.1.2
```

```
R2#show ip route
Gateway of last resort is not set

     192.168.4.0/27 is subnetted, 1 subnets
D       192.168.4.0 [90/2707456] via 192.168.100.3, 1d01h, Serial0
D    192.169.4.0/24 [90/2809856] via 192.168.100.3, 1d01h, Serial0
D EX 192.169.5.0/24 [170/2809856] via 192.168.100.3, 23:49:13, Serial0
D EX 192.168.50.0/24 [170/2697984] via 192.168.100.3, 23:49:13, Serial0
D EX 192.168.35.0/24 [170/2169856] via 192.168.100.3, 23:49:13, Serial0
C    192.168.1.0/24 is directly connected, Ethernet0
R    192.169.1.0/24 [120/1] via 192.168.1.1, 00:00:25, Ethernet0
C    192.168.2.0/24 is directly connected, Ethernet1
C    192.169.2.0/24 is directly connected, Loopback0
C    192.168.100.0/24 is directly connected, Serial0
D    192.168.3.0/24 [90/2195456] via 192.168.100.3, 1d01h, Serial0
D EX 192.169.3.0/24 [170/2169856] via 192.168.100.3, 23:49:14, Serial0
D    200.200.0.0/16 [90/2809856] via 192.168.100.3, 1d01h, Serial0
```

```
R3#show ip route
Gateway of last resort is not set

C    192.168.100.0/24 is directly connected, Serial0
C    192.168.35.0/24 is directly connected, Serial1
I    192.168.50.0/24 [100/8539] via 192.168.35.5, 00:00:25, Serial1
D EX 192.169.1.0/24 [170/2221056] via 192.168.100.2, 1d01h, Serial0
D EX 192.168.1.0/24 [170/2221056] via 192.168.100.2, 1d02h, Serial0
D EX 192.168.2.0/24 [170/2221056] via 192.168.100.2, 1d02h, Serial0
C    192.169.3.0/24 is directly connected, Loopback0
D EX 192.169.2.0/24 [170/2221056] via 192.168.100.2, 1d02h, Serial0
C    192.168.3.0/24 is directly connected, Ethernet0
     192.168.4.0/27 is subnetted, 1 subnets
D       192.168.4.0 [90/2195456] via 192.168.100.4, 2d06h, Serial0
I    192.169.5.0/24 [100/8976] via 192.168.35.5, 00:00:26, Serial1
D    192.169.4.0/24 [90/2297856] via 192.168.100.4, 1d01h, Serial0
D    200.200.0.0/16 [90/2297856] via 192.168.100.4, 2d06h, Serial0
```

```
R4#show ip route
Gateway of last resort is not set

C    200.200.1.0/24 is directly connected, Loopback1
C    200.200.2.0/24 is directly connected, Loopback2
C    192.168.100.0/24 is directly connected, Serial0
D EX 192.168.35.0/24 [170/2169856] via 192.168.100.3, 23:38:54, Serial0
D EX 192.168.50.0/24 [170/2697984] via 192.168.100.3, 23:38:54, Serial0
```

*continues*

**Example 11-20** *Routing Tables (Continued)*

```
D EX 192.169.1.0/24 [170/2733056] via 192.168.100.3, 1d01h, Serial0
D EX 192.168.1.0/24 [170/2733056] via 192.168.100.3, 1d02h, Serial0
D EX 192.169.3.0/24 [170/2169856] via 192.168.100.3, 23:38:54, Serial0
D EX 192.168.2.0/24 [170/2733056] via 192.168.100.3, 1d02h, Serial0
D EX 192.169.2.0/24 [170/2733056] via 192.168.100.3, 1d02h, Serial0
D    192.168.3.0/24 [90/2195456] via 192.168.100.3, 2d06h, Serial0
D EX 192.169.5.0/24 [170/2809856] via 192.168.100.3, 23:38:54, Serial0
     192.168.4.0/27 is subnetted, 1 subnets
C       192.168.4.0 is directly connected, Ethernet0
C    192.169.4.0/24 is directly connected, Loopback0
D    200.200.0.0/16 is a summary, 2d06h, Null0
```

```
R5#show ip route
Gateway of last resort is 192.168.35.3 to network 192.169.3.0
I    192.168.100.0/24 [100/10476] via 192.168.35.3, 00:01:14, Serial0
C    192.168.35.0/24 is directly connected, Serial0
C    192.168.50.0/24 is directly connected, TokenRing0
I    192.169.1.0/24 [100/10676] via 192.168.35.3, 00:01:14, Serial0
I    192.168.1.0/24 [100/10676] via 192.168.35.3, 00:01:14, Serial0
I    192.168.2.0/24 [100/10676] via 192.168.35.3, 00:01:14, Serial0
I*   192.169.3.0/24 [100/8976] via 192.168.35.3, 00:01:14, Serial0
I    192.168.3.0/24 [100/8576] via 192.168.35.3, 00:01:14, Serial0
I    192.169.2.0/24 [100/10676] via 192.168.35.3, 00:01:14, Serial0
I    192.168.4.0/24 [100/10576] via 192.168.35.3, 00:01:15, Serial0
C    192.169.5.0/24 is directly connected, Loopback0
I    192.169.4.0/24 [100/10976] via 192.168.35.3, 00:01:15, Serial0
```

Compare this example to Example 11-1, introduced earlier in this chapter. You will see many changes and additions to the routing tables. The next chapter provides you with the opportunity to configure ISDN dial backup between routers R5 and R6.

This chapter covers the following key topics:

- ISDN BRI and PRI
- ISDN components
- Legacy DDR concepts
- Configuring a network for ISDN

## CHAPTER 12

# Integrated Services Digital Network (ISDN)

This chapter reviews Integrated Services Digital Network (ISDN) and legacy dial-on-demand routing (DDR). This chapter specifically focuses on configuring legacy DDR using an ISDN BRI on a Cisco router. This is accomplished by configuring legacy DDR between R5 and R6 in the lab. In addition, as you configure ISDN and legacy DDR, you will understand those commands useful in verifying and troubleshooting your configuration.

## ISDN Fundamentals

Integrated Services Digital Network (ISDN) is a digital service offered by regional telephone carriers permitting voice, data, text, graphics, music, and video to be transmitted over the existing Public Switched Telephone Network (PSTN). The emergence of ISDN represents an effort to standardize subscriber services, user/network interfaces, and network and internetwork capabilities. ISDN applications include high-speed image applications, high-speed file transfer, voice services, and videoconferencing. ISDN provides many benefits without the cost of a dedicated connection. In recent years, ISDN has come under pressure from competing services such as xDSL and cable, which provide high-speed connections at competitive prices. In spite of the competition that xDSL and cable technology present, ISDN is still appealing in many areas because of the lack of availability of xDSL and cable, especially internationally. This chapter begins with a summary of the underlying technologies and services associated with ISDN and then introduces you to the lab scenario.

## ISDN BRI and PRI

ISDN can be either Basic Rate Interface (BRI) or Primary Rate Interface (PRI).

The ISDN Basic Rate Interface (BRI) service offers two B channels and one D channel (2B+D). Each BRI B channel operates at 64 kbps and is meant to carry user data. ISDN BRI can provide access at 128 kbps when using both B channels. The BRI D channel operates at 16 kbps and is meant to carry control and signaling information, although it can support user data transmission under certain circumstances. The D-channel signaling protocol comprises Layers 1 through 3 of the OSI reference model. The BRI physical layer specification is ITU-T I.430.

In North America and Japan, ISDN PRI service offers 23 B channels and 1 D channel. The PRI D channel runs at 64 kbps. ISDN PRI in Europe, Australia, and other parts of the world provides 30 B channels plus 1 64-kbps D channel. The PRI physical layer specification is ITU-T I.431.

## ISDN Components

ISDN components include:

- Terminal equipment (TE)
- Terminal adapters (TAs)
- Network-termination devices

ISDN terminals come in two types—terminal equipment (TE) and terminal adapters (TAs). TE refers to end-user devices such as digital telephones or workstations:

- Native ISDN terminals are referred to as terminal equipment type 1 (TE1). TE1s connect to the ISDN network through a four-wire, twisted-pair digital link.

- Non-ISDN terminals such as DTE that predate the ISDN standards are referred to as terminal equipment type 2 (TE2). TE2s connect to the ISDN network through terminal adapters. The ISDN TA can be either a standalone device or a board inside the TE2.

If the TE2 is implemented as a standalone device, it connects to the TA through a standard physical layer interface. Examples include EIA/TIA-232-C, V.24, and V.35. The TA performs the necessary protocol conversion to allow non-ISDN (TE2) equipment to access the ISDN network.

Beyond the TE1 and TE2 devices, the next connection point in the ISDN network is the network termination type 1 (NT1).

At the customer site, the ISDN local loop is terminated using a network termination type 1 (NT1). These are network-termination devices that connect the four-wire subscriber wiring to the conventional two-wire local loop. The NT1's responsibilities include line performance monitoring, timing, physical signaling protocol conversion, power transfer, and multiplexing of the B and D channels.

In North America, the NT1 is a customer premises equipment (CPE) device. In most other parts of the world, the NT1 is part of the network provided by the carrier. The NT2 is a more complicated device that typically is found in digital private branch exchanges (PBXs) and that performs Layer 2 and 3 protocol functions and concentration services. An NT1/2 device also exists as a single device that combines the functions of an NT1 and an NT2.

To delineate areas of responsibility within an ISDN network, ISDN defines a number of reference points within the network. Reference points define logical interfaces between functional groupings, such as TAs and NT1s. Reference points provide for a common term usage when troubleshooting a component of the local loop part of an ISDN network. Vendors and providers of ISDN equipment use the reference points R, S, T, and U. Table 12-1 illustrates the relationship between devices and ISDN reference points.

**Table 12-1**    *Reference Points Within an ISDN Network*

| Reference Point | Denotes the Following Location Within the ISDN Network |
| --- | --- |
| R | The reference point between non-ISDN equipment and a TA. The TA allows the TE2 to appear to the network as an ISDN device. There is no standard for the R reference point. Vendors can choose a variety of different physical connections and communication schemes. |
| S | The reference point between user terminals (either TE1 or TA) and the NT2. |
| T | The reference point between customer site switching equipment (NT2) and the local loop termination (NT1). |
| U | The reference point between NT1 devices and line-termination equipment in the local exchange. The U reference point is relevant only in North America, where the carrier network does not provide the NT1 function. |

Figure 12-1 illustrates a sample ISDN configuration and shows three devices attached to the local central office ISDN switch. Two of these devices are ISDN-compatible, so they can be attached through an S reference point to NT2 devices. The third device (a standard, non-ISDN telephone) attaches through an R reference point to a TA. Any of these devices also could attach to an NT1/2 device, which would replace both the NT1 and the NT2. In addition, although they are not shown, similar user stations are attached to the remote ISDN switch.

**Figure 12-1**   *Sample ISDN Configuration Demonstrates Relationship Between Devices and Reference Points*

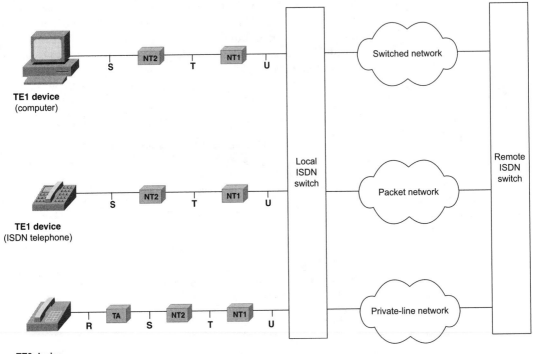

In the lab, physical connectivity between R5 and R6 occurs over ISDN BRI. Cisco implements BRI using a BRI RJ-45 interface on a router, which is enabled as a TE1 device. Both R5 and R6 have BRI RJ-45 interfaces that are connected to the ISDN simulator as TE1 devices. A detailed overview of the physical configuration between R5 and R6, and how the ISDN simulator is configured, can be found in Appendix D, "ISDN Simulator Configuration and Setup."

Now that you are familiar with ISDN components, you will next examine the key concepts necessary to understanding legacy DDR configuration.

## Legacy DDR Concepts

Dial-on-Demand Routing (DDR) addresses the need for intermittent network connections over circuit-switched WANs such as ISDN. With DDR, all traffic is classified as either interesting or uninteresting. If traffic is interesting, the packet is passed to the interface, and the router then connects by dialing to the remote router—thus, the name dial-on-demand routing.

DDR is implemented in two ways: Legacy DDR and DDR with dialer profiles. The key difference between each is that, in legacy DDR, you configure the dial details on the physical interface; with DDR dialer profiles, you configure the dial details on a virtual interface called a dialer interface. By disassociating the dial details from the physical interface, greater flexibility is permitted in your DDR configuration. For example, with one BRI interface in a router using legacy DDR, you are restricted in that all dial details are confined to the physical interface. Thus, you can configure the details for legacy DDR in one way only. However, with DDR dialer profiles, you can configure multiple dialer interfaces with different dialer details on each dialer interface. Each dialer interface uses the ISDN physical interface (BRI or PRI) for physical connectivity but applies the configuration or profile of the associated dialer. (Hence, the name *dialer profiles*.) This allows greater flexibility when more complex configurations are required.

| | |
|---|---|
| **NOTE** | The focus of this book is legacy DDR. More information on configuring DDR with dialer profiles can be found on CCO, at www.cisco.com/warp/public/793/access_dial/ddr_dialer_profile.html. |

DDR is used to cause the router to dial or receive a dialed connection. To help you remember how to configure DDR, you should remember two key questions:

- What will cause the link to dial?
- How will the dialing occur, and for how long?

Each of these questions translates to two simple steps.

What will cause the link to dial? It is important to remember that DDR cannot dial until some traffic is directed out the dialing interface. For this to occur, two steps are required:

**Step 1**  Define what traffic will trigger the link to dial. This is known as specifying interesting traffic.

**Step 2**  Specify how DDR traffic is routed out the dial interface. This involves configuring a static route so that the router will queue packets to be sent out the dialing interface.

Next, how will the dialing occur, and for how long? DDR must know what number to call to make the dialed connection and must know how long the call should remain up. These details are defined with the following two steps:

**Step 1**  Define a dialer string on the dialing interface. (Dialer maps may be used when dialing to multiple destinations.)

**Step 2**  Define a dialer idle-timeout.

The dialer string defines the number to call to get to the next-hop router. After a dialed connection is made, any type of packets can be routed across the link; however, only interesting traffic will keep the link up. The idle timer counts the time since the last interesting packet traversed the link. If the time specified as the idle-timeout expires, meaning that no interesting packets have traversed the link for the specified amount of time, the connection is brought down. The lab section of this chapter demonstrates how these steps translate to configuration commands on the router.

This completes the review of ISDN and DDR. If you feel that additional review is needed, refer to Chapter 8 of *Cisco CCNA Exam #640-607 Certification Guide* by Wendell Odom, or Chapter 12 of *Interconnecting Cisco Network Devices*.

# Lab Objectives

In the lab, R6 represents a remote office that connects to the main network (R1 through R5) over ISDN. It was unnecessary to have a permanent connection to the main office because the remote users send only sporadic amounts of data occasionally during the day. For this reason, ISDN was chosen to provide periodic connectivity to the rest of the main network using DDR. In this chapter's lab, you will learn how to configure ISDN DDR through accomplishing the following lab objectives:

- Configure the BRI interfaces on R5 and R6. See Figure 12-2 for ISDN information such as switch type and dial numbers.

- Use PPP encapsulation.

- The ISDN link should be active only when IP traffic is present. R6 should call R5. No routing protocols are to be used across the link. Use static routes on R5 and R6, but ensure that workstations on R6's Token Ring network (192.168.60.0) can reach the rest of your network.

- The link should be brought down after 5 minutes of inactivity.

- Test R6 connectivity to the rest of your network through Telnet. You must use the host name of each router, which was configured previously (that is, R1, R2, R3, and so on), to initiate the Telnet session.

Figure 12-2 depicts the routers that will be configured for DDR.

**Figure 12-2** *R5 and R6 to Be Configured for ISDN and Legacy DDR*

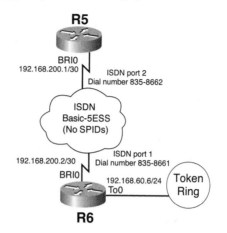

Observe in Figure 12-2 the switch type and dial numbers that will be used in the router configurations. Also note that R5 and R6 have BRI interfaces, so your configuration will be for ISDN BRI instead of ISDN PRI.

| | |
|---|---|
| **NOTE** | This lab uses an ISDN simulator to simulate a service provider's ISDN switch. The simulator can be configured to simulate various ISDN switch types and can be assigned the desired dial numbers on each ISDN simulator port. For a detailed overview of the physical configuration between R5, R6, and the ISDN simulator, including how the ISDN simulator is configured, see Appendix D. |

To enable ISDN and configure Legacy DDR, you will perform the commands outlined in Table 12-2.

**Table 12-2** *Steps to Enable ISDN and Configure Legacy DDR*

| Step | Command |
|---|---|
| 1. Enable ISDN in global configuration mode by setting the ISDN switch type. | Router(config)#**isdn switch-type** *type* |
| 2. Assign BRI0 interface an IP address from interface configuration mode, and bring up the interface. | Router#(config-if)**ip address** *address mask* <br> Router#(config-if)**no shutdown** |
| 3. Specify PPP encapsulation in interface configuration mode. | Router(config-if)#**encapsulation ppp** |

*continues*

**Table 12-2** *Steps to Enable ISDN and Configure Legacy DDR (Continued)*

| Step | Command |
|---|---|
| 4. Configure a static route pointing to the next-hop router on the opposite end of the ISDN link. | Router(config)#**ip route** *destination mask next-hop-router-ip-address* |
| 5. Specify the interesting traffic that will trigger the link by configuring a dialer list from global configuration mode. This list then is applied in interface configuration mode with the **dialer-group** command. | Router(config)#**dialer-list** [*list number*] **protocol** [*protocol*] [**deny** \| **list** \| **permit**] <br><br> Router(config)#**dialer-group** *group number* |
| 6. Configure the number that the router should call from interface configuration mode by specifying the dial string. | Router(config-if)#**dial string** *dialer-string* |
| 7. Configure the dialer idle-timeout from interface configuration mode. | Router(config-if)#**dialer idle-timeout** *idle-timeout-in-seconds* |

In previous chapters, the approach has been to perform the various configuration steps and afterward to verify their proper operation. The approach in this chapter is a little different. You will verify the configuration as you go along. In this way, you will see how the different configuration steps affect Layers 1, 2, and 3 of ISDN connectivity. Understanding ISDN in this format will help you to effectively troubleshoot ISDN connectivity at the different layers.

# Step 1: Enable ISDN in Global Configuration Mode by Setting the ISDN Switch Type

Begin the configuration by referring to the lab diagram in Figure 12-2. Notice that the ISDN switch type is basic-5ess. This information is obtained from the local service provider and must be set correctly to ensure that the router can communicate properly with the service provider's ISDN switch. If you are unsure of the correct switch type, you can use the context-sensitive help to narrow your options, as is displayed on R5 in Example 12-1.

**Example 12-1** *Context-Sensitive Help Displays the Available ISDN Switch Types*

```
R5#conf t
Enter configuration commands, one per line.  End with CNTL/Z.
R5(config)#isdn switch-type ?
  basic-1tr6    1TR6 switch type for Germany
  basic-5ess    AT&T 5ESS switch type for the U.S.
  basic-dms100  Northern DMS-100 switch type
  basic-net3    NET3 switch type for UK and Europe
  basic-ni1     National ISDN-1 switch type
  basic-nwnet3  NET3 switch type for Norway
  basic-nznet3  NET3 switch type for New Zealand
  basic-ts013   TS013 switch type for Australia
```

**Example 12-1** *Context-Sensitive Help Displays the Available ISDN Switch Types (Continued)*

```
    ntt          NTT switch type for Japan
    vn2          VN2 switch type for France
    vn3          VN3 and VN4 switch types for France

R5(config)#
```

Notice how ISDN switch types are area-specific. Normally, the local service provider provides this information. In the United States, Nortel DMS-100s, ATT 5ESSs, and National ISDN-1 are quite common; Canada uses mostly the Nortel DMS-100s. Context-sensitive help can help you narrow the possible selections, when necessary.

Begin by configuring the proper ISDN switch type on R5 and R6. By setting the ISDN switch type on the router, you are enabling ISDN on the router. Resume the connection to R5 and then R6, and set the ISDN switch type as shown in Example 12-2.

**Example 12-2** *Setting the ISDN Switch Type to Basic-5ess on R5 and R6*

```
Termserver#5
[Resuming connection 5 to r5 ... ]

R5#conf t
Enter configuration commands, one per line.  End with CNTL/Z.
R5(config)#isdn switch-type basic-5ess
R5(config)#end
R5#
%SYS-5-CONFIG_I: Configured from console by console
R5#


Termserver#6
[Resuming connection 6 to r6 ... ]

R6#conf t
Enter configuration commands, one per line.  End with CNTL/Z.
R6(config)#isdn switch-type basic-5ess
R6(config)#end
R6#
%SYS-5-CONFIG_I: Configured from console by console
R6#
```

Now if you display the running config on R5 or R6, you will see that the selected switch type is included in the configuration as shown on R6 in Example 12-3.

**Example 12-3** *Running Config on R6 Shows Where ISDN Switch Type Appears in the Config*

```
R6#show running-config
Building configuration...

Current configuration:
!
```

*continues*

**Example 12-3** *Running Config on R6 Shows Where ISDN Switch Type Appears in the Config (Continued)*

```
version 11.2
no service password-encryption
no service udp-small-servers
no service tcp-small-servers
!
hostname R6
!
enable password falcons
!
no ip domain-lookup
ip host R1 192.169.1.1
ip host R2 192.169.2.2
ip host R3 192.169.3.3
ip host R4 192.169.4.4
ip host R5 192.169.5.5
ip host R6 192.169.6.6
isdn switch-type basic-5ess
!
interface Loopback0
 ip address 192.169.6.6 255.255.255.0
```

The highlighted line in Example 12-3 confirms that the proper ISDN switch type shows up in the configuration. Another useful command in troubleshooting your ISDN configuration is the **show isdn status** command. You execute this command from global configuration mode as follows:

```
Router#show isdn status
```

Check the ISDN status as it appears on R6 after the switch type has been configured, as displayed in Example 12-4.

**Example 12-4** *ISDN Status on R6 After Switch Type Is Configured*

```
R6#show isdn status
The current ISDN Switchtype = basic-5ess
ISDN BRI0 interface
    Layer 1 Status:
        DEACTIVATED
    Layer 2 Status:
        Layer 2 NOT Activated
    Layer 3 Status:
        0 Active Layer 3 Call(s)
    Activated dsl 0 CCBs = 0
    Total Allocated ISDN CCBs = 0
R6#
```

This command tells you what the ISDN switch type is set to and also indicates what kind of ISDN interface is in the router. In this case, you can see that you have a BRI0 interface. In addition, notice that you are given Layer 1, 2, and 3 information. This is useful in troubleshooting ISDN configuration problems and determining at which layer the problem is occurring. At this point, Layer 1 is showing DEACTIVATED. Normally after configuring the ISDN switch type, Layer 1 should show ACTIVE. However, an important step has been omitted here. Examine the BRI interface on R6 using the **show interface** command, as demonstrated in Example 12-5.

**Example 12-5** *BRI0 Interface on R6 Is Administratively Down*

```
R6#show interface bri0
BRI0 is administratively down, line protocol is down
  Hardware is BRI
  MTU 1500 bytes, BW 64 Kbit, DLY 20000 usec, rely 255/255, load 1/255
  Encapsulation HDLC, loopback not set
  Last input 00:30:09, output 00:30:09, output hang never
  Last clearing of "show interface" counters never
  Input queue: 0/75/0 (size/max/drops); Total output drops: 0
  Queueing strategy: weighted fair
  Output queue: 0/1000/64/0 (size/max total/threshold/drops)
     Conversations  0/1/256 (active/max active/max total)
     Reserved Conversations 0/0 (allocated/max allocated)
  5 minute input rate 0 bits/sec, 0 packets/sec
  5 minute output rate 0 bits/sec, 0 packets/sec
     30 packets input, 131 bytes, 0 no buffer
     Received 3 broadcasts, 0 runts, 0 giants, 0 throttles
     0 input errors, 0 CRC, 0 frame, 0 overrun, 0 ignored, 0 abort
     30 packets output, 131 bytes, 0 underruns
     0 output errors, 0 collisions, 7 interface resets
     0 output buffer failures, 0 output buffers swapped out
     2 carrier transitions
R6#
```

The output in Example 12-5 indicates that R6's BRI0 is administratively down. Until this point, the interface has not been brought out of shutdown mode. So, for ISDN Layer 1 to be ACTIVE, you need to configure the ISDN switch type on the router as well as bring up the ISDN interface by doing a **no shutdown** on the interface.

# Step 2: Assign BRI0 Interface an IP Address from Interface Configuration Mode and Bring up the Interface

Return to R5 and configure an IP address on the BRI0 interface. Bring up the interface by doing a **no shutdown**, as demonstrated in Example 12-6.

**Example 12-6** *Unable to Assign R5's BRI0 Interface Its IP Address Because It Falls Within IP Subnet 0*

```
Termserver#5
[Resuming connection 5 to r5 ... ]

R5#conf t
Enter configuration commands, one per line.  End with CNTL/Z.
R5(config)#int bri0
R5(config-if)#ip address 192.168.200.1 255.255.255.252
Bad mask /30 for address 192.168.200.1
R5(config-if)#end
R5#
```

You cannot assign this address as it falls within IP subnet 0. You first must enable **ip subnet-zero** on R5 and then complete this configuration task.

**NOTE**     IP subnet 0 is enabled by default beginning in Cisco IOS Software Release 12.0. This step is necessary only for Cisco IOS Software releases earlier than 12.0.

Do this now, as shown in Example 12-7.

**Example 12-7** *Assigning R5 an IP Address and Bringing Interface Out of Shutdown Mode*

```
R5#conf t
Enter configuration commands, one per line.  End with CNTL/Z.
R5(config)#ip subnet-zero
R5(config)#int bri0
R5(config-if)#ip address 192.168.200.1 255.255.255.252
R5(config-if)#no shutdown
R5(config-if)#
%LINK-3-UPDOWN: Interface BRI0:1, changed state to down
%LINK-3-UPDOWN: Interface BRI0:2, changed state to down
%LINK-3-UPDOWN: Interface BRI0, changed state to up
R5(config-if)#
%ISDN-6-LAYER2UP: Layer 2 for Interface BR0, TEI 123 changed to up
R5(config-if)#end
R5#
%SYS-5-CONFIG_I: Configured from console by console
R5#
```

Now you are able to successfully assign this address to the interface. In addition, after doing a **no shutdown** on the interface, you receive messages that the BRI0 interface changed to up and that Layer 2 is up on the interface. Examine the ISDN status again, and see how this has changed from the initial check. Example 12-8 depicts the ISDN status after the ISDN switch type is configured and the BRI0 interface is brought up on R5.

**Example 12-8** *ISDN Status on R5 After Switch Type Is Configured and BRI0 Interface Is Up*

```
Termserver#5
[Resuming connection 5 to r5 ... ]

R5#show isdn status
The current ISDN Switchtype = basic-5ess
ISDN BRI0 interface
    Layer 1 Status:
        ACTIVE
    Layer 2 Status:
        TEI = 123, State = MULTIPLE_FRAME_ESTABLISHED
    Layer 3 Status:
        0 Active Layer 3 Call(s)
    Activated dsl 0 CCBs = 0
    Total Allocated ISDN CCBs = 0
R5#
```

The output in Example 12-8 shows that Layer 1 is now showing ACTIVE and that Layer 2 is up, as denoted by **State = MULTIPLE_FRAME_ESTABLISHED**. This means that the router's BRI0 interface is communicating at Layers 1 and 2 with the ISDN switch. Finally, Layer 3 shows that there is no current ISDN call occurring on the link.

Next, go to R6, enable **ip subnet-zero**, assign the BRI0 interface an IP address, and do a **no shutdown** on the interface, as demonstrated in Example 12-9.

**Example 12-9** *Enabling IP Subnet 0 on R6—Assigning R6's BRI0 Interface an IP Address and Bringing Up the Interface*

```
Termserver#6
[Resuming connection 6 to r6 ... ]

R6#conf t
Enter configuration commands, one per line.  End with CNTL/Z.
R6(config)#ip subnet-zero
R6(config)#int bri0
R6(config-if)#ip address 192.168.200.2 255.255.255.252
R6(config-if)#no shut
R6(config-if)#
%LINK-3-UPDOWN: Interface BRI0:1, changed state to down
%LINK-3-UPDOWN: Interface BRI0:2, changed state to down
%LINK-3-UPDOWN: Interface BRI0, changed state to up
R6(config-if)#
%ISDN-6-LAYER2UP: Layer 2 for Interface BR0, TEI 124 changed to up
R6(config-if)#end
R6#
%SYS-5-CONFIG_I: Configured from console by console
R6#
```

You can see that R6's BRI0 interface changed to up and that Layer 2 is also up. Next, verify the ISDN status on R6 as you did on R5. Example 12-10 shows the output to confirm the ISDN status on R6.

**Example 12-10**  *ISDN Status on R6 After Switch Type Is Configured and BRIO Interface Is Up*

```
Termserver#6
[Resuming connection 6 to r6 ... ]

R6#show isdn status
The current ISDN Switchtype = basic-5ess
ISDN BRI0 interface
    Layer 1 Status:
        ACTIVE
    Layer 2 Status:
        TEI = 126, State = MULTIPLE_FRAME_ESTABLISHED
    Layer 3 Status:
        0 Active Layer 3 Call(s)
    Activated dsl 0 CCBs = 0
    Total Allocated ISDN CCBs = 0
R6#
```

Layers 1 and 2 on R6 look good. R6 shows that Layer 1 is now ACTIVE and that Layer 2 is up, as denoted by **State = MULTIPLE_FRAME_ESTABLISHED**.

## Step 3: Specify PPP Encapsulation in Interface Configuration Mode

Next, you need to specify that R5 and R6's BRI0 interfaces should use PPP as the encapsulation type. Change the encapsulation to PPP on R5 and R6, as shown in Example 12-11.

**Example 12-11**  *Configuring PPP Encapsulation on R5 and R6's BRIO Interface*

```
Termserver#5
[Resuming connection 5 to r5 ... ]

R5#conf t
Enter configuration commands, one per line.  End with CNTL/Z.
R5(config)#int bri0
R5(config-if)#encapsulation ppp
R5(config-if)#end
R5#
%ISDN-6-LAYER2DOWN: Layer 2 for Interface BRI0, TEI 65 changed to down
%ISDN-6-LAYER2DOWN: Layer 2 for Interface BR0, TEI 65 changed to down
R5#
%SYS-5-CONFIG_I: Configured from console by console
R5#
%ISDN-6-LAYER2UP: Layer 2 for Interface BR0, TEI 66 changed to up
```

**Example 12-11** *Configuring PPP Encapsulation on R5 and R6's BRI0 Interface (Continued)*

```
R5#

Termserver#6
[Resuming connection 6 to r6 ... ]

R6#conf t
Enter configuration commands, one per line.  End with CNTL/Z.
R6(config)#int bri0
R6(config-if)#encapsulation ppp
R6(config-if)#end
R6#
%ISDN-6-LAYER2DOWN: Layer 2 for Interface BRI0, TEI 126 changed to down
%ISDN-6-LAYER2DOWN: Layer 2 for Interface BR0, TEI 126 changed to down
R6#
%SYS-5-CONFIG_I: Configured from console by console
R6#
%ISDN-6-LAYER2UP: Layer 2 for Interface BR0, TEI 67 changed to up
R6#
```

Notice that when you changed the encapsulation type, the interface is reset. You can see this by the fact that Layer 2 changed to down and then back up, as shown in the highlighted portions of Example 12-11. You can manually reset the interface using the following command:

```
Router#clear interface bri0
```

To demonstrate, do this on R6 and observe the results as shown in Example 12-12.

**Example 12-12** *Clearing the BRI0 Interface on R6*

```
R6#clear int bri0
R6#
%ISDN-6-LAYER2DOWN: Layer 2 for Interface BRI0, TEI 68 changed to down
%ISDN-6-LAYER2DOWN: Layer 2 for Interface BR0, TEI 68 changed to down
R6#
%ISDN-6-LAYER2UP: Layer 2 for Interface BR0, TEI 69 changed to up
R6#
```

This command is useful when you want to force the router to re-establish Layer 2 communication with the ISDN switch. In this way, when troubleshooting ISDN Layer 2 issues, you can observe whether Layer 2 comes up as expected. In addition, this command clears an existing ISDN call from the link.

# Step 4: Configure Static Routes Pointing to the Next-Hop Router on Opposite Ends of the ISDN Link

According to the lab objective, no routing protocols are to be used across the link. Instead, you must use static routes while ensuring that R6's Token Ring network (192.168.60.0) can reach the rest of the network (R1 through R4). This will require the following tasks:

- **A default route on R6**—The first task is to configure a default route on R6. R6 needs a default route pointing to the IP address of R5's BRI0 interface or, more specifically, to 192.168.200.1. This route tells R6 that when interesting traffic hits the link, it should forward packets out the dialing interface (R6's BRI0) to R5.

- **A static route on R5 pointing to R6's Token Ring network**—All IP traffic from R6 originates from R6's IP network of 192.168.60.0. Thus, R5 needs a return path back to this network. This will require a static route on R5 indicating that, to get to 192.168.60.0, packets must be forwarded to R6's BRI0 IP address of 192.168.200.2.

- **Redistribution of the static route on R5 into IGRP**—When R5 has a static route configured as a return path to R6's 192.168.60.0 network, you can redistribute this static route into the IGRP routing process of R5 so that this route is propagated to the other routers within the network (R1 through R4). By doing so, R1 through R4 will receive a route to 192.168.60.0. In addition, you will redistribute the 192.168.200.0 network into IGRP on R5 using the **redistribute connected** command. This is necessary because the 192.168.200.0 network was not added to the IGRP routing process. By redistributing this connected network into IGRP, R1 through R4 will learn the route to the 192.168.200.0 network. This is because you redistribute this connected network into IGRP, which then gets redistributed into EIGRP and eventually into RIP. This is necessary for R6 to successfully be capable of Telnetting to R1 through R4 as required by the lab objective.

Configure the default route on R6 as shown in Example 12-13.

**Example 12-13**  *Configuring a Default Route on R6 to 192.168.200.1*

```
R6#conf t
Enter configuration commands, one per line.  End with CNTL/Z.
R6(config)#ip route 0.0.0.0 0.0.0.0 192.168.200.1
R6(config)#end
R6#
```

Next, verify that the default route shows up properly in the routing table as shown on R6's in Example 12-14.

**Example 12-14** *Verifying the Default Route in R6's Routing Table*

```
R6#show ip ro
Codes: C - connected, S - static, I - IGRP, R - RIP, M - mobile, B - BGP
       D - EIGRP, EX - EIGRP external, O - OSPF, IA - OSPF inter area
       N1 - OSPF NSSA external type 1, N2 - OSPF NSSA external type 2
       E1 - OSPF external type 1, E2 - OSPF external type 2, E - EGP
       i - IS-IS, L1 - IS-IS level-1, L2 - IS-IS level-2, * - candidate default
       U - per-user static route, o - ODR

Gateway of last resort is 192.168.200.1 to network 0.0.0.0

C    192.169.6.0/24 is directly connected, Loopback0
     192.168.200.0/30 is subnetted, 1 subnets
C       192.168.200.0 is directly connected, BRI0
S*   0.0.0.0/0 [1/0] via 192.168.200.1
R6#
```

Next, resume the connection to R5, create a static route to network 192.168.60.0, and then redistribute this route into IGRP on R5. Redistribute this route on R5 using the following command:

```
Router(config-router)#redistribute static
```

In addition, redistribute connected routes using the following command:

```
Router(config-router)#redistribute connected
```

These commands will ensure that the rest of the network gets a route to R6's Token Ring network of 192.168.60.0 by using the **redistribute static** command and to the directly connected network of 192.168.200.0 by using the **redistribute connected** command. Example 12-15 shows how this is done.

**Example 12-15** *Redistributing Static and Connected Routes into IGRP on R5*

```
Termserver#5
[Resuming connection 5 to r5 ... ]

R5#conf t
Enter configuration commands, one per line.  End with CNTL/Z.
R5(config)#ip route 192.168.60.0 255.255.255.0 192.168.200.2
R5(config)#router igrp 200
R5(config-router)#redistribute static
R5(config-router)#redistribute connected
R5(config-router)#end
R5#
%SYS-5-CONFIG_I: Configured from console by console
R5#
```

At this point, you should verify that R1, R2, R3, and R4 have received each of these redistributed routes (192.168.60.0 and 192.168.200.0). Do this by displaying the IP routing table on each router, as shown in Example 12-16.

**Example 12-16** *IP Routing Table of R1, R2, R3, and R4 Shows That the Routes Redistributed on R5 into IGRP Have Been Successfully Received*

```
Termserver#1
[Resuming connection 1 to r1 ... ]

R1#sho ip ro
Codes: C - connected, S - static, I - IGRP, R - RIP, M - mobile, B - BGP
       D - EIGRP, EX - EIGRP external, O - OSPF, IA - OSPF inter area
       N1 - OSPF NSSA external type 1, N2 - OSPF NSSA external type 2
       E1 - OSPF external type 1, E2 - OSPF external type 2, E - EGP
       i - IS-IS, L1 - IS-IS level-1, L2 - IS-IS level-2, * - candidate default
       U - per-user static route, o - ODR

Gateway of last resort is 192.168.1.2 to network 0.0.0.0

R    192.168.100.0/24 [120/1] via 192.168.1.2, 00:00:10, Ethernet0
R    192.168.35.0/24 [120/1] via 192.168.1.2, 00:00:10, Ethernet0
R    192.168.60.0/24 [120/1] via 192.168.1.2, 00:00:10, Ethernet0
R    192.168.50.0/24 [120/1] via 192.168.1.2, 00:00:10, Ethernet0
C    192.169.1.0/24 is directly connected, Loopback0
C    192.168.1.0/24 is directly connected, Ethernet0
R    192.169.3.0/24 [120/1] via 192.168.1.2, 00:00:10, Ethernet0
R    192.168.2.0/24 [120/1] via 192.168.1.2, 00:00:10, Ethernet0
R    192.168.3.0/24 [120/1] via 192.168.1.2, 00:00:10, Ethernet0
R    192.169.2.0/24 [120/1] via 192.168.1.2, 00:00:10, Ethernet0
R    192.169.5.0/24 [120/1] via 192.168.1.2, 00:00:11, Ethernet0
R    192.168.4.0/24 [120/1] via 192.168.1.2, 00:00:11, Ethernet0
R    192.169.4.0/24 [120/1] via 192.168.1.2, 00:00:11, Ethernet0
R    192.168.200.0/24 [120/1] via 192.168.1.2, 00:00:11, Ethernet0
S*   0.0.0.0/0 [1/0] via 192.168.1.2
R1#


Termserver#2
[Resuming connection 2 to r2 ... ]

R2#show ip ro
Codes: C - connected, S - static, I - IGRP, R - RIP, M - mobile, B - BGP
       D - EIGRP, EX - EIGRP external, O - OSPF, IA - OSPF inter area
       N1 - OSPF NSSA external type 1, N2 - OSPF NSSA external type 2
       E1 - OSPF external type 1, E2 - OSPF external type 2, E - EGP
       i - IS-IS, L1 - IS-IS level-1, L2 - IS-IS level-2, * - candidate default
       U - per-user static route, o - ODR

Gateway of last resort is not set

D EX 192.168.60.0/24 [170/41536000] via 192.168.100.3, 00:11:15, Serial0
D EX 192.168.200.0/24 [170/41536000] via 192.168.100.3, 01:15:54, Serial0
```

**Example 12-16** *IP Routing Table of R1, R2, R3, and R4 Shows That the Routes Redistributed on R5 into IGRP Have Been Successfully Received (Continued)*

```
       192.168.4.0/27 is subnetted, 1 subnets
D         192.168.4.0 [90/2707456] via 192.168.100.3, 2w6d, Serial0
D      192.169.4.0/24 [90/2809856] via 192.168.100.3, 2w6d, Serial0
D EX 192.169.5.0/24 [170/2809856] via 192.168.100.3, 1d07h, Serial0
D EX 192.168.50.0/24 [170/2697984] via 192.168.100.3, 1d07h, Serial0
D EX 192.168.35.0/24 [170/2169856] via 192.168.100.3, 1d07h, Serial0
C      192.168.1.0/24 is directly connected, Ethernet0
R      192.169.1.0/24 [120/1] via 192.168.1.1, 00:00:21, Ethernet0
C      192.168.2.0/24 is directly connected, Ethernet1
C      192.169.2.0/24 is directly connected, Loopback0
C      192.168.100.0/24 is directly connected, Serial0
D      192.168.3.0/24 [90/2195456] via 192.168.100.3, 2w6d, Serial0
D EX 192.169.3.0/24 [170/2169856] via 192.168.100.3, 1d07h, Serial0
D      200.200.0.0/16 [90/2809856] via 192.168.100.3, 2w6d, Serial0
R2#


Termserver#3
[Resuming connection 3 to r3 ... ]
```

```
R3#show ip ro
Codes: C - connected, S - static, I - IGRP, R - RIP, M - mobile, B - BGP
Codes: C - connected, S - static, I - IGRP, R - RIP, M - mobile, B - BGP
       N1 - OSPF NSSA external type 1, N2 - OSPF NSSA external type 2
       E1 - OSPF external type 1, E2 - OSPF external type 2, E - EGP
       i - IS-IS, L1 - IS-IS level-1, L2 - IS-IS level-2, * - candidate default
       U - per-user static route, o - ODR

Gateway of last resort is not set

C      192.168.100.0/24 is directly connected, Serial0
C      192.168.35.0/24 is directly connected, Serial1
I      192.168.60.0/24 [100/160250] via 192.168.35.5, 00:01:16, Serial1
I      192.168.50.0/24 [100/8539] via 192.168.35.5, 00:01:16, Serial1
D EX 192.169.1.0/24 [170/2221056] via 192.168.100.2, 19:25:04, Serial0
D EX 192.168.1.0/24 [170/2221056] via 192.168.100.2, 19:25:04, Serial0
D EX 192.168.2.0/24 [170/2221056] via 192.168.100.2, 19:25:04, Serial0
C      192.169.3.0/24 is directly connected, Loopback0
D EX 192.169.2.0/24 [170/2221056] via 192.168.100.2, 19:25:04, Serial0
C      192.168.3.0/24 is directly connected, Ethernet0
I      192.169.5.0/24 [100/8976] via 192.168.35.5, 00:01:16, Serial1
       192.168.4.0/27 is subnetted, 1 subnets
D         192.168.4.0 [90/2195456] via 192.168.100.4, 2w6d, Serial0
D      192.169.4.0/24 [90/2297856] via 192.168.100.4, 2w6d, Serial0
I      192.168.200.0/24 [100/160250] via 192.168.35.5, 00:01:17, Serial1
D      200.200.0.0/16 [90/2297856] via 192.168.100.4, 2w6d, Serial0
R3#


Termserver#4
[Resuming connection 4 to r4 ... ]
```

*continues*

**Example 12-16**  *IP Routing Table of R1, R2, R3, and R4 Shows That the Routes Redistributed on R5 into IGRP Have Been Successfully Received (Continued)*

```
R4#show ip ro
Codes: C - connected, S - static, I - IGRP, R - RIP, M - mobile, B - BGP
       D - EIGRP, EX - EIGRP external, O - OSPF, IA - OSPF inter area
       N1 - OSPF NSSA external type 1, N2 - OSPF NSSA external type 2
       E1 - OSPF external type 1, E2 - OSPF external type 2, E - EGP
       i - IS-IS, L1 - IS-IS level-1, L2 - IS-IS level-2, * - candidate default
       U - per-user static route, o - ODR

Gateway of last resort is not set

C    200.200.1.0/24 is directly connected, Loopback1
C    200.200.2.0/24 is directly connected, Loopback2
C    192.168.100.0/24 is directly connected, Serial0
D EX 192.168.35.0/24 [170/2169856] via 192.168.100.3, 1d07h, Serial0
D EX 192.168.60.0/24 [170/41536000] via 192.168.100.3, 00:13:12, Serial0
D EX 192.168.50.0/24 [170/2697984] via 192.168.100.3, 1d07h, Serial0
D EX 192.169.1.0/24 [170/2733056] via 192.168.100.3, 19:25:59, Serial0
D EX 192.168.1.0/24 [170/2733056] via 192.168.100.3, 19:25:59, Serial0
D EX 192.168.2.0/24 [170/2733056] via 192.168.100.3, 19:25:59, Serial0
D EX 192.169.3.0/24 [170/2169856] via 192.168.100.3, 1d07h, Serial0
D EX 192.169.2.0/24 [170/2733056] via 192.168.100.3, 19:25:59, Serial0
D    192.168.3.0/24 [90/2195456] via 192.168.100.3, 2w6d, Serial0
D EX 192.169.5.0/24 [170/2809856] via 192.168.100.3, 1d07h, Serial0
     192.168.4.0/27 is subnetted, 1 subnets
C       192.168.4.0 is directly connected, Ethernet0
C    192.169.4.0/24 is directly connected, Loopback0
D EX 192.168.200.0/24 [170/41536000] via 192.168.100.3, 01:17:20, Serial0
D    200.200.0.0/16 is a summary, 2w6d, Null0
R4#
```

You can see that R1, R2, R3, and R4 have received these redistributed routes. As mentioned previously, these routes allow connectivity from R6's Token Ring network to the main network and also ensure that R6 can Telnet to R1 through R4 by the name configured previously in the host table.

# Step 5: Specify the Interesting Traffic That Will Trigger the Link by Configuring a Dialer List from Global Configuration Mode

Now that you have the proper static routes in place and have redistributed them to the rest of the network, you must define the type of traffic that will bring up the link. According to the lab objective, R6 always should initiate the ISDN call when IP traffic is present.

Because R6 should call R5 instead of the other way around, R5 will not need a dialer string because you want R6 to always be the one to initiate the call. Lastly, the objective states that only IP traffic should bring up the link, so the dialer lists on R5 and R6 should be configured so that only IP traffic is considered interesting.

You can define interesting traffic using a dialer list that explicitly permits any IP protocol. Then you can apply this dialer list to the BRI0 interface using the **dialer-group** command. Example 12-17 demonstrates how this is done on R6.

**Example 12-17** *Configuring a Dialer List on R6 and Assigning This List to the BRI0 Interface Using the* **dialer-group** *Command*

```
Termserver#6
[Resuming connection 6 to r6 ... ]

R6#conf t
Enter configuration commands, one per line.  End with CNTL/Z.
R6(config)#dialer-list 1 protocol ip permit
R6(config)#int bri0
R6(config-if)#dialer-group 1
R6(config-if)#end
R6#
%SYS-5-CONFIG_I: Configured from console by console
R6#
```

**NOTE**    Although not shown here, a dialer-list should be configured on R5 and applied to the BRI0 interface using the **dialer-group** command as demonstrated in Example 12-17. You will see this reflected in the router configurations found in Appendix A. Remember that R5 will never initiate the ISDN call as no dial string will be configured on R5. Because of this, you may wonder why a dialer this should be configured on R5. However, the dialer-list on R5 is used to define the interesting traffic that resets R5's idle-timer when interesting traffic flows in the reverse path from R5 to R6.

Next, examine the running config of R6 in Example 12-18 to familiarize yourself with where you would expect to see the **dialer-list** and **dialer-group** commands within the running configuration file.

**Example 12-18** *Running Config on R6 Shows Where You Expect to See* **dialer-group** *and* **dialer-list** *Commands*

```
Termserver#6
[Resuming connection 6 to r6 ... ]

R6#show running-config
Building configuration...

Current configuration:
!
version 11.2
no service password-encryption
no service udp-small-servers
no service tcp-small-servers
```

*continues*

**Example 12-18** *Running Config on R6 Shows Where You Expect to See* **dialer-group** *and* **dialer-list** *Commands (Continued)*

```
!
hostname R6
!
enable password falcons
!
ip subnet-zero
no ip domain-lookup
ip host R6 192.169.6.6
2
ip host R2 192.169.2.2
ip host R3 192.169.3.3
ip host R4 192.169.4.4
ip host R5 192.169.5.5
isdn switch-type basic-5ess
!
interface Loopback0
 ip address 192.169.6.6 255.255.255.0
!
interface Serial0
 no ip address
 shutdown
 no fair-queue
!
interface Serial1
 no ip address
 shutdown
!
interface TokenRing0
 description This interface does not connect with another IP device
 ip address 192.168.60.6 255.255.255.0
 ring-speed 16
!
interface BRI0
 ip address 192.168.200.2 255.255.255.252
 encapsulation ppp
 dialer-group 1
!
no ip classless
ip route 0.0.0.0 0.0.0.0 192.168.200.1
!
dialer-list 1 protocol ip permit
banner motd ^C
This is Router 6
^C
!
line con 0
 exec-timeout 0 0
 password falcons
 logging synchronous
line aux 0
line vty 0 4
```

**Example 12-18** *Running Config on R6 Shows Where You Expect to See* **dialer-group** *and*
**dialer-list** *Commands (Continued)*

```
 password falcons
 login
 !
 end

 R6#
```

Notice that the **dialer-list** statement shows up after any configured static routes, and the
**dialer-group** command appears under the BRI0 interface configuration, as highlighted in
Example 12-18.

# Step 6: Configure the Number That the Router Should Call from Interface Configuration Mode by Specifying the Dial String

Next, specify what number should be called to complete the dialed connection. R6 will call
R5, so R6 needs a dial string defined under R6's BRI0 interface, telling it to call 8358662.
Configure this as shown in Example 12-19.

**Example 12-19** *Configuring a Dial String on R6*

```
Termserver#6
[Resuming connection 6 to r6 ... ]

R6#conf t
Enter configuration commands, one per line.  End with CNTL/Z.
R6(config)#int bri0
R6(config-if)#dial string 8358662
R6(config-if)#end
R6#
%SYS-5-CONFIG_I: Configured from console by console
R6#
```

After a dial string has been configured on the interface, you can view the dialer information
with the following command:

```
Router#show dialer
```

As demonstrated in Example 12-20, the output from this command shows you the
following information:

- The dial string for the configured interface
- The status of any existing calls
- The status of the last call
- How many successes or failures have been experienced dialing the particular dial string

**Example 12-20** **show dialer** *on R6 Displays How Output Appears After Dial String Has Been Configured*

```
R6#show dialer

BRI0 - dialer type = ISDN

Dial String      Successes   Failures    Last called    Last status
8358662                  0          0     never                    -   Default
0 incoming call(s) have been screened.

BRI0:1 - dialer type = ISDN
Idle timer (120 secs), Fast idle timer (20 secs)
Wait for carrier (30 secs), Re-enable (15 secs)
Dialer state is idle

BRI0:2 - dialer type = ISDN
Idle timer (120 secs), Fast idle timer (20 secs)
Wait for carrier (30 secs), Re-enable (15 secs)
Dialer state is idle
R6#
```

You can see that the dial string is 8358662. Currently there are no successes or failures for this dial string because, up to this point, a call has never been completed to this number, as shown in the Last called column showing **never**. Currently, the dialer state is idle. When a call is made to the associated dial string, this field changes indicating the last time a dial attempt was made.

Bring up the link by initiating a **ping** from R6 to R5's BRI0 interface of 192.168.200.1, as demonstrated in Example 12-21.

**Example 12-21** **ping** *to R5 Brings Up ISDN Link*

```
R6#ping 192.168.200.1

Type escape sequence to abort.
Sending 5, 100-byte ICMP Echos to 192.168.200.1, timeout is 2 seconds:
.!!!!
Success rate is 80 percent (4/5), round-trip min/avg/max = 32/34/36 ms
R6#
%LINK-3-UPDOWN: Interface BRI0:1, changed state to up
%LINEPROTO-5-UPDOWN: Line protocol on Interface BRI0:1, changed state to up
R6#
%ISDN-6-CONNECT: Interface BRI0:1 is now connected to 8358662
R6#
```

Notice in the highlighted portion of Example 12-21 that BRI0:1 changed to up and that you now are connected to 8358662. The IP traffic initiated from R6 has caused the BRI interface to call the dial string assigned to the interface; after this, the call was placed and the link came up. Generally, you will see a certain number of your first **ping** packets fail when bringing up the ISDN connection. This was the case with the first **ping** packet sent, as denoted by the . instead of a !. This is expected because of the initial delay of bringing up the ISDN connection, causing the first **ping** packets to fail. After the link is up, four successful **ping** replies occur. Executing the **show dialer** command now shows a change in the output, as demonstrated in Example 12-22.

**Example 12-22** *Dialer Output on R6 After Call Is Connected*

```
R6#show dialer

BRI0 - dialer type = ISDN

Dial String      Successes   Failures    Last called   Last status
8358662                  1          0    00:00:17      successful   Default
0 incoming call(s) have been screened.

BRI0:1 - dialer type = ISDN
Idle timer (120 secs), Fast idle timer (20 secs)
Wait for carrier (30 secs), Re-enable (15 secs)
Dialer state is data link layer up
Dial reason: ip (s=192.168.200.2, d=192.168.200.1)
Time until disconnect 104 secs
Current call connected 00:00:17
Connected to 8358662

BRI0:2 - dialer type = ISDN
Idle timer (120 secs), Fast idle timer (20 secs)
Wait for carrier (30 secs), Re-enable (15 secs)
Dialer state is idle
R6#
```

This output shows one successful call to this dial string. In addition, the data link layer is up on the dialer. The dial reason for the call was an IP packet from the source of 192.168.200.2 destined for 192.168.200.1 (the **ping** you sent). 104 seconds remain before the link will disconnect if no IP traffic is present. The output shows that the call has been connected for 17 seconds and is connected to 8358662. This information is useful in troubleshooting the current status of the call, when it will disconnect, and the type of traffic that brought up the link. You also can see whether you are experiencing successes or failures when the dialed connection is made, whether the last attempt was a success or a failure, and when the last attempt was made. In this example, all of these values appear correctly as expected.

As another measure, examine the ISDN status after a call has been successfully made from R6 to R5, as shown in Example 12-23.

Notice that now Layer 3 has one active call on the link. This means that R6 has successfully dialed R5 across the ISDN link and now can route traffic across the connection.

**Example 12-23** *ISDN Status on R6 After Call Is Connected*

```
R6#show isdn status
The current ISDN Switchtype = basic-5ess
ISDN BRI0 interface
    Layer 1 Status:
        ACTIVE
    Layer 2 Status:
        TEI = 70, State = MULTIPLE_FRAME_ESTABLISHED
    Layer 3 Status:
        1 Active Layer 3 Call(s)
    Activated dsl 0 CCBs = 1
        CCB: callid=0x8003, sapi=0, ces=1, B-chan=1
    Total Allocated ISDN CCBs = 1
R6#
```

# Step 7: Configure the Dialer Idle-Timeout from Interface Configuration Mode

Refer back to Example 12-22. Notice that, by default, the idle timer defaults to 120 seconds. This means that if interesting traffic is not present for 120 seconds, the link is brought down. To fulfill the lab objective, change this value to 5 minutes or 300 seconds on R6 using the following command:

```
Router(config-if)#dialer idle-timeout [time-in-seconds]
```

Return to R6 and change the idle-timeout as shown in Example 12-24.

**Example 12-24** *Configuring Idle-Timeout to 5 Minutes on R6*

```
Termserver#6
[Resuming connection 6 to r6 ... ]

R6#conf t
Enter configuration commands, one per line.  End with CNTL/Z.
R6(config)#int bri0
R6(config-if)#dialer idle-timeout 300
R6(config-if)#end
%SYS-5-CONFIG_I: Configured from console by console
R6#
```

**NOTE**    Although not demonstrated here, remember to configure R5's idle-timeout to 300 as shown for R6 in Example 12-24.

Bring up the DDR connection with a **ping** to R5, and then verify that the idle timer has been changed to 300 seconds using the **show dialer** command, as demonstrated in Example 12-25.

**Example 12-25** *R6 Dialer Shows That the Idle Timer Has Been Changed to 300 Seconds*

```
R6#ping 192.168.200.1

Type escape sequence to abort.
Sending 5, 100-byte ICMP Echos to 192.168.200.1, timeout is 2 seconds:
.!!!!
Success rate is 80 percent (4/5), round-trip min/avg/max = 32/34/36 ms
R6#
%LINK-3-UPDOWN: Interface BRI0:1, changed state to up
%LINEPROTO-5-UPDOWN: Line protocol on Interface BRI0:1, changed state to up
R6#
%ISDN-6-CONNECT: Interface BRI0:1 is now connected to 8358662
R6#

R6#show dialer

BRI0 - dialer type = ISDN

Dial String      Successes    Failures    Last called    Last status
8358662                  2           0    01:29:34       successful    Default
0 incoming call(s) have been screened.

BRI0:1 - dialer type = ISDN
Idle timer (300 secs), Fast idle timer (20 secs)
Wait for carrier (30 secs), Re-enable (15 secs)
Dialer state is idle

BRI0:2 - dialer type = ISDN
Idle timer (300 secs), Fast idle timer (20 secs)
Wait for carrier (30 secs), Re-enable (15 secs)
Dialer state is idle
R6#
```

As highlighted in Example 12-24, the value has been successfully changed to 5 minutes.

When the link is up, you can display active ISDN calls using the following command:

```
Router#show isdn active
```

Do this on R6, as demonstrated in Example 12-26.

**Example 12-26** *Displaying Active Calls on R6 Using the* **show isdn active** *Command*

```
R6#show isdn active
- - - - - - - - - - - - - - - - - - - - - - - - - - - - - - - - - - - - - - - - - - -
                       ISDN ACTIVE CALLS
- - - - - - - - - - - - - - - - - - - - - - - - - - - - - - - - - - - - - - - - - - -
History Table MaxLength = 100 entries
History Retain Timer = 15 Minutes
- - - - - - - - - - - - - - - - - - - - - - - - - - - - - - - - - - - - - - - - - - -
Call Calling     Called        Duration  Remote   Time until
Type Number      Number        Seconds   Name     Disconnect
- - - - - - - - - - - - - - - - - - - - - - - - - - - - - - - - - - - - - - - - - - -
Out              8358662       Active(23)            277
- - - - - - - - - - - - - - - - - - - - - - - - - - - - - - - - - - - - - - - - - - -

R6#
```

This **show** command displays the active ISDN call. In addition, you can see that the call is going out from R6 and that the called number of 8358662 is displayed. You can see that the call is active and has been for 23 seconds, as indicated by the **Active(23)** under the Duration column. Also, the call will be disconnected in 277 seconds if interesting traffic does not hit the link.

Next, test connectivity to the remainder of the network using the host table on R6. Telnet to each lab router by the name in the host table. Remember that when this host table was configured, you mapped the router host name to the router's loopback address. Begin by returning to R6 and then testing Telnet connectivity to R1, R2, R3, R4, and R5, as shown in Example 12-27.

**Example 12-27** *Successful Telnet by Host Name from R6 to R1, R2, R3, R4, and R5*

```
Termserver#6
[Resuming connection 6 to r6 ... ]

R6#r1
Trying R1 (192.169.1.1)... Open

This is Router 1


User Access Verification

Password:
R1>quit

[Connection to r1 closed by foreign host]
R6#
%LINK-3-UPDOWN: Interface BRI0:1, changed state to up
%LINEPROTO-5-UPDOWN: Line protocol on Interface BRI0:1, changed state to up
%ISDN-6-CONNECT: Interface BRI0:1 is now connected to 8358662
```

**Example 12-27** *Successful Telnet by Host Name from R6 to R1, R2, R3, R4, and R5 (Continued)*

```
R6#r2
Trying R2 (192.169.2.2)... Open

This is Router 2


User Access Verification

Password:
R2>quit

[Connection to r2 closed by foreign host]

R6#r3
Trying R3 (192.169.3.3)... Open

This is Router 3


User Access Verification

Password:
R3>quit

[Connection to r3 closed by foreign host]

R6#r4
Trying R4 (192.169.4.4)... Open

This is Router 4


User Access Verification

Password:
R4>quit

[Connection to r4 closed by foreign host]

R6#r5
Trying R5 (192.169.5.5)... Open


User Access Verification

Password:
R5>quit

[Connection to r5 closed by foreign host]
R6#
```

Notice in Example 12-27 that the first Telnet session to R1 caused the link to become active. In addition, you were able to successfully Telnet from R6 to the remaining lab routers.

You now have successfully configured ISDN and legacy DDR between R5 and R6. You learned how to define interesting traffic to initiate the link and change the idle timer. You set up static routes and redistributed these routes where necessary to ensure connectivity to your entire network. Finally, you tested ISDN connectivity through Telnet from R6 to each other router within you network. See Appendix A, "Master Lab Configurations and Lab Diagrams," to check your router configurations for this chapter. In the next chapter, you will be configuring IPX within the network.

This chapter covers the following topics:

- Configuring IPX on Cisco routers

## CHAPTER 13

# IPX

This chapter briefly reviews the IPX protocol suite and completes the lab objectives associated with this chapter. With the release of NetWare 5 by Novell, NetWare file servers can communicate natively with TCP/IP. However, there is a substantial installed base. As a result of this install base, the need for Novell file servers that still use IPX and the need for internetworking devices to support IPX are still requirements in most enterprise networks today.

## Fundamentals of the IPX Protocol

The Internetwork Packet Exchange (IPX) protocol was developed by Novell and was derived from the Xerox Network System (XNS) protocol suite. IPX is a network layer protocol that allows a network address field in the IPX packet header. This allows IPX packets to be routed from one network to another. Figure 13-1 illustrates the IPX protocol suite as it compares to the OSI reference model.

**Figure 13-1** *IPX Protocol Suite versus OSI Reference Model*

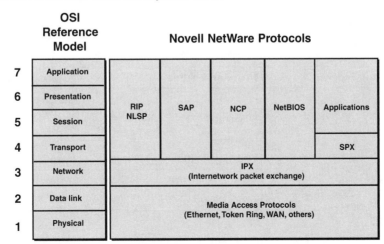

IPX uses it own version of the Routing Information Protocol (RIP) that allows the exchange of IPX routes (this will be covered in Chapter 14, "Routing IPX").

IPX also use the Service Advertisement Protocol (SAP) to announce network services such as file and print servers to Novell clients on the network. SAP advertisements are sent out every 60 seconds, and Novell file servers and clients keep a table of such services, known as a SAP table. Clients learn of Novell servers by sending Get Nearest Server (GNS) requests upon booting. The first server to respond to the request is considered the nearest server, and the Novell client uses the network address from that server as its network address as well.

IPX addresses consist of two components:

> network-number.node-number

The network number can be up to eight digits (32 bits) in length and is expressed as a hexadecimal number. Usually any preceding zeros are dropped from the network number, so the network number might appear as less than eight digits.

The node-number has 12 digits (48 bits) and is usually the MAC address of the interface on which IPX has been configured. The node number also is displayed in hexadecimal format. On serial interfaces, the node number can be manually assigned. By default, a serial interface will use the MAC address of a connected Ethernet or Token Ring interface. This does not cause a problem with Cisco routers because the network number will be different than the interface from which it borrowed the MAC address.

A valid IPX address would appear as follows:

> 2DC4AB13.0c19.ab93.0102
> or
> 1.0c32.45ce.139a

IPX does support multiple IPX networks on one interface, but each network must have a different media encapsulation. Table 13-1 lists all supported IPX media encapsulation types with their appropriate Novell and Cisco names.

**Table 13-1**   *Novell Versus Cisco Naming for Encapsulation Types*

| Media Type | Novell IPX Name | Cisco Name |
|------------|-----------------|------------|
| Ethernet | Ethernet_802.3 | novell-ether |
|  | Ethernet_802.2 | sap |
|  | Ethernet_II | ARPA |
|  | Ethernet_SNAP | snap |
| Token Ring | Token-Ring_SNAP | snap |
|  | Token-Ring | sap |
| FDDI | FDDI_SNAP | snap |
|  | FDDI_802.2 | sap |
|  | FDDI_Raw | novell-fddi |

This is a quick overview of IPX. For a complete description of the Novell IPX protocol, refer to Chapter 10 of *Interconnecting Cisco Network Devices*.

# IPX Lab Objectives

To understand better the lab objectives for this chapter, review the network topology in Figure 13-2 for configuring IPX.

**Figure 13-2**  *IPX Network Diagram*

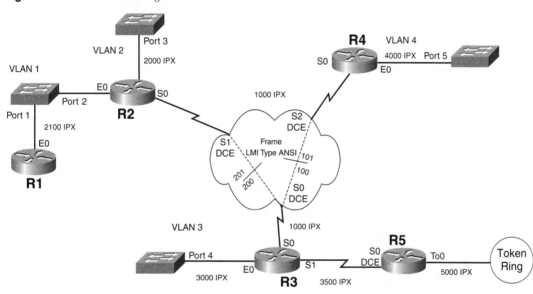

After a quick review of the diagram, you can see where IPX will be configured. This book does not cover configuration of IPX DDR, which is similar to IP DDR (covered in Chapter 12, "Integrated Services Digital Network [ISDN]"). In addition, this chapter does not cover configuration of IPX on loopback interfaces.

The objectives for this chapter's lab are as follows:

- Configure R2's S0, R3's S0, and R4's S1 with IPX network number 1000.
- Configure R3's S1 and R5's S0 for IPX network number 3500.
- Configure R5's To0 for IPX network number 5000.
- Configure R4's E0 for IPX network 4000.
- Configure R1's E0 and R2's E0 for IPX network 2100.
- Configure R2's Ethernet 1 for IPX network 2000.
- Configure R3's E0 with IPX network 3000. Use the default encapsulation type.

- Configure a secondary IPX network number 3001 on R3's E0. Make the encapsulation Novell SAP.

Now that you have seen the IPX topology and have the lab objectives, proceed with the IPX configuration.

# Configuring IPX on Cisco Routers

Several step exist for configuring IPX on a Cisco router. Knowing the steps and the proper order in which to proceed will help in configuring IPX correctly the first time. The list that follows outlines the configuration steps needed for successfully enabling IPX on a Cisco router:

**Step 1**  Enable IPX.

**Step 2**  Configure the IPX interface.

**Step 3**  Configure IPX routing (covered in Chapter 14).

**Step 4**  Verify IPX configuration.

Configuring IPX is similar to configuring IP. Each needs network and node addresses and a way to share routing information. IPX accomplishes these goals with different Cisco IOS Software commands than IP, but the end result is the same: Interfaces get assigned network and node addresses, and disparate IPX networks can communicate through Cisco routers.

Before IPX interface or IPX routing commands can be initiated, IPX must be enabled first. So let's start there.

## Enable IPX Routing

Before you can configure any IPX networks on the router interfaces, you need to enable the IPX routing process. At the same time, you can manually specify a node address for the serial interfaces (remember, serial interfaces do not have a MAC address). It is very helpful during troubleshooting to have a standard for serial link node addresses. This will ease the issue of having to look up the Ethernet or Token Ring MAC address to verify connectivity to the serial links. The naming standard for this lab is 0000.0000.1111 for R1, 0000.0000.2222 for R2, 0000.0000.3333 for R3, and so on. Go through all the routers (starting with R1), enable the IPX routing process, and manually set the node address for all the routers. Then go back and configure the individual interfaces according to the type: Frame Relay first, Ethernet second, and finally the Token Ring interfaces.

The syntax for enabling IPX on the routers, under global configuration mode, is as follows:

```
Router(config)#ipx routing [node-address]
```

The only option in this command is to specify the node address. The node address is given in hexadecimal format with a period (.) separating every 4 digits. Enable IPX routing on R1 and give it the node address of 0000.0000.1111 or 0.0.1111. Example 13-1 shows the command executed on R1.

**Example 13-1** *Enabling IPX on R1*

```
Termserver#1
[Resuming connection 1 to r1 ... ]

R1#config t
Enter configuration commands, one per line.  End with CNTL/Z.
R1(config)#ipx routing 0000.0000.1111
R1(config)#
R1(config)#end
R1#
2w4d: %SYS-5-CONFIG_I: Configured from console by console
R1#copy run start
Building configuration...
```

The command is pretty simple, but it must be entered before Cisco IOS Software will accept IPX network numbers on the interfaces. Start the IPX routing process and specify the node address. When this is completed, you can configure IPX networks on the routers' interfaces. Go through all the routers and enable IPX. Before leaving the routers, though, be sure to save the configuration, a habit that you have hopefully acquired since starting the lab. Example 13-2 displays the commands issued on the remaining routers.

**Example 13-2** *Enable IPX on All Routers*

```
Termserver#2
[Resuming connection 2 to r2 ... ]

R2#config t
Enter configuration commands, one per line.  End with CNTL/Z.
R2(config)#ipx routing 0000.0000.2222
R2(config)#end
R2#
2w4d: %SYS-5-CONFIG_I: Configured from console by console
R2#copy run start
Building configuration...

 Termserver#3
[Resuming connection 3 to r3 ... ]
```

```
R3#config t
Enter configuration commands, one per line.  End with CNTL/Z.
R3(config)#ipx routing 0000.0000.3333
R3(config)#end
R3#copy run start
Building configuration...

Termserver#4
[Resuming connection 4 to r4 ... ]
```

*continues*

**Example 13-2** *Enable IPX on All Routers (Continued)*

```
R4#config t
Enter configuration commands, one per line.  End with CNTL/Z.
R4(config)#ipx routing 0000.0000.4444
R4(config)#end
R4#copy run start
Building configuration...

Termserver#5
[Resuming connection 5 to r5 ... ]
```

```
R5#config t
Enter configuration commands, one per line.  End with CNTL/Z.
R5(config)#ipx routing 0000.0000.5555
R5(config)#end
R5#copy run start
Building configuration...
```

With IPX enabled on all the routers, you can configure the separate interfaces beginning with the Frame Relay interfaces.

# Configure IPX on Frame Relay Interfaces

Configuring IPX on Frame Relay interfaces is similar to configuring IP on Frame Relay. The first two steps already are completed: changing the encapsulation to Frame Relay on the interface and configuring the Frame Relay LMI type to be ANSI. Now you need to assign an IPX network to the interface. Because there is no such thing as Frame Relay Inverse-ARP for IPX, all IPX addresses must be manually mapped to their appropriate DLCIs on all routers.

To configure an IPX network address on an interface, under the interface configuration mode for that interface, issue this command:

```
Router(config-if)#ipx network network-address [encapsulation encapsulation-type]
```

The required field that you need to assign is the *network-address* in hexadecimal form. If there are any preceding zeros, they may be dropped. The only option here is to specify an encapsulation type. If you are using the default, there is no need to use the **encapsulation** option. If you are setting a secondary IPX network for that interface, the **encapsulation** option must be issued, and the encapsulation type must be different than the primary network address encapsulation type. Example 13-3 illustrates this command on R3's Serial 0.

**Example 13-3** *Configuring IPX Network on R3's Serial 0*

```
Termserver#3
[Resuming connection 3 to r3 ... ]
R3#config t
Enter configuration commands, one per line.  End with CNTL/Z.
R3(config)#int s0
R3(config-if)#ipx network 1000
R3(config-if)#
```

Now that an IPX network is configured on an interface, you can see whether is correctly configured by issuing this command:

```
Router#show ipx interfaces [brief]
```

This command lists all the interfaces that have IPX configured. Using the **brief** option results in less information about the interfaces. Example 13-4 shows output from this command without the **brief** option.

**Example 13-4** **show ipx interface** *Command Output*

```
R3#show ipx interface
Serial0 is up, line protocol is up
  IPX address is 1000.0000.0000.3333 [up]
  Delay of this IPX network, in ticks is 6 throughput 0 link delay 0
  IPXWAN processing not enabled on this interface.
  IPX SAP update interval is 1 minute(s)
  IPX type 20 propagation packet forwarding is disabled
  Incoming access list is not set
  Outgoing access list is not set
  IPX helper access list is not set
  SAP GNS processing enabled, delay 0 ms, output filter list is not set
  SAP Input filter list is not set
  SAP Output filter list is not set
  SAP Router filter list is not set
  Input filter list is not set
  Output filter list is not set
  Router filter list is not set
  Netbios Input host access list is not set
  Netbios Input bytes access list is not set
  Netbios Output host access list is not set
  Netbios Output bytes access list is not set
  Updates each 60 seconds, aging multiples RIP: 3 SAP: 3
  SAP interpacket delay is 55 ms, maximum size is 480 bytes
  RIP interpacket delay is 55 ms, maximum size is 432 bytes
  Watchdog processing is disabled, SPX spoofing is disabled, idle time 60
  IPX accounting is disabled
  IPX fast switching is configured (enabled)
  RIP packets received 0, RIP packets sent 1
  SAP packets received 0, SAP packets sent 0
R3#
```

The highlighted portion illustrates where the IPX address can be seen to verify that the correct IPX network was configured on the correct interface. As you notice, the IPX address is 1000.0000.0000.3333. The 1000 is the IPX network number that you just configured, and the 0000.0000.3333 is the node address that you configured earlier in the chapter when you enabled IPX for the router. Issue the same command with the **brief** option to compare the differences in the commands. Example 13-5 demonstrates the command.

**Example 13-5** **show ipx interface brief** *Command Output*

```
R3#show ipx interface brief
Interface        IPX Network Encapsulation Status          IPX State
Ethernet0        unassigned  not config'd  up              n/a
Loopback0        unassigned  not config'd  up              n/a
Serial0          1000        FRAME-RELAY   up              [up]
Serial1          unassigned  not config'd  up              n/a
```

As the highlighted output shows, only the IPX network address is revealed, not the complete IPX address with both the network address and the node address. The output also shows the encapsulation type and the status of the interface. This is a quick way to see which interfaces have IPX and what state they are in. This command is revisited later in the chapter when all the interfaces are configured for IPX. Because this is the first interface to be configured for IPX, you won't be able to IPX **ping** any other routers, so go to R2 and configure its Frame Relay interface (serial 0) for IPX and test the IPX connectivity to R3.

To configure IPX on R2's serial 0, issue the same command that you did for R3. Example 13-6 displays the commands on R2.

**Example 13-6** *Configuring IPX Network on R2's Serial 0*

```
Termserver#2
[Resuming connection 2 to r2 ... ]

R2#config t
Enter configuration commands, one per line.  End with CNTL/Z.
R2(config)#int s0
R2(config-if)#ipx network 1000
R2(config-if)#
```

Now you need to manually map the IPX address for R3 and R4 to the DLCI (201). If you have forgotten the DLCI number, you can refer back to the network diagram or you can use the **show frame-relay pvc** command. This command is the same Frame Relay map command issued in Chapter 7, "Router Interface Configuration Methodology," except that you specify the IPX protocol and the IPX address instead of the IP protocol and the IP address. Example 13-7 illustrates this command. Manually map both R3 and R4's IPX addresses, even though R4 has not yet been configured. You do know the IPX network address (1000) and the node address (0000.0000.4444) of R4 to complete the IPX address needed for the **frame-relay map** statement.

**Example 13-7** **frame-relay map** *Statements on R2*

```
R2(config-if)#frame-relay map ipx 1000.0000.0000.3333 201 broadcast
R2(config-if)#frame-relay map ipx 1000.0000.0000.4444 201 broadcast
```

With R2 having the **frame-relay map** statements, R2 should be capable of **ping**ing R3. Example 13-8 shows the results.

**Example 13-8** *R2 IPX* **ping** *to R3*

```
R2(config-if)#end
R2#ping 1000.0000.0000.3333 (or R2#ping IPX 1000.0000.0000.3333)

Type escape sequence to abort.
Sending 5, 100-byte IPXcisco Echoes to 1000.0000.0000.3333, timeout is 2 seconds:
!!!!!
Success rate is 100 percent (5/5), round-trip min/avg/max = 32/33/36 ms
R2#
```

This results in 100 percent success. It is important to note that the IPX address that was **ping**ed was that of the serial 0 interface. When IPX is configured on the Ethernet interfaces, the IPX address no longer uses the 0000.0000.3333 node address. It uses the MAC address of the Ethernet interface. The **ping** command is smart enough to understand which protocol you want to **ping** by the address format typed in after the command. Configure R4's S0 interface and verify its connectivity to R3 and R2. Example 13-9 demonstrates the configuration commands on R4.

**Example 13-9** *IPX Configuration Commands on R4's Serial 0*

```
Termserver#4
[Resuming connection 4 to r4 ... ]

R4#config t
Enter configuration commands, one per line.  End with CNTL/Z.
R4(config)#int s0
R4(config-if)#ipx network 1000
R4(config-if)#frame-relay map ipx 1000.0000.0000.3333 101 broadcast
R4(config-if)#frame-relay map ipx 1000.0000.0000.2222 101 broadcast
R4(config-if)#
```

With the configuration commands complete, verify connectivity to R3 and R2. Example 13-10 displays the results of the IPX **ping**.

**Example 13-10** *IPX* **ping** *Result from R4 to R3 and R2*

```
R4(config-if)#end
R4#ping 1000.0000.0000.3333

Type escape sequence to abort.
Sending 5, 100-byte IPX cisco Echoes to 1000.0000.0000.3333, timeout is 2 seconds:
!!!!!
Success rate is 100 percent (5/5), round-trip min/avg/max = 60/60/64 ms
R4#ping 1000.0000.0000.2222

Type escape sequence to abort.
Sending 5, 100-byte IPX cisco Echoes to 1000.0000.0000.2222, timeout is 2 seconds:
!!!!!
Success rate is 100 percent (5/5), round-trip min/avg/max = 92/94/96 ms
R4#
```

Great! IPX connectivity exists on all the Frame Relay interfaces. Take a look at what the **frame-relay map** statements now look like on R4. Example 13-11 displays the output.

**Example 13-11** **frame-relay map** *Entries on R3*

```
Termserver#3
[Resuming connection 3 to r3 ... ]

R3#show frame-relay map
Serial0 (up): ip 192.168.100.2 dlci 200(0xC8,0x3080), dynamic,
              broadcast,, status defined, active
Serial0 (up): ip 192.168.100.4 dlci 100(0x64,0x1840), dynamic,
              broadcast,, status defined, active
Serial0 (up): ipx 1000.0000.0000.2222 dlci 200(0xC8,0x3080), dynamic,
              broadcast,, status defined, active
Serial0 (up): ipx 1000.0000.0000.4444 dlci 100(0x64,0x1840), dynamic,
              broadcast,, status defined, active
R3#
```

Highlighted in Example 13-11 are the new Frame Relay map entries for the IPX address for R2 and R4. This is important because, without IPX Frame Relay map entries, R3 would not be capable of IPX **ping**ing R2 or R4.

In the next section, you will configure the Ethernet and Token Ring interfaces on all routers.

# Configure IPX on Ethernet and Token Ring Interfaces

IPX configurations are nearly the same as IP address configurations on Ethernet and Token Ring. You only need to configure the IPX network number, and the router will automatically place the MAC address of the interface in the node address portion of the IPX address. You already know how to configure an IPX network on a Frame Relay interface. The command to configure an IPX network on Ethernet and Token Ring interfaces is the same. Configure R1's Ethernet 0 and R2's Ethernet 0 interfaces for IPX. Revisiting the lab objectives, you can see that you need to assign an IPX network address of 2100. Example 13-12 illustrates the command to accomplish this.

**Example 13-12** *IPX Network Configuration on R1's Ethernet 0 and R2's Ethernet 0*

```
Termserver#1
[Resuming connection 1 to r1 ... ]

R1#config t
Enter configuration commands, one per line.  End with CNTL/Z.
R1(config)#int e0
R1(config-if)#ipx network 2100
R1(config-if)#end
R1#copy running-config startup-config
Building configuration...

Termserver#2
[Resuming connection 2 to r2 ... ]

R2#config t
Enter configuration commands, one per line.  End with CNTL/Z.

R2(config)#int e0
R2(config-if)#ipx network 2100
R2(config-if)#
```

Now that you have IPX network addresses on the interfaces, try to **ping** from R2 to R1's Ethernet 0 IPX address. To do this, you need to find the MAC address of R1's Ethernet 0. The easiest way to do this is to issue the **show interface ethernet 0** command, as demonstrated in Example 13-13.

**Example 13-13** *Output of* **show int ethernet 0** *Command on R1*

```
Termserver#1
[Resuming connection 1 to r1 ... ]
R1#show interface ethernet 0
Ethernet0 is up, line protocol is up
  Hardware is Lance, address is 00e0.1e3e.9a69 (bia 00e0.1e3e.9a69)
  Description: This interface connects to R2's E0
  Internet address is 192.168.1.1/24
  MTU 1500 bytes, BW 10000 Kbit, DLY 1000 usec, rely 255/255, load 1/255
  Encapsulation ARPA, loopback not set, keepalive set (10 sec)
  ARP type: ARPA, ARP Timeout 04:00:00
  Last input 00:00:03, output 00:00:00, output hang never
  Last clearing of "show interface" counters never
```

*continues*

**Example 13-13** *Output of* show int ethernet 0 *Command on R1 (Continued)*

```
    Queueing strategy: fifo
    Output queue 0/40, 0 drops; input queue 0/75, 0 drops
    5 minute input rate 0 bits/sec, 0 packets/sec
    5 minute output rate 0 bits/sec, 0 packets/sec
        98863 packets input, 10335188 bytes, 0 no buffer
        Received 98659 broadcasts, 0 runts, 0 giants, 0 throttles
        0 input errors, 0 CRC, 0 frame, 0 overrun, 0 ignored, 0 abort
        0 input packets with dribble condition detected
        247589 packets output, 21575438 bytes, 0 underruns
        0 output errors, 0 collisions, 2 interface resets
        0 babbles, 0 late collision, 7 deferred
        0 lost carrier, 0 no carrier
        0 output buffer failures, 0 output buffers swapped out
R1#
```

The highlighted line in Example 13-13 indicates where the MAC address is shown in the output. Go back to R2 and **ping** the interface 2100.00e0.1e3e.9a69. Example 13-14 shows the results of the **ping** to this interface.

**Example 13-14** **ping** *Result from R2 to R1's Ethernet 0 Interface*

```
Termserver#2
[Resuming connection 2 to r2 ... ]
R2#ping 2100.00e0.1e3e.9a69
Translating "2100.00e0.1e3e.9a69"

Type escape sequence to abort.
Sending 5, 100-byte IPXcisco Echoes to 2100.00e0.1e3e.9a69, timeout is 2 seconds:
!!!!!
Success rate is 100 percent (5/5), round-trip min/avg/max = 4/4/4 ms
R2#
```

Again, this results in 100 percent success. Next, configure R2's Ethernet 1 (IPX network 2000), R3's Ethernet 0 (IPX network 3000), R3's Serial 1 (IPX network 3500), R4's Ethernet 0 (IPX network 4000), R5's Serial 0 (IPX network 3500), and R5's Serial 0 (IPX network 3500) and Token Ring 0 (IPX network 5000). For Token Ring, the command is the same. Example 13-15 shows the configuration for these routers.

**Example 13-15** *IPX Configurations on the Remaining Routers*

```
R2#config t
Enter configuration commands, one per line.  End with CNTL/Z.
R2(config)#int e1
R2(config-if)#ipx network 2000
R2(config-if)#end
R2#copy running-config startup-config
Destination filename [startup-config]?
```

**Example 13-15**  *IPX Configurations on the Remaining Routers (Continued)*

```
Building configuration...

Termserver#3
[Resuming connection 3 to r3 ... ]
```

```
R3#config t
Enter configuration commands, one per line.  End with CNTL/Z.
R3(config)#int e0
R3(config-if)#ipx network 3000
R3(config-if)#exit
R3(config)#int s1
R3(config-if)#ipx network 3500
R3(config-if)#end
R3#copy running-config startup-config
Building configuration...

Termserver#4
[Resuming connection 4 to r4 ... ]
```

```
R4#config t
Enter configuration commands, one per line.  End with CNTL/Z.
R4(config)#int e0
R4(config-if)#ipx network 4000
R4(config-if)#end
R4#copy running-config startup-config
Building configuration...

Termserver#5
[Resuming connection 5 to r5 ... ]
```

```
R5#config t
Enter configuration commands, one per line.  End with CNTL/Z.
R5(config)#int s0
R5(config-if)#ipx network 3500
R5(config-if)#exit
R5(config)#int tokenRing 0
R5(config-if)#ipx network 5000
R5(config-if)#end
R5#
```

Now try to **ping** between R3's Serial 1 and R5's Serial 0 interfaces. These are the only two interfaces that are connected to another IPX device. Example 13-16 displays the results.

**Example 13-16  ping** *Result from R5 to R3's Serial 1*

```
R5(config-if)#end
R5#ping 3500.0000.0000.3333

Type escape sequence to abort.
Sending 5, 100-byte IPX cisco Echoes to 3500.0000.0000.3333, timeout is 2 seconds:
!!!!!
Success rate is 100 percent (5/5), round-trip min/avg/max = 4/5/8 ms
R5#
```

It worked. It is interesting to notice that the same node address for R3's Serial 1 interface was used as when you did the **ping** to R3's Serial 0 interface. When you manually set the node address, all serial interfaces assumed that address. The only thing that you needed to change in the **ping** command was the IPX network address that pertained to R3's Serial 1 interface (IPX network 3500).

The final lab objective is to configure a secondary IPX network number on R3's Ethernet 0 with an encapsulation type of SAP. Use the same command that you did for the primary IPX network configuration, but use the **encapsulation** option and the **secondary** option. Example 13-17 demonstrates the command on R3.

**Example 13-17** *Secondary IPX Network Configuration on R3*

```
Termserver#3
[Resuming connection 3 to r3 ... ]

R3#config t
Enter configuration commands, one per line.  End with CNTL/Z.
R3(config)#interface ethernet 0
R3(config-if)#ipx network 3001 encapsulation sap secondary
```

# Verifying IPX Configuration

Now that all the lab objectives are completed, take a look again at the output from the **show ipx interface brief** command, as displayed in Example 13-18.

**Example 13-18  show ipx interfaces brief** *Command Output*

```
R3(config-if)#end
R3#show ipx int brief
Interface          IPX Network Encapsulation Status          IPX State
Ethernet0          3000        NOVELL-ETHER  up              [up]
Ethernet0          3001        SAP           up              [up]
Loopback0          unassigned  not config'd  up              n/a
Serial0            1000        FRAME-RELAY   up              [up]
Serial1            3500        HDLC          up              [up]
R3#
```

From the output, you can see all the configured IPX interfaces and their status. This is a nice way to review the IPX configuration on the router.

Before moving on to IPX routing, take a look at the IPX routing table for R3. To see the IPX routing table, you need to issue this command:

```
Router#show ipx route
```

Example 13-19 displays the IPX routing table.

**Example 13-19** *IPX Routing Table for R3*

```
R3#show ipx route
Codes: C - Connected primary network,    c - Connected secondary network
       S - Static, F - Floating static, L - Local (internal), W - IPXWAN
       R - RIP, E - EIGRP, N - NLSP, X - External, A - Aggregate
       s - seconds, u - uses

8 Total IPX routes. Up to 1 parallel paths and 16 hops allowed.

No default route known.

C      1000 (FRAME-RELAY),   Se0
C      3000 (NOVELL-ETHER),  Et0
c      3001 (SAP),           Et0
C      3500 (HDLC),          Se1
R      2000 [07/01] via      1000.0000.0000.2222,   28s, Se0
R      2100 [07/01] via      1000.0000.0000.2222,   28s, Se0
R      4000 [07/01] via      1000.0000.0000.4444,   32s, Se0
R      5000 [07/01] via      3500.0000.0000.5555,   41s, Se1
R3#
```

Surprised? You can see all the IPX networks in the IPX routing table. How can this be if you have not yet configured a routing protocol for IPX? By default, IPX propagates all IPX networks with IPX RIP, as discussed in the next chapter.

This chapter covers the following topics:

- Configuring IPX RIP
- Configuring IPX EIGRP

## CHAPTER 14

# Routing IPX

This chapter presents an introduction to IPX routing, building on what you learned in Chapter 13, "IPX," regarding Novell's Internetwork Packet Exchange (IPX) protocol suite. This chapter begins with a brief review of IPX routing protocols, including IPX RIP and IPX EIGRP. By completing each lab objective, you will learn what is required to configure each IPX routing protocol. The lab scenario introduces you to split horizon and route redistribution in an IPX environment. You will learn how to configure IPX EIGRP and disable split horizon, where necessary. Finally, you will verify your IPX configuration by testing IPX connectivity throughout the network.

## IPX Routing Fundamentals

Within Cisco IOS Software, IPX can be routed using three possible routing protocols:

- IPX RIP
- IPX EIGRP
- Netware Link Services Protocol (NLSP)

NLSP is a link-state protocol developed by Novell based on the ISO Intermediate System-to-Intermediate System (IS-IS) routing protocol. NLSP is beyond the scope of this book, so the focus will be limited to IPX RIP and IPX EIGRP. Additional information regarding NLSP and its configuration can be found on CCO at www.cisco.com/univercd/cc/td/doc/product/software/ios121/121cgcr/atipx_c/ipx/2cdipx.htm#xtocid2449537.

## IPX RIP

Novell RIP, commonly known as IPX RIP, is a distance vector routing protocol and is the default routing protocol for IPX. IPX RIP uses two metrics to make routing decisions: ticks (a time measure equal to 1/18 second) and hop count (a count of each router traversed), to a maximum of 15. IPX RIP checks its two distance vector metrics by first comparing the ticks for path alternatives. If two or more paths have the same tick value, IPX RIP compares the hop count. Each IPX router periodically broadcasts copies of its IPX RIP routing table to its directly connected networks. The neighboring IPX routers increment the distance vector values as required before propagating their IPX RIP tables to other networks. The split-horizon algorithm prevents the neighbor from broadcasting IPX RIP routes back to the networks from where it received the information originally. IPX RIP also uses a hold-down timer to handle conditions in which an IPX router goes down without any explicit message to its neighbors. This prevents the downed link from being advertised to other routers.

Routing table updates are sent at 60-second intervals, by default. The default packet size is 576 bytes and can contain up to 50 route entries. This update frequency can cause excessive overhead traffic on some internetworks. Because of this overhead as well as the limit of 15 maximum hops, IPX RIP might not scale well in large internetworks or in WAN environments. For such cases, IPX EIGRP is a desirable alternative.

## IPX EIGRP

EIGRP is an enhanced version of IGRP developed by Cisco. Similar to IP EIGRP, IPX EIGRP uses the same distance vector algorithm and distance information. In addition, the convergence properties and the operating efficiency of EIGRP have improved significantly over other distance vector routing protocols such as IGRP or RIP.

IPX EIGRP overcomes many of the limitations of IPX RIP through the following features:

- **Fast convergence**—The DUAL algorithm allows routing information to converge as quickly as any currently available routing protocol.

- **Partial updates**—EIGRP sends incremental updates when the state of a destination changes, instead of sending the entire contents of the routing table. This feature minimizes the bandwidth required for Enhanced IGRP packets.

- **Less CPU usage**—Full update packets need not be processed each time they are received.

- **Neighbor-discovery mechanism**—This feature is a simple hello mechanism used to learn about neighboring routers. It is protocol-independent.

- **Scaling**—EIGRP scales to large networks.

For a detailed review of each feature as well as how the DUAL algorithm operates, refer to Chapter 10, "Enhanced Interior Gateway Protocol (EIGRP)."

## Routing IPX Lab Objectives

In Chapter 13, each lab router was configured with an assigned IPX network address. To ensure IPX connectivity between all IPX routers, configure IPX routing by accomplishing the following lab objectives:

- Use EIGRP as the routing protocol for the interfaces in the Frame Relay cloud and R4's Ethernet 0.

- Use IPX RIP for all other router interfaces that are *not* configured for IPX EIGRP.

- Redistribute IPX EIGRP and IPX RIP to ensure that all IPX networks are reachable by all IPX routers. Use the IPX **ping** command to verify full connectivity from each router to all IPX networks.

You will be configuring the routers shown in Figure 14-1. In addition, after you complete these lab objectives, the IPX routing domains should appear as detailed in Figure 14-1.

**Figure 14-1** *IPX EIGRP and RIP Routing Domains*

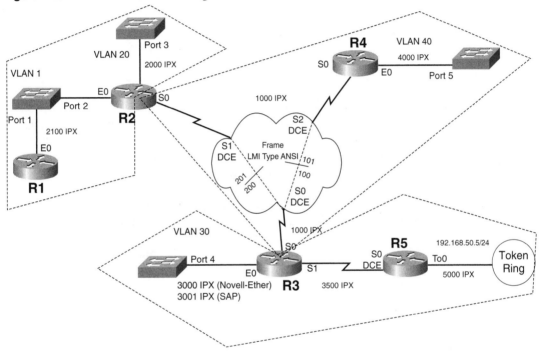

# Configuring IPX RIP

In Chapter 13, you enabled IPX routing on each router and then configured an IPX network for each interface on R1, R2, R3, R4, and R5. After that, you examined the IPX routing table of R3. Re-examine the IPX routing table of R3 as shown in Example 14-1.

**Example 14-1** *IPX Routing Table on R3*

```
Termserver#3
[Resuming connection 3 to r3 ... ]

R3#show ipx route
Codes: C - Connected primary network,    c - Connected secondary network
       S - Static, F - Floating static, L - Local (internal), W - IPXWAN
       R - RIP, E - EIGRP, N - NLSP, X - External, A - Aggregate
       s - seconds, u - uses
```

*continues*

**Example 14-1** *IPX Routing Table on R3 (Continued)*

```
8 Total IPX routes. Up to 1 parallel paths and 16 hops allowed.

No default route known.

C       1000 (FRAME-RELAY),   Se0
C       3000 (NOVELL-ETHER),  Et0
c       3001 (SAP),           Et0
C       3500 (HDLC),          Se1
R       2000 [07/01] via      1000.0000.0000.2222,   35s, Se0
R       2100 [07/01] via      1000.0000.0000.2222,   35s, Se0
R       4000 [07/01] via      1000.0000.0000.4444,   55s, Se0
R       5000 [07/01] via      3500.0000.0000.5555,   28s, Se1
R3#
```

Notice that R3 has a route to every IPX network and that all remote IPX networks have been learned through RIP. This is because, by default, when you enable IPX routing and then assign an IPX network to an interface, the network automatically is placed into IPX RIP. IPX RIP then advertises these IPX networks throughout the network. This requires no configuration on your part. The result is that R3 learns a route to every other IPX network through IPX RIP. RIP routes are denoted with the letter *R* preceding the route in the routing table, while a *C* denotes directly connected routes. Initially, this might lead you to believe that you do not need to configure a routing protocol for IPX because routes are being propagated as seen on R3. However, before making this assumption, examine the IPX routing tables of R4 and R2. Example 14-2 shows R4's IPX routing table.

**Example 14-2** *IPX Routing Table on R4*

```
Termserver#4
[Resuming connection 4 to r4 ... ]

R4#show ipx route
Codes: C - Connected primary network,    c - Connected secondary network
       S - Static, F - Floating static, L - Local (internal), W - IPXWAN
       R - RIP, E - EIGRP, N - NLSP, X - External, A - Aggregate
       s - seconds, u - uses

6 Total IPX routes. Up to 1 parallel paths and 16 hops allowed.

No default route known.

C       1000 (FRAME-RELAY),   Se0
C       4000 (NOVELL-ETHER),  Et0
R       3000 [07/01] via      1000.0000.0000.3333,   24s, Se0
R       3001 [07/01] via      1000.0000.0000.3333,   25s, Se0
R       3500 [07/01] via      1000.0000.0000.3333,   25s, Se0
R       5000 [13/02] via      1000.0000.0000.3333,   25s, Se0
R4#
```

R4 has learned all IPX networks through RIP except for networks 2000 and 2100. If you examine the IPX routing table on R2, you will find similar results, as shown in Example 14-3.

**Example 14-3** *IPX Routing Table on R2*

```
Termserver#2
[Resuming connection 2 to r2 ... ]

R2#show ipx route
Codes: C - Connected primary network,    c - Connected secondary network
       S - Static, F - Floating static, L - Local (internal), W - IPXWAN
       R - RIP, E - EIGRP, N - NLSP, X - External, A - Aggregate
       s - seconds, u - uses, U - Per-user static

7 Total IPX routes. Up to 1 parallel paths and 16 hops allowed.

No default route known.

C       1000 (FRAME-RELAY),   Se0
C       2000 (NOVELL-ETHER),  Et1
C       2100 (NOVELL-ETHER),  Et0
R       3000 [07/01] via      1000.0000.0000.3333,   47s, Se0
R       3001 [07/01] via      1000.0000.0000.3333,   47s, Se0
R       3500 [07/01] via      1000.0000.0000.3333,   47s, Se0
R       5000 [13/02] via      1000.0000.0000.3333,   47s, Se0
R2#
```

R2 has learned all IPX networks through RIP except for the IPX network 4000. Because this route is lacking, full IPX connectivity does not exist between R2 and R4. To demonstrate this, initiate a **ping** from R2 to R4's Ethernet 0 IPX address of 4000.0010.7b7f.fa6e, and observe the results shown in Example 14-4.

**Example 14-4** *IPX* **ping** *to R4's Ethernet 0 IPX Address Fails*

```
Termserver#2
[Resuming connection 2 to r2 ... ]

R2#ping ipx 4000.0010.7b7f.fa6e
Translating "4000.0010.7b7f.fa6e"

Type escape sequence to abort.
Sending 5, 100-byte IPX cisco Echoes to 4000.0010.7b7f.fa6e, timeout is 2 seconds:
.....
Success rate is 0 percent (0/5)
R2#
```

You can see that R2 cannot **ping** R4's Ethernet 0 IPX network of 4000. Although not shown, R4 also would not be capable of **ping**ing to R2's Ethernet 0 and Ethernet 1 IPX networks of 2000 or 2001. The IPX **ping** fails as a result of the fact that R4 and R2 are not receiving all IPX routes through IPX RIP. How can this be? R3 received all IPX networks through IPX RIP, but R4 and R2 did not? The answer is revealed when examining the rule of split horizon.

## Split Horizon

Split horizon blocks information about routes from being advertised out the same interface from which the route originally was learned. By default, split horizon is enabled on all interfaces. Generally, this behavior optimizes communication among multiple routers, particularly when links are broken; however, with nonbroadcast networks such as Frame Relay, situations can arise for which this behavior is less than ideal. This is particularly evident in the case of a hub-and-spoke Frame Relay environment, as exists between R3, R2, and R4. By default, IPX split horizon is enabled on R3's Serial 0 interface. Because IPX split horizon is in effect, IPX routes that R3 receives from R2 (networks 2000 and 2100) are blocked from being advertised back out R3's Serial 0 interface to R4. In addition, the IPX route that R3 receives from R4 (network 4000) is blocked from being advertised back out R3's Serial 0 interface to R2. Thus, R4 and R2 never get these routes because split horizon prevents them from being advertised out R3's Serial 0 interface.

To ensure that R2 and R4 receive these routes, you must disable split horizon on R3's Serial 0 interface. It is important to note here that split horizon cannot be disabled for IPX RIP; it can be disabled only for IPX EIGRP. So, to disable split horizon, you must first configure IPX EIGRP.

## Configuring IPX EIGRP and Disabling Split Horizon

To disable IPX split horizon, you must enable IPX EIGRP as the routing process for all interfaces in the Frame Relay cloud. When IPX EIGRP is enabled, you then will disable IPX EIGRP split horizon on the R3's Serial 0 interface. In addition, to fulfill the lab objective, you will configure R4's Ethernet 0 interface to be advertised through IPX EIGRP. To configure IPX EIGRP and disable split horizon on R3's Serial 0 interface, perform the following steps:

**Step 1**  Enable the IPX EIGRP routing process.

**Step 2**  Add the desired IPX network into the IPX EIGRP routing process.

**Step 3**  Remove the IPX network that was added to the IPX EIGRP routing process from the IPX RIP routing process.

**Step 4**  Disable split horizon on R3's Serial 0 interface.

Follow these steps starting with R2, then R4, and finally R3. First, review each step and the commands necessary to accomplish them, as shown in Table 14-1.

**Table 14-1**   *Steps to Configuring IPX EIGRP and Disabling IPX Split-Horizon*

| Step | Command |
|------|---------|
| 1. Enable the IPX EIGRP routing process from global configuration mode. | Router(config)#**ipx router eigrp** [*autonomous-system-number*] |
| 2. Add the desired IPX network into the IPX EIGRP routing process in router configuration mode. | Router(config-ipx-router)#**network** [*ipx network-number*] |
| 3. Remove the IPX EIGRP network from the IPX RIP routing process in router configuration mode. | Router(config)#**ipx router rip** <br> Router(config-ipx-router)#**no network** [*ipx-network-number*] |
| 4. Disable IPX split horizon on R3's Serial 0 interface from interface configuration mode. | Router(config-if)#**no ipx split-horizon eigrp** [*autonomous-system-number*] |

Begin with R2. Enable the IPX EIGRP routing process and use the autonomous system 100. Next, place R2's Serial 0 IPX network of 1000 into the IPX EIGRP routing process and subsequently remove IPX network 1000 from the IPX RIP routing process. This forces network 1000 to be advertised through IPX EIGRP instead of through IPX RIP. In addition, because you are using EIGRP for IPX routing, R2 will go through the process of forming neighbor relationships, as was done with IP EIGRP. For a complete review of this process, refer to Chapter 10. Return to R2 and perform these steps as shown in Example 14-5.

**Example 14-5** *Configuring R2 for IPX EIGRP AS 100, Adding IPX Network 1000, and Removing IPX Network 1000 from IPX RIP*

```
Termserver#2
[Resuming connection 2 to r2 ... ]

R2#conf t
Enter configuration commands, one per line.  End with CNTL/Z.
R2(config)#ipx router eigrp 100
R2(config-ipx-router)#network 1000
R2(config-ipx-router)#exit
R2(config)#ipx router rip
R2(config-ipx-router)#no network 1000
R2(config-ipx-router)#end
R2#
20:33:12: %SYS-5-CONFIG_I: Configured from console by console
R2#
```

If you examine the running config of R2, you can see how the IPX routing configuration appears, as shown in Example 14-6.

**Example 14-6** *R2's Running Config After Configuration of IPX EIGRP*

```
R2#show running-config
Building configuration...

Current configuration:
!
version 12.0
service timestamps debug uptime
service timestamps log uptime
no service password-encryption
!
hostname R2
!
enable password falcons
!
username all
ip subnet-zero
no ip domain-lookup
ip host R1 192.169.1.1
ip host R2 192.169.2.2
ip host R3 192.169.3.3
ip host R4 192.169.4.4
ip host R5 192.169.5.5
ip host R6 192.169.6.6
ipx routing 0000.0000.2222
!
!
!
interface Loopback0
 ip address 192.169.2.2 255.255.255.0
 no ip directed-broadcast
!
interface Ethernet0
 ip address 192.168.1.2 255.255.255.0
 no ip directed-broadcast
 ipx network 2100
!
interface Ethernet1
 description This interface does not connect with another IP device
 ip address 192.168.2.2 255.255.255.0
 no ip directed-broadcast
 ipx network 2000
!
interface Serial0
 description This interface connects to R3's S0 (201)
 ip address 192.168.100.2 255.255.255.0
 no ip directed-broadcast
 encapsulation frame-relay
 no ip mroute-cache
 ipx network 1000
 no fair-queue
 frame-relay map ip 192.168.100.3 201 broadcast
 frame-relay map ip 192.168.100.4 201 broadcast
```

**Example 14-6** *R2's Running Config After Configuration of IPX EIGRP (Continued)*

```
 frame-relay map ipx 1000.0000.0000.4444 201 broadcast
 frame-relay map ipx 1000.0000.0000.3333 201 broadcast
 frame-relay lmi-type ansi
 !
router eigrp 100
 redistribute rip metric 2000 200 255 1 1500
 network 192.168.100.0
 !
router rip
 redistribute eigrp 100 metric 1
 network 192.168.1.0
 network 192.168.2.0
 network 192.169.2.0
 !
ip classless
 !
 !
 !
ipx router eigrp 100
 network 1000
 !
 !
ipx router rip
 no network 1000
 !
 !
 !
banner motd ^C
This is Router 2
^C
 !
line con 0
 exec-timeout 0 0
 password falcons
 logging synchronous
 transport input none
line vty 0 4
 password falcons
 login
 !
end

R2#
```

The running config shows that IPX network 1000 has been added to IPX EIGRP
autonomous system 100 and has been removed from IPX RIP. It is also worthy to note that
IPX networks 2000 and 2001 do not show up explicitly under IPX RIP even though they
are properly configured on R2's Ethernet 0 and Ethernet 1, as highlighted. You just have to
remember that any IPX network configured on an interface is, by default, advertised

through IPX RIP even without adding it to the IPX RIP routing process. In addition, it is for this very reason that you must explicitly remove IPX network 1000 from IPX RIP.

Continue by configuring R4 for IPX EIGRP, and assign IPX network 1000 to be advertised through IPX EIGRP, as shown in Example 14-7.

**Example 14-7** *Configuring R4 for IPX EIGRP AS 100, Adding IPX Network 1000, and Removing IPX Network 1000 from IPX RIP*

```
R4#conf t
Enter configuration commands, one per line.  End with CNTL/Z.
R4(config)#ipx router eigrp 100
R4(config-ipx-router)#network 1000
R4(config-ipx-router)#exit
R4(config)#ipx router rip
R4(config-ipx-router)#no network 1000
R4(config-ipx-router)#end
R4#
%SYS-5-CONFIG_I: Configured from console by console
R4#
```

Next, configure R3 for IPX EIGRP, as shown in Example 14-8.

**Example 14-8** *Configuring R3 for IPX EIGRP AS 100, Adding IPX Network 1000, and Removing IPX Network 1000 from IPX RIP*

```
R3#conf t
Enter configuration commands, one per line.  End with CNTL/Z.
R3(config)#ipx router eigrp 100
R3(config-ipx-router)#network 1000
R3(config-ipx-router)#exit
R3(config)#ipx router rip
R3(config-ipx-router)#no network 1000
R3(config-ipx-router)#end
R3#
%SYS-5-CONFIG_I: Configured from console by console
R3#
```

Now that R3 has been configured for IPX EIGRP, display the IPX EIGRP neighbors, as demonstrated in Example 14-9.

**Example 14-9** *R3 Shows Established IPX EIGRP Neighbor Adjacencies with R2 and R4*

```
R3#show ipx eigrp neighbors

IPX EIGRP Neighbors for process 100
H   Address                 Interface    Hold Uptime   SRTT   RTO  Q   Seq
                                         (sec)         (ms)        Cnt Num
```

**Example 14-9** *R3 Shows Established IPX EIGRP Neighbor Adjacencies with R2 and R4 (Continued)*

```
1    1000.0000.0000.2222    Se0    179 00:01:51 724  4344  0  2
0    1000.0000.0000.4444    Se0    165 00:02:06 553  3318  0  4
R3#
```

R3 has successfully formed an IPX EIGRP neighbor adjacency with both R2 (1000.0000.0000.2222) and R4 (1000.0000.0000.4444). Now return to R4 and display the IPX routing table, to see how IPX routes are being learned. Example 14-10 shows the IPX routing table after EIGRP has been configured.

**Example 14-10** *IPX Routing Table on R4 After EIGRP Configuration*

```
R4#show ipx route
Codes: C - Connected primary network,    c - Connected secondary network
       S - Static, F - Floating static, L - Local (internal), W - IPXWAN
       R - RIP, E - EIGRP, N - NLSP, X - External, A - Aggregate
       s - seconds, u - uses

6 Total IPX routes. Up to 1 parallel paths and 16 hops allowed.

No default route known.

C       1000 (FRAME-RELAY),   Se0
C       4000 (NOVELL-ETHER),  Et0
E       3000 [2195456/1] via     1000.0000.0000.3333, age 00:09:28,
                          1u, Se0
E       3001 [2195456/1] via     1000.0000.0000.3333, age 00:09:29,
                          1u, Se0
E       3500 [2681856/1] via     1000.0000.0000.3333, age 00:09:29,
                          1u, Se0
E       5000 [276864000/2] via    1000.0000.0000.3333, age 00:09:29,
                          1u, Se0
R4#
```

The output in Example 14-10 shows that R4 is learning all remote IPX routes through IPX EIGRP. Notice that R4 has learned networks 3001, 3500, and 5000 through EIGRP, even though these networks were configured on R3 and R5 to be advertised through IPX RIP. This occurs because of IPX route redistribution and will be covered in more detail later in the chapter. Also notice that R4 still has not learned about networks 2000 and 2001, as desired. To remedy this, disable IPX EIGRP split horizon on R3's Serial 0 interface, as demonstrated in Example 14-11.

**Example 14-11** *Disabling IPX EIGRP Split Horizon on R3's Serial 0 Interface*

```
R3#conf t
%SYS-5-CONFIG_I: Configured from console by console
Enter configuration commands, one per line.  End with CNTL/Z.
R3(config)#int s0
```

*continues*

**Example 14-11**  *Disabling IPX EIGRP Split Horizon on R3's Serial 0 Interface (Continued)*

```
R3(config-if)#no ipx split-horizon eigrp 100
R3(config-if)#end
R3#
%SYS-5-CONFIG_I: Configured from console by console
R3#
```

Now that split horizon has been disabled on R3's Serial 0 interface, when you return to R4 and display the IPX routing table, you will see the results in Example 14-12.

**Example 14-12**  *R4's IPX Routing Table After Split Horizon Is Disabled on R3*

```
R4#show ipx route
Codes: C - Connected primary network,    c - Connected secondary network
       S - Static, F - Floating static, L - Local (internal), W - IPXWAN
       R - RIP, E - EIGRP, N - NLSP, X - External, A - Aggregate
       s - seconds, u - uses

8 Total IPX routes. Up to 1 parallel paths and 16 hops allowed.

No default route known.

C       1000 (FRAME-RELAY),   Se0
C       4000 (NOVELL-ETHER),  Et0
E       2000 [2707456/1] via     1000.0000.0000.3333, age 00:05:16,
                                 1u, Se0
E       2100 [2707456/1] via     1000.0000.0000.3333, age 00:05:16,
                                 1u, Se0
E       3000 [2195456/1] via     1000.0000.0000.3333, age 00:05:16,
                                 1u, Se0
E       3001 [2195456/1] via     1000.0000.0000.3333, age 00:05:16,
                                 1u, Se0
E       3500 [2681856/1] via     1000.0000.0000.3333, age 00:05:16,
                                 1u, Se0
E       5000 [276864000/2] via    1000.0000.0000.3333, age 00:05:16,
                                 1u, Se0
R4#
```

R4 has learned the IPX networks 2000 and 2001 that previously were being blocked because of split horizon. Next, examine R2's IPX routing table, as shown in Example 14-13.

**Example 14-13**  *R2's IPX Routing Table After Split Horizon Is Disabled on R3*

```
R2#show ipx route
Codes: C - Connected primary network,    c - Connected secondary network
       S - Static, F - Floating static, L - Local (internal), W - IPXWAN
       R - RIP, E - EIGRP, N - NLSP, X - External, A - Aggregate
       s - seconds, u - uses, U - Per-user static
```

**Example 14-13** *R2's IPX Routing Table After Split Horizon Is Disabled on R3 (Continued)*

```
8 Total IPX routes. Up to 1 parallel paths and 16 hops allowed.

No default route known.

C       1000 (FRAME-RELAY),   Se0
C       2000 (NOVELL-ETHER),  Et1
C       2100 (NOVELL-ETHER),  Et0
E       3000 [2195456/1] via      1000.0000.0000.3333, age 00:02:10,
                              1u, Se0
E       3001 [2195456/1] via      1000.0000.0000.3333, age 00:02:10,
                              1u, Se0
E       3500 [2681856/1] via      1000.0000.0000.3333, age 00:02:10,
                              1u, Se0
E       4000 [2707456/1] via      1000.0000.0000.3333, age 00:02:10,
                              1u, Se0
E       5000 [276864000/2] via     1000.0000.0000.3333, age 00:02:10,
                              1u, Se0
R2#
```

The IPX route table shows that R2 now has received IPX network 4000 through IPX EIGRP.

## IPX Route Redistribution

As pointed out earlier, R4 learned networks 3001, 3500, and 5000 through EIGRP, even though these networks are configured by default to be advertised through IPX RIP on R3 and R5. This occurs because, by default, Cisco IOS Software automatically redistributes IPX RIP routes into EIGRP, and vice versa. IPX route redistribution occurs at routing domain boundaries. For this lab, IPX route redistribution occurs at R3 and R2 where both IPX RIP and IPX EIGRP are configured. On R2 and R3, IPX RIP routes are redistributed into EIGRP, and vice versa. You can see this further by displaying the IPX routes on R1, as shown in Example 14-14.

**Example 14-14** *R1's IPX Routing Table Reveals That IPX Route Redistribution Is Occurring in the Network*

```
R1#show ipx route
Codes: C - Connected primary network,    c - Connected secondary network
       S - Static, F - Floating static, L - Local (internal), W - IPXWAN
       R - RIP, E - EIGRP, N - NLSP, X - External, A - Aggregate
       s - seconds, u - uses

8 Total IPX routes. Up to 1 parallel paths and 16 hops allowed.
```

*continues*

**Example 14-14** *R1's IPX Routing Table Reveals That IPX Route Redistribution Is Occurring in the Network (Continued)*

```
No default route known.

C    2100 (NOVELL-ETHER),  Et0
R    1000 [02/01] via       2100.0010.7bf9.4912,   48s, Et0
R    2000 [02/01] via       2100.0010.7bf9.4912,   48s, Et0
R    3000 [08/02] via       2100.0010.7bf9.4912,   49s, Et0
R    3001 [08/02] via       2100.0010.7bf9.4912,   49s, Et0
R    3500 [08/02] via       2100.0010.7bf9.4912,   49s, Et0
R    4000 [14/02] via       2100.0010.7bf9.4912,   49s, Et0
R    5000 [14/03] via       2100.0010.7bf9.4912,   49s, Et0
R1#
```

R1 has a route to all IPX networks. In addition, every remote network was learned through IPX RIP, as denoted by the preceding letter *R*. This is because IPX EIGRP routes are being redistributed on R3 and R2 from IPX RIP into EIGRP and from EIGRP into IPX RIP; then they subsequently are passed on through IPX RIP to R1. In this way, R1 receives all IPX routes to the rest of the network.

# Verifying IPX Configuration, Operation, and Connectivity

To verify the IPX configuration and ensure full IPX connectivity, review those IPX commands that can assist you in this task. You already have seen how the running config appears after IPX has been configured with IPX RIP and IPX EIGRP. You also have seen the usefulness of examining the IPX routing table using the **show ipx route** command, from which you verified which IPX routes have been received and from which routing protocol they were advertised—IPX RIP or IPX EIGRP. In addition, you also saw how the **show ipx eigrp neighbors** command verifies IPX EIGRP neighbor adjacencies. In addition to these commands, which have been demonstrated throughout the chapter, review the following commands used to verify the IPX configuration and ensure full IPX connectivity:

```
show ipx interface brief
show ipx interface
show ipx traffic
show ipx servers
ping ipx
```

## show ipx interface brief Command

Begin by returning to R3 and examining the IPX interfaces with the **show ipx interface brief** command, as shown in Example 14-15.

**Example 14-15**  **show ipx interface brief** *Command Output on R3 Displays IPX Summary Information for Each Interface*

```
R3#show ipx interface brief
Interface            IPX Network  Encapsulation  Status   IPX State
Ethernet0            3000         NOVELL-ETHER   up       [up]
Ethernet0            3001         SAP            up       [up]
Loopback0            unassigned   not config'd   up       n/a
Serial0              1000         FRAME-RELAY    up       [up]
Serial1              3500         HDLC           up       [up]
R3#
```

This command is similar to the IP version of the command—**show ip interface brief**—but for IPX. This command provides a summary of each interface in the router, its associated IPX network (if assigned), the encapsulation type used on the interface, the status of the interface, and the IPX state. This is helpful when you want to review IPX networks and their encapsulation types. For example, you see that R3's Ethernet0 interface has two networks assigned—3000 and 3001—and that IPX network 3000 is using the NOVELL-ETHER encapsulation while IPX network 3001 is using Service Advertising Protocol (SAP). This information could be used to ensure that neighboring routers have been set to the same encapsulation type, enabling them to share routing information. In this lab, a neighboring IPX router attached to R3's Ethernet 0 segment does not exist. However, if it did exist, you would need to assign the same IPX network and encapsulation type to both neighboring interfaces to advertise IPX routes to each other.

## show ipx interface Command

Next, take a look at the extended version of this command—**show ipx interface**. This command provides the IPX details for all IPX interfaces on the router. You could narrow the amount of information that is displayed by specifying the interface that you want to see the details for—that is, **show ipx interface Ethernet 0**. Examine the IPX details of Ethernet 0 on R3, as shown in Example 14-16.

**Example 14-16**  **show ipx interface** *on R3 Displays Detailed IPX Information for R3's Ethernet 0 Interface*

```
R3#show ipx interface
Ethernet0 is up, line protocol is up
  IPX address is 3000.0000.0c38.9306, NOVELL-ETHER [up]
  Delay of this IPX network, in ticks is 1 throughput 0 link delay 0
  IPXWAN processing not enabled on this interface.
  Secondary address is 3001.0000.0c38.9306, SAP [up]
  Delay of this Novell network, in ticks is 1
  IPX SAP update interval is 1 minute(s)
  IPX type 20 propagation packet forwarding is disabled
  Incoming access list is not set
```

*continues*

**Example 14-16** **show ipx interface** *on R3 Displays Detailed IPX Information for R3's*
*Ethernet 0 Interface (Continued)*

```
    Outgoing access list is not set
    IPX helper access list is not set
    SAP GNS processing enabled, delay 0 ms, output filter list is not set
    SAP Input filter list is not set
    SAP Output filter list is not set
    SAP Router filter list is not set
    Input filter list is not set
    Output filter list is not set
    Router filter list is not set
    Netbios Input host access list is not set
    Netbios Input bytes access list is not set
    Netbios Output host access list is not set
    Netbios Output bytes access list is not set
    Updates each 60 seconds, aging multiples RIP: 3 SAP: 3
    SAP interpacket delay is 55 ms, maximum size is 480 bytes
    RIP interpacket delay is 55 ms, maximum size is 432 bytes
    IPX accounting is disabled
    IPX fast switching is configured (enabled)
    RIP packets received 0, RIP packets sent 8207
    SAP packets received 0, SAP packets sent 8202
R3#
```

This command reveals the primary and secondary IPX addressing information, the encapsulation
type, and the complete IPX network and node address. In addition, you can see various other IPX
parameters, such as IPX access lists, SAP filters, and NetBIOS access, to name a few. These are
outside the scope of this book and have not been covered within the chapter. However, be aware
that this is where you could view such information if it were configured.

## show ipx traffic Command

Another useful command that displays IPX traffic statistics such as SAP, RIP, and EIGRP
information is **show ipx traffic**, as demonstrated on R3 in Example 14-17.

**Example 14-17** **show ipx traffic** *Command Output on R3 Displays IPX Packet Information*

```
R3#show ipx traffic
System Traffic for 0.0000.0000.0001 System-Name: R3
Rcvd:   22595 total, 0 format errors, 0 checksum errors, 0 bad hop count,
        0 packets pitched, 22550 local destination, 0 multicast
Bcast:  21761 received, 29533 sent
Sent:   30159 generated, 45 forwarded
        0 encapsulation failed, 0 no route
SAP:    0 SAP requests, 0 ignored, 0 SAP replies, 1 servers
        0 SAP Nearest Name requests, 0 replies
        0 SAP General Name requests, 0 replies
        26 SAP advertisements received, 12330 sent
        219 SAP flash updates sent, 0 SAP format errors
```

**Example 14-17**  **show ipx traffic** *Command Output on R3 Displays IPX Packet Information (Continued)*

```
RIP:       0 RIP requests, 0 ignored, 0 RIP replies, 8 routes
           4113 RIP advertisements received, 12333 sent
           223 RIP flash updates sent, 0 RIP format errors
Echo:      Rcvd 30 requests, 0 replies
           Sent 0 requests, 30 replies
           0 unknown: 0 no socket, 0 filtered, 0 no helper
           0 SAPs throttled, freed NDB len 0
Watchdog:
           0 packets received, 0 replies spoofed
Queue lengths:
           IPX input: 0, SAP 0, RIP 0, GNS 0
           SAP throttling length: 0/(no limit), 0 nets pending lost route reply
           Delayed process creation: 0
EIGRP:     Total received 18381, sent 4995
           Updates received 116, sent 152
           Queries received 9, sent 54
           Replies received 54, sent 9
           SAPs received 111, sent 146
NLSP:      Level-1 Hellos received 0, sent 0
           PTP Hello received 0, sent 0
           Level-1 LSPs received 0, sent 0
           LSP Retransmissions: 0
           LSP checksum errors received: 0
           LSP HT=0 checksum errors received: 0
           Level-1 CSNPs received 0, sent 0
           Level-1 PSNPs received 0, sent 0
           Level-1 DR Elections: 0
           Level-1 SPF Calculations: 0
           Level-1 Partial Route Calculations: 0
R3#
```

The **show ipx traffic** command displays information about the number and type of IPX packets transmitted and received. This command displays the number of broadcasts, SAPs, routing packets received, and a total of all packets received. A few of theses were highlighted in the previous example for emphasis. First, notice the fields for sent and received rows. The packet count in these fields should increment steadily. If these are not incrementing or show 0, IPX routing might not be configured properly. You should check the individual RIP, EIGRP, or SAP details for additional clues and also check your IPX routing configuration. Next, notice the SAP row. SAP is used in IPX networks to advertise available services in an IPX environment. The output in Example 14-17 shows that R3 has learned of one server through SAP. The RIP row shows that R3 has learned eight routes. The number of routes shown here should correspond to the number of routes displayed in the IPX routing table. Finally, you can see that IPX EIGRP is sending and receiving updates, queries, and replies.

## show ipx servers Command

Another useful command in verifying that IPX services are being propagated throughout the network is the **show ipx servers** command. A Novell file server is located on IPX network 2100. Verify that this server is being advertised through SAP by examining R3's SAP table, as shown in Example 14-18.

**Example 14-18** **show ipx servers** *Command Output on R3 Displays R3's SAP Table*

```
R3#show ipx servers
Codes: S - Static, P - Periodic, E - EIGRP, N - NLSP, H - Holddown, + = detail
1 Total IPX Servers

Table ordering is based on routing and server info

   Type Name                 Net     Address     Port    Route Hops Itf
E   640 NOVELLSERVER         2100.5254.00da.ee56:E885 2195456/01   2  Se0
R3#
```

NetWare nodes such as NetWare file servers and printer servers use SAP broadcasts to advertise their services and addresses every 60 seconds. SAP broadcasts are essential to a NetWare environment. Cisco routers do not forward each SAP broadcast that they receive. Instead, each router maintains a SAP table and broadcasts this table every 60 seconds. By listing the IPX servers discovered through SAP, you can see that R3 has learned about this Novell server as well as its network and node address. In addition, this command shows the port number and the number of hops to the server. In this demonstration, you are dealing with only one server. In large IPX environments, however, SAP broadcasts can consume a large portion of network bandwidth and should be managed using SAP filtering.

## ping ipx Command

Finally, assemble a table of IPX network and node address within the topology for the lab. This table will be used to test IPX connectivity throughout the network. You could gather this information either from the lab diagram (because it has been documented as you've gone along) or by going to each router and using the command **show ipx interface brief** followed by **show ipx interface**. This table should include the router name, the IPX interface, and IPX network and node information. When completed, the table should look like Table 14-2.

**NOTE** Your table will appear slightly different as the IPX node portion will correspond to the unique MAC addresses of your hardware. Serial IPX network and node information will appear the same.

**Table 14-2**    *IPX Network, Node, and Interface Information for R1 Through R5*

| Router | IPX Interface | IPX Network.Node |
|--------|---------------|------------------|
| R1 | Ethernet 0 | 2100.00e0.1e3e.9a69 |
| R2 | Ethernet 0 | 2100.0010.7bf9.4912 |
|  | Ethernet 1 | 2000.0010.7bf9.4913 |
|  | Serial 0 | 1000.0000.0000.2222 |
| R3 | Ethernet 0 | 3000.0000.0c38.9306 |
|  | Ethernet 0 (secondary) | 3001.0000.0c38.9306 |
|  | Serial 0 | 1000.0000.0000.3333 |
|  | Serial 1 | 3500.0000.0000.3333 |
| R4 | Ethernet 0 | 4000.0010.7b7f.fa6e |
|  | Serial 0 | 1000.0000.0000.4444 |
| R5 | Serial 0 | 3500.0000.0000.5555 |
|  | TokenRing 0 | 5000.0000.30b1.523b |

Using this table, you can test IPX connectivity using the **ping ipx** command followed by
the appropriate IPX network address and node. Do this from R1. From R1, begin by testing
IPX connectivity to each interface in R2, then R3, and so on. Example 14-19 shows how
this is done.

**Example 14-19**    *IPX **ping** on R1 Demonstrates Full IPX Connectivity from R1 to R2, R3, R4, and R5*

```
Termserver#1
[Resuming connection 1 to r1 ... ]

R1#ping ipx 2100.0010.7bf9.4912

Type escape sequence to abort.
Sending 5, 100-byte IPX cisco Echoes to 2100.0010.7bf9.4912, timeout is 2 seconds:
!!!!!
Success rate is 100 percent (5/5), round-trip min/avg/max = 4/4/8 ms
R1#ping ipx 2000.0010.7bf9.4913

Type escape sequence to abort.
Sending 5, 100-byte IPX cisco Echoes to 2000.0010.7bf9.4913, timeout is 2 seconds:
!!!!!
Success rate is 100 percent (5/5), round-trip min/avg/max = 4/4/4 ms
R1#ping ipx 1000.0000.0000.2222

Type escape sequence to abort.
Sending 5, 100-byte IPX cisco Echoes to 1000.0000.0000.2222, timeout is 2 seconds:
!!!!!
Success rate is 100 percent (5/5), round-trip min/avg/max = 4/8/16 ms
```

*continues*

**Example 14-19** *IPX* **ping** *on R1 Demonstrates Full IPX Connectivity from R1 to R2, R3, R4, and R5 (Continued)*

```
R1#ping ipx 3000.0000.0c38.9306

Type escape sequence to abort.
Sending 5, 100-byte IPX cisco Echoes to 3000.0000.0c38.9306, timeout is 2 seconds:
!!!!!
Success rate is 100 percent (5/5), round-trip min/avg/max = 32/35/36 ms
R1#ping ipx 3001.0000.0c38.9306

Type escape sequence to abort.
Sending 5, 100-byte IPX cisco Echoes to 3001.0000.0c38.9306, timeout is 2 seconds:
!!!!!
Success rate is 100 percent (5/5), round-trip min/avg/max = 32/57/148 ms
R1#ping ipx 1000.0000.0000.3333

Type escape sequence to abort.
Sending 5, 100-byte IPX cisco Echoes to 1000.0000.0000.3333, timeout is 2 seconds:
!!!!!
Success rate is 100 percent (5/5), round-trip min/avg/max = 32/36/40 ms
R1#ping ipx 3500.0000.0000.3333

Type escape sequence to abort.
Sending 5, 100-byte IPX cisco Echoes to 3500.0000.0000.3333, timeout is 2 seconds:
!!!!!
Success rate is 100 percent (5/5), round-trip min/avg/max = 32/34/36 ms
R1#ping ipx 4000.0010.7b7f.fa6e

Type escape sequence to abort.
Sending 5, 100-byte IPX cisco Echoes to 4000.0010.7b7f.fa6e, timeout is 2 seconds:
!!!!!
Success rate is 100 percent (5/5), round-trip min/avg/max = 92/95/96 ms
R1#ping ipx 1000.0000.0000.4444

Type escape sequence to abort.
Sending 5, 100-byte IPX cisco Echoes to 1000.0000.0000.4444, timeout is 2 seconds:
!!!!!
Success rate is 100 percent (5/5), round-trip min/avg/max = 92/96/100 ms
R1#ping ipx 3500.0000.0000.5555

Type escape sequence to abort.
Sending 5, 100-byte IPX cisco Echoes to 3500.0000.0000.5555, timeout is 2 seconds:
!!!!!
Success rate is 100 percent (5/5), round-trip min/avg/max = 32/36/40 ms
R1#ping ipx 5000.0000.30b1.523b

Type escape sequence to abort.
Sending 5, 100-byte IPX cisco Echoes to 5000.0000.30b1.523b, timeout is 2 seconds:
!!!!!
Success rate is 100 percent (5/5), round-trip min/avg/max = 36/36/40 ms
R1#
```

R1 has full IPX connectivity to every other IPX network within the network.

# Final Lab Results

You now have successfully configured IPX routing and verified its proper operation, per the lab objectives. You have configured IPX routing for both IPX RIP and IPX EIGRP, and you have seen that IPX route redistribution is occurring and that IPX EIGRP split horizon has been disabled on the hub Frame Relay router (R3's Serial 0 interface). Lastly, you have seen some commands to verify your configuration and have tested IPX connectivity using the **ping** command. Figure 14-2 shows the IPX routing domains for IPX RIP and IPX EIGRP.

In summary, review those commands that have been introduced in this chapter, as shown in Table 14-3.

**Figure 14-2**  *IPX Routing Domains*

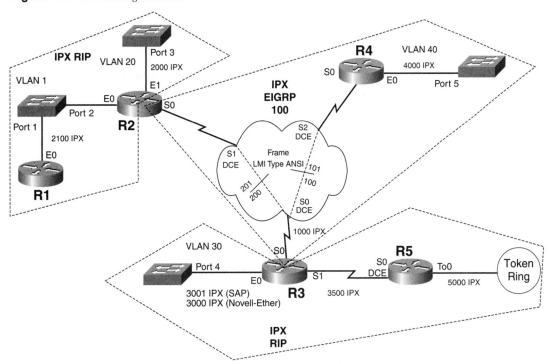

**Table 14-3**   *Command Summary for IPX Configuration and Troubleshooting*

| Command | Purpose |
|---|---|
| **ipx router eigrp** [*autonomous system number*] | Enables the IPX EIGRP routing process |
| **no ipx split-horizon eigrp** [*autonomous system number*] | Disables IPX split horizon on an IPX EIGRP interface |
| **ipx router rip** | Enters the IPX RIP routing process |
| **show ipx interface brief** | Displays a summary of configured IPX interfaces |
| **show ipx interface** | Displays a detailed status of IPX interfaces |
| **show ipx traffic** | Shows IPX packet information |
| **show ipx servers** | Lists the services discovered through SAP advertisements |
| **show ipx route** | Lists the entries in the IPX routing table |
| **ping ipx** | Verifies IPX connectivity |

The IPX routing configuration is now complete. Chapter 15, "Standard and Extended Access Lists," reviews IP standard and extended access lists and configures these in the lab environment.

PART III

# Access Lists, Cisco IOS Software Operations, and Troubleshooting

This chapter covers the following topics:

- Standard access lists
- Extended access lists

## CHAPTER 15

# Standard and Extended Access Lists

This chapter covers the difference between standard and extended access lists and their various uses. You will configure access lists according to the lab objectives stated in the chapter, verify their operation, and apply them to the router interfaces appropriately.

Network security using access list is a fundamental requirement that Cisco expects from CCNAs. Although you can use a variety of methods to write access lists, it is important that you understand the logic behind the access lists. This chapter briefly reviews the different access lists and the commands needed to configure and apply them in the appropriate manner. For a more comprehensive review of access lists, refer to Chapter 9 of *Interconnecting Cisco Network Devices*.

## Standard/Extended Access List Fundamentals

Cisco has defined two types of IP access lists: standard and extended. However, only one type can be applied to an interface at time. This means that you cannot have an inbound standard access list and an inbound extended access list applied to the same interface. Each access list must have its own number range and applications, for network security.

## Standard Access Lists

Standard access lists match packets by examining the source IP address field in the packet's IP header. Any bit positions in the 32-bit source IP address can be compared to the access list statements. However, the matching is flexible and does not consider the subnet mask in use.

Access lists use the inverse mask, sometimes called the wildcard mask or I-mask. This mask is named because it inverts the meaning of the bits. In a normal mask, ones mean "must match," while zeroes mean "may vary." For example, for two hosts to be on the same Class C network, the first 24 bits of their address must match, while the last 8 may vary. Inverse masks swap the rules so that zeroes mean "must match" and ones mean "may vary."

**TIP**   The easy way to calculate the inverse mask when you already know the normal mask is to subtract from all ones. The table that follows shows an example. The normal mask is subtracted, column by column, from the all-ones mask to determine the inverse mask.

| All Ones | 255 | 255 | 255 | 255 |
|---|---|---|---|---|
| Normal Mask | 255 | 255 | 240 | 0 |
| Inverse Mask | 0 | 0 | 15 | 255 |

The command for configuring a standard access list is as follows:

```
Router(config)# access-list {1-99} {permit | deny} source-addr [source-mask]
```

As you can see from the command syntax, the first option is to specify the access list number. The number range for standard access lists is 1 to 99. The second value that you must specify is to permit or deny the configured source IP address. The third value is the source IP address that you want to match. The fourth value is the wildcard mask that you want to apply to the IP address previously configured.

**CAUTION**   All access lists have an implicit **deny**, meaning that if a packet does not match any of the criteria that you have specified in your access list, it will be denied. If you have **deny** statements in your access lists, be sure to create **permit** statements to allow valid traffic.

When the access list has been created, you need to apply it to the appropriate interface. The command to apply the access list is as follows:

```
Router(config-if)# ip access-group {number | name [in | out] }
```

The access list is applied under the interface configuration mode. You must specify only the number or name and whether it is an incoming or an outgoing access list.

## Extended Access Lists

Extended IP access lists are almost identical to standard IP access lists in their use. The key difference between the two types is the variety of fields in the packet that can be compared for matching by extended access lists. As with standard lists, extended access lists are enabled for packets entering or exiting an interface. The list is searched sequentially; the first statement matched stops the search through the list and defines the action to be taken. All these features are true of standard access lists as well. The matching logic, however, is different than that used with standard access lists and makes extended access lists much more complex. Extended access lists can match source and destination addresses as well as different TCP and UDP ports. This gives greater flexibility and control over network access.

To configure extended access lists, the command is similar to standard access list, but with more options. The command is this:

```
Router(config)# access-list {100-199} {permit | deny} protocol source-addr [source-
mask] [operator operand] destination-addr [destination-mask] [operator operand]
[established]
```

The first value that you must configure is the access list number. Extended access lists range from 100 to 199. Then you need to permit or deny the criteria that you will specify next. The next value is the protocol type. Here, you could specify IP, TCP, UDP, or other specific IP sub-protocols. The next value is the source IP address and its wildcard mask. Next is the destination IP address and its wildcard mask. When the destination IP address and mask are configured, you can specify the port number that you want to match, by number or by a well-known port name.

As with standard access lists, after the extended access list is created, you need to apply it to an interface with the **ip access-group** command. Review the lab objectives associated with the chapter before beginning to configure the access lists.

# Lab Objectives

Note that you will not be testing the access lists because no host resides on any of the segments. Instead, you will configure, apply, and verify that the access lists are configured correctly with the appropriate **show** commands.

Here are the objectives:

- For standard access lists, create a standard outgoing access list and apply it on R2's S0 interface so that users on network 192.168.12.0 are denied access to the Frame Relay network. (Assume that this network exists off R1.)

- For extended access lists, create an extended incoming access list and apply it on R3's S0 interface to fulfill the following requirements:

    — Deny http (www) traffic from reaching R5's Token Ring network.

    — Deny SMTP traffic from reaching R3's E0 network.

    — Permit anything else.

The key terms to recognize in the lab objectives are *outgoing* and *incoming*. Remember, these keywords will affect how you build your access lists. Let's configure the standard access list first.

# Configuring Standard Access Lists

To better understand what you must accomplish with the access lists, refer to the environment in Figure 15-1.

**Figure 15-1** *Standard Access List Scenario*

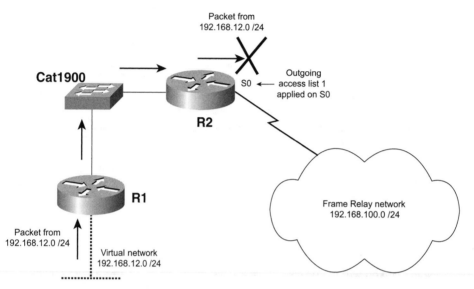

From the lab objectives, you want to do the following:

Create a standard outgoing access list and apply it on R2's S0 interface so that users on network 192.168.12.0 are denied access to the Frame Relay network. (Assume that this network exists off R1.)

From the figure, you can see that a virtual network (192.168.12.0 /24) exists off R1; you want to keep hosts on that network segment from reaching the Frame Relay network (192.168.100.0 /24). An important issue to point out is that, because this is a standard access list, there is no way to filter on the destination address. So, when you configure the access list to filter on the source IP address of 192.168.12.0 /24, you will stop that traffic from going to the Frame Relay network, as well as all other networks behind R2's S0, the interface on which you are going to apply the access list.

Because it is an outgoing access list, you will create the access list with the source address of the network 192.168.12.0 to be denied, but you will allow all other traffic to pass. Remember, there is an implicit **deny** after all access lists. Create the access list on R2, as demonstrated in Example 15-1.

**Example 15-1** *Standard Access List Configuration*

```
Termserver#2
[Resuming connection 2 to r2 ... ]

R2#config t
Enter configuration commands, one per line.  End with CNTL/Z.
R2(config)#access-list 1 deny 192.168.12.0 0.0.0.255
R2(config)#access-list 1 permit any
R2(config)#
```

The most important aspect of the **access-list** command is the wildcard mask portion. This tells the router where to match and where not to. The first three zeros in the wildcard mask (0.0.0) signify that the first three numbers of the source IP address of a packet must match the first three numbers of the IP address previously configured (192.168.12). The final .255 portion of the mask signifies that any number in the source IP address field will not be looked at for a match. In other words, any packet that has a source IP address with 192.168.12 will be matched against the access list and, therefore, will be denied, regardless of the fourth number in the source IP address field of the IP packet (0 to 255). The second line of the access list simply permits all other traffic. Without that statement, all IP traffic would be blocked because of the implicit **deny** at the end of all access lists.

The second step to configuring the access list is to apply it to the appropriate interface. From the lab objectives, you want to apply this access list on the S0 interface of R2 and make it check outgoing packets. To apply the access list, you need to be in interface mode for S0 and apply the **ip access-group** command. Example 15-2 illustrates how to apply the access lists to the interface.

**Example 15-2** *Applying the Access List to the Interface*

```
R2(config)#int s0
R2(config-if)#ip access-group 1 out
R2(config-if)#
```

This configuration applies **access-list 1** to all outgoing packets on R2's S0 interface. Because you do not have any hosts off 192.168.12.0, you cannot verify that it is working properly. However, you can use some **show** commands to make sure that the access list has been applied correctly on the interface.

The first **show** command is this one:

```
Router#show ip access-lists {number}
```

The only option here is to specify the specific access list number that you want to see. If no number is specified, all access lists are shown. Example 15-3 shows sample output from this command.

**Example 15-3 show ip access-list** *Command Output*

```
R2(config-if)#end
R2#show ip access-lists
Standard IP access list 1
    deny   192.168.12.0, wildcard bits 0.0.0.255
    permit any
R2#
```

This **show** command reveals all the important information:

- Whether it is a standard or an extended IP access list

- The access list number

- All the configured statements for that access list

You configured only one access list, so the output shows information for just **access-list 1** that you configured in Example 15-1.

Another useful **show** command is this one:

```
Router#show ip interface [interface-type] [interface-number]
```

The option that you can use here is to specify the interface type and number.

Because you have only one access list configured on S0, use that as an example. Example 15-4 demonstrates this command.

**Example 15-4 show ip interface s0** *Command Output*

```
R2#show ip interface s0
Serial0 is up, line protocol is up
  Internet address is 192.168.100.2/24
  Broadcast address is 255.255.255.255
  Address determined by setup command
  MTU is 1500 bytes
  Helper address is not set
  Directed broadcast forwarding is disabled
  Multicast reserved groups joined: 224.0.0.10
  Outgoing access list is 1
  Inbound  access list is not set
  Proxy ARP is enabled
  Security level is default
  Split horizon is disabled
  ICMP redirects are always sent
  ICMP unreachables are always sent
  ICMP mask replies are never sent
  IP fast switching is enabled
  IP fast switching on the same interface is enabled
  IP Feature Fast switching turbo vector
  IP multicast fast switching is disabled
  IP multicast distributed fast switching is disabled
  IP route-cache flags are Fast
```

**Example 15-4** **show ip interface s0** *Command Output (Continued)*

```
    Router Discovery is disabled
    IP output packet accounting is disabled
    IP access violation accounting is disabled
    TCP/IP header compression is disabled
    RTP/IP header compression is disabled
    Probe proxy name replies are disabled
    Policy routing is disabled
    Network address translation is disabled
    Web Cache Redirect is disabled
    BGP Policy Mapping is disabled
R2#
```

The command output has very useful information, but the focus here is on what IP access lists are configured for this interface. The highlighted line tells you quickly which access list(s) have been configured and whether they are incoming access lists or outgoing access lists.

Before moving on to configure the extended access list, take a look at the running configuration of R2 to see where the access list configuration commands are placed in the file. Example 15-5 displays the output of the running configuration file.

**Example 15-5** *R2's Running Config*

```
Termserver#r2
Trying r2 (192.168.10.10, 2002)... Open

R2#show running-config
Building configuration...

Current configuration:
!
version 12.0
service timestamps debug uptime
service timestamps log uptime
no service password-encryption
!
hostname R2
!
enable password falcons
!
username all
ip subnet-zero
no ip domain-lookup
ip host R1 192.169.1.1
ip host R2 192.169.2.2
ip host R3 192.169.3.3
ip host R4 192.169.4.4
ip host R5 192.169.5.5
ip host R6 192.169.6.6
```

*continues*

**Example 15-5** *R2's Running Config (Continued)*

```
ipx routing 0000.0000.2222
!
!
!
interface Loopback0
 ip address 192.169.2.2 255.255.255.0
 no ip directed-broadcast
!
interface Ethernet0
 ip address 192.168.1.2 255.255.255.0
 no ip directed-broadcast
 ipx network 2100
!
interface Ethernet1
 description This interface does not connect with another IP device
 ip address 192.168.2.2 255.255.255.0
 no ip directed-broadcast
 ipx network 2000
!
interface Serial0
 description This interface connects to R3's S0 (201)
 ip address 192.168.100.2 255.255.255.0
 ip access-group 1 out
 no ip directed-broadcast
 encapsulation frame-relay
 no ip mroute-cache
 ipx network 1000
 frame-relay map ip 192.168.100.3 201 broadcast
 frame-relay map ip 192.168.100.4 201 broadcast
 frame-relay map ipx 1000.0000.0000.4444 201 broadcast
 frame-relay map ipx 1000.0000.0000.3333 201 broadcast
 frame-relay lmi-type ansi
!
router eigrp 100
 redistribute rip metric 2000 200 255 1 1500
 network 192.168.100.0
!
router rip
 redistribute eigrp 100 metric 1
 network 192.168.1.0
 network 192.168.2.0
 network 192.169.2.0
!
ip classless
!
access-list 1 deny    192.168.12.0 0.0.0.255
access-list 1 permit any
!
!
!
banner motd ^CCCC
This is Router 2
```

**Example 15-5** *R2's Running Config (Continued)*

```
^C
!
line con 0
 exec-timeout 0 0
 password falcons
 logging synchronous
 transport input none
line vty 0 4
 password falcons
 login
!
end

R2#
```

From the highlighted text, you see that the **ip access-group** command is located under the configuration of S0 and that the definition command lines are toward the end of the configuration file.

## Configuring Extended Access Lists

The process of configuring extended access lists is much the same as that for standard access lists, except for the additional options to provide with the command. Figure 15-2 illustrates the environment that the access list should create.

**Figure 15-2** *Extended Access List Environment*

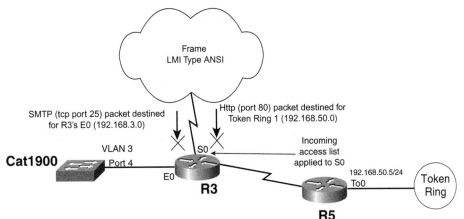

From the lab objectives, you want to create an extended incoming access list and apply it on R3's S0 interface to fulfill the following requirements:

- Deny http (www) traffic from reaching R5's Token Ring network.
- Deny SMTP traffic from reaching R3's E0 network.
- Permit anything else.

This extended access list is a little different from the standard access list. You will be filtering on the destination network address instead of the source address, and you want to filter only certain services (HTTP and FTP), not all traffic destined to these networks. Look at each requirement for the access list individually.

The first criterion is to deny TCP HTTP traffic (port 80) from reaching the Token Ring network on R5. The network address for the network is 192.168.50.0, and the wildcard mask is 0.0.0.255 because you want to match the entire network on R5's To0. Use 101 as the access list number for the extended access list. Example 15-6 demonstrates the configuration of the first line of the access list on R3.

**Example 15-6** *Extended Access List Configuration*

```
Termserver#3
[Resuming connection 3 to r3 ... ]

R3#config t
Enter configuration commands, one per line.  End with CNTL/Z.
R3(config)#access-list 101 deny tcp any 192.168.50.0 0.0.0.255 eq 80
R3(config)#
```

Because you are not concerned about the source IP address, you can use the **any** option, meaning that any source will be filtered if the destination IP address falls within the destination IP address and wildcard mask. It is interesting to note that the port on the access list may be either the port number (80) or the name for that port (www). With that objective criteria complete, look at the second portion of the access list requirement.

---

**TIP**

The well-known industry name for TCP port 80 is http, but Cisco has used www in the Cisco IOS Software code. As a practical tip, use the port numbers instead of well-known port names when configuring access lists, in case Cisco changes the well-known names in the IOS Software code.

---

The second criterion is to deny TCP SMTP traffic (port 25) from reaching R3's E0 network. The network address is 192.168.3.0, and the wildcard mask is 0.0.0.255 because you want to match against the entire network on R3's E0. To add to the access list, you only need to use the same access list number as previously used, 101. Remember to permit all other traffic! Example 15-7 shows the commands on R3.

**Example 15-7** *Extended Access List Configuration Completed*

```
R3(config)#access-list 101 deny tcp any 192.168.3.0 0.0.0.255 eq 25

R3(config)#access-list 101 permit ip any any
R3(config)#
```

The final command line is to permit all IP traffic, coming from anyone and going to anyone. That is why you use **any** for both the source and the destination addresses.

Now that the access list is configured with the correct filtering criteria, apply it to R3's S0 interface as an incoming access list. Example 15-8 demonstrates how to do this.

**Example 15-8** *Applying Extended Access Lists on R3*

```
R3(config)#int s0
R3(config-if)#ip access-group 101 in
R3(config-if)#
```

Remember to match the **ip access-group** command with the correct access list number (101) that you want to apply to the interface. The **in** option tells the router to apply this access list to any incoming packets.

Now take a look at the interface to make sure that the configuration is correctly applied. Example 15-9 shows the output from the **show ip interface s0** command.

**Example 15-9 show ip interface s0** *Command Output*

```
R3(config-if)#end
R3#show ip interface s0
Serial0 is up, line protocol is up
  Internet address is 192.168.100.3/24
  Broadcast address is 255.255.255.255
  Address determined by non-volatile memory
  MTU is 1500 bytes
  Helper address is not set
  Directed broadcast forwarding is enabled
  Multicast reserved groups joined: 224.0.0.10
  Outgoing access list is not set
  Inbound  access list is 101
  Proxy ARP is enabled
  Security level is default
  Split horizon is disabled
  ICMP redirects are always sent
  ICMP unreachables are always sent
```

*continues*

**Example 15-9 show ip interface s0** *Command Output (Continued)*

```
    ICMP mask replies are never sent
    IP fast switching is enabled
    IP fast switching on the same interface is enabled
    IP multicast fast switching is enabled
    Router Discovery is disabled
    IP output packet accounting is disabled
    IP access violation accounting is disabled
    TCP/IP header compression is disabled
    Probe proxy name replies are disabled
    Gateway Discovery is disabled
    Policy routing is disabled
    Network address translation is disabled
  R3#
```

The highlighted text confirms that the correct access list, 101, has been applied as an incoming access list. Because you do not have any Web hosts or FTP hosts on these segments, you will not be able to test the access lists. However, the configurations are correct and you have completed the lab objectives for this chapter.

# Summary

This chapter briefly reviewed the differences between standard and extended access lists and completed the lab objectives associated with this chapter. Hopefully you now have a better understanding of how to configure and apply access lists. The next chapter reviews basic router operations used to manage Cisco IOS Software images and configuration files for backup and recovery.

This chapter covers the following topics:

- Cisco router boot sequence and configuration
- Backing up Cisco IOS Software image files
- Upgrading Cisco IOS Software image files from TFTP servers
- Backing up/restoring configuration files to/from TFTP servers

## CHAPTER 16

# Cisco Router Operations

This chapter reviews some basic router operations necessary to manage Cisco IOS Software images and configuration files. This chapter begins by reviewing Cisco router boot order and then focuses on the practical application of controlling the router boot sequence, upgrading Cisco IOS Software image files, and managing router configuration files. If you need an in-depth review on these topics, refer to Chapter 4 of *Interconnecting Cisco Network Devices* or Chapter 2 of *Cisco CCNA Exam #640-607 Certification Guide*.

## Lab Objectives

In this chapter, you will perform the following lab objectives:

- **Cisco router boot configuration**—Configure R1 to boot from the TFTP server and then Flash. (Use the Cisco IOS Software image filename igs-j-l.111-18.bin.)

- **Cisco router IOS Software backup**—Backup the Cisco IOS Software image on R1 to the TFTP server 192.168.1.5.

- **Cisco router IOS Software upgrade**—Upgrade the Cisco IOS Software on R1 to image c2500-js-l_112-17.bin from the TFTP server.

- **Cisco router configuration backup**—Back up the current configurations of R1 to the TFTP server.

- **Cisco router configuration restore**—Restore the startup config on R1 from the saved image on the TFTP server.

Begin by examining the lab environment. Figure 16-1 displays those routers that will be used to accomplish the lab objectives and shows where the TFTP server is located within the network.

**Figure 16-1** *TFTP Server Within Lab Environment*

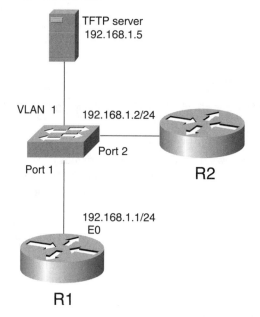

The lab objectives can be performed from any router within the network as long as IP connectivity to the TFTP server (192.168.1.5) exists before performing the router operation. The lab objectives deal specifically with R1. Begin by ensuring that IP connectivity from R1 to the TFTP server exists by issuing a **ping** to 192.168.1.5, as demonstrated in Example 16-1.

**Example 16-1** *R1 Successfully **ping**s TFTP Server's IP Address 192.168.1.5*

```
Termserver#1
[Resuming connection 1 to r1 ... ]

R1#ping 192.168.1.5

Type escape sequence to abort.
Sending 5, 100-byte ICMP Echos to 192.168.1.5, timeout is 2 seconds:
!!!!!
Success rate is 100 percent (5/5), round-trip min/avg/max = 1/3/4 ms
R1#
```

Now you know that R1 can successfully reach the TFTP server.

| NOTE | If you are unable to **ping** the TFTP server, check the cabling to ensure physical connectivity. Next, make sure that the Ethernet interface on R1 is up and has the proper IP address assigned. Ensure that the TFTP server is plugged into the switch and that the port is configured within VLAN 1. Finally, make sure that no access lists have been configured on R1 that could be blocking ICMP or TFTP. |
|---|---|

# Cisco Router Boot Sequence and Configuration

Before configuring R1 to boot from the TFTP server and then Flash, briefly review the events that occur during router initialization

## Router Boot Sequence

The sequence of events that occurs during the powerup (also known as the booting of a router) is important to understand. Knowledge of this sequence can help you accomplish operational tasks and troubleshoot router problems. When power initially is applied to a router, the following events occur in the order shown:

1  **Power-on self-test (POST)**—This event is a series of hardware tests to verify that all the router's components are functional. During this test, the router also determines what hardware is present. POST executes from microcode resident in the system ROM.

2  **Load and run bootstrap code**—Bootstrap code is used to perform subsequent events, such as finding the Cisco IOS Software, loading it, and then running it. After Cisco IOS Software is loaded and running, the bootstrap code is not used until the next time the router is reloaded or power-cycled.

3  **Finding Cisco IOS Software**—The bootstrap code determines where Cisco IOS Software to be run is located. The Flash memory is the normal place where a Cisco IOS Software image is found. The configuration register and configuration file in NVRAM help determine where the Cisco IOS Software images are and what image file should be used.

4  **Load Cisco IOS Software**—After the bootstrap code has found the proper image, it loads that image into RAM and starts **Cisco IOS Software** running. Some routers (such as the 2500 series) do not load the Cisco IOS Software image into RAM but execute it directly from Flash memory.

5  **Find the configuration**—The default is to look in NVRAM for a valid configuration. A parameter can be set to have the router attempt to locate a configuration file from another location, such as a TFTP server.

6 **Load the configuration**—The desired configuration for the router is loaded and executed. If no configuration exists or the configuration is being ignored, the router will enter the setup utility or attempt an autoinstall. Autoinstall will be attempted if a router is connected to a functioning serial link and can resolve an address through a process of the Serial Line Address Resolution Protocol (SLARP).

7 **Run**—The router now is running the configured Cisco IOS Software.

Use the **show version** command to determine where R1 booted its Cisco IOS Software image from, as shown in Example 16-2.

**Example 16-2** *show version Command Indicates That R1 Booted Cisco IOS Software Image Through Flash*

```
R1#show version
Cisco Internetwork Operating System Software
IOS (tm) 2500 Software (C2500-JS-L), Version 11.2(17), RELEASE SOFTWARE (fc1)
Copyright (c) 1986-1999 by cisco Systems, Inc.
Compiled Mon 04-Jan-99 17:27 by ashah
Image text-base: 0x03040148, data-base: 0x00001000

ROM: System Bootstrap, Version 11.0(10c), SOFTWARE
BOOTFLASH: 3000 Bootstrap Software (IGS-BOOT-R), Version 11.0(10c), RELEASE SOFTWARE
  (fc1)

R1 uptime is 1 minute
System restarted by reload
System image file is "igs-j-l.111-18.bin", booted via flash

cisco 2500 (68030) processor (revision N) with 14336K/2048K bytes of memory.
Processor board ID 06158021, with hardware revision 00000000
Bridging software.
SuperLAT software copyright 1990 by Meridian Technology Corp).
X.25 software, Version 2.0, NET2, BFE and GOSIP compliant.
TN3270 Emulation software.
1 Ethernet/IEEE 802.3 interface(s)
2 Serial network interface(s)
32K bytes of non-volatile configuration memory.
8192K bytes of processor board System flash (Read ONLY)

Configuration register is 0x2102
R1#
```

As indicated by the highlighted line, R1 is a 2500 series router and the system image was booted from Flash memory. You want to modify this so that R1 loads Cisco IOS Software from the TFTP server and then Flash. This can be done using the following command:

```
Router(config)#boot system [tftp | flash]
```

Example 16-3 demonstrates this process on R1.

**Example 16-3** *Modifying R1's Boot Order to Boot First from TFTP and Then from Flash*

```
R1#conf t
Enter configuration commands, one per line.  End with CNTL/Z.
R1(config)#boot system tftp igs-j-1.111-18.bin
R1(config)#boot system flash igs-j-1.111-18.bin
R1(config)#
```

| | |
|---|---|
| **NOTE** | For R1, it is not essential to specify the filename after the **boot system flash** command. By default, R1 tries to boot using this file because it's the only file in Flash. However, it is recommended to get in the habit of making the filename distinction because many routers have a sufficient Flash size to contain more than one Cisco IOS Software image at a time in Flash. By specifying the filename, you ensure that the exact Cisco IOS Software image you desire will be loaded. |

If you examine the first portion of the running config on R1, you will see that the boot system configuration statements have been added and are placed in the same sequence that the router will look for its Cisco IOS Software image. This is shown in the highlighted portion of Example 16-4.

**Example 16-4** *R1's Running Config Shows Boot System Commands*

```
R1#show running-config
Building configuration...

Current configuration:
!
version 11.2
no service password-encryption
no service udp-small-servers
no service tcp-small-servers
!
hostname R1
!
boot system igs-j-1.111-18.bin 255.255.255.255
boot system flash igs-j-1.111-18.bin
enable password falcons
!
no ip domain-lookup
ip host R1 192.169.1.1
ip host R2 192.169.2.2
ip host R3 192.169.3.3
ip host R4 192.169.4.4
ip host R5 192.169.5.5
ip host R6 192.169.6.6
ipx routing 0000.0000.1111
!
```

Next, reload R1 and observe whether Cisco IOS Software is loaded from TFTP instead of Flash, as shown in Example 16-5.

**Example 16-5** *After Boot System Configuration Changes, R1 Boots from TFTP*

```
R1#reload

System configuration has been modified. Save? [yes/no]: y
Building configuration...
[OK]
Proceed with reload? [confirm] [Enter]

System Bootstrap, Version 11.0(10c), SOFTWARE
Copyright (c) 1986-1996 by cisco Systems
2500 processor with 14336 Kbytes of main memory

%SYS-4-CONFIG_NEWER: Configurations from version 11.2 may not be correctly under
stood.
Loading igs-j-1.111-18.bin from 192.168.1.5 (via Ethernet0): !!!!!!!!!!!!!!!!!!
!!!!!!!!!!!!!!!!!!!!!!!!!!!!!!!!!!!!!!!!!!!!!!!!!!!!!!!!!!!!!!!!!!!!!!!!!!!!!!!!!!
!!!!!!!!!!!!!!!!!!!!!!!!!!!!!!!!!!!!!!!!!!!!!!!!!!!!!!!!!!!!!!!!!!!!!!!!!!!!!!!!!!
!!!!!!!!!!!!!!!!!!!!!!!!!!!!!!!!!!!!!!!!!!!!!!!!!!!!!!!!!!!!!!!!!!!!!!!!!!!!!!!!!!
!!!!!!!!!!!!!!!!!!!!!!!!!!!!!!!!!!!!!!!!!!!!!!!!!!!!!!!!!!!!!!!!!!!!!!!!!!!!!!!!!!
!!!!!!!!!!!!!!!!!!!!!!!!!!!!!!!!!!!!!!!!!!!!!!!!!!!!!!!!!!!!!!!!!!!!!!!!!!!!!!!!!!
!!!!!!!!!!!!!!!!!!!!!!!!!!!!!!!!!!!!!!!!!!!!!!!!!!!!!!!!!!!!!!!!!!!!!!!!!!!!!!!!!!
!!!!!!!!!!!!!!!!!!!!!!!!!!!!!!!!!!!!!!!!!!!!!!!!!!!!!!!!!!!!!!!!!!!!!!!!!!!!!!!!!!
!!!!!!!!!!!!!!!!!!!!!!!!!!!!!!!!!!!!!!!!!!!!!!!!!!!!!!!!!!!!!!!!!!!!!!!!!!!!!!!!!!
!!!!!!!!!!!!!!!!!!!!!!!!!!!!!!!!!!!!!!!!!!!!!!!!!!!!!!!!!!!!!!!!!!!!!!!!!!!!!!!!!!
!!!!!!!!!!!!!!!!!!!!!!!!!!!!!!!!!!!!!!!!!!!!!!!!!!!!!!!!!!!!!!!!!!!!!!!!!!!!!!!!!!
!!!!!!!!!!!!!!!!!!!!!!!!!!!!!!!!!!!!!!!!!!!!!!!!!!!!!!!!!!!!!!!!!!!!!!!!!!!!!!!!!!
!!!!!!!!!!!!!!!!!!!!!!!!!!!!!!!!!!!!!!!!!!!!!!!!!!!!!!!!!!!!!!!!!!!!!!!!!!!!!!!!!!
!!!!!!!!!!!!!!!!!!!!!!!!!!!!!!!!!!!!!!!!!!!!!!!!!!!!!!!!!!!!!!!!!!!!!!!!!!!!!!!!!!
!!!!!!!!!!!!!!!!!!!!!!!!!!!!!!!!!!!!!!!!!!!!!!!!!!!!!!!!!!!!!!!!!!!!!!!!!!!!!!!!!!
!!!!!!!!!!!!!!!!!!!!!!!!!!!!!!!!!!!!!!!!!!!!!!!!!!!!!!!!!!!!!!!!!!!!!!!!!!!!!!!!!!
!!!!!!!!!!!!!!!!!!!!!!!!!!!!!!!!!!!!!!!!!!!!!!!!!!!!!!!!!!!!!!!!!!!!!!!!!!!!!!!!!!
!!!!!!!!!!!!!!!!!!!!!!!!!!!!!!!!!!!!!!!!!!!!!!!!!!!!!!!
[OK - 8108960/13879830 bytes]
F3: 8010312+98616+315708 at 0x1000

                  Restricted Rights Legend

Use, duplication, or disclosure by the Government is
subject to restrictions as set forth in subparagraph
(c) of the Commercial Computer Software - Restricted
Rights clause at FAR sec. 52.227-19 and subparagraph
(c) (1) (ii) of the Rights in Technical Data and Computer
Software clause at DFARS sec. 252.227-7013.
```

**Example 16-5** *After Boot System Configuration Changes, R1 Boots from TFTP (Continued)*

```
                    cisco Systems, Inc.
                    170 West Tasman Drive
                    San Jose, California 95134-1706


    Cisco Internetwork Operating System Software
    IOS (tm) 2500 Software, Version 11.1(18), RELEASE SOFTWARE (fc1)
    Copyright (c) 1986-1999 by cisco Systems, Inc.
    Compiled Mon 04-Jan-99 17:27 by ashah
    Image text-base: 0x00001448, data-base: 0x00764DA8


    cisco 2500 (68030) processor (revision N) with 14336K/2048K bytes of memory.
    Processor board ID 06158021, with hardware revision 00000000
    Bridging software.
    SuperLAT software copyright 1990 by Meridian Technology Corp).
    X.25 software, Version 2.0, NET2, BFE and GOSIP compliant.
    TN3270 Emulation software.
    1 Ethernet/IEEE 802.3 interface(s)
    2 Serial network interface(s)
    32K bytes of non-volatile configuration memory.
    8192K bytes of processor board System flash (Read/Write)



    Press RETURN to get started!


    This is Router 1

    R1>
```

Notice that you are asked first to save the configuration changes and then to confirm the
request to reload R1. When the router reboots, you can see that the Cisco IOS Software
image is loaded from the TFTP server at 192.168.1.5, as highlighted in Example 16-5.
Additionally, if you do a **show version**, you can see that R1 was booted from the TFTP
server, as highlighted in Example 16-6.

**Example 16-6 show version** *Command Verifies That R1 Booted from TFTP*

```
R1#show version
Cisco Internetwork Operating System Software
IOS (tm) 2500 Software, Version 11.1(18), RELEASE SOFTWARE (fc1)
Copyright (c) 1986-1999 by cisco Systems, Inc.
```

*continues*

**Example 16-6 show version** *Command Verifies That R1 Booted from TFTP (Continued)*

```
Compiled Mon 04-Jan-99 17:27 by ashah
Image text-base: 0x00001448, data-base: 0x00764DA8

ROM: System Bootstrap, Version 11.0(10c), SOFTWARE
BOOTFLASH: 3000 Bootstrap Software (IGS-BOOT-R), Version 11.0(10c), RELEASE SOFTWARE
  (fc1)

R1 uptime is 4 minutes
System restarted by reload
System image file is "igs-j-1.111-18.bin", booted via tftp from 192.168.1.5

cisco 2500 (68030) processor (revision N) with 14336K/2048K bytes of memory.
Processor board ID 06158021, with hardware revision 00000000
Bridging software.
SuperLAT software copyright 1990 by Meridian Technology Corp).
X.25 software, Version 2.0, NET2, BFE and GOSIP compliant.
TN3270 Emulation software.
1 Ethernet/IEEE 802.3 interface(s)
2 Serial network interface(s)
32K bytes of non-volatile configuration memory.
8192K bytes of processor board System flash (Read/Write)

Configuration register is 0x2102

R1#
```

If the TFTP server were unavailable, R1 would load Cisco IOS Software from Flash. You can simulate this by making the TFTP server unavailable by simply shutting down Ethernet 0 on R1 and then reloading R1. Observe the results as shown in Example 16-7.

**Example 16-7** *Cisco IOS Software Loaded from Flash Times Out and Is Instead Booted from Flash*

```
R1#conf t
Enter configuration commands, one per line.  End with CNTL/Z.
R1(config)#int e0
R1(config-if)#shut
R1(config-if)#
%LINEPROTO-5-UPDOWN: Line protocol on Interface Ethernet0, changed state to down
R1(config-if)#
%LINK-5-CHANGED: Interface Ethernet0, changed state to administratively down
R1(config-if)#^Z
R1#
%SYS-5-CONFIG_I: Configured from console by console
R1#reload

System configuration has been modified. Save? [yes/no]: y
Building configuration...
[OK]
Proceed with reload? [confirm] [Enter]
```

**Example 16-7** *Cisco IOS Software Loaded from Flash Times Out and Is Instead Booted from Flash (Continued)*

```
System Bootstrap, Version 11.0(10c), SOFTWARE
Copyright (c) 1986-1996 by cisco Systems
2500 processor with 14336 Kbytes of main memory

%SYS-4-CONFIG_NEWER: Configurations from version 11.1 may not be correctly under
stood.
Loading igs-j-1.111-18.bin ... [timed out]
F3: 8010312+98616+315708 at 0x3000060

                   Restricted Rights Legend

Use, duplication, or disclosure by the Government is
subject to restrictions as set forth in subparagraph
(c) of the Commercial Computer Software - Restricted
Rights clause at FAR sec. 52.227-19 and subparagraph
(c) (1) (ii) of the Rights in Technical Data and Computer
Software clause at DFARS sec. 252.227-7013.

            cisco Systems, Inc.
            170 West Tasman Drive
            San Jose, California 95134-1706




Cisco Internetwork Operating System Software
IOS (tm) 2500 Software (C2500-JS-L), Version 11.2(17), RELEASE SOFTWARE (fc1)
Copyright (c) 1986-1999 by cisco Systems, Inc.
Compiled Mon 04-Jan-99 17:27 by ashah
Image text-base: 0x03040148, data-base: 0x00001000

cisco 2500 (68030) processor (revision N) with 14336K/2048K bytes of memory.
Processor board ID 06158021, with hardware revision 00000000
Bridging software.
SuperLAT software copyright 1990 by Meridian Technology Corp).
X.25 software, Version 2.0, NET2, BFE and GOSIP compliant.
TN3270 Emulation software.
1 Ethernet/IEEE 802.3 interface(s)
2 Serial network interface(s)
32K bytes of non-volatile configuration memory.
8192K bytes of processor board System flash (Read ONLY)




Press RETURN to get started!

 This is Router 1

R1>
```

You can see that R1 attempts to load Cisco IOS Software from Flash but cannot do so and times out, as shown in the highlighted portion of Example 16-7. If you do a **show version**, you will see that R1 failed to load Cisco IOS Software from TFTP and then loaded the image from Flash instead. This is shown in the highlighted portion of Example 16-8.

**Example 16-8** **show version** *Command Verifies That R1 Booted from Flash After Boot from TFTP Server Failed*

```
R1#show version
Cisco Internetwork Operating System Software
IOS (tm) 2500 Software (C2500-JS-L), Version 11.2(17), RELEASE SOFTWARE (fc1)
Copyright (c) 1986-1999 by cisco Systems, Inc.
Compiled Mon 04-Jan-99 17:27 by ashah
Image text-base: 0x03040148, data-base: 0x00001000

ROM: System Bootstrap, Version 11.0(10c), SOFTWARE
BOOTFLASH: 3000 Bootstrap Software (IGS-BOOT-R), Version 11.0(10c), RELEASE SOFT
WARE (fc1)

R1 uptime is 2 minutes
System restarted by reload
System image file is "flash:igs-j-l.111-18.bin", booted via flash

cisco 2500 (68030) processor (revision N) with 14336K/2048K bytes of memory.
Processor board ID 06158021, with hardware revision 00000000
Bridging software.
SuperLAT software copyright 1990 by Meridian Technology Corp).
X.25 software, Version 2.0, NET2, BFE and GOSIP compliant.
TN3270 Emulation software.
1 Ethernet/IEEE 802.3 interface(s)
2 Serial network interface(s)
32K bytes of non-volatile configuration memory.
8192K bytes of processor board System flash (Read ONLY)

Configuration register is 0x2102

R1#
```

Now that you have verified that R1 attempts to boot first from TFTP and then from Flash, bring Ethernet 0 back up on R1 and save the configuration as demonstrated in Example 16-9.

**Example 16-9** *Bring Up Ethernet 0 and Save Running Config on R1*

```
R1#conf t
Enter configuration commands, one per line.  End with CNTL/Z.
R1(config)#int e0
R1(config-if)#no shut
R1(config-if)#
%LINEPROTO-5-UPDOWN: Line protocol on Interface Ethernet0, changed state to up
R1(config-if)#
%LINK-3-UPDOWN: Interface Ethernet0, changed state to up
```

**Example 16-9** *Bring Up Ethernet 0 and Save Running Config on R1 (Continued)*

```
R1(config-if)#^Z
R1#
%SYS-5-CONFIG_I: Configured from console by console
R1#copy run start
Building configuration...
[OK]
R1#
```

# Backing Up Your Cisco IOS Software Image File

You can create a software backup image of Cisco IOS Software by copying the image file from a router to a network TFTP server. Later in this chapter, you will upgrade the Cisco IOS Software image on R1. Before the upgrade, you will back up the existing Cisco IOS Software image on R1 to the TFTP server. In this way, you have a backup of R1's Cisco IOS Software that could be restored from the TFTP server, if necessary. To copy the current system image file from R1 to the network server, you would use the following command in privileged EXEC mode:

```
Router#copy flash tftp
```

The **copy flash tftp** command requires you to enter the IP address of the remote host and the name of the source and destination system image file. Resume the connection to R1, enter 192.168.1.5 as the address of the remote host, identify the source file that you want to copy to the TFTP server as igs-j-l.111-18.bin, and then change the destination filename to be igs-j-l.111-18backup.bin, as demonstrated in Example 16-10.

---

**TIP**

Typing the name of the Cisco IOS Software image is often error-prone because the number 1 and letter *l* look the same in the Courier font typical on terminal emulators such as HyperTerminal. To avoid a typo when entering the filename that you want to copy to the TFTP server, it is recommended that you execute the **show flash** command, highlight the IOS Software filename as it appears in the output, and then copy and paste it following the **copy flash tftp** command.

---

**Example 16-10** *Copying the Current Cisco IOS Software Image on R1 to TFTP Server*

```
Termserver#1
[Resuming connection 1 to r1 ... ]

R1#copy flash tftp

System flash directory:
File  Length    Name/status
  1   7101640   igs-j-l.111-18.bin
```

*continues*

**Example 16-10** *Copying the Current Cisco IOS Software Image on R1 to TFTP Server (Continued)*

```
[7101704 bytes used, 1286904 available, 8388608 total]
Address or name of remote host? 192.168.1.5
Source file name? igs-j-l.111-18.bin
Destination file name [igs-j-l.111-18.bin]? igs-j-l.111-18backup.bin
Verifying checksum for 'igs-j-l.111-18.bin' (file # 1)...  OK
Copy 'igs-j-l.111-18.bin' from Flash to server
  as 'igs-j-l.111-18backup.bin'? [yes/no]y
.!!!!!!!!!!!!!!!!!!!!!!!!!!!!!!!!!!!!!!!!!!!!!!!!!!!!!!!!!!!!!!!!!!!!!!!!!!!!!!!!!!!!!!!!!!!!
!!!!!!!!!!!!!!!!!!!!!!!!!!!!!!!!!!!!!!!!!!!!!!!!!!!!!!!!!!!!!!!!!!!!!!!!!!!!!!!!!!!!!!!!!!!!!!
!!!!!!!!!!!!!!!!!!!!!!!!!!!!!!!!!!!!!!!!!!!!!!!!!!!!!!!!!!!!!!!!!!!!!!!!!!!!!!!!!!!!!!!!!!!!!!
!!!!!!!!!!!!!!!!!!!!!!!!!!!!!!!!!!!!!!!!!!!!!!!!!!!!!!!!!!!!!!!!!!!!!!!!!!!!!!!!!!!!!!!!!!!!!!
!!!!!!!!!!!!!!!!!!!!!!!!!!!!!!!!!!!!!!!!!!!!!!!!!!!!!!!!!!!!!!!!!!!!!!!!!!!!!!!!!!!!!!!!!!!!!!
!!!!!!!!!!!!!!!!!!!!!!!!!!!!!!!!!!!!!!!!!!!!!!!!!!!!!!!!!!!!!!!!!!!!!!!!!!!!!!!!!!!!!!!!!!!!!!
!!!!!!!!!!!!!!!!!!!!!!!!!!!!!!!!!!!!!!!!!!!!!!!!!!!!!!!!!!!!!!!!!!!!!!!!!!!!!!!!!!!!!!!!!!!!!!
!!!!!!!!!!!!!!!!!!!!!!!!!!!!!!!!!!!!!!!!!!!!!!!!!!!!!!!!!!!!!!!!!!!!!!!!!!!!!!!!!!!!!!!!!!!!!!
!!!!!!!!!!!!!!!!!!!!!!!!!!!!!!!!!!!!!!!!!!!!!!!!!!!!!!!!!!!!!!!!!!!!!!!!!!!!!!!!!!!!!!!!!!!!!!
!!!!!!!!!!!!!!!!!!!!!!!!!!!!!!!!!!!!!!!!!!!!!!!!!!!!!!!!!!!!!!!!!!!!!!!!!!!!!!!!!!!!!!!!!!!!!!
!!!!!!!!!!!!!!!!!!!!!!!!!!!!!!!!!!!!!!!!!!!!!!!!!!!!!!!!!!!!!!!!!!!!!!!!!!!!!!!!!!!!!!!!!!!!!!
!!!!!!!!!!!!!!!!!!!!!!!!!!!!!!!!!!!!!!!!!!!!!!!!!!!!!!!!!!!!!!!!!!!!!!!!!!!!!!!!!!!!!!!!!!!!!!
!!!!!!!!!!!!!!!!!!!!!!!!!!!!!!!!!!!!!!!!!!!!!!!!!!!!!!!!!!!!!!!!!!!!!!!!!!!!!!!!!!!!!!!!!!!!!!
!!!!!!!!!!!!!!!!!!!!!!!!!!!!!!!!!!!!!!!!!!!!!!!!!!!!!!!!!!!!!!!!!!!!!!!!!!!!!!!!!!!!!!!!!!!!!!
!!!!!!!!!!!!!!!!!!!!!!!!!!!!!!!!!!!!!!!!!!!!!!!!!!!!!!!!!!!!!!!!!!!!!!!!!!!!!!!!!!!!!!!!!!!!!!
!!!!!!!!!!!!!!!!!!!!!!!!!!!!!!!!!!!!!!!!!!!!!!!!!!!!!!!!!!!!!!!!!!!!!!!!!!!!!!!!!!!!!!!!!!!!!!
!!!!!!!!!!!!!!!!!!!!!!!!!!!!!!!!!!!!!!!!!!!!!!!!!!!!!!!!!!!!!!!!!!!!!!!!!!!!!!!!!!!!!!!!!!!!!!
!!!!!!!!!!!!!!!!!!!!!!!!!!!!!!!!!!!!!!!
Upload to server done
Flash copy took 00:02:17 [hh:mm:ss]
R1#
```

After confirming your choices, the copy from Flash to the network TFTP server begins. Each exclamation point (!) means that one User Datagram Protocol (UDP) segment has been successfully transferred. When the backup from Flash to TFTP is finished, you receive the message that the upload to the TFTP server is completed, as highlighted. The file that you backed up now resides on the TFTP server as igs-j-l.111-18backup.bin. This is the filename that you would use when doing a restore of this image from the TFTP server to the router.

## Upgrading a Cisco IOS Software Image File from the TFTP Server

Before upgrading the existing Flash image, examine the Flash of R1. You can view existing images contained in Flash memory with the **show flash** command, as demonstrated in Example 16-11.

**Example 16-11** **show flash** *on R1 Details the Size and Name of the Existing Image in R1's Flash*

```
R1#show flash

System flash directory:
File   Length   Name/status
  1   7101640  igs-j-l.111-18.bin
[7101704 bytes used, 1286904 available, 8388608 total]
8192K bytes of processor board System flash (Read ONLY)

R1#
```

Notice that R1 currently is running igs-j-l.111-18.bin, consuming 7,101,640 bytes of the 8192K total available in Flash. The **show flash** command shows any existing images in Flash and also gives details regarding the total size of Flash. This command also can help you ensure that the Flash size is sufficient to handle new images that you might want to download to the router.

You can load a new system image file on your router if the existing image file has become damaged or if you simply want to upgrade the image to a newer software version.

You want to download the new image c2500-js-l_112-17.bin to R1. You download the new image from the network TFTP server using the following command:

```
Router#copy tftp flash
```

When this command is executed, you are informed that if you are connected to the router through Telnet, your connection will be terminated after the copy operation completes when the router automatically is rebooted. Because you are connected to the console port of R1 through the terminal server, you will be able to see the entire process without being disconnected. Next, you are prompted for the IP address of the remote host (network TFTP server) and the name of the source and destination system image file. Enter the appropriate filename of the image as it appears on the TFTP server. In this case, you will enter **192.168.1.5** as the address of the TFTP server and **c2500-js-l_112-17.bin** as the image that you want to download to R1. Example 16-12 demonstrates how this is done on R1.

**Example 16-12** *Upgrading Cisco IOS Software Image on R1 from TFTP Server*

```
R1#copy tftp flash
                    ****  NOTICE  ****
Flash load helper v1.0
This process will accept the copy options and then terminate
the current system image to use the ROM based image for the copy.
Routing functionality will not be available during that time.
If you are logged in via telnet, this connection will terminate.
Users with console access can see the results of the copy operation.
                 ---- ******** ----
Proceed? [confirm] [Enter]

System flash directory:
```

*continues*

**Example 16-12** *Upgrading Cisco IOS Software Image on R1 from TFTP Server (Continued)*

```
File  Length    Name/status
  1   7101640   igs-j-l.111-18.bin
[7101704 bytes used, 1286904 available, 8388608 total]
Address or name of remote host [255.255.255.255]? 192.168.1.5
Source file name? c2500-js-l_112-17.bin
Destination file name [c2500-js-l_112-17.bin]? [Enter]
Accessing file 'c2500-js-l_112-17.bin' on 192.168.1.5...
Loading c2500-js-l_112-17.bin .from 192.168.1.5 (via Ethernet0): ! [OK]

Erase flash device before writing? [confirm] [Enter]
Flash contains files. Are you sure you want to erase? [confirm] [Enter]
Copy 'c2500-js-l_112-17.bin' from server
  as 'c2500-js-l_112-17.bin' into Flash WITH erase? [yes/no] yes

%SYS-4-CONFIG_NEWER: Configurations from version 11.2 may not be correctly under
stood.
%FLH: c2500-js-l_112-17.bin from 192.168.1.5 to flash ...

System flash directory:
File  Length    Name/status
  1   7101640   igs-j-l.111-18.bin
[7101704 bytes used, 1286904 available, 8388608 total]
Accessing file 'c2500-js-l_112-17.bin' on 192.168.1.5...
Loading c2500-js-l_112-17.bin from 192.168.1.5 (via Ethernet0): ! [OK]
Erasing device... eeeeeeeeeeeeeeeeeeeeeeeeeeeeeeeeee ...erased
Loading c2500-js-l_112-17.bin from 192.168.1.5 (via Ethernet0): !!!!!!!!!!!!!!!!!!
!!!!!!!!!!!!!!!!!!!!!!!!!!!!!!!!!!!!!!!!!!!!!!!!!!!!!!!!!!!!!!!!!!!!!!!!!!!!!!!!!!!!!
!!!!!!!!!!!!!!!!!!!!!!!!!!!!!!!!!!!!!!!!!!!!!!!!!!!!!!!!!!!!!!!!!!!!!!!!!!!!!!!!!!!!!!
!!!!!!!!!!!!!!!!!!!!!!!!!!!!!!!!!!!!!!!!!!!!!!!!!!!!!!!!!!!!!!!!!!!!!!!!!!!!!!!!!!!!!!
!!!!!!!!!!!!!!!!!!!!!!!!!!!!!!!!!!!!!!!!!!!!!!!!!!!!!!!!!!!!!!!!!!!!!!!!!!!!!!!!!!!!!!
!!!!!!!!!!!!!!!!!!!!!!!!!!!!!!!!!!!!!!!!!!!!!!!!!!!!!!!!!!!!!!!!!!!!!!!!!!!!!!!!!!!!!!
!!!!!!!!!!!!!!!!!!!!!!!!!!!!!!!!!!!!!!!!!!!!!!!!!!!!!!!!!!!!!!!!!!!!!!!!!!!!!!!!!!!!!!
!!!!!!!!!!!!!!!!!!!!!!!!!!!!!!!!!!!!!!!!!!!!!!!!!!!!!!!!!!!!!!!!!!!!!!!!!!!!!!!!!!!!!!
!!!!!!!!!!!!!!!!!!!!!!!!!!!!!!!!!!!!!!!!!!!!!!!!!!!!!!!!!!!!!!!!!!!!!!!!!!!!!!!!!!!!!!
!!!!!!!!!!!!!!!!!!!!!!!!!!!!!!!!!!!!!!!!!!!!!!!!!!!!!!!!!!!!!!!!!!!!!!!!!!!!!!!!!!!!!!
!!!!!!!!!!!!!!!!!!!!!!!!!!!!!!!!!!!!!!!!!!!!!!!!!!!!!!!!!!!!!!!!!!!!!!!!!!!!!!!!!!!!!!
!!!!!!!!!!!!!!!!!!!!!!!!!!!!!!!!!!!!!!!!!!!!!!!!!!!!!!!!!!!!!!!!!!!!!!!!!!!!!!!!!!!!!!
!!!!!!!!!!!!!!!!!!!!!!!!!!!!!!!!!!!!!!!!!!!!!!!!!!!!!!!!!!!!!!!!!!!!!!!!!!!!!!!!!!!!!!
!!!!!!!!!!!!!!!!!!!!!!!!!!!!!!!!!!!!!!!!!!!!!!!!!!!!!!!!!!!!!!!!!!!!!!!!!!!!!!!!!!!!!!
!!!!!!!!!!!!!!!!!!!!!!!!!!!!!!!!!!!!!!!!!!!!!!!!!!!!!!!!!!!!!!!!!!!!!!!!!!!!!!!!!!!!!!
!!!!!!!!!!!!!!!!!!!!!!!!!!!!!!!!!!!!!!!!!!!!!!!!!!!!!!!!!!!!!!!!!!!!!!!!!!!!!!!!!!!!!!
!!!!!!!!!!!!!!!!!!!!!!!!!!!!!!!!!!!!!!!!!!!!!!!!!!!!!!!!!!!!!!!!!!!!!!!!!!!!!!!!!!!!!!
!!!!!!!!!!!!!!!!!!!!!!!!!!!!!!!!!!!!!!!!!!!!!!!!!!!
[OK - 8108960/8388608 bytes]

Verifying checksum... OK (0x619E)
Flash copy took 0:03:59 [hh:mm:ss]
%FLH: Re-booting system after download
F3: 8010312+98616+315708 at 0x3000060
```

**Example 16-12** *Upgrading Cisco IOS Software Image on R1 from TFTP Server (Continued)*

```
Restricted Rights Legend

Use, duplication, or disclosure by the Government is
subject to restrictions as set forth in subparagraph
(c) of the Commercial Computer Software - Restricted
Rights clause at FAR sec. 52.227-19 and subparagraph
(c) (1) (ii) of the Rights in Technical Data and Computer
Software clause at DFARS sec. 252.227-7013.

            cisco Systems, Inc.
            170 West Tasman Drive
            San Jose, California 95134-1706


Cisco Internetwork Operating System Software
IOS (tm) 2500 Software (C2500-JS-L), Version 11.2(17), RELEASE SOFTWARE (fc1)
Copyright (c) 1986-1999 by cisco Systems, Inc.
Compiled Mon 04-Jan-99 17:27 by ashah
Image text-base: 0x03040148, data-base: 0x00001000

cisco 2500 (68030) processor (revision N) with 14336K/2048K bytes of memory.
Processor board ID 06158021, with hardware revision 00000000
Bridging software.
SuperLAT software copyright 1990 by Meridian Technology Corp).
X.25 software, Version 2.0, NET2, BFE and GOSIP compliant.
TN3270 Emulation software.
1 Ethernet/IEEE 802.3 interface(s)
2 Serial network interface(s)
32K bytes of non-volatile configuration memory.
8192K bytes of processor board System flash (Read ONLY)


Press RETURN to get started!


This is Router 1

R1>
```

Now examine the highlighted portion of Example 16-12. Notice that after you enter the IP address of the TFTP server and the name of source and destination image file, the procedure asks if you want to erase Flash. Erasing Flash makes room for the new image if there is insufficient Flash memory for more than one Cisco IOS Software image. In addition, if no free Flash memory space is available, or if the Flash memory never has been written to, the Flash must be erased before new files can be copied. The system informs you of these conditions and prompts you for a response. Answer yes to erase the Flash; the erase begins as indicated by the sequence of *e*'s. When this process is complete, the existing image in

Flash (igs-j-l.111-18.bin) is erased, allowing sufficient space for the new image (c2500-js-l-112-17.bin) to be copied to Flash memory. As the new image begins to be downloaded from the TFTP server, you see each exclamation point (!), meaning that one UDP segment successfully has been transferred. When the TFTP download is finished, the checksum is verified to guarantee the integrity of the file. Then the router is rebooted and you are put into user EXEC mode.

## Backing Up/Restoring Your Configuration Files to/from a TFTP Server

The Cisco IOS Software **copy** commands are used to move configuration files from one component or device to another. The syntax of the **copy** commands requires that the first argument indicate the source (from where the configuration is to be copied) and then the destination (to where the configuration is to be copied). Throughout the book, you have seen how this is performed with the command **copy running startup**. This command is used when configuration changes are made and you want to save them. You now want to back up the running config of R1 to the TFTP server by executing the following command:

```
Router#copy running-config tftp
```

This command allows you to copy the running config to a TFTP server, where it later can be retrieved as a backup, if necessary. In production environments, backups always should be made before making configuration changes. In this way, if the changes are unsuccessful or have undesirable results, or the configuration file becomes corrupted, the configuration can be restored from backup.

Back up the running config of R1, as demonstrated in Example 16-13.

**Example 16-13** *Backing Up Running Config of R1 to TFTP Server*

```
R1#copy running-config tftp
Remote host []? 192.168.1.5
Name of configuration file to write [r1-confg]? [Enter]
Write file r1-confg on host 192.168.1.5? [confirm] [Enter]
Building configuration...

Writing r1-confg !! [OK]
R1#
```

You are asked to confirm your choices, and the copy begins. Now suppose that R1's startup config has become corrupted. You can restore R1's startup config from backup using the file that you just backed up to the TFTP server. To restore R1's startup config, you would execute the following command:

```
Router#copy tftp startup-config
```

This is demonstrated in Example 16-14.

**Example 16-14** *Restoring Configuration from TFTP Server to R1's Startup Config*

```
R1#copy tftp startup-config
Address of remote host [255.255.255.255]? 192.168.1.5
Name of configuration file [r1-confg]? [Enter]
Configure using r1-confg from 192.168.1.5? [confirm] [Enter]
Loading r1-confg from 192.168.1.5 (via Ethernet0): !
[OK - 885/32723 bytes]
[OK]
R1#
%SYS-5-CONFIG_NV: Non-volatile store configured from r1-confg by console tftp fr
om 192.168.1.5
R1#
```

Again, you enter the address of the TFTP server and then confirm the name that you want
to restore from the TFTP server as r1-confg. Lastly, you confirm your choices and the file
is copied from the TFTP server to the startup config of R1.

# Summary

You now have successfully completed the lab objectives for this chapter. You have learned
how to control the router boot sequence and have configured R1 to boot from TFTP and
then Flash. You have seen how to manage Cisco IOS Software images and configuration
files, and you have used a TFTP server to back up as well as upgrade Cisco IOS Software
images and configuration files within your network. Table 16-1 is a command summary,
reviewing the commands used throughout the chapter.

**Table 16-1** *Chapter Command Summary*

| Command | Purpose |
| --- | --- |
| **boot system tftp** | Specifies that the router should load the system image from a TFTP server at startup |
| **boot system flash** | Specifies that the router should load the system image from Flash at startup |
| **Reload** | Reloads the Cisco IOS Software |
| **show flash** | Displays any files currently in Flash memory and shows the amounts of Flash memory used and remaining |
| **show version** | Displays the names and sources of configuration files and the boot images |
| **copy flash tftp** | Copies a Cisco IOS Software image from Flash to a TFTP server |
| **copy tftp flash** | Copies a Cisco IOS Software image from a TFTP server to Flash |
| **copy running-config tftp** | Copies the running config to a TFTP server |
| **copy tftp startup-config** | Copies a configuration file from a TFTP server to the startup config |

## CHAPTER 17

# Troubleshooting

In this chapter you will have the opportunity to troubleshoot different internetworking problems. The chapter presents four scenarios in which you identify the problem, isolate where the issue resides, and then resolve the problem.

Before beginning with the scenarios, you should familiarize yourself with a few basic troubleshooting steps. One of the most important items to remember about troubleshooting is to have a process or a methodology that you can repeat for every internetworking problem that you might encounter. From our own experiences and studies, we recommend using the OSI reference model to isolate these problems. That is, always start at the physical layer, verify that no problems exist, and then move on to the data link layer, on to the network layer, and so on. This provides a repeatable process to all internetworking problems.

Another helpful hint is to always start the troubleshooting process closest to where the symptom is experienced. For instance, if users on router R6 are having problems accessing a resource off router R1, start the troubleshooting process on R6 and then move on to the next router in the path to the destination router, R1. This will follow the path of the symptom until the source of the problem is isolated and can be resolved. These processes are demonstrated in the scenarios included in this chapter.

To troubleshoot properly, you will need to understand the physical topology, the logical addressing, and routing domain boundaries. This chapter refers to the complete lab diagram, shown in Figure 17-1, that you should have been developing throughout the book.

**Figure 17-1**  *Completed Lab Diagram*

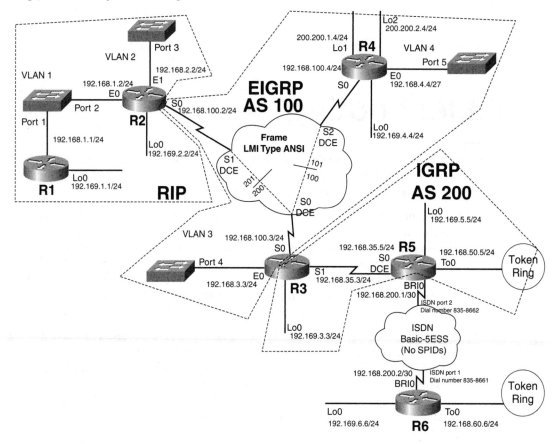

# Scenario 1

**Symptom:** Users off R4's Ethernet 0 network (192.168.4.0) cannot access IP-based resources located off R2's Ethernet 1 network (192.168.2.0).

**Objective:** Resolve the issue so that users can access those resources again. This is completed when R4 successfully can **ping** R2's Ethernet 1 interface IP address.

The first step in troubleshooting the issue is to verify that R4 and R2 are physically up and that the respective interfaces are in the UP and UP states. Look at R4 first and then R2. One thing that you want to be aware of is that R3 is the hub router for the Frame Relay network. (See Figure 17-1 for the physical path for these networks.) All packets from R4 going to R2 must traverse R3, so you might as well verify that R3 is operational and that the pertinent interfaces are both up.

Example 17-1 illustrates the output.

**Example 17-1** show ip interface brief *Command Output on R4*

```
R4#show ip interface brief
Interface          IP-Address      OK? Method Status               Protocol

Ethernet0          192.168.4.4     YES NVRAM  up                       up

Loopback0          192.169.4.4     YES NVRAM  up                       up

Loopback1          200.200.1.4     YES NVRAM  up                       up

Loopback2          200.200.2.4     YES NVRAM  up                       up

Serial0            192.168.100.4   YES NVRAM  up                       up

Serial1            unassigned      YES unset  administratively down down

R4#
```

First, you know that R4 is up and operational because you could Reverse Telnet to it. If the router had lost power, you would not have been able to Reverse Telnet to it from the terminal server. Second, from the output, you see that the Ethernet interface Ethernet 0 is up and up. You then will assume that users can access R4's Ethernet 0's interface.

**NOTE**    This scenario assumes that no LAN problems occur, such as a bad switch, hub, or cabling.

Third, you can see that the serial interface Serial 0 is up and up. So, the connection to the Frame Relay appears to not have any physical problems.

From this information, you can safely assume that the physical and data link layers are physically up. If there had been a physical issue with either of the layers, the status of the interface would have been down, down or up, down. You will verify correct configurations later; at this point, you just want to make sure that no physical problems are present on R4, R3, and R2, so next go to R3. See Example 17-2.

**Example 17-2** show ip interface brief *Command Output on R3*

```
R3#show ip interface brief
Interface          IP-Address      OK? Method Status               Protocol

Ethernet0          192.168.3.3     YES NVRAM  up                       up

Loopback0          192.169.3.3     YES NVRAM  up                       up
```

*continues*

**Example 17-2 show ip interface brief** *Command Output on R3 (Continued)*

```
Serial0               192.168.100.3   YES NVRAM  up              up

Serial1               192.168.35.3    YES NVRAM  up              up

R3#
```

The only interface of concern on R3 is Serial 0, the hub interface for the Frame Relay network. The status is up and up, so no physical issues are present here. Next, go to R2. See Example 17-3.

**Example 17-3 show ip interface brief** *Command Output on R2*

```
R2#show ip interface brief
Interface            IP-Address      OK? Method Status          Protocol

Ethernet0            192.168.1.2     YES NVRAM  up              up

Ethernet1            192.168.2.2     YES NVRAM  up              up

Loopback0            192.169.2.2     YES NVRAM  up              up

Serial0              192.168.100.2   YES NVRAM  up              up

R2#
```

By virtue of connecting to the router, you verified that it has power and that the status of interface Ethernet 1 and Serial 0 are both up and up; no physical issues are present on R4 or R2. Before you start checking for configuration errors, isolate where the communication fails. Because users on R4 cannot access IP resources on R2's Ethernet 1 interface, **ping** from R4 to R2's Ethernet 1 interface, then R2's Serial 0, then R3's Serial 0 interface, and so forth until you have isolated the failure.

**NOTE**     Remember, in the Frame Relay network, R4 must send to R3 all packets destined to R2. This is because no direct PVC connects R4 to R2.

Example 17-4 demonstrates this process.

**Example 17-4 ping** *R2's Ethernet 1 from R4*

```
R4#ping 192.168.2.2

Type escape sequence to abort.
Sending 5, 100-byte ICMP Echos to 192.168.2.2, timeout is 2 seconds:
.....
Success rate is 0 percent (0/5)
R4#
```

That failed. Next try R2's Serial 0. See Example 17-5.

**Example 17-5 ping** *R2's Serial 0 from R4*

```
R4#ping 192.168.100.2

Type escape sequence to abort.
Sending 5, 100-byte ICMP Echos to 192.168.100.2, timeout is 2 seconds:
.....
Success rate is 0 percent (0/5)
R4#
```

That failed as well. Next try R3's Serial 0, which is the next hop in the routing path. See Example 17-6.

**Example 17-6 ping** *R3's Serial 0 from R4*

```
R4#ping 192.168.100.3

Type escape sequence to abort.
Sending 5, 100-byte ICMP Echos to 192.168.100.3, timeout is 2 seconds:
.....
Success rate is 0 percent (0/5)
R4#
```

This failed, too. Because this is the next hop from R4, you know that there is a communication breakdown between R4 and R3. Because R4 must send all packets destined for R2 through R3, you need to resolve the communication issue between R4 and R3 first. When that is resolved, you should test to see if that corrects the problem of R4 not being capable of **ping**ing R2's Ethernet 1 network. If it does not resolve the issue, further troubleshooting will be needed; however, first resolve the communication problem between R4 and R3.

As mentioned in the introduction to this chapter, you want to start each troubleshooting step at the physical layer of the OSI reference model and start the troubleshooting process closest to where the symptom occurs. In this case, users on R4's Ethernet 0 network cannot communicate with R2's Ethernet 1 network. So, according to the prescribed troubleshooting process, look at R4's data link layer configurations because you have already dismissed physical layer issues.

From your initial troubleshooting steps, you found a communication breakdown between R3's Serial 0 and R4's Serial 0 interfaces. This is the Frame Relay network, so you need to recall the configuration tasks and issues that pertain to Frame Relay.

First, you need to verify that you are receiving the correct DLCI from the Frame Relay switch. If are not receiving LMI, the interface would be in an UP DOWN state; you know that you are receiving LMI, so you just need to make sure that the LMI information is correct. Issue a **show frame-relay pvc** command to verify that you are receiving DLCI 101 on interface Serial 0. Example 17-7 displays the output from the command.

**Example 17-7 show frame-relay pvc** *Output on R4*

```
R4#show frame-relay pvc

PVC Statistics for interface Serial0 (Frame Relay DTE)

DLCI = 101, DLCI USAGE = LOCAL, PVC STATUS = ACTIVE, INTERFACE = Serial0

  input pkts 60          output pkts 75          in bytes 6040
  out bytes 6930         dropped pkts 0          in FECN pkts 0
  in BECN pkts 0         out FECN pkts 0         out BECN pkts 0
  in DE pkts 0           out DE pkts 0
  out bcast pkts 51       out bcast bytes 3690
  pvc create time 00:20:26, last time pvc status changed 00:20:26
R4#
```

You are receiving DLCI 101, which is correct, and it is in ACTIVE status. This means that the DLCI that the Frame Relay switch is sending you through LMI is valid and is on Serial 0, the correct interface.

Frame Relay also needs mappings that map DLCIs to IP addresses. These tell the router how to forward the frame out the appropriate PVC. Verify the DLCI-to-IP address mappings on R4 by issuing the command **show frame-relay map**. See Example 17-8.

**Example 17-8 show frame-relay map** *Output on R4*

```
R4#show frame-relay map
Serial0 (up): ipx 1000.0000.0000.2222 dlci 101(0x65,0x1850), static,
              broadcast,
              CISCO, status defined, active
Serial0 (up): ipx 1000.0000.0000.3333 dlci 101(0x65,0x1850), static,
              broadcast,
              CISCO, status defined, active
R4#
```

Here is a problem. You see DLCI-to-IPX address mappings, but you do not see DLCI-to-IP address mappings. Remember, you need mappings for each protocol that you are using on that interface. The mappings have two ways of occurring. You can rely on Frame Relay

Inverse ARP, or you can statically assign the mappings. If you recall, you used static **frame-relay map** statements for R4 and R2, but you let Frame Relay Inverse ARP dynamically create the mappings on R3. Frame Relay Inverse ARP is utilized on R3 because R3 has two PVCs, one to each router. Take a look at R4's configuration to verify that the **frame-relay map** statements are still there. See Example 17-9.

**Example 17-9** *R4's Running Config File*

```
R4#show running-config
Building configuration...

Current configuration:
!
version 11.2
no service password-encryption
no service udp-small-servers
no service tcp-small-servers
!
hostname R4
!
enable password falcons
!
ip subnet-zero
ip telnet source-interface Serial0
no ip domain-lookup
ip host R4 192.169.4.4
ip host R1 192.169.1.1
ip host R2 192.169.2.2
ip host R3 192.169.3.3
ip host R5 192.169.5.5
ip host R6 192.169.6.6
ipx routing 0000.0000.4444
!
interface Loopback0
 ip address 192.169.4.4 255.255.255.0
!
interface Loopback1
 ip address 200.200.1.4 255.255.255.0
!
interface Loopback2
 ip address 200.200.2.4 255.255.255.0
!
interface Ethernet0
 description This interface does not connect to another IP device
 ip address 192.168.4.4 255.255.255.224
 ipx network 4000
!
interface Serial0
 description This interface connects to R3's S0 (DLCI 101)
 ip address 192.168.100.4 255.255.255.0
 ip summary-address eigrp 100 200.200.0.0 255.255.0.0
 encapsulation frame-relay
```

*continues*

**Example 17-9** *R4's Running Config File (Continued)*

```
 ipx network 1000
 no fair-queue
 frame-relay map ipx 1000.0000.0000.2222 101 broadcast
 frame-relay map ipx 1000.0000.0000.3333 101 broadcast
 no frame-relay inverse-arp
 frame-relay lmi-type ansi
!
interface Serial1
 no ip address
 shutdown
!
router eigrp 100
 network 192.168.100.0
 network 192.168.4.0
 network 200.200.1.0
 network 200.200.2.0
 network 192.169.4.0
 no auto-summary
!
no ip classless
!
!
!
ipx router eigrp 100
 network 1000
!
!
ipx router rip
 no network 1000
!
!
!
banner motd ^C
This is Router 4
^C
!
line con 0
 exec-timeout 0 0
 password falcons
 logging synchronous
line aux 0
line vty 0 4
 password falcons
 login
!
end

R4#
```

From the highlighted section, you can see that Serial 0 has the **frame-relay map** statements for IPX but not for IP. Somehow they were removed, either by a configuration change not saved since the last reload or from a corrupt configuration file—from our experience, you will probably never know.

To resolve this issue, you just need to add back the **frame-relay map** statements for R2's Serial 0 and R3's Serial 0. Example 17-10 takes you through the process of adding the **frame-relay map** statements. Don't forget to save the configuration after you have added the **frame-relay map** statements.

**Example 17-10** *Adding* **frame-relay map** *Statements on R4*

```
R4#conf t
Enter configuration commands, one per line.  End with CNTL/Z.
R4(config)#interface serial 0
R4(config-if)#frame-relay map ip 192.168.100.2 101 broadcast
R4(config-if)#frame-relay map ip 192.168.100.3 101 broadcast
R4(config-if)#end
R4#copy running-config startup-config
Building configuration...
[OK]
R4#
```

To verify that the mappings are correct, again issue the **show frame-relay map** command. See Example 17-11.

**Example 17-11** *Verify Frame Relay Mappings on R4*

```
R4#show frame-relay map
Serial0 (up): ip 192.168.100.2 dlci 101(0x65,0x1850), static,
              broadcast,
              CISCO, status defined, active
Serial0 (up): ip 192.168.100.3 dlci 101(0x65,0x1850), static,
              broadcast,
              CISCO, status defined, active
Serial0 (up): ipx 1000.0000.0000.2222 dlci 101(0x65,0x1850), static,
              broadcast,
              CISCO, status defined, active
Serial0 (up): ipx 1000.0000.0000.3333 dlci 101(0x65,0x1850), static,
              broadcast,
              CISCO, status defined, active
R4#
```

From the highlighted text, you see that the mappings are correct. Verify that you can **ping** to R3's Serial 0 and R2's Serial 0 to see if this resolves the initial problem of R4's Ethernet 0 users not being able to access IP-based resources on R2's Ethernet 1 network. Example 17-12 illustrates the results.

**Example 17-12** *Verify Connectivity to R3's Serial 0 and R2's Ethernet 1*

```
R4#ping 192.168.100.3

Type escape sequence to abort.
Sending 5, 100-byte ICMP Echos to 192.168.100.3, timeout is 2 seconds:
!!!!!
Success rate is 100 percent (5/5), round-trip min/avg/max = 60/60/60 ms
R4#ping 192.168.2.2

Type escape sequence to abort.
Sending 5, 100-byte ICMP Echos to 192.168.2.2, timeout is 2 seconds:
!!!!!
Success rate is 100 percent (5/5), round-trip min/avg/max = 88/92/104 ms
R4#
```

Success on both interfaces! You have resolved the problem. To quickly review, you verified that the routers in the routing path, R4, R3, and R2, were operational and that all pertinent interfaces were in the UP and UP state, removing concerns that there were physical layer issues. You then did a series of **ping** commands to isolate where the communication breakdown occurred. After isolating the communication breakdown, you verified data link layer configuration commands with a **show frame-relay pvc** command and a **show frame-relay map** command. From the **show frame-relay map** command, you found that the Frame Relay mappings were missing and added those mappings manually. This was the cause of the problem.

# Scenario 2

**Symptom:** It has been reported that users on network 192.168.4.0 (R4's E0 network) cannot reach IP resources on network 192.168.3.0 (R3's Ethernet 0 network).

**Objective:** You will have resolved this issue when you can successfully **ping** 192.168.3.3 from R4.

**Isolate the problem:** Begin by verifying that the reported symptoms are a network issue instead of an end-user configuration problem. You can do this by issuing a **ping** from R4 to R3's Ethernet 0 interface of 192.168.3.3, as shown in Example 17-13.

**Example 17-13** *Verify Symptom by pinging on R4 to 192.168.3.3*

```
R4#ping 192.168.3.3

Type escape sequence to abort.
Sending 5, 100-byte ICMP Echos to 192.168.3.3, timeout is 2 seconds:
.....
Success rate is 0 percent (0/5)
R4#
```

The request has failed. Now that you have verified the problem, follow the prescribed troubleshooting methodology by starting at R4 and verifying Layer 1, Layer 2, and finally Layer 3.

Examine physical connectivity on R4 and verify that Ethernet 0 and Serial 0 are up by doing a **show ip interfaces brief**, as shown in Example 17-14.

**Example 17-14  show ip int brief** *on R4 Shows That Ethernet 0 and Serial 0 Are Up*

```
R4#show ip int brief
Interface            IP-Address       OK? Method Status                 Protocol
Ethernet0            192.168.4.4      YES NVRAM  up                     up
Loopback0            192.169.4.4      YES NVRAM  up                     up
Loopback1            200.200.1.4      YES NVRAM  up                     up
Loopback2            200.200.2.4      YES NVRAM  up                     up
Serial0              192.168.100.4    YES NVRAM  up                     up
Serial1              unassigned       YES unset  administratively down  down
R4#
```

Of particular concern here is Ethernet 0 and Serial 0 because if either of these interfaces were down or if the line protocol were down, you would have a Layer 1 or 2 issue to resolve. However, you can see in the highlighted sections of Example 17-14 that both Ethernet 0 and Serial 0 interfaces are up and that the line protocol on each is up. Additionally, you can verify that R4's PVC to R3 is ACTIVE by doing a **show frame-relay pvc**, as shown in Example 17-15.

**Example 17-15** *R4's PVC to R3 Shows ACTIVE as Verified by* **show frame-relay pvc** *Command on R4*

```
R4#show frame-relay pvc

PVC Statistics for interface Serial0 (Frame Relay DTE)

DLCI = 101, DLCI USAGE = LOCAL, PVC STATUS = ACTIVE, INTERFACE = Serial0

  input pkts 12250        output pkts 23980       in bytes 878122
  out bytes 1677066       dropped pkts 0          in FECN pkts 0
  in BECN pkts 0          out FECN pkts 0         out BECN pkts 0
  in DE pkts 0            out DE pkts 0
  out bcast pkts 23474     out bcast bytes 1619636
  pvc create time 3d18h, last time pvc status changed 2d16h
R4#
```

From the highlighted portions of Example 17-15, you see that the PVC to R3 is ACTIVE and that the PVC has been up for 2 days and 16 hours, as shown by the last PVC status change in the example. Thus, to this point, you know that Layer 1 and 2 appear as you would expect them to on R4.

Next, look for a route to the 192.168.3.0 network in R4's routing table by doing a **show ip route 192.168.3.0** on R4, as shown in Example 17-16.

**Example 17-16** *Network 192.168.3.0 Is Not in R4's Routing Table*

```
R4#show ip route 192.168.3.0
% Network not in table
R4#
```

It is apparent that R4 is not receiving this route. If you examine the IP routing table of R4, you can determine whether you are lacking just this one route or whether you aren't learning routes to other networks as shown in Example 17-17.

**Example 17-17** *Routing Table Shows R4's Routes to Other Networks*

```
R4#show ip route
Codes: C - connected, S - static, I - IGRP, R - RIP, M - mobile, B - BGP
       D - EIGRP, EX - EIGRP external, O - OSPF, IA - OSPF inter area
       N1 - OSPF NSSA external type 1, N2 - OSPF NSSA external type 2
       E1 - OSPF external type 1, E2 - OSPF external type 2, E - EGP
       i - IS-IS, L1 - IS-IS level-1, L2 - IS-IS level-2, * - candidate default
       U - per-user static route, o - ODR

Gateway of last resort is not set

C    200.200.1.0/24 is directly connected, Loopback1
C    200.200.2.0/24 is directly connected, Loopback2
C    192.168.100.0/24 is directly connected, Serial0
D EX 192.168.35.0/24 [170/2169856] via 192.168.100.3, 02:03:34, Serial0
D EX 192.168.60.0/24 [170/41536000] via 192.168.100.3, 02:03:34, Serial0
D EX 192.168.50.0/24 [170/2697984] via 192.168.100.3, 02:03:34, Serial0
D EX 192.169.1.0/24 [170/2733056] via 192.168.100.3, 01:48:05, Serial0
D EX 192.168.1.0/24 [170/2733056] via 192.168.100.3, 01:48:05, Serial0
D EX 192.168.2.0/24 [170/2733056] via 192.168.100.3, 01:48:05, Serial0
D EX 192.169.3.0/24 [170/2169856] via 192.168.100.3, 02:03:34, Serial0
D EX 192.169.2.0/24 [170/2733056] via 192.168.100.3, 01:48:06, Serial0
D EX 192.169.5.0/24 [170/2809856] via 192.168.100.3, 02:03:35, Serial0
     192.168.4.0/27 is subnetted, 1 subnets
C       192.168.4.0 is directly connected, Ethernet0
C    192.169.4.0/24 is directly connected, Loopback0
D EX 192.168.200.0/24 [170/41536000] via 192.168.100.3, 02:03:38, Serial0
D    200.200.0.0/16 is a summary, 02:03:38, Null0
R4#
```

You can see that all EIGRP routes have been learned through 192.168.100.3, as highlighted. This tells you that R3's Serial 0 interface and the Frame Relay PVC must be up to be propagating these routes to R4. Refer back to the routing protocol diagram in Figure 17-1.

Network 192.168.3.0 should be a part of EIGRP AS 100. Because it is not being propagated, you might have an EIGRP configuration issue on R3 or Ethernet 0 on R3 could be down, causing the route not to be advertised by EIGRP. Ensure that Ethernet 0 is up on R3 by doing a **show ip interface brief**, as demonstrated in Example 17-18.

**Example 17-18** *Verify That Ethernet 0 on R3 Is up Using the* **show ip interface brief** *Command*

```
R3#show ip interface brief
Interface            IP-Address       OK? Method Status            Protocol
Ethernet0            192.168.3.3      YES NVRAM  up                up
Loopback0            192.169.3.3      YES NVRAM  up                up
Serial0              192.168.100.3    YES NVRAM  up                up
Serial1              192.168.35.3     YES NVRAM  up                up
R3#
```

Because R3's Ethernet 0 interface is up and the line protocol is up, you might suspect the issue to be with the EIGRP configuration of R3. Do a **show ip eigrp interfaces** to see which interfaces on R3 are part of EIGRP AS 100, as demonstrated in Example 17-19.

**Example 17-19** *Examine Which Interfaces Are a Part of EIGRP 100 Using the* **show ip eigrp interfaces** *Command on R3*

```
R3#show ip eigrp interfaces
IP-EIGRP interfaces for process 100

                     Xmit Queue   Mean   Pacing Time   Multicast    Pending
Interface    Peers   Un/Reliable  SRTT   Un/Reliable   Flow Timer   Routes
Se0          2       0/0          91     0/15          262          0
R3#
```

You can see that Serial 0 is a part of EIGRP process (AS) 100, but R3's Ethernet 0 is not. At this point, the EIGRP configuration is definitely suspect. Examine the running config of R3, as shown in Example 17-20.

**Example 17-20** *Examine the Running Configuration on R3*

```
R3#show running-config
Building configuration...

Current configuration:
!
version 11.2
no service password-encryption
no service udp-small-servers
no service tcp-small-servers
!
hostname R3
!
```

*continues*

**Example 17-20** *Examine the Running Configuration on R3 (Continued)*

```
enable password falcons
!
username all
no ip domain-lookup
ip host R3 192.169.3.3
ip host R1 192.169.1.1
ip host R2 192.169.2.2
ip host R4 192.169.4.4
ip host R5 192.169.5.5
ip host R6 192.169.6.6
ipx routing 0000.0000.3333
!
interface Loopback0
 ip address 192.169.3.3 255.255.255.0
!
interface Ethernet0
 ip address 192.168.3.3 255.255.255.0
 ipx network 3000
 ipx network 3001 encapsulation SAP secondary
!
interface Serial0
 description This interface connects to R2's S0(DLCI 200) and R4's S0 (DLCI 100)
 ip address 192.168.100.3 255.255.255.0
 ip access-group 101 in
 encapsulation frame-relay
 no ip split-horizon eigrp 100
 ipx network 1000
 no ipx split-horizon eigrp 100
 no fair-queue
 frame-relay lmi-type ansi
!
interface Serial1
 description This interface connects to R5's S0 (DCE)
 ip address 192.168.35.3 255.255.255.0
 ipx network 3500
!
router eigrp 100
 redistribute igrp 200 metric 200 200 255 1 1500
 network 192.168.100.0
!
router igrp 200
 redistribute eigrp 100 metric 2000 200 255 1 1500
 network 192.168.35.0
 network 192.169.3.0
!
no ip classless
access-list 101 deny   tcp any 192.168.50.0 0.0.0.255 eq www
access-list 101 deny   tcp any 192.168.30.0 0.0.0.255 eq ftp
access-list 101 deny   tcp any 192.168.30.0 0.0.0.255 eq ftp-data
access-list 101 permit ip any any
!
!
```

**Example 17-20** *Examine the Running Configuration on R3 (Continued)*

```
!
ipx router eigrp 100
 network 1000
!
!
ipx router rip
 no network 1000
!
!
!
banner motd ^C
This is Router 3
^C
!
line con 0
 exec-timeout 0 0
 password falcons
 logging synchronous
line aux 0
line vty 0 4
 password falcons
 login
!
end

R3#
```

In Example 17-20, the EIGRP configuration has been highlighted. Notice that network 192.168.3.0 is not a part of EIGRP AS 100. It sure is difficult to get good help these days. Someone must have incorrectly removed this network from EIGRP. Correct this error by adding the network back into EIGRP AS 100, saving the configuration, and then doing a **show ip eigrp interfaces**, as shown in Example 17-21.

**Example 17-21** *Adding Network 192.168.3.0 Back into EIGRP 100, Saving Configuration, and Then Verify Configuration Using* **show ip eigrp interfaces** *Command on R3*

```
R3#conf t
Enter configuration commands, one per line.  End with CNTL/Z.
R3(config)#router eigrp 100
R3(config-router)#network 192.168.3.0
R3(config-router)#^Z
R3#
%SYS-5-CONFIG_I: Configured from console by console
R3#copy run start
Building configuration...
[OK]
R3#sho ip eigrp int
IP-EIGRP interfaces for process 100
```

*continues*

**Example 17-21** *Adding Network 192.168.3.0 Back into EIGRP 100, Saving Configuration, and Then Verify Configuration Using* **show ip eigrp interfaces** *Command on R3 (Continued)*

```
                    Xmit Queue   Mean   Pacing Time   Multicast    Pending
Interface   Peers   Un/Reliable  SRTT   Un/Reliable   Flow Timer   Routes
Se0          2         0/0       114       0/15          50          0
Et0          0         0/0         0       0/10           0          0
R3#
```

Now you see that R3's Ethernet 0 network of 192.168.3.0 is being advertised in EIGRP process 100. You can verify that R4 receives this route as you expect by returning to R4 and doing a **show ip route 192.168.3.0**, as demonstrated in Example 17-22.

**Example 17-22** **show ip route 192.168.3.0** *Now Shows That R4 Is Receiving This Route*

```
R4#show ip route 192.168.3.0
Routing entry for 192.168.3.0/24
  Known via "eigrp 100", distance 90, metric 2195456, type internal
  Redistributing via eigrp 100
  Last update from 192.168.100.3 on Serial0, 00:04:15 ago
  Routing Descriptor Blocks:
  * 192.168.100.3, from 192.168.100.3, 00:04:15 ago, via Serial0
      Route metric is 2195456, traffic share count is 1
      Total delay is 21000 microseconds, minimum bandwidth is 1544 Kbit
      Reliability 255/255, minimum MTU 1500 bytes
      Loading 1/255, Hops 1

R4#
```

R4 has now received this route, which was learned through 192.168.100.3, as highlighted. Now **ping** 192.168.3.3 from R4, as shown in Example 17-23.

**Example 17-23** *Successful* **ping** *to 192.168.3.3*

```
R4#ping 192.168.3.3

Type escape sequence to abort.
Sending 5, 100-byte ICMP Echos to 192.168.3.3, timeout is 2 seconds:
!!!!!
Success rate is 100 percent (5/5), round-trip min/avg/max = 60/60/60 ms
R4#
```

You got 100 percent success! You have successfully resolved this issue.

# Scenario 3

**Symptom:** In the lab, R6 represents a remote office that connects to the main network over ISDN. You configured legacy DDR to connect these remote users on network 192.168.60.0 (R6's Token Ring network) to the main corporate network when IP traffic was present to send. You receive a call reporting that remote users on network 192.168.60.0 are unable to access IP resources on network 192.168.3.0 (R3's Ethernet 0 network).

**Objective:** You will have resolved this issue when you can successfully **ping** 192.168.3.3 from R6.

First, isolate the problem and verify that the reported symptom is accurate by issuing a **ping** from R6 to 192.168.3.3, as shown in Example 17-24.

**Example 17-24** *Verify Symptom by Issuing a* **ping** *to 192.168.3.3*

```
R6#ping 192.168.3.3

Type escape sequence to abort.
Sending 5, 100-byte ICMP Echos to 192.168.3.3, timeout is 2 seconds:
.....
Success rate is 0 percent (0/5)
R6#
```

You definitely have an issue. Next, you need to determine the layer at which you are having problems. To begin, examine the interfaces on R6 to ensure that the BRI 0 interface is up, as shown in Example 17-25.

**Example 17-25** *Using* **show ip interface brief** *Command to Determine Current Interface Status*

```
R6#show ip interface brief
Interface         IP-Address       OK? Method Status                Protocol
BRI0              192.168.200.2    YES NVRAM  up                    up
BRI0:1            unassigned       YES unset  down                  down
BRI0:2            unassigned       YES unset  down                  down
Loopback0         192.169.6.6      YES NVRAM  up                    up
Serial0           unassigned       YES unset  administratively down down
Serial1           unassigned       YES unset  administratively down down
TokenRing0        192.168.60.6     YES NVRAM  up                    up
R6#
```

You can see that interface BRI 0 is up, has not been administratively shut down, and has the correct IP address of 192.168.200.2 assigned. Next, do a **show isdn status** to verify that ISDN Layers 1, 2, and 3 appear as you would expect, as demonstrated in Example 17-26.

**Example 17-26** *Checking ISDN Layers 1, 2, and 3 with* **show isdn status** *Command*

```
R6#show isdn status
The current ISDN Switchtype = basic-5ess
ISDN BRI0 interface
    Layer 1 Status:
        ACTIVE
    Layer 2 Status:
        TEI = 101, State = MULTIPLE_FRAME_ESTABLISHED
    Layer 3 Status:
        0 Active Layer 3 Call(s)
    Activated dsl 0 CCBs = 0
    Total Allocated ISDN CCBs = 0
R6#
```

As the highlighted output indicates, the ISDN switch type (basic-5ess) is correct and Layer 1 shows ACTIVE. Also, Layer 2 appears okay, as indicated by State = MULTIPLE_FRAME_ESTABLISHED. So far, it appears that the issue might be at Layer 3. Review those items configured on R6 applicable to legacy DDR configuration at Layer 3:

- The BRI 0 interface IP address and subnet mask
- A default route pointing to R5's BRI0 interface
- A **dialer-list** statement defining IP as interesting traffic
- Applying a dialer group defining interesting traffic for the interface

Examine each of these four items to determine whether you can find something that might be causing the problem. Verify that the mask on R6's BRI0 has not been changed using the command **show interface bri0**, as shown in Example 17-27.

**Example 17-27** *Check IP Address and Mask of Interface BRI 0 Using* **show interface bri0** *Command*

```
R6#show interface bri0
BRI0 is up, line protocol is up (spoofing)
  Hardware is BRI
  Internet address is 192.168.200.2/30
  MTU 1500 bytes, BW 64 Kbit, DLY 20000 usec, rely 255/255, load 1/255
  Encapsulation PPP, loopback not set
  Last input 00:00:23, output 00:00:23, output hang never
  Last clearing of "show interface" counters never
  Input queue: 0/75/0 (size/max/drops); Total output drops: 0
  Queueing strategy: weighted fair
  Output queue: 0/1000/64/0 (size/max total/threshold/drops)
     Conversations  0/1/256 (active/max active/max total)
     Reserved Conversations 0/0 (allocated/max allocated)
  5 minute input rate 0 bits/sec, 0 packets/sec
  5 minute output rate 0 bits/sec, 0 packets/sec
     3058 packets input, 12254 bytes, 0 no buffer
     Received 6 broadcasts, 0 runts, 0 giants, 0 throttles
     0 input errors, 0 CRC, 0 frame, 0 overrun, 0 ignored, 0 abort
     3058 packets output, 12249 bytes, 0 underruns
```

**Example 17-27** *Check IP Address and Mask of Interface BRI 0 Using* **show interface bri0** *Command (Continued)*

```
       0 output errors, 0 collisions, 7 interface resets
       0 output buffer failures, 0 output buffers swapped out
       3 carrier transitions
R6#
```

The IP address and mask are correct. Next, ensure that R6 has a default route pointing to
R5's BRI 0 interface's IP address of 192.168.200.1 using the **show ip route** command, as
demonstrated in Example 17-28.

**Example 17-28** *Verify That R6 Has a Default Route Pointing to 192.168.200.1*

```
R6#show ip route
Codes: C - connected, S - static, I - IGRP, R - RIP, M - mobile, B - BGP
       D - EIGRP, EX - EIGRP external, O - OSPF, IA - OSPF inter area
       N1 - OSPF NSSA external type 1, N2 - OSPF NSSA external type 2
       E1 - OSPF external type 1, E2 - OSPF external type 2, E - EGP
       i - IS-IS, L1 - IS-IS level-1, L2 - IS-IS level-2, * - candidate default
       U - per-user static route, o - ODR

Gateway of last resort is 192.168.200.1 to network 0.0.0.0

C       192.168.60.0/24 is directly connected, TokenRing0
C       192.169.6.0/24 is directly connected, Loopback0
        192.168.200.0/30 is subnetted, 1 subnets
C          192.168.200.0 is directly connected, BRI0
S*      0.0.0.0/0 [1/0] via 192.168.200.1
R6#
```

You can see that the default route pointing to R5's BRI 0 shows up as expected. Third, debug
the dialer packets and then issue a **ping** to 192.168.3.3. Do this using the command **debug
dialer packets** and then examine the results of the output as displayed in Example 17-29.

**Example 17-29** *Use* **debug dialer packets** *to Determine Status of Outgoing IP Packets over
the ISDN Link*

```
R6#debug dialer packets
Dial on demand packets debugging is on
R6#ping 192.168.3.3

Type escape sequence to abort.
Sending 5, 100-byte ICMP Echos to 192.168.3.3, timeout is 2 seconds:
.....
Success rate is 0 percent (0/5)
R6#
BRI0: ip (s=192.168.200.2, d=192.168.3.3), 100 bytes, uninteresting (dialer-list 1
  not defined)
BRI0: ip (s=192.168.200.2, d=192.168.3.3), 100 bytes, uninteresting (dialer-list 1
  not defined)
```

*continues*

**Example 17-29** *Use* **debug dialer packets** *to Determine Status of Outgoing IP Packets over the ISDN Link (Continued)*

```
BRI0: ip (s=192.168.200.2, d=192.168.3.3), 100 bytes, uninteresting (dialer-list 1
  not defined)
BRI0: ip (s=192.168.200.2, d=192.168.3.3), 100 bytes, uninteresting (dialer-list 1
  not defined)
BRI0: ip (s=192.168.200.2, d=192.168.3.3), 100 bytes, uninteresting (dialer-list 1
  not defined)
R6#
```

Notice from the highlighted portion of Example 17-29 that each **ping** packet fails. You are given the additional debug output indicating that the packets are considered "uninteresting" because dialer-list 1 is not defined. This points to the dialer list configuration. Examine the running config of R6 as shown in Example 17-30.

**Example 17-30** *Examine the Running Configuration on R6 to Verify Configuration of dialer-list 1*

```
R6#show running-config
Building configuration...

Current configuration:
!
version 11.2
no service password-encryption
no service udp-small-servers
no service tcp-small-servers
!
hostname R6
!
enable password falcons
!
ip subnet-zero
no ip domain-lookup
ip host R6 192.169.6.6
ip host R1 192.169.1.1
ip host R2 192.169.2.2
ip host R3 192.169.3.3
ip host R4 192.169.4.4
ip host R5 192.169.5.5
isdn switch-type basic-5ess
!
interface Loopback0
 ip address 192.169.6.6 255.255.255.0
!
interface Serial0
 no ip address
 shutdown
 no fair-queue
!
interface Serial1
 no ip address
```

**Example 17-30** *Examine the Running Configuration on R6 to Verify Configuration of dialer-list 1 (Continued)*

```
 shutdown
!
interface TokenRing0
 description This interface does not connect with another IP device
 ip address 192.168.60.6 255.255.255.0
 ring-speed 16
!
interface BRI0
 ip address 192.168.200.2 255.255.255.252
 encapsulation ppp
 dialer idle-timeout 300
 dialer string 8358662
 dialer-group 1
!
no ip classless
ip route 0.0.0.0 0.0.0.0 192.168.200.1
!
banner motd ^C
This is Router 6
^C
!
line con 0
 exec-timeout 0 0
 password falcons
 logging synchronous
line aux 0
line vty 0 4
 password falcons
 login
!
end

R6#
```

The highlighted portion of R6's running config indicates that the BRI0 interface has the appropriate dialer group assigned. However, when you examine the configuration more closely, you notice that the **dialer-list** statement defining all IP traffic as interesting has been removed from the configuration. Normally, you would expect to see the dialer list after the static routes and before the banner configuration. Correct this on R6, as demonstrated in Example 17-31.

**Example 17-31** *Correcting the dialer-list 1 Configuration*

```
R6#conf t
Enter configuration commands, one per line.  End with CNTL/Z.
R6(config)#dialer-list 1 protocol ip permit
R6(config)#^Z
R6#
```

Now that the appropriate dialer list has been configured, **ping** 192.168.3.3 and observe the debug output as shown in Example 17-32.

**Example 17-32** **debug** *Output Now Shows That IP Traffic Is Considered "Interesting," in Turn Bringing Up the ISDN Link*

```
R6#ping 192.168.3.3

Type escape sequence to abort.
Sending 5, 100-byte ICMP Echos to 192.168.3.3, timeout is 2 seconds:
..!!!
Success rate is 60 percent (3/5), round-trip min/avg/max = 40/44/48 ms
R6#
BRI0: ip (s=192.168.200.2, d=192.168.3.3), 100 bytes, interesting (ip PERMIT)
%LINK-3-UPDOWN: Interface BRI0:1, changed state to up
BRI0: ip (s=192.168.200.2, d=192.168.3.3), 100 bytes, interesting (ip PERMIT)
BRI0: ip (s=192.168.200.2, d=192.168.3.3), 100 bytes, interesting (ip PERMIT)
BRI0: ip (s=192.168.200.2, d=192.168.3.3), 100 bytes, interesting (ip PERMIT)
%LINEPROTO-5-UPDOWN: Line protocol on Interface BRI0:1, changed state to up
BRI0: cdp, 284 bytes, uninteresting (no list matched)
BRI0: sending broadcast to default destination
BRI0: ip (s=192.168.200.2, d=192.168.3.3), 100 bytes, interesting (ip PERMIT)
R6#
%ISDN-6-CONNECT: Interface BRI0:1 is now connected to 8358662
R6#
```

Notice the three highlighted sections. The first shows that the initial **ping** packets fail and that then you get three successful **ping**s. At this point, you know that the link is up. Next, you can see that the traffic now is considered interesting, causing the link to come up. Lastly, you see that you are connected to 8358662. Turn off debugging using **undebug all**, and then save the changes, as shown in Example 17-33.

**Example 17-33** *Turning Off All Debugging and Saving the Configuration*

```
R6#undebug all
All possible debugging has been turned off
R6#copy run start
Building configuration...
[OK]
R6#
```

You now have successfully resolved this ISDN issue.

# Scenario 4

**Symptom:** As a network administrator, you need to have access to all the routers in the internetwork. For some reason, the enable password on R1 is not working. No one in the IT department remembers changing it. You need to gain access to the router and change the enable password so that you can correctly manage the router.

**Objective:** Successfully break into the router and change the enable password to falcons.

The first issue is to research how to initiate the password-recovery process for the Cisco router model that you have. R1 is a Cisco 2500 series router. With this information, you can search on Cisco CCO (www.cisco.com/) with the keywords **password recovery 2500** to find the password-recovery document for the 2500 series routers. Review the steps that follow outlined in the document for password recovery.

Attach a terminal or PC with terminal emulation to the console port of the router. Use the following terminal settings:

> 9600 baud rate
> No parity
> 8 data bits
> 1 stop bit
> No flow control

The required console cable specifications are described in the *Cabling Guide for RJ-45 Console and AUX Ports* (Cisco's 1000 series, 2500 series, and AS5100).

**Step 1**  Type **show version** and record the setting of the configuration register.

The configuration register setting is usually 0x2102 or 0x102.

**Step 2**  Using the switch, turn off the router and then turn it on.

**Step 3**  Press Break on the terminal keyboard within 60 seconds of the powerup to put the router into ROMMON.

**Step 4**  Type **o/r 0x2142** at the > prompt to boot from Flash without loading the configuration. (For a review of the purpose of the configuration register, see Chapter 2, "Cisco Router Review.")

**Step 5**  Type **i** at the > prompt.

The router reboots but ignores its saved configuration.

**Step 6**  Type **no** after each setup question, or press Ctrl-C to skip the initial setup procedure.

**Step 7**  Type **enable** at the Router> prompt.

You'll be in enable mode and see the Router# prompt.

**Step 8**  *Important:* Type **config mem** or **copy start running** to copy the nonvolatile RAM (NVRAM) into memory. Do *not* type **config term**.

**Step 9** Type **wr term** or **show runnin**g. The **show running** and **wr term** commands show the configuration of the router. In this configuration, you see under all the interfaces the **shutdown** command, which means that all interfaces are currently shutdown. Also, you can see the passwords in either encrypted or unencrypted format.

**Step 10** Type **config term** and make the changes.

The prompt is now hostname(config)#.

**Step 11** Type **enable** <*password*.

**Step 12** Issue the **no shutdown** command on every interface that is used. If you issue a **show ip interface brief** command, every interface that you want to use should be up, up.

**Step 13** Type **config-register 0x2102** or the value that you recorded in step 2.

**Step 14** Press Ctrl-z to leave the configuration mode.

The prompt is now hostname#.

**Step 15** Type **write mem** or **copy running startup** to commit the changes.

---

**NOTE** You also can find documentation on password recovery at www.cisco.com/warp/public/474/pswdrec_2500.html. For password recovery, a laptop or PC will be connected directly into the router. A terminal server will not be used.

---

Now that you have reviewed the procedures, connect your PC to the console port of the router with the following terminal parameters:

- 9600 baud rate
- No parity
- 8 data bits
- 1 stop bit
- No flow control

When this is done, you can follow the steps according to the document for password recovery:

**Step 1** Type **show version** and record the setting of the configuration register. See Example 17-34.

**Example 17-34** **show version** *Command Output*

```
R1>show version
Cisco Internetwork Operating System Software
IOS (tm) 2500 Software (C2500-JS-L), Version 11.2(17), RELEASE SOFTWARE (fc1)
Copyright (c) 1986-1999 by cisco Systems, Inc.
Compiled Mon 04-Jan-99 17:27 by ashah
Image text-base: 0x00001448, data-base: 0x00764DA8

ROM: System Bootstrap, Version 11.0(10c), SOFTWARE
BOOTFLASH: 3000 Bootstrap Software (IGS-BOOT-R), Version 11.0(10c), RELEASE SOFT
WARE (fc1)

R1 uptime is 1 minute
System restarted by power-on
System image file is "c2500-js-l_112-17.bin", booted via tftp from 192.168.1.5

cisco 2500 (68030) processor (revision N) with 14336K/2048K bytes of memory.
Processor board ID 06158021, with hardware revision 00000000
Bridging software.
SuperLAT software copyright 1990 by Meridian Technology Corp).
X.25 software, Version 2.0, NET2, BFE and GOSIP compliant.
TN3270 Emulation software.
1 Ethernet/IEEE 802.3 interface(s)
2 Serial network interface(s)
32K bytes of non-volatile configuration memory.
8192K bytes of processor board System flash (Read/Write)

Configuration register is 0x2102

R1>
```

The configuration register is 0x2102. You need to note this so that you can set it back to the original setting when you are finished with the password recovery procedure.

**Step 2**  Using the switch, turn off the router and then turn it on.

**Step 3**  Press Break on the terminal keyboard within 60 seconds of the powerup to put the router into ROMMON. (For HyperTerminal, the break sequence is Ctrl-Break. The Break key is in the upper-right of your keyboard, usually the same key as the Pause key.) See Example 17-35.

**Example 17-35** *Rebooting R1 and Initiating the Break Sequence*

```
R1>

System Bootstrap, Version 11.0(10c), SOFTWARE
Copyright (c) 1986-1996 by cisco Systems
2500 processor with 14336 Kbytes of main memory
```

*continues*

**Example 17-35** *Rebooting R1 and Initiating the Break Sequence (Continued)*

```
<ctrl-Break>
Abort at 0x1098FEC (PC)
>
```

The > prompt indicates that you are in ROMMON mode.

**Step 4**  Type **o/r 0x2142** at the > prompt to boot from Flash without loading the configuration. See Example 17-36.

**Example 17-36** *Changing the Configuration Register to Bypass the Startup Confg File*

```
>o/r 0x2142
>
```

**Step 5**  Type **i** at the > prompt.

The router reboots but ignores its saved configuration. See Example 17-37.

**Example 17-37** *Reinitialize R1 and Ignore Saved Configuration*

```
>i

System Bootstrap, Version 11.0(10c), SOFTWARE
Copyright (c) 1986-1996 by cisco Systems
2500 processor with 14336 Kbytes of main memory

F3: 8010312+98616+315708 at 0x3000060


               Restricted Rights Legend

Use, duplication, or disclosure by the Government is
subject to restrictions as set forth in subparagraph
(c) of the Commercial Computer Software - Restricted
Rights clause at FAR sec. 52.227-19 and subparagraph
(c) (1) (ii) of the Rights in Technical Data and Computer
Software clause at DFARS sec. 252.227-7013.


          cisco Systems, Inc.
          170 West Tasman Drive
          San Jose, California 95134-1706



Cisco Internetwork Operating System Software
IOS (tm) 2500 Software (C2500-JS-L), Version 11.2(17), RELEASE SOFTWARE (fc1)
Copyright (c) 1986-1999 by cisco Systems, Inc.
Compiled Mon 04-Jan-99 17:27 by ashah
Image text-base: 0x03040148, data-base: 0x00001000
```

**Example 17-37** *Reinitialize R1 and Ignore Saved Configuration (Continued)*

```
cisco 2500 (68030) processor (revision N) with 14336K/2048K bytes of memory.
Processor board ID 06158021, with hardware revision 00000000
Bridging software.
SuperLAT software copyright 1990 by Meridian Technology Corp).
X.25 software, Version 2.0, NET2, BFE and GOSIP compliant.
TN3270 Emulation software.
1 Ethernet/IEEE 802.3 interface(s)
2 Serial network interface(s)
32K bytes of non-volatile configuration memory.
8192K bytes of processor board System flash (Read ONLY)
        --- System Configuration Dialog ---

At any point you may enter a question mark '?' for help.
Use ctrl-c to abort configuration dialog at any prompt.
Default settings are in square brackets '[]'.
Would you like to enter the initial configuration dialog? [yes]:
```

**Step 6**   Type **no** or press Ctrl-C to skip the initial setup procedure. See Example 17-38.

**Example 17-38** *Exiting Setup Configuration Mode on R1*

```
Would you like to enter the initial configuration dialog? [yes]: no

Press RETURN to get started!


%LINK-3-UPDOWN: Interface Ethernet0, changed state to up
%LINK-3-UPDOWN: Interface Serial0, changed state to down
%LINK-3-UPDOWN: Interface Serial1, changed state to down
%LINEPROTO-5-UPDOWN: Line protocol on Interface Ethernet0, changed state to up
%LINEPROTO-5-UPDOWN: Line protocol on Interface Serial0, changed state to down
%LINEPROTO-5-UPDOWN: Line protocol on Interface Serial1, changed state to down
%SYS-5-RESTART: System restarted --
Cisco Internetwork Operating System Software
IOS (tm) 25
Router>00 Software (C2500-JS-L), Version 11.2(17), RELEASE SOFTWARE (fc1)
Copyright (c) 1986-1999 by cisco Systems, Inc.
Compiled Mon 04-Jan-99 17:27 by ashah
%LINEPROTO-5-UPDOWN: Line protocol on Interface Ethernet0, changed state to down

%LINK-5-CHANGED: Interface Ethernet0, changed state to administratively down
%LINK-5-CHANGED: Interface Serial0, changed state to administratively down
%LINK-5-CHANGED: Interface Serial1, changed state to administratively down
Router>
```

**Step 7**   Type **enable** at the Router> prompt.

You'll be in enable mode and see the Router# prompt. See Example 17-39.

**Example 17-39** *Gaining Access to Privileged Exec Mode (Enable Mode)*

```
Router>enable
Router#
```

Remember, by bypassing the configuration on the router, there is no enable password, so you never get prompted for a password.

**Step 8**   *This is very important.* Type **config mem** or **copy start running** to copy the nonvolatile RAM (NVRAM) into memory. Do *not* type **config term**. This will overwrite your configuration in the startup config file. See Example 17-40.

**Example 17-40** *Placing the Startup Config File into R1's RAM (Running Confg)*

```
Router#copy startup-config running-config

R1#
%LINEPROTO-5-UPDOWN: Line protocol on Interface Loopback0, changed state to up
%SYS-5-CONFIG_I: Configured from memory by console
R1#
```

You are still in privileged EXEC mode, but with the startup config now copied into running config.

**Step 9**   Type **show running**.

The **show running** command shows the configuration of the router. In this configuration, you see under all the interfaces the **shutdown** command, which means that all interfaces currently are shut down. Also, if **service password-encryption** is enabled, you will see the password in the output, but it will encrypted. If **no service password-encryption** is in the config file, the password will be in clear text. By initiating the password-recovery procedure, you will not change whether the passwords appear encrypted or in clear text in the output. See Example 17-41.

**Example 17-41  show running-config** *Output*

```
R1#show running-config
Building configuration...

Current configuration:
!
version 11.2
```

**Example 17-41  show running-config** *Output (Continued)*

```
no service password-encryption
no service udp-small-servers
no service tcp-small-servers
!
hostname R1
!
boot system c2500-js-l_112-17.bin 255.255.255.255
boot system flash c2500-js-l_112-17.bin
enable password ducks
!
no ip domain-lookup
ip host R1 192.169.1.1
ip host R2 192.169.2.2
ip host R3 192.169.3.3
ip host R4 192.169.4.4
ip host R5 192.169.5.5
ip host R6 192.169.6.6
ipx routing 0000.0000.1111
!
interface Loopback0
 ip address 192.169.1.1 255.255.255.0
!
interface Ethernet0
 description This interface connects to R2's E0
 ip address 192.168.1.1 255.255.255.0
 shutdown
 ipx network 2100
!
interface Serial0
 no ip address
 shutdown
 no fair-queue
!
interface Serial1
 no ip address
 shutdown
!
router rip
 network 192.168.1.0
 network 192.169.1.0
!
no ip classless
ip route 0.0.0.0 0.0.0.0 192.168.1.2
!
!
!
!
banner motd ^C
This is Router 1
^C
!
```

*continues*

**Example 17-41** **show running-config** *Output (Continued)*

```
line con 0
 exec-timeout 0 0
 password falcons
 logging synchronous
line aux 0
line vty 0 4
 password falcons
 login
!
end

R1#
```

From the highlighted text, you see that the enable password was changed to ducks. You now know the enable password.

**Step 10** Type **config term** and make the changes. The prompt is now hostname(config)#. See Example 17-42.

**Example 17-42** *Entering Global Configuration Mode on R1*

```
R1#config terminal
Enter configuration commands, one per line.  End with CNTL/Z.
R1(config)#
```

**Step 11** Type **enable** *password*. Use just the **enable password** command, not the **enable secret password** command. Change the password back to the original password of falcons. See Example 17-43.

**Example 17-43** *Changing the Enable Password on R1*

```
R1(config)#enable password falcons
R1(config)#
```

**Step 12** Issue the **no shutdown** command on every interface that is used. If you issue a **show ip interface brief** command, every interface that you want to use should be up, up. See Example 17-44.

**Example 17-44** *Remove Interfaces from Shutdown State*

```
R1(config)#interface ethernet 0
R1(config-if)#no shut
R1(config-if)#
%LINEPROTO-5-UPDOWN: Line protocol on Interface Ethernet0, changed state to up
R1(config-if)#
%LINK-3-UPDOWN: Interface Ethernet0, changed state to up
R1(config-if)#exit
```

**Example 17-44** *Remove Interfaces from Shutdown State (Continued)*

```
R1#sho ip interface brief
Interface              IP-Address      OK? Method Status                 Protocol

Ethernet0              192.168.1.1     YES NVRAM  up                          up

Loopback0              192.169.1.1     YES NVRAM  up                          up

Serial0                unassigned      YES unset  administratively down down

Serial1                unassigned      YES unset  administratively down down

R1#
```

As you recall, the only interfaces that should be active on R1 is Ethernet 0 and Loopback 0. If other interfaces were being used, you would need to remove those from the shutdown state as well.

**Step 13** Type **config-register 0x2102** or the value that you recorded in Step 2. See Example 17-45.

**Example 17-45** *Resetting the Original Configuration Register on R1*

```
R1(config)#config-register 0x2102
R1(config)#
```

**Step 14** Press Ctrl-z to leave the configuration mode. The prompt is now hostname#.

**Step 15** Type **write mem** or **copy running startup** to commit the changes. See Example 17-46.

**Example 17-46** *Exiting Configuration Mode and Saving Configuration*

```
R1(config)#^Z
R1#
%SYS-5-CONFIG_I: Configured from console by console
R1#copy running-config startup-config
Building configuration...
[OK]
R1#
```

You now have completed the password-recovery procedure. To verify that you have successfully changed the enable password, you can exit the router and re-enter privileged mode. Example 17-47 demonstrates this process.

**Example 17-47** *Exiting and Re-entering Privileged EXEC Mode*

```
R1#exit




R1 con0 is now available




Press RETURN to get started.




This is Router 1

R1>enable
Password:falcons
R1#
```

Success! The enable password has been successfully changed.

# Summary

Proficiency in troubleshooting Cisco routers comes through experience as well as following a defined troubleshooting methodology. In this chapter, you learned to troubleshoot in a systematic manner beginning with Layers 1, 2, and then 3. In addition, you learned that it is often helpful to begin the troubleshooting process closest to where the problem seems to originate. As you gain more experience, you will be able to diagnose the problem based on your knowledge and experience, often allowing you to go right to the heart of the problem and correct it. Table 17-1 reviews those troubleshooting commands referenced in the chapter.

**Table 17-1** *Troubleshooting Scenarios Command Summary*

| Command | Purpose |
|---------|---------|
| Router#**show ip interface brief** | Displays a summary of configured IP interfaces |
| Router#**ping** | Tests IP connectivity |
| Router#**show frame-relay pvc** | Verifies status of the Frame Relay PVC |
| Router#**show frame-relay map** | Verifies Frame Relay IP or IPX mappings |
| Router#**show running-config** | Verifies that the running configuration file is correct |
| Router#**show ip route** | Displays the IP routing table to ensure that the correct routes are being received |
| Router#**show ip eigrp interfaces** | Verifies which interfaces are being advertised within a particular EIGRP autonomous system |
| Router#**show isdn status** | Verifies ISDN switch type, Layers 1, 2, and 3 |
| Router#**show interface** *interface* | Displays detailed interface information |
| Router#**debug dialer packets** | Displays dialer packet output showing whether packets are classified as "interesting" or "uninteresting" |
| Router#**undebug all** | Turns off all debugging on the router |
| Router#**show version** | Displays the current configurations register setting |
| >**o/r 0x2142** | Within ROMMON mode, changes the configuration register to a value that bypasses the startup config file |
| >**I** | Reinitializes (reboots) the router from ROMMON mode |
| Router(config)#**config-register 0x2102** | Changes the configuration register back to the original setting, permitting the router to load the startup config file upon next router reboot |

PART IV

# Appendixes

# APPENDIX A

# Master Lab Configurations and Lab Diagrams

This appendix contains completed router configurations and diagrams by chapter, including the completed lab router configurations, their routing tables, and a completed lab diagram of what the diagram should show at the end of the lab. Use this appendix to check your configurations before moving on to the next chapter.

## Chapter 4 Terminal Server Configuration

**Example A-1** *Terminal Server Configuration*

```
!
version 11.2
service password-encryption
no service udp-small-servers
no service tcp-small-servers
!
hostname Termserver
!
enable password 7 0200055708090132
!
no ip domain-lookup
ip host r1 2001 192.168.10.10
ip host r2 2002 192.168.10.10
ip host r3 2003 192.168.10.10
ip host r4 2004 192.168.10.10
ip host r5 2005 192.168.10.10
ip host r6 2006 192.168.10.10
ip host cat19 2007 192.168.10.10
!
interface Loopback0
 ip address 192.168.10.10 255.255.255.0
!
interface Ethernet0
ip address 192.168.1.10 255.255.255.0
!
interface Serial0
 no ip address
 shutdown
!
interface Serial1
```

*continues*

**Example A-1** *Terminal Server Configuration (Continued)*

```
 no ip address
 shutdown
!
ip classless
ip route 0.0.0.0 0.0.0.0 192.168.1.100
!
!
line con 0
 password 7 11051C111A170202
 login
line 1 16
 transport input telnet
line aux 0
line vty 0
 exec-timeout 15 0
 password 7 110F1809141D051F
 login
line vty 1 4
 exec-timeout 30 0
 password 7 110F1809141D051F
 logging synchronous
 login
!
end
```

# Chapter 6 Router Configurations
## R1 Configuration

**Example A-2** *R1's Configuration*

```
!
version 11.1
no service password-encryption
no service udp-small-servers
no service tcp-small-servers
!
hostname R1
!
enable password falcons
!
no ip domain-lookup
ip host R1 192.169.1.1
ip host R2 192.169.2.2
ip host R3 192.169.3.3
ip host R4 192.169.4.4
ip host R5 192.169.5.5
ip host R6 192.169.6.6
!
interface Ethernet0
 no ip address
```

**Example A-2** *R1's Configuration (Continued)*

```
 shutdown
!
interface Serial0
 no ip address
 shutdown
!
interface Serial1
 no ip address
 shutdown
!
no ip classless
!
banner motd #
This is Router 1
#
!
line con 0
 exec-timeout 0 0
 password falcons
 logging synchronous
line aux 0
line vty 0 4
 password falcons
 login
!
end
```

# R2 Configuration

**Example A-3** *R2's Configuration*

```
!
version 12.0
service timestamps debug uptime
service timestamps log uptime
no service password-encryption
!
hostname R2
!
enable password falcons
!
ip subnet-zero
no ip domain-lookup
ip host R1 192.169.1.1
ip host R2 192.169.2.2
ip host R3 192.169.3.3
ip host R4 192.169.4.4
ip host R5 192.169.5.5
ip host R6 192.169.6.6
!
!
```

*continues*

**Example A-3** *R2's Configuration (Continued)*

```
!
interface Ethernet0
 no ip address
 shutdown
!
interface Ethernet1
 no ip address
 shutdown
!
interface Serial0
 no ip address
 shutdown
!
ip classless
!
banner motd #
This is Router 2
#
!
line con 0
 exec-timeout 0 0
 password falcons
 logging synchronous
line vty 0 4
 password falcons
 login
!
end
```

# R3 Configuration

**Example A-4** *R3's Configuration*

```
!
version 11.2
no service password-encryption
no service udp-small-servers
no service tcp-small-servers
!
hostname R3
!
enable password falcons
!
no ip domain-lookup
ip host R1 192.169.1.1
ip host R2 192.169.2.2
ip host R3 192.169.3.3
ip host R4 192.169.4.4
ip host R5 192.169.5.5
ip host R6 192.169.6.6
```

**Example A-4**  *R3's Configuration (Continued)*

```
!
!
interface Ethernet0
 no ip address
 shutdown
!
interface Serial0
 no ip address
 shutdown
!
interface Serial1
 no ip address
 shutdown
!
no ip classless
!
banner motd #
This is Router 3
#
!
line con 0
 exec-timeout 0 0
 password falcons
 logging synchronous
line aux 0
line vty 0 4
 password falcons
 login
!
end
```

# R4 Configuration

**Example A-5**  *R4's Configuration*

```
!
version 11.2
no service password-encryption
no service udp-small-servers
no service tcp-small-servers
!
hostname R4
!
enable password falcons
!
ip subnet-zero
no ip domain-lookup
ip host R1 192.169.1.1
ip host R2 192.169.2.2
ip host R3 192.169.3.3
ip host R4 192.169.4.4
```

*continues*

**Example A-5**    *R4's Configuration (Continued)*

```
ip host R5 192.169.5.5
ip host R6 192.169.6.6
!
!
interface Ethernet0
 no ip address
 shutdown
!
interface Serial0
 no ip address
 shutdown
!
interface Serial1
 no ip address
 shutdown
!
no ip classless
!
banner motd #
This is Router 4
#
!
line con 0
 exec-timeout 0 0
 password falcons
 logging synchronous
line aux 0
line vty 0 4
 password falcons
 login
!
end
```

# R5 Configuration

**Example A-6**    *R5's Configuration*

```
!
version 11.2
no service password-encryption
no service udp-small-servers
no service tcp-small-servers
!
hostname R5
!
enable password falcons
!
no ip domain-lookup
ip host R1 192.169.1.1
ip host R2 192.169.2.2
ip host R3 192.169.3.3
```

**Example A-6**  *R5's Configuration (Continued)*

```
ip host R4 192.169.4.4
ip host R5 192.169.5.5
ip host R6 192.169.6.6
!
!
interface Serial0
 no ip address
 shutdown
!
interface Serial1
 no ip address
 shutdown
!
interface TokenRing0
 no ip address
 shutdown
!
interface BRI0
 no ip address
 shutdown
!
no ip classless
!
banner motd #
This is Router 5
#
!
line con 0
 exec-timeout 0 0
 password falcons
 logging synchronous
line aux 0
line vty 0 4
 password falcons
 login
!
end
```

# R6 Configuration

**Example A-7**  *R6's Configuration*

```
!
version 11.2
no service password-encryption
no service udp-small-servers
no service tcp-small-servers
!
hostname R6
!
enable password falcons
```

*continues*

**Example A-7** *R6's Configuration (Continued)*

```
!
no ip domain-lookup
ip host R1 192.169.1.1
ip host R2 192.169.2.2
ip host R3 192.169.3.3
ip host R4 192.169.4.4
ip host R5 192.169.5.5
ip host R6 192.169.6.6

!
interface Serial0
 no ip address
 shutdown
 no fair-queue
!
interface Serial1
 no ip address
 shutdown
!
interface TokenRing0
 no ip address
 shutdown
!
interface BRI0
 no ip address
 shutdown
!
no ip classless
!
banner motd #
This is Router 6
#
!
line con 0
 exec-timeout 0 0
 password falcons
 logging synchronous
line aux 0
line vty 0 4
 password falcons
 login
!
end
```

# Chapter 7 Router Configurations
## R1 Configuration

**Example A-8**  *R1's Configuration*

```
!
version 11.1
no service password-encryption
no service udp-small-servers
no service tcp-small-servers
!
hostname R1
!
enable password falcons
!
no ip domain-lookup
ip host R1 192.169.1.1
ip host R2 192.169.2.2
ip host R3 192.169.3.3
ip host R4 192.169.4.4
ip host R5 192.169.5.5
ip host R6 192.169.6.6
!
interface Loopback0
 ip address 192.169.1.1 255.255.255.0
!
interface Ethernet0
 description This interface connects to R2's E0
 ip address 192.168.1.1 255.255.255.0
!
interface Serial0
 no ip address
 shutdown
!
interface Serial1
 no ip address
 shutdown
!
no ip classless
!
banner motd #
This is Router 1
#
!
line con 0
 exec-timeout 0 0
 password falcons
 logging synchronous
line aux 0
line vty 0 4
 password falcons
```

*continues*

**Example A-8** *R1's Configuration (Continued)*

```
 login
 !
end
```

# R2 Configuration

**Example A-9** *R2's Configuration*

```
!
version 12.0
service timestamps debug uptime
service timestamps log uptime
no service password-encryption
!
hostname R2
!
enable password falcons
!
ip subnet-zero
no ip domain-lookup
ip host R1 192.169.1.1
ip host R2 192.169.2.2
ip host R3 192.169.3.3
ip host R4 192.169.4.4
ip host R5 192.169.5.5
ip host R6 192.169.6.6
!
!
!
interface Loopback0
 ip address 192.169.2.2 255.255.255.0
 no ip directed-broadcast
!
interface Ethernet0
 ip address 192.168.1.2 255.255.255.0
 no ip directed-broadcast
!
interface Ethernet1
 description This interface does not connect with another IP device
 ip address 192.168.2.2 255.255.255.0
 no ip directed-broadcast
!
interface Serial0
 description This interface connects to R3's S0 (201)
 ip address 192.168.100.2 255.255.255.0
 no ip directed-broadcast
 encapsulation frame-relay
 no ip mroute-cache
 frame-relay map ip 192.168.100.3 201 broadcast
 frame-relay map ip 192.168.100.4 201 broadcast
 frame-relay lmi-type ansi
```

**Example A-9**  *R2's Configuration (Continued)*

```
!
ip classless
!
banner motd #
This is Router 2
#
!
line con 0
 exec-timeout 0 0
 password falcons
 logging synchronous
line vty 0 4
 password falcons
 login
!
end
```

# R3 Configuration

**Example A-10** *R3's Configuration*

```
!
version 11.2
no service password-encryption
no service udp-small-servers
no service tcp-small-servers
!
hostname R3
!
enable password falcons
!
no ip domain-lookup
ip host R1 192.169.1.1
ip host R2 192.169.2.2
ip host R3 192.169.3.3
ip host R4 192.169.4.4
ip host R5 192.169.5.5
ip host R6 192.169.6.6
!
interface Loopback0
 ip address 192.169.3.3 255.255.255.0
!
interface Ethernet0
 ip address 192.168.3.3 255.255.255.0
!
interface Serial0
 description This interface connects to R2's S0 (DLCI 200) and R4's S0 (DLCI 100)
 ip address 192.168.100.3 255.255.255.0
 encapsulation frame-relay
 frame-relay lmi-type ansi
```

*continues*

**Example A-10** *R3's Configuration (Continued)*

```
!
interface Serial1
 description This interface connects to R5's S0 (DCE)
 ip address 192.168.35.3 255.255.255.0
!
no ip classless
!
banner motd #
This is Router 3
#
!
line con 0
 exec-timeout 0 0
 password falcons
 logging synchronous
line aux 0
line vty 0 4
 password falcons
 login
!
end
```

# R4 Configuration

**Example A-11** *R4's Configuration*

```
!
version 11.2
no service password-encryption
no service udp-small-servers
no service tcp-small-servers
!
hostname R4
!
enable password falcons
!
ip subnet-zero
no ip domain-lookup
ip host R1 192.169.1.1
ip host R2 192.169.2.2
ip host R3 192.169.3.3
ip host R4 192.169.4.4
ip host R5 192.169.5.5
ip host R6 192.169.6.6
!
interface Loopback0
 ip address 192.169.4.4 255.255.255.0
!
interface Ethernet0
 description This interface does not connect to another IP device
 ip address 192.168.4.4 255.255.255.224
```

**Example A-11** *R4's Configuration (Continued)*

```
!
interface Serial0
 description This interface connects to R3's S0 (DLCI 101)
 ip address 192.168.100.4 255.255.255.0
 encapsulation frame-relay
 frame-relay map ip 192.168.100.2 101 broadcast
 frame-relay map ip 192.168.100.3 101 broadcast
 frame-relay lmi-type ansi
!
interface Serial1
 no ip address
 shutdown
!
no ip classless
!
banner motd #
This is Router 4
#
!
line con 0
 exec-timeout 0 0
 password falcons
 logging synchronous
line aux 0
line vty 0 4
 password falcons
 login
!
end
```

# R5 Configuration

**Example A-12** *R5's Configuration*

```
!
version 11.2
no service password-encryption
no service udp-small-servers
no service tcp-small-servers
!
hostname R5
!
enable password falcons
!
no ip domain-lookup
ip host R1 192.169.1.1
ip host R2 192.169.2.2
ip host R3 192.169.3.3
ip host R4 192.169.4.4
ip host R5 192.169.5.5
ip host R6 192.169.6.6
```

*continues*

**Example A-12** *R5's Configuration (Continued)*

```
!
interface Loopback0
 ip address 192.169.5.5 255.255.255.0
!
interface Serial0
 description This interface connects to R3's S1 (DTE)
 ip address 192.168.35.5 255.255.255.0
 no fair-queue
 clockrate 2000000
!
interface Serial1
 no ip address
 shutdown
!
interface TokenRing0
 description This interface does not connect with another IP device
 ip address 192.168.50.5 255.255.255.0
 ring-speed 16
!
interface BRI0
 no ip address
 shutdown
!
no ip classless
!
banner motd ^C
This is Router 5
^C
!
line con 0
 exec-timeout 0 0
 password falcons
 logging synchronous
line aux 0
line vty 0 4
 password falcons
 login
!
end
```

# R6 Configuration

**Example A-13** *R6's Configuration*

```
!
version 11.2
no service password-encryption
no service udp-small-servers
no service tcp-small-servers
!
hostname R6
```

**Example A-13** *R6's Configuration (Continued)*

```
!
enable password falcons
!
no ip domain-lookup
ip host R1 192.169.1.1
ip host R2 192.169.2.2
ip host R3 192.169.3.3
ip host R4 192.169.4.4
ip host R5 192.169.5.5
ip host R6 192.169.6.6
!
interface Loopback0
 ip address 192.169.6.6 255.255.255.0
!
interface Serial0
 no ip address
 shutdown
 no fair-queue
!
interface Serial1
 no ip address
 shutdown
!
interface TokenRing0
 description This interface does not connect with another IP device
 ip address 192.168.60.6 255.255.255.0
 ring-speed 16
!
interface BRI0
 no ip address
 shutdown
!
no ip classless
!
banner motd ^C
This is Router 6
^C
!
line con 0
 exec-timeout 0 0
 password falcons
 logging synchronous
line aux 0
line vty 0 4
 password falcons
 login
!
end
```

# Chapter 8 Router Configurations and Diagrams

Figure A-1 shows the network diagram for RIP.

**Figure A-1** *RIP Diagram*

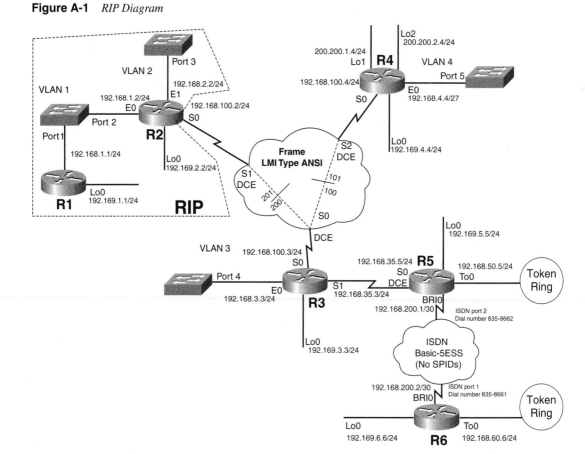

## R1 Configuration

**Example A-14** *R1's Configuration*

```
!
version 11.1
no service password-encryption
no service udp-small-servers
no service tcp-small-servers
!
hostname R1
!
enable password falcons
!
```

**Example A-14** *R1's Configuration (Continued)*

```
no ip domain-lookup
ip host R1 192.169.1.1
ip host R2 192.169.2.2
ip host R3 192.169.3.3
ip host R4 192.169.4.4
ip host R5 192.169.5.5
ip host R6 192.169.6.6
!
interface Loopback0
 ip address 192.169.1.1 255.255.255.0
!
interface Ethernet0
 description This interface connects to R2's E0
 ip address 192.168.1.1 255.255.255.0
!
interface Serial0
 no ip address
 shutdown
!
interface Serial1
 no ip address
 shutdown
!
router rip
 network 192.168.1.0
 network 192.169.1.0
!
no ip classless
!
banner motd #
This is Router 1
#
!
line con 0
 exec-timeout 0 0
 password falcons
 logging synchronous
line aux 0
line vty 0 4
 password falcons
 login
!
end
```

# R2 Configuration

**Example A-15** *R2's Configuration*

```
!
version 12.0
service timestamps debug uptime
service timestamps log uptime
no service password-encryption
!
hostname R2
!
enable password falcons
!
ip subnet-zero
no ip domain-lookup
ip host R1 192.169.1.1
ip host R2 192.169.2.2
ip host R3 192.169.3.3
ip host R4 192.169.4.4
ip host R5 192.169.5.5
ip host R6 192.169.6.6
!
!
!
interface Loopback0
 ip address 192.169.2.2 255.255.255.0
 no ip directed-broadcast
!
interface Ethernet0
 ip address 192.168.1.2 255.255.255.0
 no ip directed-broadcast
!
interface Ethernet1
 description This interface does not connect with another IP device
 ip address 192.168.2.2 255.255.255.0
 no ip directed-broadcast
!
interface Serial0
 description This interface connects to R3's S0 (201)
 ip address 192.168.100.2 255.255.255.0
 no ip directed-broadcast
 encapsulation frame-relay
 no ip mroute-cache
 frame-relay map ip 192.168.100.3 201 broadcast
 frame-relay map ip 192.168.100.4 201 broadcast
 frame-relay lmi-type ansi
!
router rip
 network 192.168.1.0
 network 192.168.2.0
 network 192.169.2.0
!
ip classless
```

**Example A-15** *R2's Configuration (Continued)*

```
!
banner motd #
This is Router 2
#
!
line con 0
 exec-timeout 0 0
 password falcons
 logging synchronous
line vty 0 4
 password falcons
 login
!
end
```

# Chapter 9 Router Configurations and Diagrams

Figure A-2 shows the network diagram for IGRP.

**Figure A-2**  *IGRP Diagram*

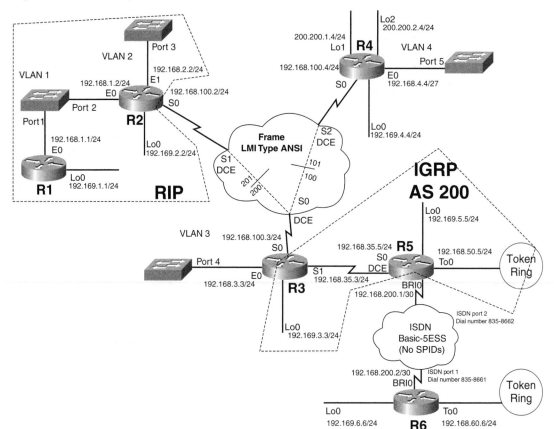

## R3 Configuration

**Example A-16** *R3's Configuration*

```
!
version 11.2
no service password-encryption
no service udp-small-servers
no service tcp-small-servers
!
hostname R3
!
enable password falcons
!
```

**Example A-16** *R3's Configuration (Continued)*

```
no ip domain-lookup
ip host R1 192.169.1.1
ip host R2 192.169.2.2
ip host R3 192.169.3.3
ip host R4 192.169.4.4
ip host R5 192.169.5.5
ip host R6 192.169.6.6
!
interface Loopback0
 ip address 192.169.3.3 255.255.255.0
!
interface Ethernet0
 ip address 192.168.3.3 255.255.255.0
!
interface Serial0
 description This interface connects to R2's S0(DLCI 200) and R4's S0 (DLCI 100
 ip address 192.168.100.3 255.255.255.0
 encapsulation frame-relay
 frame-relay lmi-type ansi
!
interface Serial1
 description This interface connects to R5's S0 (DCE)
 ip address 192.168.35.3 255.255.255.0
!
router igrp 200
 network 192.168.35.0
 network 192.169.3.0
!
no ip classless
!
banner motd #
This is Router 3
#
!
line con 0
 exec-timeout 0 0
 password falcons
 logging synchronous
line aux 0
line vty 0 4
 password falcons
 login
!
end
```

# R5 Configuration

**Example A-17** *R5's Configuration*

```
!
version 11.2
no service password-encryption
no service udp-small-servers
no service tcp-small-servers
!
hostname R5
!
enable password falcons
!
no ip domain-lookup
ip host R5 192.169.5.5
ip host R1 192.169.1.1
ip host R2 192.169.2.2
ip host R3 192.169.3.3
ip host R4 192.169.4.4
ip host R6 192.169.6.6
!
interface Loopback0
 ip address 192.169.5.5 255.255.255.0
!
interface Serial0
 description This interface connects to R3's S1 (DTE)
 ip address 192.168.35.5 255.255.255.0
 no fair-queue
 clockrate 2000000
!
interface Serial1
 no ip address
 shutdown
!
interface TokenRing0
 description This interface does not connect with another IP device
 ip address 192.168.50.5 255.255.255.0
 ring-speed 16
!
interface BRI0
 no ip address
 shutdown
!
router igrp 200
 passive-interface Loopback0
 network 192.168.35.0
 network 192.168.50.0
 network 192.169.5.0
!
no ip classless
!
banner motd #
This is Router 5
```

**Example A-17** *R5's Configuration (Continued)*

```
#
!
line con 0
 exec-timeout 0 0
 password falcons
 logging synchronous
line aux 0
line vty 0 4
 password falcons
 login
!
end
```

# Chapter 10 Router Configurations and Diagrams

Figure A-3 shows the network diagram for EIGRP.

**Figure A-3**    *EIGRP Diagram*

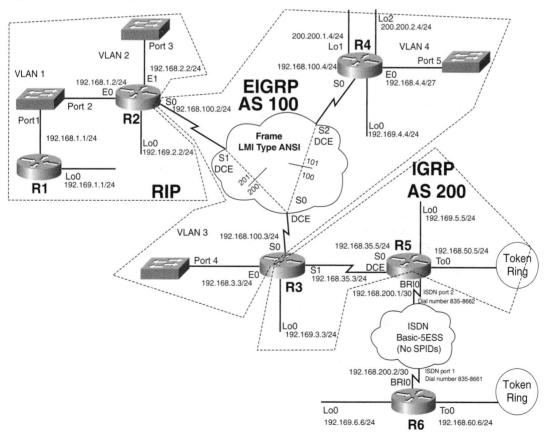

## R2 Configuration

**Example A-18** *R2's Configuration*

```
!
version 12.0
service timestamps debug uptime
service timestamps log uptime
no service password-encryption
!
hostname R2
!
enable password falcons
!
ip subnet-zero
no ip domain-lookup
ip host R1 192.169.1.1
ip host R2 192.169.2.2
ip host R3 192.169.3.3
ip host R4 192.169.4.4
ip host R5 192.169.5.5
ip host R6 192.169.6.6
!
!
!
interface Loopback0
 ip address 192.169.2.2 255.255.255.0
 no ip directed-broadcast
!
interface Ethernet0
 ip address 192.168.1.2 255.255.255.0
 no ip directed-broadcast
!
interface Ethernet1
 description This interface does not connect with another IP device
 ip address 192.168.2.2 255.255.255.0
 no ip directed-broadcast
!
interface Serial0
 description This interface connects to R3's S0 (201)
 ip address 192.168.100.2 255.255.255.0
 no ip directed-broadcast
 encapsulation frame-relay
 no ip mroute-cache
 frame-relay map ip 192.168.100.3 201 broadcast
 frame-relay map ip 192.168.100.4 201 broadcast
 frame-relay lmi-type ansi
!
router eigrp 100
 network 192.168.100.0
!
router rip
 network 192.168.1.0
 network 192.168.2.0
```

**Example A-18** *R2's Configuration (Continued)*

```
   network 192.169.2.0
 !
 ip classless
 !
 banner motd #
 This is Router 2
 #
 !
 line con 0
  exec-timeout 0 0
  password falcons
  logging synchronous
 line vty 0 4
  password falcons
  login
 !
 end
```

# R3 Configuration

**Example A-19** *R3's Configuration*

```
 !
 version 11.2
 no service password-encryption
 no service udp-small-servers
 no service tcp-small-servers
 !
 hostname R3
 !
 enable password falcons
 !
 no ip domain-lookup
 ip host R1 192.169.1.1
 ip host R2 192.169.2.2
 ip host R3 192.169.3.3
 ip host R4 192.169.4.4
 ip host R5 192.169.5.5
 ip host R6 192.169.6.6
 !
 interface Loopback0
  ip address 192.169.3.3 255.255.255.0
 !
 interface Ethernet0
  ip address 192.168.3.3 255.255.255.0
 !
 interface Serial0
  description This interface connects to R2's S0(DLCI 200) and R4's S0 (DLCI 100)
```

*continues*

**Example A-19** *R3's Configuration (Continued)*

```
 ip address 192.168.100.3 255.255.255.0
 encapsulation frame-relay
 no ip split-horizon eigrp 100
 frame-relay lmi-type ansi
!
interface Serial1
 description This interface connects to R5's S0 (DCE)
 ip address 192.168.35.3 255.255.255.0
!
router eigrp 100
 network 192.168.100.0
 network 192.168.3.0
!
router igrp 200
 network 192.168.35.0
 network 192.169.3.0
!
no ip classless
!
banner motd #
This is Router 3
#
!
line con 0
 exec-timeout 0 0
 password falcons
 logging synchronous
line aux 0
line vty 0 4
 password falcons
 login
!
end
```

# R4 Configuration

**Example A-20** *R4's Configuration*

```
!
version 11.2
no service password-encryption
no service udp-small-servers
no service tcp-small-servers
!
hostname R4
!
enable password falcons
!
ip subnet-zero
no ip domain-lookup
ip host R1 192.169.1.1
```

**Example A-20** *R4's Configuration (Continued)*

```
ip host R2 192.169.2.2
ip host R3 192.169.3.3
ip host R4 192.169.4.4
ip host R5 192.169.5.5
ip host R6 192.169.6.6
!
interface Loopback0
 ip address 192.169.4.4 255.255.255.0
!
interface Loopback1
 ip address 200.200.1.4 255.255.255.0
!
interface Loopback2
 ip address 200.200.2.4 255.255.255.0
!
interface Ethernet0
 description This interface does not connect to another IP device
 ip address 192.168.4.4 255.255.255.224
!
interface Serial0
 description This interface connects to R3's S0 (DLCI 101)
 ip address 192.168.100.4 255.255.255.0
 ip summary-address eigrp 100 200.200.0.0 255.255.0.0
 encapsulation frame-relay
 frame-relay map ip 192.168.100.2 101 broadcast
 frame-relay map ip 192.168.100.3 101 broadcast
 frame-relay lmi-type ansi
!
interface Serial1
 no ip address
 shutdown
!
router eigrp 100
 network 192.168.100.0
 network 192.168.4.0
 network 200.200.1.0
 network 200.200.2.0
 network 192.169.4.0
 no auto-summary
!
no ip classless
!
banner motd #
This is Router 4
#
!
line con 0
 exec-timeout 0 0
 password falcons
 logging synchronous
line aux 0
line vty 0 4
```

*continues*

**Example A-20** *R4's Configuration (Continued)*

```
 password falcons
 login
 !
end
```

# Chapter 11 Router Configurations
## R2 Configuration

**Example A-21** *R2's Configuration*

```
!
version 12.0
service timestamps debug uptime
service timestamps log uptime
no service password-encryption
!
hostname R2
!
enable password falcons
!
ip subnet-zero
no ip domain-lookup
ip host R1 192.169.1.1
ip host R2 192.169.2.2
ip host R3 192.169.3.3
ip host R4 192.169.4.4
ip host R5 192.169.5.5
ip host R6 192.169.6.6
!
!
!
interface Loopback0
 ip address 192.169.2.2 255.255.255.0
 no ip directed-broadcast
!
interface Ethernet0
 ip address 192.168.1.2 255.255.255.0
 no ip directed-broadcast
!
interface Ethernet1
 description This interface does not connect with another IP device
 ip address 192.168.2.2 255.255.255.0
 no ip directed-broadcast
!
interface Serial0
 description This interface connects to R3's S0 (201)
 ip address 192.168.100.2 255.255.255.0
 no ip directed-broadcast
 encapsulation frame-relay
 no ip mroute-cache
```

**Example A-21** *R2's Configuration (Continued)*

```
 frame-relay map ip 192.168.100.3 201 broadcast
 frame-relay map ip 192.168.100.4 201 broadcast
 frame-relay lmi-type ansi
!
router eigrp 100
 redistribute rip metric 2000 200 255 1 1500
 network 192.168.100.0
!
router rip
 redistribute eigrp 100 metric 1
 network 192.168.1.0
 network 192.168.2.0
 network 192.169.2.0
!
ip classless
!
banner motd #
This is Router 2
#
!
line con 0
 exec-timeout 0 0
 password falcons
 logging synchronous
line vty 0 4
 password falcons
 login
!
end
```

# R3 Configuration

**Example A-22** *R3's Configuration*

```
!
version 11.2
no service password-encryption
no service udp-small-servers
no service tcp-small-servers
!
hostname R3
!
enable password falcons
!
no ip domain-lookup
ip host R1 192.169.1.1
ip host R2 192.169.2.2
ip host R3 192.169.3.3
ip host R4 192.169.4.4
```

*continues*

**Example A-22** *R3's Configuration (Continued)*

```
ip host R5 192.169.5.5
ip host R6 192.169.6.6
!
interface Loopback0
 ip address 192.169.3.3 255.255.255.0
!
interface Ethernet0
 ip address 192.168.3.3 255.255.255.0
!
interface Serial0
 description This interface connects to R2's S0(DLCI 200) and R4's S0 (DLCI 100)
 ip address 192.168.100.3 255.255.255.0
 encapsulation frame-relay
 no ip split-horizon eigrp 100
 frame-relay lmi-type ansi
!
interface Serial1
 description This interface connects to R5's S0 (DCE)
 ip address 192.168.35.3 255.255.255.0
!
router eigrp 100
 redistribute igrp 200 metric 2000 200 255 1 1500
 network 192.168.100.0
 network 192.168.3.0
!
router igrp 200
 redistribute eigrp 100 metric 2000 200 255 1 1500
 network 192.168.35.0
 network 192.169.3.0
!
no ip classless
!
banner motd #
This is Router 3
#
!
line con 0
 exec-timeout 0 0
 password falcons
 logging synchronous
line aux 0
line vty 0 4
 password falcons
 login
!
end
```

# Chapter 12 Router Configurations

## R5 Configuration

**Example A-23** *R5's Configuration*

```
!
version 11.2
no service password-encryption
no service udp-small-servers
no service tcp-small-servers
!
hostname R5
!
enable password falcons
!
ip subnet-zero
no ip domain-lookup
ip host R5 192.169.5.5
ip host R1 192.169.1.1
ip host R2 192.169.2.2
ip host R3 192.169.3.3
ip host R4 192.169.4.4
ip host R6 192.169.6.6
isdn switch-type basic-5ess
!
interface Loopback0
 ip address 192.169.5.5 255.255.255.0
!
interface Serial0
 description This interface connects to R3's S1 (DTE)
 ip address 192.168.35.5 255.255.255.0
 no fair-queue
 clockrate 2000000
!
interface Serial1
 no ip address
 shutdown
!
interface TokenRing0
 description This interface does not connect with another IP device
 ip address 192.168.50.5 255.255.255.0
 ring-speed 16
!
interface BRI0
 ip address 192.168.200.1 255.255.255.252
 encapsulation ppp
 dialer idle-timeout 300
 dialer-group 1
!
router igrp 200
 redistribute connected
 redistribute static
 passive-interface Loopback0
```

*continues*

**Example A-23** *R5's Configuration (Continued)*

```
 network 192.168.35.0
 network 192.168.50.0
 network 192.169.5.0
 !
no ip classless
ip default-network 192.169.3.0
ip route 192.168.60.0 255.255.255.0 192.168.200.2
 !
dialer-list 1 protocol ip permit
banner motd#
This is Router 5
#
 !
line con 0
 exec-timeout 0 0
 password falcons
 logging synchronous
line aux 0
line vty 0 4
 password falcons
 login
 !
end
```

# R6 Configuration

**Example A-24** *R6's Configuration*

```
 !
version 11.2
no service password-encryption
no service udp-small-servers
no service tcp-small-servers
 !
hostname R6
 !
enable password falcons
 !
ip subnet-zero
no ip domain-lookup
ip host R6 192.169.6.6
ip host R1 192.169.1.1
ip host R2 192.169.2.2
ip host R3 192.169.3.3
ip host R4 192.169.4.4
ip host R5 192.169.5.5
isdn switch-type basic-5ess
 !
interface Loopback0
 ip address 192.169.6.6 255.255.255.0
 !
interface Serial0
```

**Example A-24** *R6's Configuration (Continued)*

```
 no ip address
 shutdown
 no fair-queue
!
interface Serial1
 no ip address
 shutdown
!
interface TokenRing0
 description This interface does not connect with another IP device
 ip address 192.168.60.6 255.255.255.0
 ring-speed 16
!
interface BRI0
 ip address 192.168.200.2 255.255.255.252
 encapsulation ppp
 dialer idle-timeout 300
 dialer string 8358662
 dialer-group 1
!
no ip classless
ip route 0.0.0.0 0.0.0.0 192.168.200.1
!
dialer-list 1 protocol ip permit
banner motd #
This is Router 6
#
!
line con 0
 exec-timeout 0 0
 password falcons
 logging synchronous
line aux 0
line vty 0 4
 password falcons
 login
!
end
```

# Chapter 13 Router Configurations
## R1 Configuration

**Example A-25** *R1's Configuration*

```
!
version 11.1
no service password-encryption
no service udp-small-servers
no service tcp-small-servers
!
```

*continues*

**Example A-25** *R1's Configuration (Continued)*

```
hostname R1
!
enable password falcons
!
no ip domain-lookup
ip host R1 192.169.1.1
ip host R2 192.169.2.2
ip host R3 192.169.3.3
ip host R4 192.169.4.4
ip host R5 192.169.5.5
ip host R6 192.169.6.6
ipx routing 0000.0000.1111
!
interface Loopback0
 ip address 192.169.1.1 255.255.255.0
!
interface Ethernet0
 description This interface connects to R2's E0
 ip address 192.168.1.1 255.255.255.0
 ipx network 2100
 no shut
!
interface Serial0
 no ip address
 shutdown
 no fair-queue
!
interface Serial1
 no ip address
 shutdown
!
router rip
 network 192.168.1.0
 network 192.169.1.0
!
no ip classless
ip route 0.0.0.0 0.0.0.0 192.168.1.2
!
!
!
!
banner motd #
This is Router 1
#
!
line con 0
 exec-timeout 0 0
 password falcons
 logging synchronous
line aux 0
line vty 0 4
 password falcons
 login
!
end
```

# R2 Configuration

**Example A-26** *R2's Configuration*

```
!
version 12.0
service timestamps debug uptime
service timestamps log uptime
no service password-encryption
!
hostname R2
!
enable password falcons
!
ip subnet-zero
no ip domain-lookup
ip host R1 192.169.1.1
ip host R2 192.169.2.2
ip host R3 192.169.3.3
ip host R4 192.169.4.4
ip host R5 192.169.5.5
ip host R6 192.169.6.6
ipx routing 0000.0000.2222
!
!
!
interface Loopback0
 ip address 192.169.2.2 255.255.255.0
 no ip directed-broadcast
!
interface Ethernet0
 ip address 192.168.1.2 255.255.255.0
 no ip directed-broadcast
 ipx network 2100
 no shut
!
interface Ethernet1
 description This interface does not connect with another IP device
 ip address 192.168.2.2 255.255.255.0
 no ip directed-broadcast
 ipx network 2000
 no shut
!
interface Serial0
 description This interface connects to R3's S0 (201)
 ip address 192.168.100.2 255.255.255.0
 no ip directed-broadcast
 encapsulation frame-relay
 no ip mroute-cache
 ipx network 1000
 frame-relay map ip 192.168.100.3 201 broadcast
 frame-relay map ip 192.168.100.4 201 broadcast
 frame-relay map ipx 1000.0000.0000.4444 201 broadcast
```

*continues*

**Example A-26** *R2's Configuration (Continued)*

```
 frame-relay map ipx 1000.0000.0000.3333 201 broadcast
 frame-relay lmi-type ansi
 no shut
!
router eigrp 100
 redistribute rip metric 2000 200 255 1 1500
 network 192.168.100.0
!
router rip
 redistribute eigrp 100 metric 1
 network 192.168.1.0
 network 192.168.2.0
 network 192.169.2.0
!
ip classless
!
!
!
!
banner motd #
This is Router 2
#
!
line con 0
 exec-timeout 0 0
 password falcons
 logging synchronous
line vty 0 4
 password falcons
 login
!
end
```

# R3 Configuration

**Example A-27** *R3's Configuration*

```
!
version 11.2
no service password-encryption
no service udp-small-servers
no service tcp-small-servers
!
hostname R3
!
enable password falcons
!
no ip domain-lookup
ip host R3 192.169.3.3
ip host R1 192.169.1.1
```

**Example A-27** *R3's Configuration (Continued)*

```
ip host R2 192.169.2.2
ip host R4 192.169.4.4
ip host R5 192.169.5.5
ip host R6 192.169.6.6
ipx routing 0000.0000.3333
!
interface Loopback0
 ip address 192.169.3.3 255.255.255.0
!
interface Ethernet0
 ip address 192.168.3.3 255.255.255.0
 ipx network 3000
 ipx network 3001 encapsulation SAP secondary
 no shut
!
interface Serial0
 description This interface connects to R2's S0(DLCI 200) and R4's S0 (DLCI 100)
 ip address 192.168.100.3 255.255.255.0
 encapsulation frame-relay
 no ip split-horizon eigrp 100
 ipx network 1000
 frame-relay lmi-type ansi
 no shut
!
interface Serial1
 description This interface connects to R5's S0 (DCE)
 ip address 192.168.35.3 255.255.255.0
 ipx network 3500
 no shut
!
router eigrp 100
 redistribute igrp 200 metric 2000 200 255 1 1500
 network 192.168.100.0
 network 192.168.3.0
!
router igrp 200
 redistribute eigrp 100 metric 2000 200 255 1 1500
 network 192.168.35.0
 network 192.169.3.0
!
no ip classless
!
!
!
!
banner motd #
This is Router 3
#
!
line con 0
 exec-timeout 0 0
 password falcons
```

*continues*

**Example A-27** *R3's Configuration (Continued)*

```
 logging synchronous
line aux 0
line vty 0 4
 password falcons
 login
!
end
```

# R4 Configuration

**Example A-28** *R4's Configuration*

```
!
version 11.2
no service password-encryption
no service udp-small-servers
no service tcp-small-servers
!
hostname R4
!
enable password falcons
!
ip subnet-zero
no ip domain-lookup
ip host R1 192.169.1.1
ip host R2 192.169.2.2
ip host R3 192.169.3.3
ip host R4 192.169.4.4
ip host R5 192.169.5.5
ip host R6 192.169.6.6
ipx routing 0000.0000.4444
!
interface Loopback0
 ip address 192.169.4.4 255.255.255.0
!
interface Loopback1
 ip address 200.200.1.4 255.255.255.0
!
interface Loopback2
 ip address 200.200.2.4 255.255.255.0
!
interface Ethernet0
 description This interface does not connect to another IP device
 ip address 192.168.4.4 255.255.255.224
 ipx network 4000
 no shut
!
interface Serial0
 description This interface connects to R3's S0 (DLCI 101)
 ip address 192.168.100.4 255.255.255.0
 ip summary-address eigrp 100 200.200.0.0 255.255.0.0
```

**Example A-28** *R4's Configuration (Continued)*

```
 encapsulation frame-relay
 ipx network 1000
 frame-relay map ip 192.168.100.2 101 broadcast
 frame-relay map ip 192.168.100.3 101 broadcast
 frame-relay map ipx 1000.0000.0000.2222 101 broadcast
 frame-relay map ipx 1000.0000.0000.3333 101 broadcast
 frame-relay lmi-type ansi
 no shut
!
interface Serial1
 no ip address
 shutdown
!
router eigrp 100
 network 192.168.100.0
 network 192.168.4.0
 network 200.200.1.0
 network 200.200.2.0
 network 192.169.4.0
 no auto-summary
!
no ip classless
!
!
!
!
banner motd #
This is Router 4
#
!
line con 0
 exec-timeout 0 0
 password falcons
 logging synchronous
line aux 0
line vty 0 4
 password falcons
 login
!
end
```

# R5 Configuration

**Example A-29** *R5's Configuration*

```
R5#show running-config
Building configuration...

Current configuration:
!
version 11.2
```

*continues*

**Example A-29** *R5's Configuration (Continued)*

```
no service password-encryption
no service udp-small-servers
no service tcp-small-servers
!
hostname R5
!
enable password falcons
!
ip subnet-zero
no ip domain-lookup
ip host R5 192.169.5.5
ip host R1 192.169.1.1
ip host R2 192.169.2.2
ip host R3 192.169.3.3
ip host R4 192.169.4.4
ip host R6 192.169.6.6
ipx routing 0000.0000.5555
isdn switch-type basic-5ess
!
interface Loopback0
 ip address 192.169.5.5 255.255.255.0
!
interface Serial0
 description This interface connects to R3's S1 (DTE)
 ip address 192.168.35.5 255.255.255.0
 ipx network 3500
 no fair-queue
 clockrate 2000000
 no shut
!
interface Serial1
 no ip address
 shutdown
!
interface TokenRing0
 description This interface does not connect with another IP device
 ip address 192.168.50.5 255.255.255.0
 ipx network 5000
 ring-speed 16
 no shut
!
interface BRI0
 ip address 192.168.200.1 255.255.255.252
 encapsulation ppp
 dialer idle-timeout 300
 dialer-group 1
 no shut
!
router igrp 200
 redistribute connected
 redistribute static
 passive-interface Loopback0
```

**Example A-29** *R5's Configuration (Continued)*

```
 network 192.168.35.0
 network 192.168.50.0
 network 192.169.5.0
 !
no ip classless
ip default-network 192.169.3.0
ip route 192.168.60.0 255.255.255.0 192.168.200.2
 !
 !
dialer-list 1 protocol ip permit
 !
 !
banner motd #
This is Router 5
#
 !
line con 0
 exec-timeout 0 0
 password falcons
 logging synchronous
line aux 0
line vty 0 4
 password falcons
 login
 !
end

R5#
```

# Chapter 14 Router Configurations
## R2 Configuration

**Example A-30** *R2's Configuration*

```
 !
version 12.0
service timestamps debug uptime
service timestamps log uptime
no service password-encryption
 !
hostname R2
 !
enable password falcons
 !
ip subnet-zero
no ip domain-lookup
ip host R1 192.169.1.1
ip host R2 192.169.2.2
ip host R3 192.169.3.3
ip host R4 192.169.4.4
```

*continues*

**Example A-30** *R2's Configuration (Continued)*

```
ip host R5 192.169.5.5
ip host R6 192.169.6.6
ipx routing 0000.0000.2222
!
!
!
interface Loopback0
 ip address 192.169.2.2 255.255.255.0
 no ip directed-broadcast
!
interface Ethernet0
 ip address 192.168.1.2 255.255.255.0
 no ip directed-broadcast
 ipx network 2100
!
interface Ethernet1
 description This interface does not connect with another IP device
 ip address 192.168.2.2 255.255.255.0
 no ip directed-broadcast
 ipx network 2000
!
interface Serial0
 description This interface connects to R3's S0 (201)
 ip address 192.168.100.2 255.255.255.0
 no ip directed-broadcast
 encapsulation frame-relay
 no ip mroute-cache
 ipx network 1000
 no fair-queue
 service-module t1 clock source internal
 frame-relay map ip 192.168.100.3 201 broadcast
 frame-relay map ip 192.168.100.4 201 broadcast
 frame-relay map ipx 1000.0000.0000.4444 201 broadcast
 frame-relay map ipx 1000.0000.0000.3333 201 broadcast
 frame-relay lmi-type ansi
!
router eigrp 100
 redistribute rip metric 2000 200 255 1 1500
 network 192.168.100.0
!
router rip
 redistribute eigrp 100 metric 1
 network 192.168.1.0
 network 192.168.2.0
 network 192.169.2.0
!
ip classless
!
!
!
ipx router eigrp 100
 network 1000
```

**Example A-30** *R2's Configuration (Continued)*

```
!
!
ipx router rip
 no network 1000
 !
 !
 !
banner motd #
This is Router 2
#
!
line con 0
 exec-timeout 0 0
 password falcons
 logging synchronous
line vty 0 4
 password falcons
 login
 !
end
```

# R3 Configuration

**Example A-31** *R3's Configuration*

```
!
version 11.2
no service password-encryption
no service udp-small-servers
no service tcp-small-servers
!
hostname R3
!
enable password falcons
!
no ip domain-lookup
ip host R3 192.169.3.3
ip host R1 192.169.1.1
ip host R2 192.169.2.2
ip host R4 192.169.4.4
ip host R5 192.169.5.5
ip host R6 192.169.6.6
ipx routing 0000.0000.3333
!
interface Loopback0
 ip address 192.169.3.3 255.255.255.0
 !
interface Ethernet0
 ip address 192.168.3.3 255.255.255.0
 ipx network 3000
```

*continues*

**Example A-31** *R3's Configuration (Continued)*

```
 ipx network 3001 encapsulation SAP secondary
 !
interface Serial0
 description This interface connects to R2's S0(DLCI 200) and R4's S0 (DLCI 100)
 ip address 192.168.100.3 255.255.255.0
 encapsulation frame-relay
 no ip split-horizon eigrp 100
 ipx network 1000
 no ipx split-horizon eigrp 100
 no fair-queue
 frame-relay lmi-type ansi
 !
interface Serial1
 description This interface connects to R5's S0 (DCE)
 ip address 192.168.35.3 255.255.255.0
 ipx network 3500
 !
router eigrp 100
 redistribute igrp 200 metric 2000 200 255 1 1500
 network 192.168.100.0
 network 192.168.3.0
 !
router igrp 200
 redistribute eigrp 100 metric 2000 200 255 1 1500
 network 192.168.35.0
 network 192.169.3.0
 !
no ip classless
 !
 !
 !
ipx router eigrp 100
 network 1000
 !
 !
ipx router rip
 no network 1000
 !
 !
 !
banner motd #
This is Router 3
#
 !
line con 0
 exec-timeout 0 0
 password falcons
 logging synchronous
line aux 0
line vty 0 4
 password falcons
```

**Example A-31** *R3's Configuration (Continued)*

```
 login
 !
 end
```

# R4 Configuration

**Example A-32** *R4's Configuration*

```
 !
 version 11.2
 no service password-encryption
 no service udp-small-servers
 no service tcp-small-servers
 !
 hostname R4
 !
 enable password falcons
 !
 ip subnet-zero
 ip telnet source-interface Serial0
 no ip domain-lookup
 ip host R1 192.169.1.1
 ip host R2 192.169.2.2
 ip host R3 192.169.3.3
 ip host R4 192.169.4.4
 ip host R5 192.169.5.5
 ip host R6 192.169.6.6
 ipx routing 0000.0000.4444
 !
 interface Loopback0
  ip address 192.169.4.4 255.255.255.0
 !
 interface Loopback1
  ip address 200.200.1.4 255.255.255.0
 !
 interface Loopback2
  ip address 200.200.2.4 255.255.255.0
 !
 interface Ethernet0
  description This interface does not connect to another IP device
  ip address 192.168.4.4 255.255.255.224
  ipx network 4000
 !
 interface Serial0
  description This interface connects to R3's S0 (DLCI 101)
  ip address 192.168.100.4 255.255.255.0
  ip summary-address eigrp 100 200.200.0.0 255.255.0.0
  encapsulation frame-relay
  ipx network 1000
  no fair-queue
  frame-relay map ip 192.168.100.2 101 broadcast
```

*continues*

**Example A-32** *R4's Configuration (Continued)*

```
 frame-relay map ip 192.168.100.3 101 broadcast
 frame-relay map ipx 1000.0000.0000.2222 101 broadcast
 frame-relay map ipx 1000.0000.0000.3333 101 broadcast
 frame-relay lmi-type ansi
!
interface Serial1
 no ip address
 shutdown
!
router eigrp 100
 network 192.168.100.0
 network 192.168.4.0
 network 200.200.1.0
 network 200.200.2.0
 network 192.169.4.0
 no auto-summary
!
no ip classless
!
!
!
ipx router eigrp 100
 network 1000
!
!
ipx router rip
 no network 1000
!
!
!
banner motd #
This is Router 4
#
!
line con 0
 exec-timeout 0 0
 password falcons
 logging synchronous
line aux 0
line vty 0 4
 password falcons
 login
!
end
```

# Chapter 15 Router Configurations and Diagrams
## R2 Configuration

**Example A-33** *R2's Configuration*

```
!
version 12.0
service timestamps debug uptime
service timestamps log uptime
no service password-encryption
!
hostname R2
!
enable password falcons
!
ip subnet-zero
no ip domain-lookup
ip host R1 192.169.1.1
ip host R2 192.169.2.2
ip host R3 192.169.3.3
ip host R4 192.169.4.4
ip host R5 192.169.5.5
ip host R6 192.169.6.6
ipx routing 0000.0000.2222
!
!
!
interface Loopback0
 ip address 192.169.2.2 255.255.255.0
 no ip directed-broadcast
!
interface Ethernet0
 ip address 192.168.1.2 255.255.255.0
 no ip directed-broadcast
 ipx network 2100
!
interface Ethernet1
 description This interface does not connect with another IP device
 ip address 192.168.2.2 255.255.255.0
 no ip directed-broadcast
 ipx network 2000
!
interface Serial0
 description This interface connects to R3's S0 (201)
 ip address 192.168.100.2 255.255.255.0
 ip access-group 1 out
 no ip directed-broadcast
 encapsulation frame-relay
 no ip mroute-cache
 ipx network 1000
 frame-relay map ip 192.168.100.3 201 broadcast
 frame-relay map ip 192.168.100.4 201 broadcast
```

*continues*

**Example A-33** *R2's Configuration (Continued)*

```
 frame-relay map ipx 1000.0000.0000.4444 201 broadcast
 frame-relay map ipx 1000.0000.0000.3333 201 broadcast
 frame-relay lmi-type ansi
!
router eigrp 100
 redistribute rip metric 2000 200 255 1 1500
 network 192.168.100.0
!
router rip
 redistribute eigrp 100 metric 1
 network 192.168.1.0
 network 192.168.2.0
 network 192.169.2.0
!
ip classless
!
access-list 1 deny   192.168.12.0 0.0.0.255
access-list 1 permit any
!
!
!
banner motd #
This is Router 2
#
!
line con 0
 exec-timeout 0 0
 password falcons
 logging synchronous
line vty 0 4
 password falcons
 login
!
end
```

# R3 Configuration

**Example A-34** *R3's Configuration*

```
!
version 11.2
no service password-encryption
no service udp-small-servers
no service tcp-small-servers
!
hostname R3
!
enable password falcons
!
```

**Example A-34** *R3's Configuration (Continued)*

```
no ip domain-lookup
ip host R3 192.169.3.3
ip host R1 192.169.1.1
ip host R2 192.169.2.2
ip host R4 192.169.4.4
ip host R5 192.169.5.5
ip host R6 192.169.6.6
ipx routing 0000.0000.3333
!
interface Loopback0
 ip address 192.169.3.3 255.255.255.0
!
interface Ethernet0
 ip address 192.168.3.3 255.255.255.0
 ipx network 3000
 ipx network 3001 encapsulation SAP secondary
!
interface Serial0
 description This interface connects to R2's S0(DLCI 200) and R4's S0 (DLCI 100)

 ip address 192.168.100.3 255.255.255.0
 ip access-group 101 in
 encapsulation frame-relay
 no ip split-horizon eigrp 100
 ipx network 1000
 frame-relay lmi-type ansi
!
interface Serial1
 description This interface connects to R5's S0 (DCE)
 ip address 192.168.35.3 255.255.255.0
 ipx network 3500
!
router eigrp 100
 redistribute igrp 200 metric 2000 200 255 1 1500
 network 192.168.100.0
 network 192.168.3.0
!
router igrp 200
 redistribute eigrp 100 metric 2000 200 255 1 1500
 network 192.168.35.0
 network 192.169.3.0
!
no ip classless
access-list 101 deny   tcp any 192.168.50.0 0.0.0.255 eq www
access-list 101 deny   tcp any 192.168.30.0 0.0.0.255 eq smtp

access-list 101 permit ip any any
!
!
!
!
banner motd #
```

*continues*

**Example A-34** *R3's Configuration (Continued)*

```
This is Router 3
#
!
line con 0
 exec-timeout 0 0

R3#
```

# Master Router Configurations, Diagrams, and Routing Tables

## R1 Configuration, IP Routing Table, and IPX Routing Table

**Example A-35** *R1's Configuration*

```
Building configuration...

Current configuration:
!
version 11.2
no service password-encryption
no service udp-small-servers
no service tcp-small-servers
!
hostname R1
!
enable password falcons
!
no ip domain-lookup
ip host R1 192.169.1.1
ip host R2 192.169.2.2
ip host R3 192.169.3.3
ip host R4 192.169.4.4
ip host R5 192.169.5.5
ip host R6 192.169.6.6
ipx routing 0000.0000.1111
!
interface Loopback0
 ip address 192.169.1.1 255.255.255.0
!
interface Ethernet0
 description This interface connects to R2's E0
 ip address 192.168.1.1 255.255.255.0
 ipx network 2100
!
interface Serial0
 no ip address
 shutdown
 no fair-queue
!
```

**Example A-35** *R1's Configuration (Continued)*

```
interface Serial1
 no ip address
 shutdown
!
router rip
 network 192.168.1.0
 network 192.169.1.0
!
no ip classless
ip route 0.0.0.0 0.0.0.0 192.168.1.2
!
!
!
!
banner motd #
This is Router 1
#
!
line con 0
 exec-timeout 0 0
 password falcons
 logging synchronous
line aux 0
line vty 0 4
 password falcons
 login
!
end
```

**Example A-36** *R1's IP Routing Table*

```
Codes: C - connected, S - static, I - IGRP, R - RIP, M - mobile, B - BGP
       D - EIGRP, EX - EIGRP external, O - OSPF, IA - OSPF inter area
       N1 - OSPF NSSA external type 1, N2 - OSPF NSSA external type 2
       E1 - OSPF external type 1, E2 - OSPF external type 2, E - EGP
       i - IS-IS, L1 - IS-IS level-1, L2 - IS-IS level-2, * - candidate default
       U - per-user static route, o - ODR

Gateway of last resort is 192.168.1.2 to network 0.0.0.0

R    192.168.100.0/24 [120/1] via 192.168.1.2, 00:00:02, Ethernet0
R    192.168.35.0/24 [120/1] via 192.168.1.2, 00:00:03, Ethernet0
R    192.168.60.0/24 [120/1] via 192.168.1.2, 00:00:03, Ethernet0
R    192.168.50.0/24 [120/1] via 192.168.1.2, 00:00:03, Ethernet0
C    192.169.1.0/24 is directly connected, Loopback0
C    192.168.1.0/24 is directly connected, Ethernet0
R    192.169.3.0/24 [120/1] via 192.168.1.2, 00:00:03, Ethernet0
R    192.168.2.0/24 [120/1] via 192.168.1.2, 00:00:03, Ethernet0
R    192.168.3.0/24 [120/1] via 192.168.1.2, 00:00:03, Ethernet0
R    192.169.2.0/24 [120/1] via 192.168.1.2, 00:00:03, Ethernet0
R    192.169.5.0/24 [120/1] via 192.168.1.2, 00:00:03, Ethernet0
```

*continues*

**Example A-36** *R1's IP Routing Table (Continued)*

```
R     192.168.4.0/24 [120/1] via 192.168.1.2, 00:00:03, Ethernet0
R     192.169.4.0/24 [120/1] via 192.168.1.2, 00:00:03, Ethernet0
R     192.168.200.0/24 [120/1] via 192.168.1.2, 00:00:03, Ethernet0
S*    0.0.0.0/0 [1/0] via 192.168.1.2
```

**Example A-37** *R1's IPX Routing Table*

```
Codes: C - Connected primary network,   c - Connected secondary network
       S - Static, F - Floating static, L - Local (internal), W - IPXWAN
       R - RIP, E - EIGRP, N - NLSP, X - External, A - Aggregate
       s - seconds, u - uses

8 Total IPX routes. Up to 1 parallel paths and 16 hops allowed.

No default route known.

C       2100 (NOVELL-ETHER),  Et0
R       1000 [02/01] via      2100.0010.7bf9.4912,   41s, Et0
R       2000 [02/01] via      2100.0010.7bf9.4912,   41s, Et0
R       3000 [08/02] via      2100.0010.7bf9.4912,   41s, Et0
R       3001 [08/02] via      2100.0010.7bf9.4912,   41s, Et0
R       3500 [08/02] via      2100.0010.7bf9.4912,   41s, Et0
R       4000 [14/02] via      2100.0010.7bf9.4912,   41s, Et0
R       5000 [14/03] via      2100.0010.7bf9.4912,   41s, Et0
```

# R2 Configuration, IP Routing Table, and IPX Routing Table

**Example A-38** *R2's Configuration*

```
R2#show running-config
Building configuration...

Current configuration:
!
version 12.0
service timestamps debug uptime
service timestamps log uptime
no service password-encryption
!
hostname R2
!
enable password falcons
!
ip subnet-zero
no ip domain-lookup
ip host R1 192.169.1.1
ip host R2 192.169.2.2
ip host R3 192.169.3.3
ip host R4 192.169.4.4
ip host R5 192.169.5.5
```

**Example A-38** *R2's Configuration (Continued)*

```
ip host R6 192.169.6.6
ipx routing 0000.0000.2222
!
!
!
interface Loopback0
 ip address 192.169.2.2 255.255.255.0
 no ip directed-broadcast
!
interface Ethernet0
 ip address 192.168.1.2 255.255.255.0
 no ip directed-broadcast
 ipx network 2100
!
interface Ethernet1
 description This interface does not connect with another IP device
 ip address 192.168.2.2 255.255.255.0
 no ip directed-broadcast
 ipx network 2000
!
interface Serial0
 description This interface connects to R3's S0 (201)
 ip address 192.168.100.2 255.255.255.0
 ip access-group 1 out
 no ip directed-broadcast
 encapsulation frame-relay
 no ip mroute-cache
 ipx network 1000
 no fair-queue
 service-module t1 clock source internal
 frame-relay map ip 192.168.100.3 201 broadcast
 frame-relay map ip 192.168.100.4 201 broadcast
 frame-relay map ipx 1000.0000.0000.4444 201 broadcast
 frame-relay map ipx 1000.0000.0000.3333 201 broadcast
 frame-relay lmi-type ansi
!
router eigrp 100
 redistribute rip metric 2000 200 255 1 1500
 network 192.168.100.0
!
router rip
 redistribute eigrp 100 metric 1
 network 192.168.1.0
 network 192.168.2.0
 network 192.169.2.0
!
ip classless
!
access-list 1 deny   192.168.12.0 0.0.0.255
access-list 1 permit any
!
!
```

*continues*

**Example A-38** *R2's Configuration (Continued)*

```
ipx router eigrp 100
 network 1000
!
!
ipx router rip
 no network 1000
!
!
!
banner motd #
This is Router 2
#
!
line con 0
 exec-timeout 0 0
 password falcons
 logging synchronous
line vty 0 4
 password falcons
 login
!
end
```

**Example A-39** *R2's IP Routing Table*

```
Codes: C - connected, S - static, I - IGRP, R - RIP, M - mobile, B - BGP
       D - EIGRP, EX - EIGRP external, O - OSPF, IA - OSPF inter area
       N1 - OSPF NSSA external type 1, N2 - OSPF NSSA external type 2
       E1 - OSPF external type 1, E2 - OSPF external type 2, E - EGP
       i - IS-IS, L1 - IS-IS level-1, L2 - IS-IS level-2, * - candidate default
       U - per-user static route, o - ODR

Gateway of last resort is not set

D EX 192.168.60.0/24 [170/41536000] via 192.168.100.3, 00:05:06, Serial0
D EX 192.168.200.0/24 [170/41536000] via 192.168.100.3, 00:05:06, Serial0
     192.168.4.0/27 is subnetted, 1 subnets
D       192.168.4.0 [90/2707456] via 192.168.100.3, 00:05:06, Serial0
D    192.169.4.0/24 [90/2809856] via 192.168.100.3, 00:05:06, Serial0
D EX 192.169.5.0/24 [170/2809856] via 192.168.100.3, 00:05:06, Serial0
D EX 192.168.50.0/24 [170/2697984] via 192.168.100.3, 00:05:06, Serial0
D EX 192.168.35.0/24 [170/2169856] via 192.168.100.3, 00:05:06, Serial0
C    192.168.1.0/24 is directly connected, Ethernet0
R    192.169.1.0/24 [120/1] via 192.168.1.1, 00:00:00, Ethernet0
C    192.168.2.0/24 is directly connected, Ethernet1
C    192.169.2.0/24 is directly connected, Loopback0
C    192.168.100.0/24 is directly connected, Serial0
D    192.168.3.0/24 [90/2195456] via 192.168.100.3, 00:05:07, Serial0
D EX 192.169.3.0/24 [170/2169856] via 192.168.100.3, 00:05:08, Serial0
D    200.200.0.0/16 [90/2809856] via 192.168.100.3, 00:05:08, Serial0
```

**Example A-40** *R2's IPx Routing Table*

```
Codes: C - Connected primary network,    c - Connected secondary network
       S - Static, F - Floating static, L - Local (internal), W - IPXWAN
       R - RIP, E - EIGRP, N - NLSP, X - External, A - Aggregate
       s - seconds, u - uses, U - Per-user static

8 Total IPX routes. Up to 1 parallel paths and 16 hops allowed.

No default route known.

C       1000 (FRAME-RELAY),   Se0
C       2000 (NOVELL-ETHER),  Et1
C       2100 (NOVELL-ETHER),  Et0
E       3000 [2195456/1] via     1000.0000.0000.3333, age 00:02:34,
                           1u, Se0
E       3001 [2195456/1] via     1000.0000.0000.3333, age 00:02:34,
                           1u, Se0
E       3500 [2681856/1] via     1000.0000.0000.3333, age 00:02:34,
                           1u, Se0
E       4000 [2707456/1] via     1000.0000.0000.3333, age 00:02:34,
                           1u, Se0
E       5000 [276864000/2] via    1000.0000.0000.3333, age 00:02:34,
                           1u, Se0
```

# R3 Configuration, IP Routing Table, and IPX Routing Table

**Example A-41** *R3's Configuration*

```
R3#show running-config
Building configuration...

Current configuration:
!
version 11.2
no service password-encryption
no service udp-small-servers
no service tcp-small-servers
!
hostname R3
!
enable password falcons
!
no ip domain-lookup
ip host R3 192.169.3.3
ip host R1 192.169.1.1
ip host R2 192.169.2.2
ip host R4 192.169.4.4
ip host R5 192.169.5.5
ip host R6 192.169.6.6
ipx routing 0000.0000.3333
!
```

*continues*

**Example A-41** *R3's Configuration (Continued)*

```
interface Loopback0
 ip address 192.169.3.3 255.255.255.0
!
interface Ethernet0
 ip address 192.168.3.3 255.255.255.0
 ipx network 3000
 ipx network 3001 encapsulation SAP secondary
!
interface Serial0
 description This interface connects to R2's S0(DLCI 200) and R4's S0 (DLCI 100)

 ip address 192.168.100.3 255.255.255.0
 ip access-group 101 in
 encapsulation frame-relay
 no ip split-horizon eigrp 100
 ipx network 1000
 no ipx split-horizon eigrp 100
 no fair-queue
 frame-relay lmi-type ansi
!
interface Serial1
 description This interface connects to R5's S0 (DCE)
 ip address 192.168.35.3 255.255.255.0
 ipx network 3500
!
router eigrp 100
 redistribute igrp 200 metric 2000 200 255 1 1500
 network 192.168.100.0
 network 192.168.3.0
!
router igrp 200
 redistribute eigrp 100 metric 2000 200 255 1 1500
 network 192.168.35.0
 network 192.169.3.0
!
no ip classless
access-list 101 deny   tcp any 192.168.50.0 0.0.0.255 eq www
access-list 101 deny   tcp any 192.168.30.0 0.0.0.255 eq smtp
access-list 101 permit ip any any
!
!
!
ipx router eigrp 100
 network 1000
!
!
ipx router rip
 no network 1000
!
!
!
banner motd #
```

**Example A-41** *R3's Configuration (Continued)*

```
This is Router 3
#
!
line con 0
 exec-timeout 0 0
 password falcons
 logging synchronous
line aux 0
line vty 0 4
 password falcons
 login
!
end
```

**Example A-42** *R3's IP Routing Table*

```
Codes: C - connected, S - static, I - IGRP, R - RIP, M - mobile, B - BGP
       D - EIGRP, EX - EIGRP external, O - OSPF, IA - OSPF inter area
       N1 - OSPF NSSA external type 1, N2 - OSPF NSSA external type 2
       E1 - OSPF external type 1, E2 - OSPF external type 2, E - EGP
       i - IS-IS, L1 - IS-IS level-1, L2 - IS-IS level-2, * - candidate default
       U - per-user static route, o - ODR

Gateway of last resort is not set

C    192.168.100.0/24 is directly connected, Serial0
C    192.168.35.0/24 is directly connected, Serial1
I    192.168.60.0/24 [100/160250] via 192.168.35.5, 00:00:15, Serial1
I    192.168.50.0/24 [100/8539] via 192.168.35.5, 00:00:15, Serial1
D EX 192.169.1.0/24 [170/2221056] via 192.168.100.2, 00:06:19, Serial0
D EX 192.168.1.0/24 [170/2221056] via 192.168.100.2, 00:06:19, Serial0
D EX 192.168.2.0/24 [170/2221056] via 192.168.100.2, 00:06:19, Serial0
C    192.169.3.0/24 is directly connected, Loopback0
D EX 192.169.2.0/24 [170/2221056] via 192.168.100.2, 00:06:19, Serial0
C    192.168.3.0/24 is directly connected, Ethernet0
     192.168.4.0/27 is subnetted, 1 subnets
D       192.168.4.0 [90/2195456] via 192.168.100.4, 00:06:19, Serial0
I    192.169.5.0/24 [100/8976] via 192.168.35.5, 00:00:16, Serial1
D    192.169.4.0/24 [90/2297856] via 192.168.100.4, 00:06:19, Serial0
I    192.168.200.0/24 [100/160250] via 192.168.35.5, 00:00:17, Serial1
D    200.200.0.0/16 [90/2297856] via 192.168.100.4, 00:06:21, Serial0
```

**Example A-43** *R3's IPX Routing Table*

```
Codes: C - Connected primary network,    c - Connected secondary network
       S - Static, F - Floating static, L - Local (internal), W - IPXWAN
       R - RIP, E - EIGRP, N - NLSP, X - External, A - Aggregate
       s - seconds, u - uses

8 Total IPX routes. Up to 1 parallel paths and 16 hops allowed.
```

*continues*

**Example A-43** *R3's IPX Routing Table (Continued)*

```
No default route known.

C       1000 (FRAME-RELAY),   Se0
C       3000 (NOVELL-ETHER),  Et0
c       3001 (SAP),           Et0
C       3500 (HDLC),          Se1
E       2000 [2195456/1] via    1000.0000.0000.2222, age 00:03:41,
                           1u, Se0
E       2100 [2195456/1] via    1000.0000.0000.2222, age 00:03:41,
                           3u, Se0
E       4000 [2195456/1] via    1000.0000.0000.4444, age 00:06:26,
                           1u, Se0
R       5000 [07/01] via    3500.0000.0000.5555,    38s, Se1
```

# R4 Configuration, IP Routing Table, and IPX Routing Table

**Example A-44** *R4's Configuration*

```
R4#show running-config
Building configuration...

Current configuration:
!
version 11.2
no service password-encryption
no service udp-small-servers
no service tcp-small-servers
!
hostname R4
!
enable password falcons
!
ip subnet-zero
ip telnet source-interface Serial0
no ip domain-lookup
ip host R1 192.169.1.1
ip host R2 192.169.2.2
ip host R3 192.169.3.3
ip host R4 192.169.4.4
ip host R5 192.169.5.5
ip host R6 192.169.6.6
ipx routing 0000.0000.4444
!
interface Loopback0
 ip address 192.169.4.4 255.255.255.0
!
interface Loopback1
 ip address 200.200.1.4 255.255.255.0
!
interface Loopback2
 ip address 200.200.2.4 255.255.255.0
```

**Example A-44** *R4's Configuration (Continued)*

```
!
interface Ethernet0
 description This interface does not connect to another IP device
 ip address 192.168.4.4 255.255.255.224
 ipx network 4000
!
interface Serial0
 description This interface connects to R3's S0 (DLCI 101)
 ip address 192.168.100.4 255.255.255.0
 ip summary-address eigrp 100 200.200.0.0 255.255.0.0
 encapsulation frame-relay
 ipx network 1000
 no fair-queue
 frame-relay map ip 192.168.100.2 101 broadcast
 frame-relay map ip 192.168.100.3 101 broadcast
 frame-relay map ipx 1000.0000.0000.2222 101 broadcast
 frame-relay map ipx 1000.0000.0000.3333 101 broadcast
 frame-relay lmi-type ansi
!
interface Serial1
 no ip address
 shutdown
!
router eigrp 100
 network 192.168.100.0
 network 192.168.4.0
 network 200.200.1.0
 network 200.200.2.0
 network 192.169.4.0
 no auto-summary
!
no ip classless
!
!
!
ipx router eigrp 100
 network 1000
!
!
ipx router rip
 no network 1000
!
!
!
banner motd #
This is Router 4
#
!
line con 0
 exec-timeout 0 0
 password falcons
 logging synchronous
```

*continues*

**Example A-44** *R4's Configuration (Continued)*

```
line aux 0
line vty 0 4
 password falcons
 login
!
end
```

**Example A-45** *R4's IP Routing Table*

```
Codes: C - connected, S - static, I - IGRP, R - RIP, M - mobile, B - BGP
       D - EIGRP, EX - EIGRP external, O - OSPF, IA - OSPF inter area
       N1 - OSPF NSSA external type 1, N2 - OSPF NSSA external type 2
       E1 - OSPF external type 1, E2 - OSPF external type 2, E - EGP
       i - IS-IS, L1 - IS-IS level-1, L2 - IS-IS level-2, * - candidate default
       U - per-user static route, o - ODR

Gateway of last resort is not set

C    200.200.1.0/24 is directly connected, Loopback1
C    200.200.2.0/24 is directly connected, Loopback2
C    192.168.100.0/24 is directly connected, Serial0
D EX 192.168.35.0/24 [170/2169856] via 192.168.100.3, 00:07:17, Serial0
D EX 192.168.60.0/24 [170/41536000] via 192.168.100.3, 00:07:17, Serial0
D EX 192.168.50.0/24 [170/2697984] via 192.168.100.3, 00:07:17, Serial0
D EX 192.169.1.0/24 [170/2733056] via 192.168.100.3, 00:07:17, Serial0
D EX 192.168.1.0/24 [170/2733056] via 192.168.100.3, 00:07:17, Serial0
D EX 192.168.2.0/24 [170/2733056] via 192.168.100.3, 00:07:17, Serial0
D EX 192.169.3.0/24 [170/2169856] via 192.168.100.3, 00:07:17, Serial0
D EX 192.169.2.0/24 [170/2733056] via 192.168.100.3, 00:07:17, Serial0
D    192.168.3.0/24 [90/2195456] via 192.168.100.3, 00:07:17, Serial0
D EX 192.169.5.0/24 [170/2809856] via 192.168.100.3, 00:07:17, Serial0
     192.168.4.0/27 is subnetted, 1 subnets
C       192.168.4.0 is directly connected, Ethernet0
C    192.169.4.0/24 is directly connected, Loopback0
D EX 192.168.200.0/24 [170/41536000] via 192.168.100.3, 00:07:19, Serial0
D    200.200.0.0/16 is a summary, 00:07:19, Null0
```

**Example A-46** *R4's IPX Routing Table*

```
Codes: C - Connected primary network,    c - Connected secondary network
       S - Static, F - Floating static, L - Local (internal), W - IPXWAN
       R - RIP, E - EIGRP, N - NLSP, X - External, A - Aggregate
       s - seconds, u - uses

8 Total IPX routes. Up to 1 parallel paths and 16 hops allowed.

No default route known.

C     1000 (FRAME-RELAY),   Se0
C     4000 (NOVELL-ETHER),  Et0
E     2000 [2707456/1] via     1000.0000.0000.3333, age 00:04:42,
```

**Example A-46** *R4's IPX Routing Table (Continued)*

```
                              1u, Se0
E         2100 [2707456/1] via      1000.0000.0000.3333, age 00:04:43,
                              2u, Se0
E         3000 [2195456/1] via      1000.0000.0000.3333, age 00:07:23,
                              1u, Se0
E         3001 [2195456/1] via      1000.0000.0000.3333, age 00:07:23,
                              1u, Se0
E         3500 [2681856/1] via      1000.0000.0000.3333, age 00:07:23,
                              1u, Se0
E         5000 [276864000/2] via     1000.0000.0000.3333, age 00:07:23,
                              1u, Se0
```

# R5 Configuration, IP Routing Table, and IPX Routing Table

**Example A-47** *R5's Configuration*

```
R5#show running-config
Building configuration...

Current configuration:
!
version 11.2
no service password-encryption
no service udp-small-servers
no service tcp-small-servers
!
hostname R5
!
enable password falcons
!
ip subnet-zero
no ip domain-lookup
ip host R5 192.169.5.5
ip host R1 192.169.1.1
ip host R2 192.169.2.2
ip host R3 192.169.3.3
ip host R4 192.169.4.4
ip host R6 192.169.6.6
ipx routing 0000.0000.5555
isdn switch-type basic-5ess
!
interface Loopback0
 ip address 192.169.5.5 255.255.255.0
!
interface Serial0
 description This interface connects to R3's S1 (DTE)
 ip address 192.168.35.5 255.255.255.0
 ipx network 3500
 no fair-queue
 clockrate 2000000
!
```

*continues*

**Example A-47** *R5's Configuration (Continued)*

```
interface Serial1
 no ip address
 shutdown
!
interface TokenRing0
 description This interface does not connect with another IP device
 ip address 192.168.50.5 255.255.255.0
 ipx network 5000
 ring-speed 16
!
interface BRI0
 ip address 192.168.200.1 255.255.255.252
 encapsulation ppp
 dialer idle-timeout 300
 dialer-group 1
!
router igrp 200
 redistribute connected
 redistribute static
 passive-interface Loopback0
 network 192.168.35.0
 network 192.168.50.0
 network 192.169.5.0
!
no ip classless
ip default-network 192.169.3.0
ip route 192.168.60.0 255.255.255.0 192.168.200.2
!
!
dialer-list 1 protocol ip permit
!
!
banner motd #
This is Router 5
#
!
line con 0
 exec-timeout 0 0
 password falcons
 logging synchronous
line aux 0
line vty 0 4
 password falcons
 login
!
end
```

**Example A-48** *R5's IP Routing Table*

```
Codes: C - connected, S - static, I - IGRP, R - RIP, M - mobile, B - BGP
       D - EIGRP, EX - EIGRP external, O - OSPF, IA - OSPF inter area
       N1 - OSPF NSSA external type 1, N2 - OSPF NSSA external type 2
```

**Example A-48** *R5's IP Routing Table (Continued)*

```
           E1 - OSPF external type 1, E2 - OSPF external type 2, E - EGP
           i - IS-IS, L1 - IS-IS level-1, L2 - IS-IS level-2, * - candidate default
           U - per-user static route, o - ODR

Gateway of last resort is 192.168.35.3 to network 192.169.3.0

I    192.168.100.0/24 [100/10476] via 192.168.35.3, 00:00:51, Serial0
C    192.168.35.0/24 is directly connected, Serial0
S    192.168.60.0/24 [1/0] via 192.168.200.2
C    192.168.50.0/24 is directly connected, TokenRing0
I    192.169.1.0/24 [100/10676] via 192.168.35.3, 00:00:51, Serial0
I    192.168.1.0/24 [100/10676] via 192.168.35.3, 00:00:51, Serial0
I    192.168.2.0/24 [100/10676] via 192.168.35.3, 00:00:51, Serial0
I*   192.169.3.0/24 [100/8976] via 192.168.35.3, 00:00:51, Serial0
I    192.168.3.0/24 [100/8576] via 192.168.35.3, 00:00:51, Serial0
I    192.169.2.0/24 [100/10676] via 192.168.35.3, 00:00:51, Serial0
I    192.168.4.0/24 [100/10576] via 192.168.35.3, 00:00:52, Serial0
C    192.169.5.0/24 is directly connected, Loopback0
I    192.169.4.0/24 [100/10976] via 192.168.35.3, 00:00:52, Serial0
     192.168.200.0/30 is subnetted, 1 subnets
C        192.168.200.0 is directly connected, BRI0
```

**Example A-49** *R5's IPX Routing Table*

```
Codes: C - Connected primary network,    c - Connected secondary network
       S - Static, F - Floating static, L - Local (internal), W - IPXWAN
       R - RIP, E - EIGRP, N - NLSP, X - External, A - Aggregate
       s - seconds, u - uses

8 Total IPX routes. Up to 1 parallel paths and 16 hops allowed.

No default route known.

C       3500 (HDLC),       Se0
C       5000 (SAP),        To0
R       1000 [07/01] via   3500.0000.0000.3333,   25s, Se0
R       2000 [13/02] via   3500.0000.0000.3333,   25s, Se0
R       2100 [13/02] via   3500.0000.0000.3333,   25s, Se0
R       3000 [07/01] via   3500.0000.0000.3333,   25s, Se0
R       3001 [07/01] via   3500.0000.0000.3333,   25s, Se0
R       4000 [13/02] via   3500.0000.0000.3333,   25s, Se0
```

# R6 Configuration and IP Routing Table

**Example A-50** *R6's Configuration*

```
Current configuration:
!
version 11.2
no service password-encryption
no service udp-small-servers
```

*continues*

**Example A-50** *R6's Configuration (Continued)*

```
no service tcp-small-servers
!
hostname R6
!
enable password falcons
!
ip subnet-zero
no ip domain-lookup
ip host R6 192.169.6.6
ip host R1 192.169.1.1
ip host R2 192.169.2.2
ip host R3 192.169.3.3
ip host R4 192.169.4.4
ip host R5 192.169.5.5
isdn switch-type basic-5ess
!
interface Loopback0
 ip address 192.169.6.6 255.255.255.0
!
interface Serial0
 no ip address
 shutdown
 no fair-queue
!
interface Serial1
 no ip address
 shutdown
!
interface TokenRing0
 description This interface does not connect with another IP device
 ip address 192.168.60.6 255.255.255.0
 ring-speed 16
!
interface BRI0
 ip address 192.168.200.2 255.255.255.252
 encapsulation ppp
 dialer idle-timeout 300
 dialer string 8358662
 dialer-group 1
!
no ip classless
ip route 0.0.0.0 0.0.0.0 192.168.200.1
!
dialer-list 1 protocol ip permit
banner motd #
This is Router 6
#
!
line con 0
 exec-timeout 0 0
 password falcons
 logging synchronous
```

**Example A-50** *R6's Configuration (Continued)*

```
line aux 0
line vty 0 4
 password falcons
 login
!
end
```

**Example A-51** *R6's IP Routing Table*

```
Codes: C - connected, S - static, I - IGRP, R - RIP, M - mobile, B - BGP
       D - EIGRP, EX - EIGRP external, O - OSPF, IA - OSPF inter area
       N1 - OSPF NSSA external type 1, N2 - OSPF NSSA external type 2
       E1 - OSPF external type 1, E2 - OSPF external type 2, E - EGP
       i - IS-IS, L1 - IS-IS level-1, L2 - IS-IS level-2, * - candidate default
       U - per-user static route, o - ODR

Gateway of last resort is 192.168.200.1 to network 0.0.0.0

C    192.168.60.0/24 is directly connected, TokenRing0
C    192.169.6.0/24 is directly connected, Loopback0
     192.168.200.0/30 is subnetted, 1 subnets
C       192.168.200.0 is directly connected, BRI0
S*   0.0.0.0/0 [1/0] via 192.168.200.1
```

# Master Diagram

Figure A-4 shows the master lab diagram.

**Figure A-4** *Master Lab Diagram*

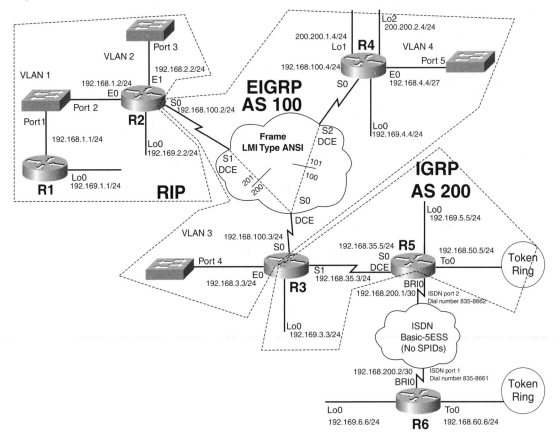

# Frame Relay Switch Configuration

One of the most common WAN protocols used today is Frame Relay. This appendix provides an overview of Frame Relay, its components, and its implementations. It also details how to configure a Cisco router to simulate a Frame Relay switch.

Frame Relay is a high-performance WAN protocol that operates at the physical and data link layers of the OSI reference model. Frame Relay originally was designed for use across Integrated Services Digital Network (ISDN) interfaces. Today it is used over a variety of other network interfaces as well. This section focuses on Frame Relay's specifications and applications in the context of WAN services.

Frame Relay is an example of a packet-switched technology. Packet-switched networks enable end stations to dynamically share the network medium and the available bandwidth. Variable-length packets are used for more efficient and flexible transfers. These packets then are switched among the various network segments until the destination is reached. Statistical multiplexing techniques control network access in a packet-switched network. The advantage of this technique is that it accommodates more flexibility and more efficient use of bandwidth. Most of today's popular LANs, such as Ethernet and Token Ring, are packet-switched networks.

Frame Relay often is described as a streamlined version of X.25, offering fewer of the robust capabilities, such as windowing and retransmission of lost data, which are offered in X.25. This is because Frame Relay typically operates over WAN facilities that offer more reliable connection services and a higher degree of reliability than the facilities available during the late 1970s and early 1980s that served as the common platforms for X.25 WANs. As mentioned earlier, Frame Relay is strictly a Layer 2 protocol suite, whereas X.25 provides services at Layer 3 (the network layer) as well. This enables Frame Relay to offer higher performance and greater transmission efficiency than X.25, and it makes Frame Relay suitable for current WAN applications, such as LAN interconnection.

Initial proposals for the standardization of Frame Relay were presented to the Consultative Committee on International Telephone and Telegraph (CCITT) in 1984. Because of a lack of interoperability and lack of complete standardization, however, Frame Relay did not experience significant deployment during the late 1980s.

A major development in Frame Relay's history occurred in 1990 when Cisco Systems, Digital Equipment, Northern Telecom, and StrataCom formed a consortium to focus on

Frame Relay technology development. This consortium developed a specification that conformed to the basic Frame Relay protocol that was being discussed in CCITT, but it extended the protocol with features that provide additional capabilities for complex internetworking environments. These Frame Relay extensions are referred to collectively as the Local Management Interface (LMI).

Since the consortium's specification was developed and published, many vendors have announced their support of this extended Frame Relay definition. ANSI and CCITT subsequently have standardized their own variations of the original LMI specification, and these standardized specifications now are more commonly used than the original version.

Internationally, Frame Relay was standardized by the International Telecommunications Union-Telecommunications Sector (ITU-T). In the United States, Frame Relay is an American National Standards Institute (ANSI) standard.

# Frame Relay Devices

Devices attached to a Frame Relay WAN fall into two general categories: data terminal equipment (DTE) and data circuit-terminating equipment (DCE). DTEs generally are considered to be terminating equipment for a specific network and typically are located on the premises of a customer. In fact, the customer can own them. Examples of DTE devices are terminals, personal computers, routers, and bridges.

DCEs are carrier-owned internetworking devices. The purpose of DCE equipment is to provide clocking and switching services in a network, which are the devices that actually transmit data through the WAN. In most cases, these are packet switches. Figure B-1 shows the relationship between the two categories of devices.

**Figure B-1**    *DCEs Generally Reside Within Carrier-operated WANs*

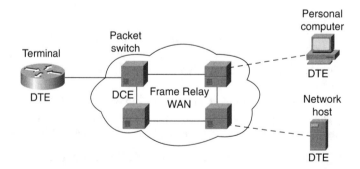

The connection between a DTE device and a DCE device consists of both a physical layer component and a data link layer component. The physical component defines the mechanical, electrical, functional, and procedural specifications for the connection between the devices. One of the most commonly used physical layer interface specifications is the recommended standard RS232 specification. The data link layer component defines the protocol that establishes the connection between the DTE device, such as a router, and the DCE device, such as a switch. This appendix examines a commonly utilized protocol specification used in WAN networking—the Frame Relay protocol.

# Frame Relay Virtual Circuits

Frame Relay provides connection-oriented data link layer communication. This means that a defined communication exists between each pair of devices and that these connections are associated with a connection identifier. This service is implemented by using a *Frame Relay virtual circuit*, which is a logical connection created between two data terminal equipment (DTE) devices across a Frame Relay packet-switched network (PSN).

Virtual circuits provide a bidirectional communications path from one DTE device to another and are uniquely identified by a data-link connection identifier (DLCI). A number of virtual circuits can be multiplexed into a single physical circuit for transmission across the network. This capability often can reduce the equipment and network complexity required to connect multiple DTE devices.

A virtual circuit can pass through any number of intermediate DCE devices (switches) located within the Frame Relay PSN.

Frame Relay virtual circuits fall into two categories:

- Switched virtual circuits (SVCs)
- Permanent virtual circuits (PVCs)

## Switched Virtual Circuits

Switched virtual circuits (SVCs) are temporary connections used in situations requiring only sporadic data transfer between DTE devices across the Frame Relay network. A communication session across an SVC consists of four operational states:

- **Call setup**—The virtual circuit between two Frame Relay DTE devices is established.
- **Data transfer**—Data is transmitted between the DTE devices over the virtual circuit.
- **Idle**—The connection between DTE devices is still active, but no data is transferred. If an SVC remains in an idle state for a defined period of time, the call can be terminated.
- **Call termination**—The virtual circuit between DTE devices is terminated.

After the virtual circuit is terminated, the DTE devices must establish a new SVC if there is additional data to be exchanged. It is expected that SVCs will be established, maintained, and terminated using the same signaling protocols used in ISDN. Few manufacturers of

Frame Relay DCE equipment, however, support SVCs. Therefore, their actual deployment is minimal in today's Frame Relay networks.

## Permanent Virtual Circuits

*Permanent virtual circuits (PVCs)* are permanently established connections that are used for frequent and consistent data transfers between DTE devices across the Frame Relay network. Communication across a PVC does not require the call setup and termination states that are used with SVCs. PVCs always operate in one of the following two operational states:

- **Data transfer**—Data is transmitted between the DTE devices over the virtual circuit.
- **Idle**—The connection between DTE devices is active, but no data is transferred. Unlike SVCs, PVCs are not terminated under any circumstances if they are in an idle state. DTE devices can begin transferring data whenever they are ready because the circuit is permanently established.

## Data-Link Connection Identifier

Frame Relay virtual circuits are identified by data-link connection identifiers (DLCIs). The Frame Relay service provider (for example, the telephone company) typically assigns DLCI values. Frame Relay DLCIs have local significance, which means that the values themselves are not unique in the Frame Relay WAN. Two DTE devices connected by a virtual circuit, for example, may use a different DLCI value to refer to the same connection. Figure B-2 illustrates how a single virtual circuit can be assigned a different DLCI value on each end of the connection.

**Figure B-2**   *A Single Frame Relay Virtual Circuit Can Be Assigned Different DLCIs on Each End of a VC*

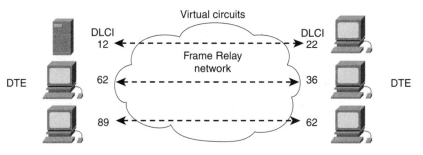

# Congestion-Control Mechanisms

Frame Relay reduces network overhead by implementing simple congestion-notification mechanisms rather than explicit, per-virtual-circuit flow control. Frame Relay typically is implemented on reliable network media. Thus, data integrity is not sacrificed because flow control can be left to higher-layer protocols. Frame Relay implements two congestion-notification mechanisms:

- Forward-explicit congestion notification (FECN)
- Backward-explicit congestion notification (BECN)

A single bit contained in the Frame Relay frame header controls FECN and BECN. The Frame Relay frame header also contains a *discard eligibility (DE)* bit, which is used to identify less important traffic that can be dropped during periods of congestion.

The FECN bit is part of the Address field in the Frame Relay frame header. The FECN mechanism is initiated when a DTE device sends Frame Relay frames into the network. If the network is congested, DCE devices (switches) set the value of the frames' FECN bit to 1. When the frames reach the destination DTE device, the Address field (with the FECN bit set) indicates that the frame experienced congestion in the path from source to destination. The DTE device can relay this information to a higher-layer protocol for processing. Depending on the implementation, flow-control can be initiated or the indication might be ignored.

The BECN bit is part of the Address field in the Frame Relay frame header. DCE devices set the value of the BECN bit to 1 in frames traveling in the opposite direction of frames with their FECN bit set. This informs the receiving DTE device that a particular path through the network is congested. The DTE device then can relay this information to a higher-layer protocol for processing. Depending on the implementation, flow control can be initiated or the indication might be ignored.

## Frame Relay Discard Eligibility

The discard eligibility (DE) bit is used to indicate that a frame has lower importance than other frames. The DE bit is part of the Address field in the Frame Relay frame header.

DTE devices can set the value of the DE bit of a frame to 1 to indicate that the frame has lower importance than other frames. When the network becomes congested, DCE devices will discard frames with the DE bit set before discarding those that do not. This reduces the likelihood of critical data being dropped by Frame Relay DCE devices during periods of congestion.

## Frame Relay Error Checking

Frame Relay uses a common error-checking mechanism known as the *cyclic redundancy check (CRC)*. The CRC compares two calculated values to determine whether errors occurred during the transmission from source to destination. Frame Relay reduces network overhead by implementing error checking rather than error correction. Frame Relay typically is implemented on reliable network media, so data integrity is not sacrificed because error correction can be left to higher-layer protocols running on top of Frame Relay.

# Frame Relay Local Management Interface

The *Local Management Interface (LMI)* is a set of enhancements to the basic Frame Relay specification. Cisco Systems, StrataCom, Northern Telecom, and Digital Equipment Corporation developed the LMI in 1990. It offers a number of features (called *extension*s) for managing complex internetworks. Key Frame Relay LMI extensions include global addressing, virtual circuit status messages, and multicasting.

The LMI global addressing extension gives Frame Relay DLCI values global rather than local significance. DLCI values become DTE addresses that are unique in the Frame Relay WAN. The global addressing extension adds functionality and manageability to Frame Relay internetworks. Individual network interfaces and the end nodes attached to them, for example, can be identified by using standard address-resolution and discovery techniques. In addition, the entire Frame Relay network appears to be a typical LAN to routers on its periphery.

LMI virtual circuit status messages provide communication and synchronization between Frame Relay DTE and DCE devices. These messages are used to periodically report on the status of PVCs, which prevents data from being sent into *black holes* (that is, over PVCs that no longer exist).

The LMI multicasting extension allows multicast groups to be assigned. *Multicasting* saves bandwidth by allowing routing updates and address-resolution messages to be sent only to specific groups of routers. The extension also transmits reports on the status of multicast groups in update messages.

# Frame Relay Network Implementation

A common private Frame Relay network implementation is to equip a T1 multiplexer with both Frame Relay and non–Frame Relay interfaces. Frame Relay traffic is forwarded out the Frame Relay interface and onto the data network. Non–Frame Relay traffic is forwarded to the appropriate application or service, such as a *private branch exchange* (PBX) for telephone service or to a video-teleconferencing application.

A typical Frame Relay network consists of a number of DTE devices, such as routers, connected to remote ports on multiplexer equipment by traditional point-to-point services such as T1, fractional T1, or 56-kbps circuits. Figure B-3 shows an example of a simple Frame Relay network.

**Figure B-3**    *A Simple Frame Relay Network Connects Various Devices to Different Services over a WAN*

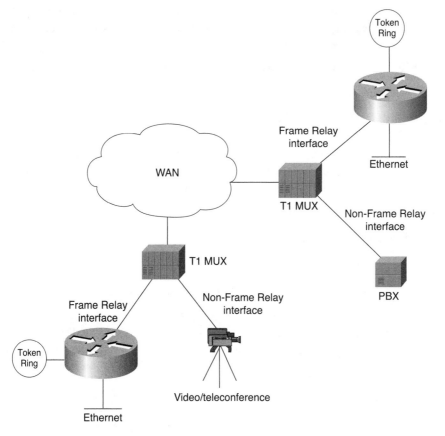

Service providers who intend to offer transmission services to customers provision the majority of Frame Relay networks deployed today. This is often referred to as a public Frame Relay service. Frame Relay is implemented in both public carrier–provided networks and in private enterprise networks. The following section examines the two methodologies for deploying Frame Relay.

## Public Carrier–Provided Networks

In public carrier–provided Frame Relay networks, the Frame Relay switching equipment is located in the central offices of a telecommunications carrier. Subscribers are charged based on their network use but are relieved from administering and maintaining the Frame Relay network equipment and service.

Generally, the telecommunications provider also owns the DCE equipment. DCE equipment either is customer-owned or perhaps is owned by the telecommunications provider as a service to the customer.

The majority of today's Frame Relay networks are public carrier–provided networks.

## Private Enterprise Networks

More frequently, organizations worldwide are deploying private Frame Relay networks. In private Frame Relay networks, the administration and maintenance of the network are the responsibilities of the enterprise (a private company). The customer owns all the equipment, including the switching equipment.

# Frame Relay Frame Formats

To understand much of the functionality of Frame Relay, it is helpful to understand the structure of the Frame Relay frame. Figure B-4 depicts the basic format of the Frame Relay frame, and Figure B-5 illustrates the LMI version of the Frame Relay frame.

Flags indicate the beginning and end of the frame. Three primary components make up the Frame Relay frame: the header and address area, the user-data portion, and the frame-check sequence (FCS). The address area, which is 2 bytes in length, is comprised of 10 bits representing the actual circuit identifier and 6 bits of fields related to congestion management. This identifier commonly is referred to as the data-link connection identifier (DLCI). Each of these is discussed in the descriptions that follow.

## Standard Frame Relay Frame

Standard Frame Relay frames consist of the fields illustrated in Figure B-4.

**Figure B-4**    *Five Fields Comprise the Frame Relay Frame*

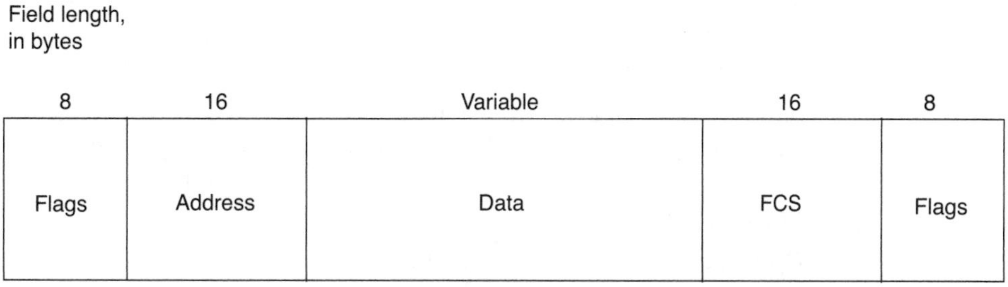

Field length,
in bytes

| 8 | 16 | Variable | 16 | 8 |
|---|---|---|---|---|
| Flags | Address | Data | FCS | Flags |

The following descriptions summarize the basic Frame Relay frame fields illustrated in Figure B-4.

- **Flags**—Delimits the beginning and end of the frame. The value of this field is always the same and is represented either as the hexadecimal number 7E or as the binary number 01111110.

- **Address**—Contains the following information:

  — **DLCI**—The 10-bit DLCI is the essence of the Frame Relay header. This value represents the virtual connection between the DTE device and the switch. Each virtual connection that is multiplexed onto the physical channel is represented by a unique DLCI. The DLCI values have local significance only, which means that they are unique only to the physical channel on which they reside. Therefore, devices at opposite ends of a connection can use different DLCI values to refer to the same virtual connection.

  — **Extended Address (EA)**—Indicates whether the byte in which the EA value is 1 is the last addressing field. If the value is 1, the current byte is determined to be the last DLCI octet. Although current Frame Relay implementations all use a two-octet DLCI, this capability does allow for longer DLCIs to be used in the future. The eighth bit of each byte of the Address field is used to indicate the EA.

  — **C/R**—Is the bit that follows the most significant DLCI byte in the Address field. The C/R bit is not currently defined.

  — **Congestion Control**—This consists of the 3 bits that control the Frame Relay congestion-notification mechanisms. These are the FECN, BECN, and DE bits, which are the last 3 bits in the Address field.

    *Forward-explicit congestion notification (FECN)* is a single-bit field that can be set to a value of 1 by a switch to indicate to an end DTE device, such as a router, that congestion was experienced in the direction of the frame transmission from source to destination. The primary benefit of the use of the FECN and BECN fields is that higher-layer protocols can react intelligently to these congestion indicators. Today, DECnet and OSI are the only higher-layer protocols that implement these capabilities.

*Backward-explicit congestion notification (BECN)* is a single-bit field that, when set to a value of 1 by a switch, indicates that congestion was experienced in the network in the direction opposite of the frame transmission from source to destination.

*Discard eligibility (DE)* is set by the DTE device, such as a router, to indicate that the marked frame is of lesser importance relative to other frames being transmitted. Frames that are marked as "discard eligible" should be discarded before other frames in a congested network. This allows for a fairly basic prioritization mechanism in Frame Relay networks.

- **Data**—Contains encapsulated upper-layer data. Each frame in this variable-length field includes a user data or payload field that will vary in length up to 16,000 octets. This field serves to transport the higher-layer protocol packet (PDU) through a Frame Relay network.

- **Frame Check Sequence**—Ensures the integrity of transmitted data. This value is computed by the source device and is verified by the receiver to ensure integrity of transmission.

## LMI Frame Format

Frame Relay frames that conform to the LMI specifications consist of the fields illustrated in Figure B-5.

**Figure B-5**   *Nine Fields Comprise the Frame Relay That Conforms to the LMI Format*

Field length, in bytes

| 1 | 2 | 1 | 1 | 1 | 1 | Variable | 2 | 1 |
|---|---|---|---|---|---|----------|---|---|
| Flag | LMI DLCI | Unnumbered information indicator | Protocol discriminator | Call reference | Message type | Information elements | FCS | Flag |

The following descriptions summarize the fields illustrated in Figure 10-5.

- **Flag**—Delimits the beginning and end of the frame.

- **LMI DLCI**—Identifies the frame as an LMI frame instead of a basic Frame Relay frame. The LMI-specific DLCI value defined in the LMI consortium specification is DLCI = 1023.

- **Unnumbered Information Indicator**—Sets the poll/final bit to 0.

- **Protocol Discriminator**—Always contains a value indicating that the frame is an LMI frame.

- **Call Reference**—Always contains zeros. This field currently is not used for any purpose.

- **Message Type**—Labels the frame as one of the following message types:

  — **Status-inquiry message**—Allows a user device to inquire about the status of the network.

  — **Status message**—Responds to status-inquiry messages. Status messages include keepalives and PVC status messages.

- **Information Elements**—Contains a variable number of individual information elements (IEs). IEs consist of the following fields:

  — **IE Identifier**—Uniquely identifies the IE.

  — **IE Length**—Indicates the length of the IE.

  — **Data**—Consists of 1 or more bytes containing encapsulated upper-layer data.

- **Frame Check Sequence (FCS)**—Ensures the integrity of transmitted data.

# Frame Relay Switch Overview

Frame Relay switches are very complex and complicated devices used by telecom services providers to provide cheap, reliable access to the service provider's network. The Frame Relay switch is the device that Cisco routers communicate with to negotiate packet transmissions. There are several important aspects to understanding how a Frame Relay switch operates.

First, you need to review two of the components of Frame Relay that involve the switch. Although there are several more, you need not be well versed in these for the CCNA exam. This appendix restricts definition of these terms in the perspective of the Frame Relay switch. The two components in question are as follows:

- **Data-Link Control Identifier (DLCI)**—The identifying number of the PVC on the Frame Relay switch. This has local significance only.

- **Local Management Interface (LMI)**—The Frame Relay Switch responds to LMI requests sent by a Frame Relay DTE device. This is the mechanism by which the Frame Relay switch announces to the Frame Relay DTE device (usually a router) the DLCI that the Frame Relay switch has been configured to propagate. This DLCI is only locally significant, meaning that the destination PVC does not need to have the same DLCI number.

A Frame Relay switch announces on the appropriate port the correct DLCI to a Frame Relay DTE device (router). Because Frame Relay is a Layer 1 and Layer 2 technology, Layer 3 protocols can be transported independently. The Frame Relay switch provides the physical layer path and the format specification for the Layer 2 frame.

Figure B-6 reviews the sequence of events that transpires between a Frame Relay switch and a Frame Relay DTE device.

**Figure B-6**   *Frame Relay Events*

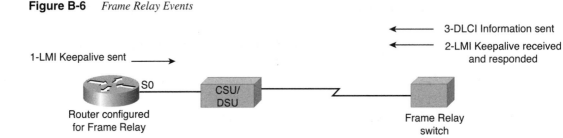

As you can see in Figure B-6, the router sends an LMI keepalive to the Frame Relay switch, and then the Frame Relay switch responds to the keepalives and sends the appropriate DLCI information to the router.

# Configuring a Cisco Router as a Frame Relay Switch

A Cisco router now has the capability to simulate a Frame Relay switch. Although this appendix will not show you how configure all of the features that a true Frame Relay switch will have, it will show you how to configure a Cisco router to propagate DLCIs and match them to the appropriate outgoing interfaces to make the router act as a Frame Relay switch.

The most important thing to remember about a Frame Relay switch in the lab is that the DLCI is sent through LMI out a particular interface, and then that DLCI and interface are mapped to an outgoing DLCI and interface.

## Physical Connections to the Frame Relay Switch (Cisco 2523)

Before you start configuring the Frame Relay switch, take a look at how the lab routers are connected to the Cisco 2523 acting as the Frame Relay switch. Figure B-7 illustrates the physical connections.

**Figure B-7**   *Frame Relay Physical Connections*

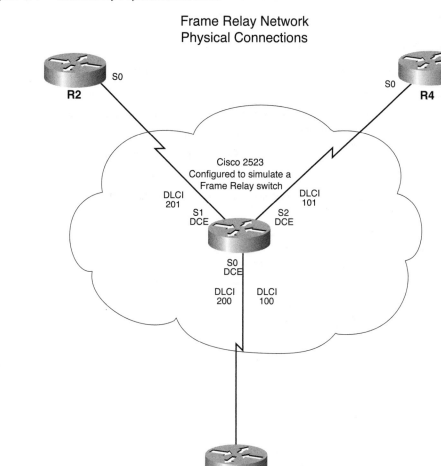

Frame Relay Network
Physical Connections

As you can see from Figure B-7, R3 will be the "hub" site and requires two PVCs and DLCIs to be configured on interface S0 of the Cisco 2523. R2 and R4 need only one PVC and one DLCI. Begin by configuring the router as a Frame Relay switch.

# Steps for Configuring a Cisco Router as a Frame Relay Switch

Table B-1 defines the steps to configuring a Cisco router as a Frame Relay switch.

**Table B-1** *Configuring a Cisco Router as a Frame Relay Switch*

| Step | Description | Command |
|------|-------------|---------|
| Step 1 | Enable Frame Relay switching. | **frame-relay switching** |
| Step 2 | Configure Frame Relay encapsulation, Frame Relay LMI type, Frame Relay DCE interface mode, and clock rate on individual interfaces. | **encapsulation frame-relay** <br> **frame-relay lmi-type ansi** <br> **frame-relay intf-type dce** <br> **clock rate 64000**[1] |
| Step 3 | Configure DLCI to interface mappings on individual interfaces. | **frame-relay route** {*local-dlci*} **interface** {*outgoing interface and number*} {*outgoing-dlci*} |

1  The clock rate is 64000 because the Cisco 2523 has both synchronous and asynchronous serial interfaces, and the asynchronous interfaces support only 64000 bps.

The first thing is to connect to the Cisco 2523's console port. There is no configuration on the router at this point. You should be in setup mode or at the **Router>** prompt. If you are in setup mode, just exit this mode (Ctrl-c).

When you are into the router, give it a host name of Frame-Switch.

```
Router>en
Router#config t
Enter configuration commands, one per line.  End with CNTL/Z.
Router(config)#hostname Frame-Switch
```

Do not worry about passwords and Telnet connectivity. This router will be a standalone Frame Relay switch. If you need to access it, you will connect to the console port.

Begin with the first step documented in Table B-1, and enable Frame Relay switching on the router. Example B-1 illustrates this configuration step.

**Example B-1** *Enable Frame Relay Switching*

```
Frame-Switch(config)#frame-relay switching
Frame-Switch(config)#
```

After the Frame Relay switching process has been started, configure the individual interfaces for the Frame Relay switch. This includes changing the encapsulation type to **frame-relay** and changing the LMI type to ANSI. Because all interfaces on the Frame Relay switch are DCEs (refer to the Figure B-7), they will need to be changed to the Frame

Relay type DCE and must have the **clock rate** command issued as well. Example B-2 demonstrates these commands for interface Serial0.

**Example B-2** *Frame-Relay Commands for Serial0*

```
Frame-Switch(config)#int serial0
Frame-Switch(config-if)#encapsulation frame-relay
Frame-Switch(config-if)#frame-relay lmi-type ansi
Frame-Switch(config-if)#frame-relay intf-type dce
Frame-Switch(config-if)#clock rate 64000
```

Now that all the Frame Relay commands have been set, you need to map the local DLCI of this interface to the outgoing DLCI and port. Because the Serial0 interface has two PVCs, it needs two mappings. Example B-3 shows the commands.

**Example B-3** *DLCI-to-Interface Mappings for Serial0*

```
Frame-Switch(config-if)#frame-relay route 100 interface serial 2 101
Frame-Switch(config-if)#frame-relay route 200 interface serial 1 201
Frame-Switch(config-if)#no shutdown
```

From Figure B-7, you know that Serial 0 has two PVCs, one to R2 and one to R4. The first highlighted portion of lines 1 and 2 in Example B-3 point out the local DLCI that will be advertised out Serial 0. Therefore, R3 will see DLCI 100 and DLCI 200 because R3 is connected to the Frame Relay switch on Serial0. The second portion of highlighting in lines 1 and 2 marks the outgoing interface to which each DLCI is mapped. Therefore, anything coming from R3 on DLCI 100 will be sent to Serial2, and anything coming from R3 on DLCI 200 will be sent to Serial1. The last portion of highlighting in lines 1 and 2 indicates the DLCI assigned to the outgoing port. So, anything coming from R3 on DLCI 100 will go out Serial2 to DLCI 101, and anything coming from R3 on DLCI 200 will go out Serial1 to DLCI 201. Don't forget to remove the interfaces from shutdown mode.

The next thing you need to do is perform a similar mapping statement on interfaces Serial1 and Serial2, except that the numbers will be reversed. See Example B-4.

**Example B-4** *Frame Relay Commands and DLCI-to-Interface Mappings for Serial1*

```
Frame-Switch(config)#interface serial1
Frame-Switch(config-if)#encapsulation frame-relay
Frame-Switch(config-if)#frame-relay lmi-type ansi
Frame-Switch(config-if)#frame-relay intf-type dce
Frame-Switch(config-if)#clock rate 64000
Frame-Switch(config-if)#frame-relay route 201 interface serial 0 200
Frame-Switch(config-if)#no shutdown
```

The highlighted portion of the configuration shows the local DLCI (201), the outgoing interface (Serial0), and the outgoing DLCI (200). Next, do the same for interface Serial2. See Example B-5.

**Example B-5** *Frame-Relay Commands and DLCI-to-Interface Mappings on Serial2*

```
Frame-Switch(config)#interface serial2
Frame-Switch(config-if)#encapsulation frame-relay
Frame-Switch(config-if)#frame-relay lmi-type ansi
Frame-Switch(config-if)#frame intf-type dce
Frame-Switch(config-if)#clock rate 64000
Frame-Switch(config-if)#frame-relay route 101 interface serial 0 100
Frame-Switch(config-if)#no shut
Frame-Switch(config-if)#
```

The highlighted portion of the configuration shows the local DLCI (101), the outgoing interface (Serial0), and the outgoing DLCI (100). At this point, you have a functional Frame Relay switch. You will be able to verify the connections in Chapter 7, "Router Interface Configuration," but for now, take a look at the configuration and do a **show frame-relay route** to verify that the configuration matches the lab diagram. Example B-6 shows the running-config file. Notice where the commands are located in the configuration file.

**Example B-6** *Output from* **show running-config**

```
Frame-Switch#show running-config
Building configuration...

Current configuration:
!
version 11.2
no service password-encryption
no service udp-small-servers
no service tcp-small-servers
!
hostname Frame-Switch
!
!
frame-relay switching
!
interface Serial0
 no ip address
 encapsulation frame-relay
 clockrate 64000
 frame-relay lmi-type ansi
 frame-relay intf-type dce
 frame-relay route 100 interface serial2 101
 frame-relay route 200 interface Serial1 201
!
interface Serial1
 no ip address
 encapsulation frame-relay
 clockrate 64000
 frame-relay lmi-type ansi
 frame-relay intf-type dce
 frame-relay route 201 interface Serial0 200
!
interface Serial2
```

**Example B-6**  *Output from* **show running-config** *(Continued)*

```
 no ip address
 encapsulation frame-relay
 clockrate 64000
 frame-relay lmi-type ansi
 frame-relay intf-type dce
 frame-relay route 101 interface Serial0 100
!
interface Serial3
 no ip address
 shutdown
!
interface Serial4
 no ip address
 shutdown
!
interface Serial5
 no ip address
 shutdown
!
interface Serial6
 no ip address
 shutdown
!
interface Serial7
 no ip address
 shutdown
!
interface Serial8
 no ip address
 shutdown
!
interface Serial9
 no ip address
 shutdown
!
interface TokenRing0
 no ip address
 shutdown
!
interface BRI0
 no ip address
 shutdown
!
no ip classless
!
!
line con 0
 exec-timeout 0 0
line aux 0
line vty 0 4
 login
```

*continues*

**Example B-6** *Output from* **show running-config** *(Continued)*

```
!
end

Frame-Switch#
```

The highlighted portions illustrate all the Frame Relay configuration tasks that you completed. Notice that none of the interfaces has IP addresses, nor do any of the interfaces need them. You are only mapping DLCIs to interfaces. This is a Layer 2 function, not a Layer 3 function, therefore, no IP address are needed.

The **show frame-relay route** command is a useful command in determining that your configuration is correct. Example B-7 shows the output from this command.

**Example B-7** *Output from* **show frame-relay route** *Command*

```
Frame-Switch#show frame-relay route
Input Intf     Input Dlci     Output Intf     Output Dlci     Status
Serial0        100            Serial2         101             inactive
Serial0        200            Serial1         201             inactive
Serial1        201            Serial0         200             inactive
Serial2        101            Serial0         100             inactive
Frame-Switch#
```

From this output, you can see that the **Input Dlci** matches the correct interfaces from the lab diagram in Figure B-7. You also can see that **Output Intf** and **Output Dlci** match to the correct interfaces and DLCIs as well. From here, you can assume that everything is configured correctly. The status will be inactive until you configure the Frame Relay interfaces on R2, R3, and R4 and remove them from shutdown mode.

# Summary

This appendix provided a review of Frame Relay technology and its components, such as PVCs, DLCIs, and LMI. You also learned how to configure a Cisco router to act as a Frame Relay switch, giving you the opportunity to simulate a Frame Relay network for the lab.

# APPENDIX C

# Self-Study Lab

This appendix is a complete self-study lab. You will have the opportunity to configure a network lab according to the lab objectives outlined in this appendix. Hints have been provided to help if you get stuck. This appendix also contains the completed router configurations for the lab so that you can check your configs or, if you need help completing an objective, refer to the completed router configuration for guidance.

Draw the entire lab environment. Label all routers, interfaces, connections, IP addresses, subnet masks, and routing domains. Be sure to update the diagram as you progress through the lab. Figure C-1 shows the physical connections and IP addressing for the lab.

**Figure C-1** *Self-Study Lab Diagram*

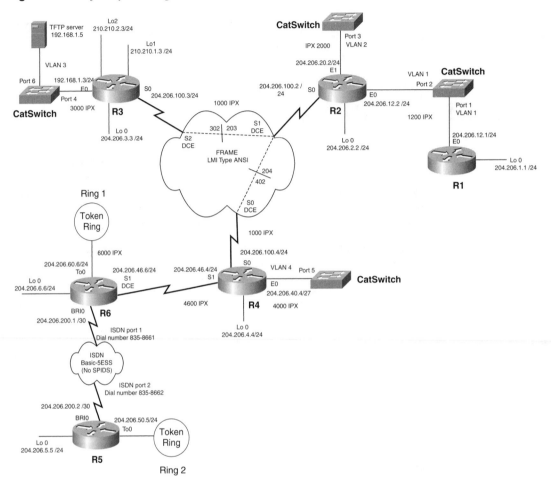

# Lab Objectives

## Terminal Server Configuration

Configure the Cisco 2511 router to be the terminal server for this lab. The terminal server is connected to each device's console port (see Hint 1). Port assignments are as follows:

- R1 2001
- R2 2002
- R3 2003

- R4 2004
- R5 2005
- R6 2006
- Catalyst switch 2007

# Cisco Catalyst Switch Configuration

- Configure the switch with a host name of Catswitch.
- Set the management console password to letmein.
- Assign the management console to an IP address of 192.168.1.4/24 and a default gateway of 192.168.1.10 (the terminal server).
- Configure ports 1 and 2 (refer to the diagram, if needed) to be in VLAN 1. Name the VLAN Vlan1.
- Configure port 3 for VLAN 2, and name the VLAN Vlan2.
- Configure port 4 for VLAN 3, name the VLAN Vlan3.
- Configure port 5 for VLAN 4, and name the VLAN Vlan4.
- *Note:* If you have a TFTP server, you will need to place that port into VLAN 3 for this lab.

# Cisco Router Configuration

Configure all routers to have the following:

- A host name (that is, host names are to be according to the number r1, r2, r3, and so on).
- An enable secret password of allpower.
- An enable console login with password letmein.
- Telnet access (vty 0 4) password falcons.
- No DNS resolution (no domain name lookups).
- Configure all routers so that the console port will not time out your connection.
- Configure all routers so that messages from the router to the console screen will not be appended to the command line.
- Configure all routers to show a banner when you log into the router (from console port or Telnet). (In the banner, state which router you are logging into. As an example, on Router 1, the banner should read "This is router 1.")

- Create loopback interfaces on all routers. Use IP address 204.206.*X.X*/24 (where *X* is the router number). So, R1 would have a loopback address of 204.206.1.1/24, R2 would be 204.206.2.2/24, and so on.)
- Create a host table on all routers using the loopback addresses that you just created for each router.

## IP Addressing Assignment

- Look at the network diagram for IP addressing assignments for each interface, and assign them to the appropriate interfaces. Don't forget to look at the netmasks!
- While configuring IP addresses on the interfaces, configure the data link layer (Frame Relay, if appropriate—see Hint 2) and place a description on each interface (except loopback interfaces) stating the router that they are connected to and which interface they are. Remove the interface from shutdown mode.

## RIP

- Place R4's Ethernet 0, Serial 1, and Loopback 0 networks into RIP.
- Place R6's Serial 1, Token Ring 0, and Loopback 0 networks into RIP as well.

## IGRP

- Place R2's Ethernet 0 and Ethernet 1 into IGRP AS 20.
- Configure R1 so that IGRP AS 20 propagates the networks from R1's Ethernet 0 and Loopback 0 interfaces.

## EIGRP

- Place R2's Serial 0, R2's Loopback 0, R3's Serial 0, and R4's Serial 0 networks into EIGRP autonomous system 10.
- Place R3's Ethernet 0 network into EIGRP 10 (see Hint 3).
- Create two loopback interfaces on R3 with the following addresses:
    — loopback 1=210.210.1.3/24
    — loopback 2=210.210.2.3/24
- Add these two networks into the EIGRP routing domain, and configure R3 so that all other routers see only one route to these two addresses (see Hint 4).

# Route Redistribution

- On R4, redistribute RIP into EIGRP and redistribute EIGRP into RIP. On R2, redistribute EIGRP into IGRP and redistribute IGRP into EIGRP (see Hint 5).

- Fix the problem of R6 and R1 not being capable of **ping**ing the two loopback addresses on R3 with either a default route or a default network statement.

# ISDN DDR

- Configure the BRI interfaces on R5 and R6 with IP addresses. See Figure C-1 for IP address and ISDN information (switch type and dial numbers).

- Use PPP encapsulation.

- Make sure that R5 is the only one to initiate a call.

- The ISDN link should be active when any IP traffic needs to cross the link. No routing protocols are to be used across the link. Use static routes, but make sure that R5 can **ping** all interfaces on all routers (See Hint 6).

# IPX

- Configure R2's Serial 0, R3's Serial 0, and R4's Serial 0 with IPX network number 1000 (see Hint 7).

- Configure R3's Ethernet 0 for IPX network 3000

- Configure R4's Serial 1 and R6's Serial 1 for IPX network number 4600.

- Configure R4's Ethernet 0 for IPX network 4000.

- Configure a secondary IPX network number 4001 on R4's Ethernet 0. Make the encapsulation Novell SAP (see Hint 8).

- Configure R1's Ethernet 0 and R2's Ethernet 0 for IPX network 1200.

- Configure R6's To0 network number to be 6000.

# IPX EIGRP

Use EIGRP as the routing protocol for the interfaces in the Frame-Relay cloud and R3's Ethernet 0 (see Hints 9, 10, and 11).

## IPX RIP

Use IPX RIP for all other router interfaces that are *not* configured for IPX EIGRP.

## Standard Access List

Create a standard outgoing access list and apply it on R4's Serial 0 to fulfill the following requirements:

- Deny access to users on network 192.168.111.32/27 to the Frame Relay network. (Assume that this network exists off R6. See Hint 12.)

## Extended Access List

Create an extended incoming access list, and apply it on R3's Serial 0 to fulfill the following requirements:

- Deny http (www) requests from reaching R3's Ethernet 0 network, where several Web servers reside.
- Deny FTP traffic from reaching R3's E0 network.
- Permit anything else (see Hint 13).

## Cisco Router Operations

- **Cisco router IOS backup**—Back up the current Cisco IOS Software image on R3 to the TFTP server at 192.168.1.5.
- **Cisco router IOS upgrade**—Upgrade the Cisco IOS Software on R3 to image c2500-js-l_112-17.bin on TFTP server 192.168.1.5.
- **Cisco router configuration backup**—Back up the current configuration on R3 to the same TFTP server. Name your file r3-confg.
- **Cisco router network configuration**—Suppose that your startup-config has become corrupted. Configure R3 from the TFTP server (use the filename that you just backed up).

# Hints

1  Don't forget to place the command **transport input all** under lines 1 through 7.

2  Be sure to have **frame-relay map** statements for the opposite two routers. See the completed router configurations for R2, R3, or R4 if you cannot get Frame Relay working.

**3**  Don't forget to disable IP split horizon for EIGRP. Use **no ip split-horizon eigrp 10** under the interface S0 on R2.

**4**  The command begins with **ip summary**. It is configured under the interface configuration mode.

**5**  Do not forget the metric option on the **redistribute** command. The metric for RIP is hops, and the metrics for IGRP and EIGRP for this lab are Bandwidth=2000 Delay=200 Reliability=255 Load=1 MTU=1500.

**6**  You might need to redistribute static or connected routes on R6. This will inform the other routers of the existence of R5's networks (204.206.200.0/30 and 204.206.50.0/24). Don't forget to define and apply interesting traffic with the **dialer-list** and **dialer-group** commands.

**7**  You must enable IPX routing before you can assign any IPX networks to interfaces. You also can assign a default node address for IPX to use on serial links. The command **ipx routing 0000.0000.1111** would be used on R1, for example.

**8**  Do not forget to use the **secondary** option at the end of the **ipx network** command when configuring a secondary IPX address. Otherwise, it will overwrite the primary IPX address.

**9**  For IPX to function correctly over the Frame Relay network, you need **frame-relay map ipx** commands. This is just like IP, but you will use IPX addresses instead of IP address. An example of this on R4 is **frame-relay map ipx 1000.0000.0000.2222 402 broadcast**.

**10**  IPX split horizon is real. Be sure to disable it for IPX as you did for IP.

**11**  By default, all IPX networks were placed into IPX RIP. So that you don't have EIGRP and RIP propagating the routes; you need to remove them from the IPX RIP process with the **no network** command under the **IPX router RIP** process and add them to IPX EIGRP.

**12**  All access lists have an implicit **deny** at the end of the list. Be sure to permit the rest of the traffic.

**13**  Don't forget to apply the access list to the appropriate interface in the appropriate direction.

# Completed Lab Diagram

**Figure C-2** *Completed Lab*

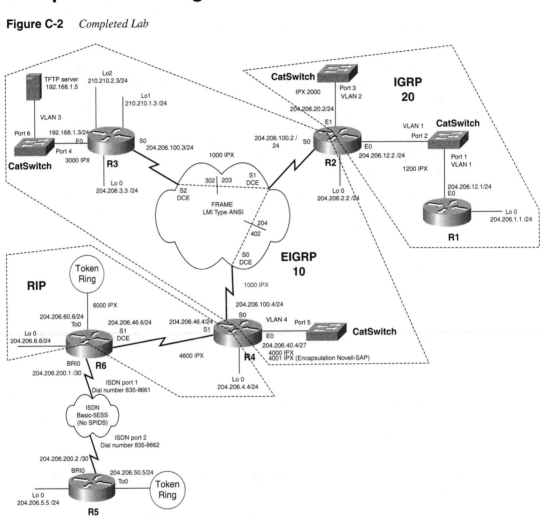

# Completed Router Configurations

Termserver

| NOTE | The terminal server is located on the same segment as R3's E0 here. Yours might be different. |
| --- | --- |

```
Current configuration:
!
version 11.2
service password-encryption
no service udp-small-servers
no service tcp-small-servers
!
hostname Termserver
!
enable password 7 0200055708090132
!
no ip domain-lookup
ip host r1 2001 192.168.10.10
ip host r2 2002 192.168.10.10
ip host r3 2003 192.168.10.10
ip host r4 2004 192.168.10.10
ip host r5 2005 192.168.10.10
ip host r6 2006 192.168.10.10
ip host cat19 2007 192.168.10.10
!
interface Loopback0
 ip address 192.168.10.10 255.255.255.0
!
interface Ethernet0
 ip address 192.168.1.10 255.255.255.0
!
interface Serial0
 no ip address
 shutdown
!
interface Serial1
 no ip address
 shutdown
!
ip classless
ip route 0.0.0.0 0.0.0.0 192.168.1.100
!
!
line con 0
 password 7 11051C111A170202
 logging synchronous
 login
line 1 16
 transport input all
line aux 0
line vty 0
 exec-timeout 15 0
 password 7 110F1809141D051F
 logging synchronous
 login
line vty 1 4
 exec-timeout 30 0
 password 7 110F1809141D051F
 logging synchronous
 login
!
end
```

## Catalyst Switch

```
Catalyst 1900 - System Configuration
        System Revision:  0   Address Capacity:  1024
        System Last Reset:   Sun Jul 01 10:12:01 2001

        ------------------Settings-----------------
        [N] Name of system                      Catswitch
        [C] Contact name
        [L] Location
        [D] Date/time                           Sun Jul 01 11:25:21 2001
        [S] Switching mode                      FastForward
        [U] Use of store-and-forward for multicast   Disabled
        [A] Action upon address violation       Suspend
        [G] Generate alert on address violation Enabled
        [M] Management Console inactivity timeout   None
        [I] Address aging time                  300 second(s)
        [P] Network Port                        A


        ------------------Actions------------------
        [R] Reset system                [F] Reset to factory defaults

        ----------------Related Menus--------------
        [B] Broadcast storm control     [X] Exit to Main Menu

Enter Selection:


Catalyst 1900 - IP Configuration

        Ethernet Address:  00-C0-1D-80-C7-5E

        ------------------Settings-----------------
        [I] IP address                          192.168.1.4
        [S] Subnet mask                         255.255.255.0
        [G] Default gateway                     192.168.1.10
        [V] Management VLAN                     1

        [X] Exit to previous menu

Enter Selection:



Catalyst 1900 - Virtual LAN Configuration

        VLAN  Name                        Member ports
        ----  --------------------------  -----------
          1   VLAN1                       1-2, 7-24, AUI, A, B
          2   VLAN2                       3
          3   VLAN3                       4,6
          4   VLAN4                       5

        ------------------Actions------------------
        [C] Configure VLAN
        [X] Exit to Main Menu

Enter Selection:
```

## Frame Relay Switch

```
version 11.2
no service password-encryption
no service udp-small-servers
no service tcp-small-servers
!
hostname Frame-Switch
!
!
frame-relay switching
!
interface Serial0
 no ip address
 encapsulation frame-relay
 no fair-queue
 clockrate 2000000
 frame-relay lmi-type ansi
 frame-relay intf-type dce
 frame-relay route 402 interface Serial1 204
!
interface Serial1
 no ip address
 encapsulation frame-relay
 clockrate 64000
 frame-relay lmi-type ansi
 frame-relay intf-type dce
 frame-relay route 203 interface Serial2 302
 frame-relay route 204 interface Serial0 402
!
interface Serial2
 no ip address
 encapsulation frame-relay
 clockrate 64000
 frame-relay lmi-type ansi
 frame-relay intf-type dce
 frame-relay route 302 interface Serial1 203
!
interface Serial3
 no ip address
 shutdown
!
interface Serial4
 no ip address
 shutdown
!
interface Serial5
 no ip address
 shutdown
!
interface Serial6
 no ip address
 shutdown
!
interface Serial7
 no ip address
 shutdown
!
interface Serial8
 no ip address
 shutdown
!
interface Serial9
 no ip address
 shutdown
```

```
!
interface TokenRing0
 no ip address
 shutdown
!
interface BRI0
 no ip address
 shutdown
!
no ip classless
 !
 !
line con 0
line aux 0
line vty 0 4
 login
!
end
```

# R1

```
!
version 11.2
no service password-encryption
no service udp-small-servers
no service tcp-small-servers
!
hostname r1
!
enable secret 5 $1$KT.D$FHsm6ry/Nsa8NgMqGoJ0e/
 !
no ip domain-lookup
ip host r1 204.206.1.1
ip host r2 204.206.2.2
ip host r3 204.206.3.3
ip host r4 204.206.4.4
ip host r5 204.206.5.5
ip host r6 204.206.6.6
ipx routing 0000.0000.1111
!
interface Loopback0
 ip address 204.206.1.1 255.255.255.0
!
interface Ethernet0
 description This interface connects with R2's E0.
 ip address 204.206.12.1 255.255.255.0
 ipx network 1200
!
interface Serial0
 no ip address
 shutdown
 no fair-queue
!
interface Serial1
 no ip address
 shutdown
!
router igrp 20
 network 204.206.12.0
 network 204.206.1.0
!
no ip classless
```

```
ip route 0.0.0.0 0.0.0.0 204.206.12.2
!
!
!
!
banner motd #
This is Router 1
#
!
line con 0
 exec-timeout 0 0
 password letmein
 logging synchronous
 login
line aux 0
line vty 0 4
 password falcons
 login
!
end
```

## R2

```
!
version 12.0
service timestamps debug uptime
service timestamps log uptime
no service password-encryption
!
hostname r2
!
enable secret 5 $1$wi9S$tfPkl0EU5/6WAyedtP/O3.
!
ip subnet-zero
no ip domain-lookup
ip host r1 204.206.1.1
ip host r2 204.206.2.2
ip host r3 204.206.3.3
ip host r4 204.206.4.4
ip host r5 204.206.5.5
ip host r6 204.206.6.6
ipx routing 0000.0000.2222
!
!
!
interface Loopback0
 ip address 204.206.2.2 255.255.255.0
 no ip directed-broadcast
!
interface Ethernet0
 description This interface connects to R1's E0
 ip address 204.206.12.2 255.255.255.0
 no ip directed-broadcast
 ipx network 1200
!
interface Ethernet1
 description This interface does not connect to another device.
 ip address 204.206.20.2 255.255.255.0
 no ip directed-broadcast
 ipx network 2000
!
interface Serial0
```

```
    description This interface connects to R4's S0 and R3's S0 (Frame-Relay)
    ip address 204.206.100.2 255.255.255.0
    no ip directed-broadcast
    encapsulation frame-relay
    no ip split-horizon eigrp 10
    no ip mroute-cache
    ipx network 1000
    no ipx split-horizon eigrp 10
    no fair-queue
    frame-relay map ip 204.206.100.3 203 broadcast
    frame-relay map ip 204.206.100.4 204 broadcast
    frame-relay map ipx 1000.0000.0000.4444 204 broadcast
    frame-relay map ipx 1000.0000.0000.3333 203 broadcast
    frame-relay lmi-type ansi
!
router eigrp 10
  redistribute igrp 20 metric 2000 200 255 1 1500
  network 204.206.2.0
  network 204.206.100.0
!
router igrp 20
  redistribute eigrp 10 metric 2000 200 255 1 1500
  network 204.206.12.0
  network 204.206.20.0
!
ip classless
!
!
!
ipx router eigrp 10
  network 1000
!
!
ipx router rip
  no network 1000
!
!
!
banner motd #
This is Router 2
#
!
line con 0
  exec-timeout 0 0
  password letmein
  logging synchronous
  login
  transport input none
line vty 0 4
  password falcons
  login
!
end
```

# R3

```
!
version 11.2
no service password-encryption
no service udp-small-servers
no service tcp-small-servers
!
```

```
hostname r3
!
enable secret 5 $1$XIPn$bRgZg3BayP2MswmQqh2nJ/
!
no ip domain-lookup
ip host r3 204.206.3.3
ip host r1 204.206.1.1
ip host r2 204.206.2.2
ip host r4 204.206.4.4
ip host r5 204.206.5.5
ip host r6 204.206.6.6
ipx routing 0000.0000.3333
!
interface Loopback0
 ip address 204.206.3.3 255.255.255.0
!
interface Loopback1
 ip address 210.210.1.3 255.255.255.0
!
interface Loopback2
 ip address 210.210.2.3 255.255.255.0
!
interface Ethernet0
 description This interface connects to the management network (192.168.1.0)
 ip address 192.168.1.3 255.255.255.0
 ipx network 3000
!
interface Serial0
 description This interface connects to R2's S0 and R4's S0 (Frame-Relay)
 ip address 204.206.100.3 255.255.255.0
 ip access-group 101 in
 ip summary-address eigrp 10 210.210.0.0 255.255.0.0
 encapsulation frame-relay
 ipx network 1000
 no fair-queue
 frame-relay map ip 204.206.100.2 302 broadcast
 frame-relay map ip 204.206.100.4 302 broadcast
 frame-relay map ipx 1000.0000.0000.2222 302 broadcast
 frame-relay map ipx 1000.0000.0000.4444 302 broadcast
 frame-relay lmi-type ansi
!
interface Serial1
 no ip address
 shutdown
!
router eigrp 10
 network 192.168.1.0
 network 204.206.3.0
 network 204.206.100.0
 network 210.210.1.0
 network 210.210.2.0
!
no ip classless
access-list 101 deny   tcp any 192.168.1.0 0.0.0.255 eq www
access-list 101 deny   tcp any 192.168.1.0 0.0.0.255 eq ftp-data
access-list 101 deny   tcp any 192.168.1.0 0.0.0.255 eq ftp
access-list 101 permit ip any any
!
!
!
ipx router eigrp 10
 network 1000
 network 3000
!
```

```
!
ipx router rip
 no network 1000
 no network 3000
 !
 !
 !
banner motd #
This is Router 3
#
!
line con 0
 exec-timeout 0 0
 password letmein
 logging synchronous
 login
line aux 0
line vty 0 4
 password falcons
 login
!
end
```

## R4

```
!
version 11.2
no service password-encryption
no service udp-small-servers
no service tcp-small-servers
!
hostname r4
!
enable secret 5 $1$MEQG$jpIIxk/ppZWA7yos3cXQk0
!
ip subnet-zero
no ip domain-lookup
ip host r1 204.206.1.1
ip host r2 204.206.2.2
ip host r3 204.206.3.3
ip host r4 204.206.4.4
ip host r5 204.206.5.5
ip host r6 204.206.6.6
ipx routing 0000.0000.4444
!
interface Loopback0
 ip address 204.206.4.4 255.255.255.0
!
interface Ethernet0
 description This interface does not connect with another one.
 ip address 204.206.40.4 255.255.255.224
 ipx network 4000
 ipx network 4001 encapsulation SAP secondary
!
interface Serial0
 description This interface connects to R2's S0 and R3's S0 (Frame-Relay)
 ip address 204.206.100.4 255.255.255.0
 ip access-group 1 out
 encapsulation frame-relay
 ipx network 1000
 frame-relay map ip 204.206.100.2 402 broadcast
 frame-relay map ip 204.206.100.3 402 broadcast
```

```
 frame-relay map ipx 1000.0000.0000.2222 402 broadcast
 frame-relay map ipx 1000.0000.0000.3333 402 broadcast
 frame-relay lmi-type ansi
!
interface Serial1
 description This interface connects to R6's S1.
 ip address 204.206.46.4 255.255.255.0
 ipx network 4600
!
router eigrp 10
 redistribute rip metric 2000 200 255 1 1500
 network 204.206.100.0
!
router rip
 redistribute eigrp 10 metric 1
 network 204.206.40.0
 network 204.206.4.0
 network 204.206.46.0
!
no ip classless
access-list 1 deny   192.168.111.32 0.0.0.31
access-list 1 permit any
!
!
!
ipx router eigrp 10
 network 1000
!
!
ipx router rip
 no network 1000
!
!
!
banner motd #
This is Router 4
#
!
line con 0
 exec-timeout 0 0
 password letmein
 logging synchronous
 login
line aux 0
line vty 0 4
 password falcons
 login
!
end
```

# R5

```
!
version 11.2
no service password-encryption
no service udp-small-servers
no service tcp-small-servers
!
hostname r5
!
enable secret 5 $1$DKBm$xUF3Aq0wLUZYXv4wnOFzG0
!
```

```
ip subnet-zero
no ip domain-lookup
ip host r1 204.206.1.1
ip host r2 204.206.2.2
ip host r3 204.206.3.3
ip host r4 204.206.4.4
ip host r5 204.206.5.5
ip host r6 204.206.6.6
isdn switch-type basic-5ess
!
interface Loopback0
 ip address 204.206.5.5 255.255.255.0
!
interface Serial0
 no ip address
 shutdown
 no fair-queue
!
interface Serial1
 no ip address
 shutdown
!
interface TokenRing0
 description This interface does not connect to another router
 ip address 204.206.50.5 255.255.255.0
 ring-speed 16
!
interface BRI0
 ip address 204.206.200.2 255.255.255.252
 encapsulation ppp
 dialer map ip 204.206.200.1 8358661
 dialer-group 1
!
no ip classless
ip route 0.0.0.0 0.0.0.0 204.206.200.1
!
dialer-list 1 protocol ip permit
banner motd #
This is Router 5
#
!
line con 0
 exec-timeout 0 0
 password letmein
 logging synchronous
 login
line aux 0
line vty 0 4
 password falcons
 login
!
end
```

## R6

```
!
version 11.2
no service password-encryption
no service udp-small-servers
no service tcp-small-servers
!
hostname r6
```

```
!
enable secret 5 $1$eD2v$4sSaZ1eH1XcjODRVDdcm01
!
ip subnet-zero
no ip domain-lookup
ip host r1 204.206.1.1
ip host r2 204.206.2.2
ip host r3 204.206.3.3
ip host r4 204.206.4.4
ip host r5 204.206.5.5
ip host r6 204.206.6.6
ipx routing 0000.0000.6666
isdn switch-type basic-5ess
!
interface Loopback0
 ip address 204.206.6.6 255.255.255.0
!
interface Serial0
 no ip address
 shutdown
 no fair-queue
!
interface Serial1
 description This interface connects to R4's Serial 1.
 ip address 204.206.46.6 255.255.255.0
 ipx network 4600
 clockrate 2000000
!
interface TokenRing0
 description This interface does not connect to another device.
 ip address 204.206.60.6 255.255.255.0
 ipx network 6000
 ring-speed 16
!
interface BRI0
 ip address 204.206.200.1 255.255.255.252
 encapsulation ppp
 dialer-group 1
!
router rip
 redistribute connected metric 1
 redistribute static metric 1
 network 204.206.46.0
 network 204.206.6.0
 network 204.206.60.0
!
no ip classless
ip default-network 204.206.4.0
ip route 204.205.50.0 255.255.255.0 204.206.200.2
!
!
!
!
dialer-list 1 protocol ip permit
banner motd #
This is Router 6
#
!
line con 0
 exec-timeout 0 0
 password letmein
 logging synchronous
 login
line aux 0
```

```
line vty 0 4
 password falcons
 login
 !
end
```

# IP and IPX Routing Tables

## R1

```
r1#show ip route
Codes: C - connected, S - static, I - IGRP, R - RIP, M - mobile, B - BGP
       D - EIGRP, EX - EIGRP external, O - OSPF, IA - OSPF inter area
       N1 - OSPF NSSA external type 1, N2 - OSPF NSSA external type 2
       E1 - OSPF external type 1, E2 - OSPF external type 2, E - EGP
       i - IS-IS, L1 - IS-IS level-1, L2 - IS-IS level-2, * - candidate default
       U - per-user static route, o - ODR

Gateway of last resort is 204.206.12.2 to network 0.0.0.0

I    204.206.2.0/24 [100/1600] via 204.206.12.2, 00:00:25, Ethernet0
I    204.206.3.0/24 [100/9076] via 204.206.12.2, 00:00:26, Ethernet0
C    204.206.1.0/24 is directly connected, Loopback0
I    204.206.6.0/24 [100/8776] via 204.206.12.2, 00:00:26, Ethernet0
I    204.206.4.0/24 [100/8776] via 204.206.12.2, 00:00:26, Ethernet0
C    204.206.12.0/24 is directly connected, Ethernet0
I    204.206.20.0/24 [100/1200] via 204.206.12.2, 00:00:26, Ethernet0
I    204.206.40.0/24 [100/8776] via 204.206.12.2, 00:00:26, Ethernet0
I    204.206.46.0/24 [100/8776] via 204.206.12.2, 00:00:26, Ethernet0
I    204.205.50.0/24 [100/8776] via 204.206.12.2, 00:00:27, Ethernet0
I    204.206.60.0/24 [100/8776] via 204.206.12.2, 00:00:27, Ethernet0
I    204.206.100.0/24 [100/8576] via 204.206.12.2, 00:00:27, Ethernet0
I    192.168.1.0/24 [100/8676] via 204.206.12.2, 00:00:27, Ethernet0
I    204.206.200.0/24 [100/8776] via 204.206.12.2, 00:00:27, Ethernet0
S*   0.0.0.0/0 [1/0] via 204.206.12.2
r1#show ipx route
Codes: C - Connected primary network,    c - Connected secondary network
       S - Static, F - Floating static, L - Local (internal), W - IPXWAN
       R - RIP, E - EIGRP, N - NLSP, X - External, A - Aggregate
       s - seconds, u - uses

8 Total IPX routes. Up to 1 parallel paths and 16 hops allowed.

No default route known.
```

## R2

```
r2#show ip route
Codes: C - connected, S - static, I - IGRP, R - RIP, M - mobile, B - BGP
       D - EIGRP, EX - EIGRP external, O - OSPF, IA - OSPF inter area
       N1 - OSPF NSSA external type 1, N2 - OSPF NSSA external type 2
       E1 - OSPF external type 1, E2 - OSPF external type 2, E - EGP
       i - IS-IS, L1 - IS-IS level-1, L2 - IS-IS level-2, * - candidate default
       U - per-user static route, o - ODR

Gateway of last resort is not set

I    204.206.1.0/24 [100/1600] via 204.206.12.1, 00:00:53, Ethernet0
D EX 204.205.50.0/24 [170/2221056] via 204.206.100.4, 01:27:43, Serial0
C    204.206.2.0/24 is directly connected, Loopback0
```

```
C       204.206.100.0/24 is directly connected, Serial0
D       204.206.3.0/24 [90/2297856] via 204.206.100.3, 00:08:27, Serial0
D EX 204.206.4.0/24 [170/2221056] via 204.206.100.4, 01:37:52, Serial0
D EX 204.206.200.0/24 [170/2221056] via 204.206.100.4, 01:27:43, Serial0
C       204.206.20.0/24 is directly connected, Ethernet1
D EX 204.206.6.0/24 [170/2221056] via 204.206.100.4, 01:37:52, Serial0
        204.206.40.0/27 is subnetted, 1 subnets
D EX    204.206.40.0 [170/2221056] via 204.206.100.4, 01:37:53, Serial0
C       204.206.12.0/24 is directly connected, Ethernet0
D EX 204.206.46.0/24 [170/2221056] via 204.206.100.4, 01:37:53, Serial0
D       192.168.1.0/24 [90/2195456] via 204.206.100.3, 00:08:27, Serial0
D EX 204.206.60.0/24 [170/2221056] via 204.206.100.4, 01:37:54, Serial0
D EX 204.206.60.0/24 [170/2221056] via 204.206.100.4, 01:37:54, Serial0
r2#show ipx route
Codes: C - Connected primary network,    c - Connected secondary network
       S - Static, F - Floating static, L - Local (internal), W - IPXWAN
       R - RIP, E - EIGRP, N - NLSP, X - External, A - Aggregate
       s - seconds, u - uses, U - Per-user static

8 Total IPX routes. Up to 1 parallel paths and 16 hops allowed.

No default route known.

C       1000 (FRAME-RELAY),    Se0
C       1200 (NOVELL-ETHER),   Et0
C       2000 (NOVELL-ETHER),   Et1
E       3000 [2195456/0] via    1000.0000.0000.3333, age 00:09:11,
                                1u, Se0
E       4000 [2195456/1] via    1000.0000.0000.4444, age 01:20:12,
                                1u, Se0
E       4001 [2195456/1] via    1000.0000.0000.4444, age 01:20:12,
                                1u, Se0
E       4600 [2681856/1] via    1000.0000.0000.4444, age 01:20:12,
                                11u, Se0
E       6000 [276864000/2] via    1000.0000.0000.4444, age 01:20:12,
                                1u, Se0
r2#
```

## R3

```
r3#show ip route
Codes: C - connected, S - static, I - IGRP, R - RIP, M - mobile, B - BGP
       D - EIGRP, EX - EIGRP external, O - OSPF, IA - OSPF inter area
       N1 - OSPF NSSA external type 1, N2 - OSPF NSSA external type 2
       E1 - OSPF external type 1, E2 - OSPF external type 2, E - EGP
       i - IS-IS, L1 - IS-IS level-1, L2 - IS-IS level-2, * - candidate default
       U - per-user static route, o - ODR

Gateway of last resort is not set

D       204.206.2.0/24 [90/2297856] via 204.206.100.2, 00:14:00, Serial0
C       210.210.1.0/24 is directly connected, Loopback1
C       204.206.3.0/24 is directly connected, Loopback0
C       210.210.2.0/24 is directly connected, Loopback2
D EX 204.206.1.0/24 [170/2221056] via 204.206.100.2, 00:14:01, Serial0
D EX 204.206.6.0/24 [170/2733056] via 204.206.100.2, 00:14:01, Serial0
D EX 204.206.4.0/24 [170/2733056] via 204.206.100.2, 00:14:01, Serial0
D EX 204.206.12.0/24 [170/2221056] via 204.206.100.2, 00:14:01, Serial0
D EX 204.206.20.0/24 [170/2221056] via 204.206.100.2, 00:14:01, Serial0
        204.206.40.0/27 is subnetted, 1 subnets
D EX    204.206.40.0 [170/2733056] via 204.206.100.2, 00:14:01, Serial0
D EX 204.206.46.0/24 [170/2733056] via 204.206.100.2, 00:14:01, Serial0
```

```
D EX 204.205.50.0/24 [170/2733056] via 204.206.100.2, 00:14:01, Serial0
D EX 204.206.60.0/24 [170/2733056] via 204.206.100.2, 00:14:01, Serial0
C    204.206.100.0/24 is directly connected, Serial0
C    192.168.1.0/24 is directly connected, Ethernet0
D EX 204.206.200.0/24 [170/2733056] via 204.206.100.2, 00:14:02, Serial0
D    210.210.0.0/16 is a summary, 00:14:02, Null0
r3#show ipx route
Codes: C - Connected primary network,    c - Connected secondary network
       S - Static, F - Floating static, L - Local (internal), W - IPXWAN
       R - RIP, E - EIGRP, N - NLSP, X - External, A - Aggregate
       s - seconds, u - uses

8 Total IPX routes. Up to 1 parallel paths and 16 hops allowed.

No default route known.

C    1000 (FRAME-RELAY),   Se0
C    3000 (NOVELL-ETHER),   Et0
E    1200 [2195456/1] via    1000.0000.0000.2222, age 00:14:40,
                             1u, Se0
E    2000 [2195456/1] via    1000.0000.0000.2222, age 00:14:41,
                             1u, Se0
E    4000 [2707456/1] via    1000.0000.0000.2222, age 00:14:41,
                             1u, Se0
E    4001 [2707456/1] via    1000.0000.0000.2222, age 00:14:41,
                             1u, Se0
E    4600 [3193856/1] via    1000.0000.0000.2222, age 00:14:41,
                             1u, Se0
E    6000 [277376000/2] via   1000.0000.0000.2222, age 00:14:41,
                             1u, Se0
r3#
```

## R4

```
r4#show ip route
Codes: C - connected, S - static, I - IGRP, R - RIP, M - mobile, B - BGP
       D - EIGRP, EX - EIGRP external, O - OSPF, IA - OSPF inter area
       N1 - OSPF NSSA external type 1, N2 - OSPF NSSA external type 2
       E1 - OSPF external type 1, E2 - OSPF external type 2, E - EGP
       i - IS-IS, L1 - IS-IS level-1, L2 - IS-IS level-2, * - candidate default
       U - per-user static route, o - ODR

Gateway of last resort is not set

D    204.206.2.0/24 [90/2297856] via 204.206.100.2, 01:46:46, Serial0
D    204.206.3.0/24 [90/2809856] via 204.206.100.2, 00:14:29, Serial0
D EX 204.206.1.0/24 [170/2221056] via 204.206.100.2, 01:44:18, Serial0
R    204.206.6.0/24 [120/1] via 204.206.46.6, 00:00:20, Serial1
C    204.206.4.0/24 is directly connected, Loopback0
D EX 204.206.12.0/24 [170/2221056] via 204.206.100.2, 01:44:18, Serial0
D EX 204.206.20.0/24 [170/2221056] via 204.206.100.2, 01:44:18, Serial0
     204.206.40.0/27 is subnetted, 1 subnets
C       204.206.40.0 is directly connected, Ethernet0
C    204.206.46.0/24 is directly connected, Serial1
R    204.205.50.0/24 [120/1] via 204.206.46.6, 00:00:21, Serial1
R    204.206.60.0/24 [120/1] via 204.206.46.6, 00:00:21, Serial1
C    204.206.100.0/24 is directly connected, Serial0
D    192.168.1.0/24 [90/2707456] via 204.206.100.2, 00:14:30, Serial0
R    204.206.200.0/24 [120/1] via 204.206.46.6, 00:00:22, Serial1
D    210.210.0.0/16 [90/2809856] via 204.206.100.2, 00:14:31, Serial0
r4#show ipx route
Codes: C - Connected primary network,    c - Connected secondary network
```

```
        S - Static, F - Floating static, L - Local (internal), W - IPXWAN
        R - RIP, E - EIGRP, N - NLSP, X - External, A - Aggregate
        s - seconds, u - uses

8 Total IPX routes. Up to 1 parallel paths and 16 hops allowed.

No default route known.

C       1000 (FRAME-RELAY),   Se0
C       4000 (NOVELL-ETHER),  Et0
c       4001 (SAP),           Et0
C       4600 (HDLC),          Se1
E       1200 [2195456/1] via      1000.0000.0000.2222, age 01:25:36,
                             1u, Se0
E       2000 [2195456/1] via      1000.0000.0000.2222, age 01:25:36,
                             1u, Se0
E       3000 [2707456/0] via      1000.0000.0000.2222, age 00:15:12,
                             1u, Se0
R       6000 [07/01] via      4600.0000.0000.6666,   10s, Se1
r4#
```

# R5

```
r5#show ip route
Codes: C - connected, S - static, I - IGRP, R - RIP, M - mobile, B - BGP
       D - EIGRP, EX - EIGRP external, O - OSPF, IA - OSPF inter area
       N1 - OSPF NSSA external type 1, N2 - OSPF NSSA external type 2
       E1 - OSPF external type 1, E2 - OSPF external type 2, E - EGP
       i - IS-IS, L1 - IS-IS level-1, L2 - IS-IS level-2, * - candidate default
       U - per-user static route, o - ODR

Gateway of last resort is 204.206.200.1 to network 0.0.0.0

C    204.206.5.0/24 is directly connected, Loopback0
C    204.206.50.0/24 is directly connected, TokenRing0
     204.206.200.0/30 is subnetted, 1 subnets
C       204.206.200.0 is directly connected, BRI0
S*   0.0.0.0/0 [1/0] via 204.206.200.1
r5#show ipx route
%IPX not running
r5#
```

# R6

```
r6#show ip route
Codes: C - connected, S - static, I - IGRP, R - RIP, M - mobile, B - BGP
       D - EIGRP, EX - EIGRP external, O - OSPF, IA - OSPF inter area
       N1 - OSPF NSSA external type 1, N2 - OSPF NSSA external type 2
       E1 - OSPF external type 1, E2 - OSPF external type 2, E - EGP
       i - IS-IS, L1 - IS-IS level-1, L2 - IS-IS level-2, * - candidate default
       U - per-user static route, o - ODR

Gateway of last resort is 204.206.46.4 to network 204.206.4.0

R    204.206.2.0/24 [120/1] via 204.206.46.4, 00:00:09, Serial1
R    204.206.3.0/24 [120/1] via 204.206.46.4, 00:00:09, Serial1
R    204.206.1.0/24 [120/1] via 204.206.46.4, 00:00:09, Serial1
C    204.206.6.0/24 is directly connected, Loopback0
R*   204.206.4.0/24 [120/1] via 204.206.46.4, 00:00:09, Serial1
R    204.206.12.0/24 [120/1] via 204.206.46.4, 00:00:09, Serial1
```

```
R    204.206.20.0/24 [120/1] via 204.206.46.4, 00:00:09, Serial1
R    204.206.40.0/24 [120/1] via 204.206.46.4, 00:00:09, Serial1
C    204.206.46.0/24 is directly connected, Serial1
S    204.205.50.0/24 [1/0] via 204.206.200.2
C    204.206.60.0/24 is directly connected, TokenRing0
R    204.206.100.0/24 [120/1] via 204.206.46.4, 00:00:10, Serial1
R    192.168.1.0/24 [120/1] via 204.206.46.4, 00:00:10, Serial1
     204.206.200.0/30 is subnetted, 1 subnets
C       204.206.200.0 is directly connected, BRI0
r6#show ipx route
Codes: C - Connected primary network,    c - Connected secondary network
       S - Static, F - Floating static, L - Local (internal), W - IPXWAN
       R - RIP, E - EIGRP, N - NLSP, X - External, A - Aggregate
       s - seconds, u - uses

8 Total IPX routes. Up to 1 parallel paths and 16 hops allowed.

No default route known.

C       4600 (HDLC),        Se1
C       6000 (SAP),         To0
R       1000 [07/01] via    4600.0000.0000.4444,    22s, Se1
R       1200 [13/02] via    4600.0000.0000.4444,    22s, Se1
R       2000 [13/02] via    4600.0000.0000.4444,    22s, Se1
R       3000 [06/01] via    4600.0000.0000.4444,    22s, Se1
R       4000 [07/01] via    4600.0000.0000.4444,    22s, Se1
R       4001 [07/01] via    4600.0000.0000.4444,    22s, Se1
r6#
```

# Completed Cisco Router Operations

## Cisco Router IOS Backup

```
r3#copy flash tftp

System flash directory:
File  Length   Name/status
  1   8108960  c2500-js-l_112-17.bin
[8109024 bytes used, 279584 available, 8388608 total]
Address or name of remote host [255.255.255.255]? 192.168.1.5
Source file name? c2500-js-l_112-17.bin
Destination file name [c2500-js-l_112-17.bin]?
Verifying checksum for 'c2500-js-l_112-17.bin' (file # 1)...  OK
Copy 'c2500-js-l_112-17.bin' from Flash to server
  as 'c2500-js-l_112-17.bin'? [yes/no]y
!!!!!!!!!!!!!!!!!!!!!!!!!!!!!!!!!!!!!!!!!!!!!!!!!!!!!!!!!!!!!!!!!!!!!!!!!!!!!!!!!!!!!!!!
!!!!!!!!!!!!!!!!!!!!!!!!!!!!!!!!!!!!!!!!!!!!!!!!!!!!!!!!!!!!!!!!!!!!!!!!!!!!!!!!!!!!!!!!
!!!!!!!!!!!!!!!!!!!!!!!!!!!!!!!!!!!!!!!!!!!!!!!!!!!!!!!!!!!!!!!!!!!!!!!!!!!!!!!!!!!!!!!!
!!!!!!!!!!!!!!!!!!!!!!!!!!!!!!!!!!!!!!!!!!!!!!!!!!!!!!!!!!!!!!!!!!!!!!!!!!!!!!!!!!!!!!!!
!!!!!!!!!!!!!!!!!!!!!!!!!!!!!!!!!!!!!!!!!!!!!!!!!!!!!!!!!!!!!!!!!!!!!!!!!!!!!!!!!!!!!!!!
!!!!!!!!!!!!!!!!!!!!!!!!!!!!!!!!!!!!!!!!!!!!!!!!!!!!!!!!!!!!!!!!!!!!!!!!!!!!!!!!!!!!!!!!
!!!!!!!!!!!!!!!!!!!!!!!!!!!!!!!!!!!!!!!!!!!!!!!!!!!!!!!!!!!!!!!!!!!!!!!!!!!!!!!!!!!!!!!!
!!!!!!!!!!!!!!!!!!!!!!!!!!!!!!!!!!!!!!!!!!!!!!!!!!!!!!!!!!!!!!!!!!!!!!!!!!!!!!!!!!!!!!!!
!!!!!!!!!!!!!!!!!!!!!!!!!!!!!!!!!!!!!!!!!!!!!!!!!!!!!!!!!!!!!!!!!!!!!!!!!!!!!!!!!!!!!!!!
!!!!!!!!!!!!!!!!!!!!!!!!!!!!!!!!!!!!!!!!!!!!!!!!!!!!!!!!!!!!!!!!!!!!!!!!!!!!!!!!!!!!!!!!
!!!!!!!!!!!!!!!!!!!!!!!!!!!!!!!!!!!!!!!!!!!!!!!!!!!!!!!!!!!!!!!!!!!!!!!!!!!!!!!!!!!!!!!!
!!!!!!!!!!!!!!!!!!!!!!!!!!!!!!!!!!!!!!!!!!!!!!!!!!!!!!!!!!!!!!!!!!!!!!!!!!!!!!!!!!!!!!!!
!!!!!!!!!!!!!!!!!!!!!!!!!!!!!!!!!!!!!!!!!!!!!!!!!!!!!!!!!!!!!!!!!!!!!!!!!!!!!!!!!!!!!!!!
!!!!!!!!!!!!!!!!!!!!!!!!!!!!!!!!!!!!!!!!!!!!!!!!!!!!!!!!!!!!!!!!!!!!!!!!!!!!!!!!!!!!!!!!
!!!!!!!!!!!!!!!!!!!!!!!!!!!!!!!!!!!!!!!!!!!!!!!!!!!!!!!!!!!!!!!!!!!!!!!!!!!!!!!!!!!!!!!!
!!!!!!!!!!!!!!!!!!!!!!!!!!!!!!!!!!!!!!!!!!!!!!!!!!!!!!!!!!!!!!!!!!!!!!!
```

```
Upload to server done
Flash copy took 00:01:53 [hh:mm:ss]
r3#
```

## Cisco Router IOS Upgrade

```
r3#copy tftp flash
                          **** NOTICE ****
Flash load helper v1.0
This process will accept the copy options and then terminate
the current system image to use the ROM based image for the copy.
Routing functionality will not be available during that time.
If you are logged in via telnet, this connection will terminate.
Users with console access can see the results of the copy operation.
                     ---- ******** ----
Proceed? [confirm]

System flash directory:
File  Length   Name/status
  1   8108960  c2500-js-l_112-17.bin
[8109024 bytes used, 279584 available, 8388608 total]
Address or name of remote host []? 192.168.1.5
Source file name? c2500-js-l_112-17.bin
Destination file name [c2500-js-l_112-17.bin]?
Accessing file 'c2500-js-l_112-17.bin' on 192.168.1.5...
Loading c2500-js-l_112-17.bin from 192.168.1.5 (via Ethernet0): ! [OK]

Erase flash device before writing? [confirm]
Flash contains files. Are you sure you want to erase? [confirm]

Copy 'c2500-js-l_112-17.bin' from server
  as 'c2500-js-l_112-17.bin' into Flash WITH erase? [yes/no]y

%SYS-4-CONFIG_NEWER: Configurations from version 11.2 may not be correctly under
stood.
%FLH: c2500-js-l_112-17.bin from 192.168.1.5 to flash ...

System flash directory:
File  Length   Name/status
  1   8108960  c2500-js-l_112-17.bin
[8109024 bytes used, 279584 available, 8388608 total]
Accessing file 'c2500-js-l_112-17.bin' on 192.168.1.5...
Loading c2500-js-l_112-17.bin from 192.168.1.1 (via Ethernet0): ! [OK]

Erasing device... eeeeeeeeeeeeeeeeeeeeeeeeeeeeeeee ...erased
Loading c2500-js-l_112-17.bin from 10.10.10.1 (via Ethernet0):
!!!!!!!!!!!!!!!!!!!!!!!!!!!!!!!!!!!!!!!!!!!!!!!!!!!!!!!!!!!!!!!!!!!!!!!!!!!!!!!!!!!!!
!!!!!!!!!!!!!!!!!!!!!!!!!!!!!!!!!!!!!!!!!!!!!!!!!!!!!!!!!!!!!!!!!!!!!!!!!!!!!!!!!!!!!
!!!!!!!!!!!!!!!!!!!!!!!!!!!!!!!!!!!!!!!!!!!!!!!!!!!!!!!!!!!!!!!!!!!!!!!!!!!!!!!!!!!!!
!!!!!!!!!!!!!!!!!!!!!!!!!!!!!!!!!!!!!!!!!!!!!!!!!!!!!!!!!!!!!!!!!!!!!!!!!!!!!!!!!!!!!
!!!!!!!!!!!!!!!!!!!!!!!!!!!!!!!!!!!!!!!!!!!!!!!!!!!!!!!!!!!!!!!!!!!!!!!!!!!!!!!!!!!!!
!!!!!!!!!!!!!!!!!!!!!!!!!!!!!!!!!!!!!!!!!!!!!!!!!!!!!!!!!!!!!!!!!!!!!!!!!!!!!!!!!!!!!
!!!!!!!!!!!!!!!!!!!!!!!!!!!!!!!!!!!!!!!!!!!!!!!!!!!!!!!!!!!!!!!!!!!!!!!!!!!!!!!!!!!!!
!!!!!!!!!!!!!!!!!!!!!!!!!!!!!!!!!!!!!!!!!!!!!!!!!!!!!!!!!!!!!!!!!!!!!!!!!!!!!!!!!!!!!
!!!!!!!!!!!!!!!!!!!!!!!!!!!!!!!!!!!!!!!!!!!!!!!!!!!!!!!!!!!!!!!!!!!!!!!!!!!!!!!!!!!!!
!!!!!!!!!!!!!!!!!!!!!!!!!!!!!!!!!!!!!!!!!!!!!!!!!!!!!!!!!!!!!!!!!!!!!!!!!!!!!!!!!!!!!
!!!!!!!!!!!!!!!!!!!!!!!!!!!!!!!!!!!!!!!!!!!!!!!!!!!!!!!!!!!!!!!!!!!!!!!!!!!!!!!!!!!!!
!!!!!!!!!!!!!!!!!!!!!!!!!!!!!!!!!!!!!!!!!!!!!!!!!!!!!!!!!!!!!!!!!!!!!!!!!!!!!!!!!!!!!
!!!!!!!!!!!!!!!!!!!!!!!!!!!!!!!!!!!!!!!!!!!!!!!!!!!!!!!!!!!!!!!!!!!!!!!!!!!!!!!!!!!!!
!!!!!!!!!!!!!!!!!!!!!!!!!!!!!!!!!!!!!!!!!!!!!!!!!!!!!!!!!!!!!!!!!!!!!!!!!!!!!!!!!!!!!
```

```
!!!!!!!!!!!!!!!!!!!!!!!!!!!!!!!!!!!!!!!!!!!!!!!!!!!!!!!!!!!!!!!!!!!!!!!!!!!!!!!!!!!!!!!!!!!!!!!!!!!!!!!
!!!!!!!!!!!!!!!!!!!!!!!!!!!!!!!!!!!!!!!!!!!!!!!!!!!!!!!!!!!!!!!!!!!!!!!!!!!!!!!!!!!!!!!!!!!!!!!!!!!!!!!
!!!!!!!!!!!!!!!!!!!!!!!!!!!!!!!!!!!!!!!!!!!!!!!!!!!!!!!!!!!!!!!!
[OK - 8108960/8388608 bytes]

Verifying checksum...  OK (0x619E)
Flash copy took 0:03:59 [hh:mm:ss]
%FLH: Re-booting system after download
```

## Cisco Router Configuration Backup

```
r3#copy start tftp
Remote host []? 192.168.1.5
Name of configuration file to write [r3-confg]?
Write file r3-confg on host 192.168.1.5? [confirm]
Writing r3-confg .!! [OK]
r3#
```

## Cisco Router Network Configuration

```
R3#copy tftp running-config
Host or network configuration file [host]? host
Address of remote host []? 192.168.1.5
Name of configuration file [r3-config]? R3-config
Configure using r1-config from 192.168.1.5? [confirm]
Loading r1-config from 192.168.1.5 (via Ethernet0): !
[OK - 780/32723 bytes]

r3#
%SYS-5-CONFIG: Configured from r1-config by console tftp from 192.168.1.5
r3#
```

# ISDN Simulator
# Configuration and Setup

This appendix will assist you in configuring your Black Box ISDN Simulator with the correct ISDN features needed for the lab. If you are using a different vendor ISDN simulator, please refer to its user guide for proper configuration. We recommend that you read the user guide thoroughly before attempting to configure the ISDN switch. Many of the features of the ISDN simulator are beyond the scope of this book, so we will show you only the correct values needed for successful operation in the lab environment. If you want to learn more about the advanced features of the ISDN simulator, refer to the user guide.

**NOTE**    For additional product or purchasing information on the ISDN Line Simulator, visit www.blackbox.com.

## ISDN Simulator Physical Connections

Before you configure the ISDN simulator, take a look at the physical layout of the ISDN environment. Figure D-1 illustrates the physical layout.

**Figure D-1** *Physical Connections for ISDN*

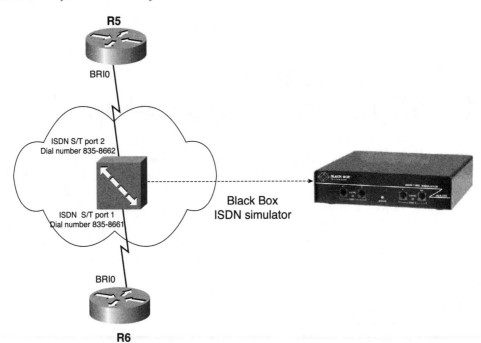

From the figure, you can see that R5 is connected to the S/T port 2 of the ISDN switch and that R6 is connected to the S/T port 1 of the ISDN switch. You do not need to use the N port because the routers already have the N interface within the BRI interface. The dial numbers to reach each of these ports appear on the diagram. For R5 to be capable of calling R6, it must dial 835-8661; for R6 to call R5, it must dial 835-8662. Because you are using the ISDN switch type AT&T Custom 5-ESS, no SPIDs are needed. If you want to use SPIDs at a later date, you will need to change the ISDN switch type to one that supports SPIDs; refer to your user manual for the SPID numbers for the individual B channels.

# ISDN Simulator Configuration

To configure the Black Box ISDN Simulator, you need to install the configuration tool on a PC or laptop and then connect to the ISDN simulator with the serial cable provided. You also must configure the correct properties for the ISDN switch.

To install the configuration software provided by Black Box, remove the 3.5-inch floppy labeled ISDN Simulator Configuration Software for Windows. Place it into the floppy drive, initiate the setup.exe program, and accept the default values during the installation process. When the installation is complete, connect the serial cable (RS-232 to DB 9) to the back of the ISDN simulator and to your COM1 port on the PC, and initiate the configuration program previously installed (DLS Configuration is the name of the program within the Windows Start menu).

After the configuration program has fully loaded and retrieved the current configuration off the ISDN simulator, set the values to match those shown in Figure D-2, and click the Download button. This downloads the configuration to the ISDN switch.

**NOTE**    The initial configuration will show QUERY in the Configuration Name property box, meaning that the configuration program has queried the ISDN simulator for its current configuration parameters. You can disregard this for now. Change the other values; when you save the configuration, it will then prompt you to name the configuration file.

**Figure D-2**    *DLS Configuration Screen for ISDN Simulator*

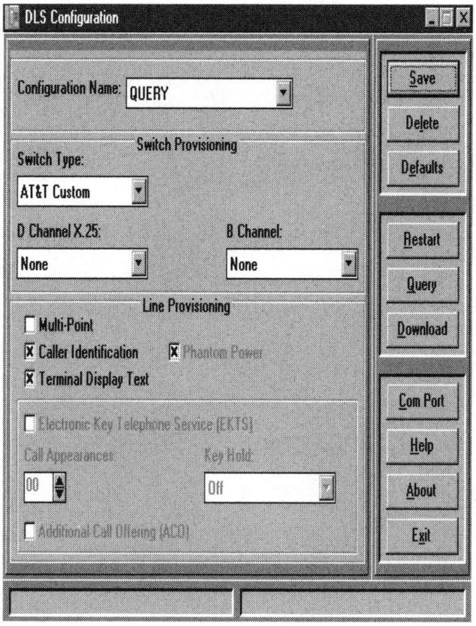

When this is complete, you can choose to save the configuration in case the ISDN simulator loses its configuration in the future. You might want to save the configuration file to something meaningful, such as CCNA Lab.

# INDEX

## A

access
Catalyst 1900 switches, 74–75
console ports, 41–44
lists, 35–36
command, 317
configuring, 315–324
extended, 313–314
standard, 313–314
networks, 346–353
remote users, 361–366
routers, 366–376
Telnet
configuring vty lines, 50–52
creating host tables, 101–103
terminal servers, 46–54
adding
frame-relay map statements, 131
network, 201–208
addresses
EA, 457
IP, 30
assigning, 48, 59, 472
BRIO interfaces, 249–252
Catalyst 1900 switches, 78–81
interfaces, 115–116
management consoles, 78–81
mapping, 118
loopback, 203
MAC
switching, 70
transparent bridging, 69
summary, 204
administrative distances by routing protocols, 224
advertisement receipts, confirming, 165
algorithms, 187–192, 288
analysis, routers, 167–168
ANSI (American National Standards Institute), 450
applications, 6
Cisco IOS
backing up, 337–338, 492
executing, 330
loading, 329
searching, 329

upgrading, , 338–341, 493–494
HyperTerminal, 43. *See also* HyperTerminal
Notepad. *See* Notepad
applying ping command, 354–360
ARP (Address Resolution Protocol), 118
AS (autonomous system), 191, 197
assignment of
BRIO interfaces, 249–252
IP addresses, 48, 59, 472
asynchronous lines, 62
clearing, 64
Telnet, 61
autosummary, disabling, 204
AUX (auxiliary), 15

## B

backing up
Cisco IOS software
diagrams, 492
image files, 337–338
configuration files, 342–343
router diagrams, 494
banner motd command, 97
basic scripts, writing, 103–104, 108–113
BECN (backward-explicit congestion notification), 453, 457
bits
buckets, 206
C/R, 457
Black Box ISDN Simulator, 27, 497–498
boot sequences, routers, 329–337
boot system flash command, 331
bootstrap code, loading, 329
BRI (Basic Rate Interface), 239
bridging, 69
brief option, 277
BRIO interfaces
IP addresses, 249–252
PPP encapsulation, 252–253
broadcast option, 130
buckets, 206

# D

# L

# M

# N

# O

# S

# Train with authorized Cisco Learning Partners.

## Discover all that's possible on the Internet.

One of the biggest challenges facing networking professionals is how to stay current with today's ever-changing technologies in the global Internet economy. Nobody understands this better than Cisco Learning Partners, the only companies that deliver training developed by Cisco Systems.

Just go to **www.cisco.com/go/training_ad**. You'll find more than 120 Cisco Learning Partners in over 90 countries worldwide.* Only Cisco Learning Partners have instructors that are certified by Cisco to provide recommended training on Cisco networks and to prepare you for certifications.

To get ahead in this world, you first have to be able to keep up. Insist on training that is developed and authorized by Cisco, as indicated by the Cisco Learning Partner or Cisco Learning Solutions Partner logo.

Visit **www.cisco.com/go/training_ad** today.

EMPOWERING THE
INTERNET GENERATION℠

# Hey, you've got enough worries.

## Don't let IT training be one of them.

Get on the fast track to IT training at InformIT,
your total Information Technology training network.

 | **www.informit.com** | Pearson Education

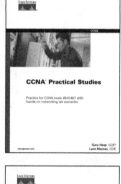

# Cisco Press CCNA® Solutions

### Interconnecting Cisco Network Devices
Cisco Systems, Edited by Steve McQuerry, CCIE®
1-57870-111-2 • **Available Now**

Based on the Cisco-recommended CCNA training course taught worldwide, this is the official Coursebook from Cisco Systems that teaches you how to configure Cisco switches and routers in multiprotocol internetworks. This book provides you with the knowledge needed to identify and recommend the best Cisco solutions for small- to medium-sized businesses. Prepare for CCNA exam #640-607 while learning the fundamentals of setting up, configuring, maintaining, and troubleshooting Cisco networks.

### CCNA Practical Studies
Gary Heap, CCIE and Lynn Maynes, CCIE
1-58720-046-5 • **Available April 2002**

You learned the concepts Cisco says a CCNA should know, but can you put those concepts into practice? Gain critical hands-on experience with *CCNA Practical Studies*. This title provides practice scenarios that you can experiment with on lab equipment, a networking simulator, or a remote-access networking lab. It is the only practical lab book recommended by Cisco Systems for CCNA preparation.

### Cisco CCNA Exam #640-607 Flash Card Practice Kit
Eric Rivard
1-58720-048-1 • **Available Now**

CCNA test time is rapidly approaching. You learned the concepts, you have the experience to put them into practice, and now you want to practice, practice, practice until exam time. Cisco *CCNA Exam #640-607 Flash Card Practice Kit* is an essential final-stage study tool with more than 350 flash cards for memory retention, 550 practice exam questions to verify your knowledge, and 54 study sheets for review of complex topics. Flash cards come in print and electronic formats, including PC, Palm® OS, and Pocket PC for optimal flexibility.

**Cisco Press**

# Cisco Press CCNA Solutions

### Cisco CCNA #640-607 Preparation Library
Wendell Odom, CCIE; Steven McQuerry, CCIE; Cisco Systems
1-58705-093-5 • **Available May 2002**

The *Cisco CCNA #640-607 Preparation Library* is a comprehensive study package that combines the Cisco-recommended CCNA Coursebooks—*Interconnecting Cisco Network Devices* and *Internetworking Technologies Handbook*, Third Edition, with *Cisco CCNA Exam #640-607 Certification Guide* to form a value-priced library for CCNA preparation. Learn what you need to know, prepare for the exam, and succeed.

### Cisco CCNA Exam #640-607 Certification Guide
Wendell Odom, CCIE
1-58720-055-4 • **Available Now**

A comprehensive late-stage study tool for CCNA #640-607 preparation, this new edition is completely updated to include technology advancements and new learning elements. Key updates and additions include hands-on lab exercises; updates to LAN, subnetting, and Frame Relay sections; "Credit" sections highlighting content that is beyond the scope of the exam but critical for you to know in your daily job; and a subnetting appendix. The accompanying CD-ROM includes a comprehensive CCNA #640-607 test bank of practice exam questions.

For the latest on Cisco Press resources and Certification and Training guides, or for information on publishing opportunities, **visit www.ciscopress.com.**

**Skyline Computer Corporation**

# Skyline Computer—Integrated Solutions and Learning

Skyline Computer is a leading provider of integrated solutions for Cisco® internetworking technologies delivering Cisco Certified training, hardware, and professional services. Skyline's dedication to customer service will keep you coming back—as evidenced by Skyline Computer being selected as Cisco Training Partner of the Year in 2001.

As a Certified Cisco Training Partner, Skyline offers the full range of educational curriculum for the Cisco Certification tracks CCNA®, CCDA®, CCNP®, CCDP®, CQS, CCIP™, and CCIE®. Skyline also specializes in customized education for all Cisco-based technologies and disciplines, such as SNA, CIP, WAN, AVVID, and Security.

## Skyline Computer expands to include remote network lab access

With this book, you can learn how to build and use networking labs. Skyline Computer will enhance your learning experience with a series of remote networking labs available now. These labs are actual networking hardware arranged in a variety of designs, including some identical to scenarios in this book. You work on actual equipment without having to invest in additional hardware. With a basic Internet connection you can work through scenarios and labs from this book, as well as test and experiment with other network designs assembled by the experts at Skyline Computer.

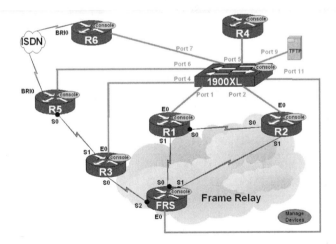

## Cisco Press

Go to **www.ciscopress.com/getexperience** in May 2002 to learn how you can try out these exciting labs at a discounted price, and register for a chance to win prizes from Cisco Press and Skyline Computer. You can also go directly to **www.skylinecomputer.com/skylabs.htm** to discover what innovative learning solutions can do for your growth as a networking professional.

### Get Experience.    Get Certified.